WAVELL IN THE MIDDLE EAST 1939–1941

A STUDY IN GENERALSHIP

By
Harold E. Raugh, Jr

Foreword
by
Field Marshal The Rt. Hon. Lord Carver
GCB CBE DSO MC

BRASSEY'S (UK)

LONDON · NEW YORK

Copyright © Brassey's (UK) 1993

First English edition 1993

UK editorial offices: Brassey's, 165 Great Dover Street, London SE1 4YA
Orders: Marston Book Services, Po Box 87, Oxford OX2 ODT

USA orders: Macmillan Publishing Company, Front and Brown Streets,
Riverside, NJ 08075

Distributed in North America to booksellers and wholesalers by the
Macmillan Publishing Company, NY 10022

Library of Congress Cataloging in Publication Data
Available

British Library Cataloguing in Publication Data
A catalogue record for this book is
available from the British Library

ISBN 0-08-040983-0   Hardcover

*Harold E. Raugh, Jr has asserted his moral right to be identified
as author of this work.*

Printed in Great Britain by BPCC Wheatons Ltd., Exeter

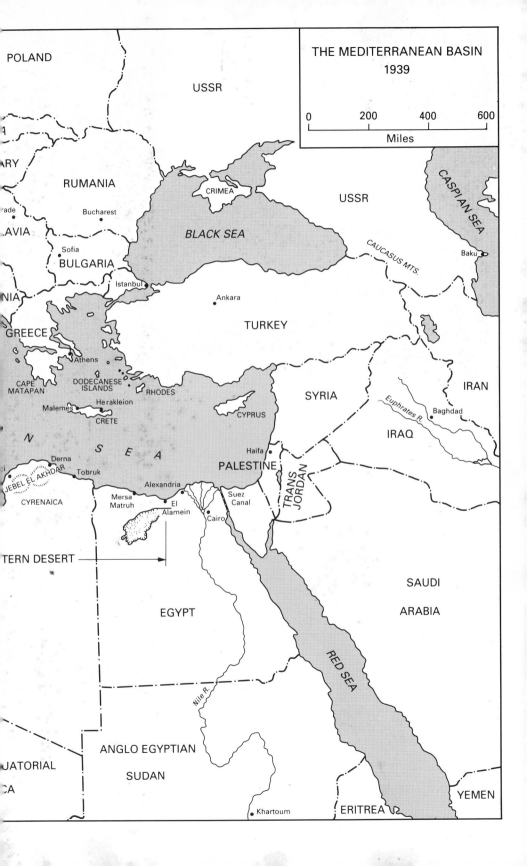

POLAND

USSR

THE MEDITERRANEAN BASIN
1939

0   200   400   600
Miles

RUMANIA

ARY

Bucharest

rade

AVIA

CRIMEA

USSR

CASPIAN SEA

BLACK SEA

NIA

Sofia

BULGARIA

Istanbul

CAUCASUS MTS.

Baku

Ankara

GREECE

TURKEY

Athens

CAPE
MATAPAN

DODECANESE
ISLANDS

RHODES

SYRIA

IRAN

Euphrates R.

Baghdad

Malemes

Herakleion

CRETE

CYPRUS

IRAQ

N

S   E   A

Haifa

PALESTINE

Derna

JEBEL EL AKHDAR

Tobruk

i

CYRENAICA

Mersa
Matruh

Alexandria

El
Alamein

Suez
Canal

TRANS
JORDAN

TERN DESERT

Cairo

SAUDI

ARABIA

EGYPT

RED SEA

Nile R.

JATORIAL

CA

ANGLO EGYPTIAN

SUDAN

Khartoum

ERITREA

YEMEN

WAVELL IN THE MIDDLE EAST 1939–1941

A STUDY IN GENERALSHIP

THE BLACK WATCH
(Royal Highland Regiment)

Field Marshal The Earl Wavell PC GCB GCSI GCIE CMG
MC (*From the portrait by James Gunn. Reproduced by courtesy of the
Colonel, The Black Watch*)

To my wife, Si Ho
for her love, patience, and understanding.

Contents

Foreword

by
Field Marshal The Rt. Hon. Lord Carver,
GCB, CBE, DSO, MC

In this extensively researched and meticulously documented book, Harold Raugh has made a major contribution to military history; to the record of the Second World War; and to a balanced assessment of Field Marshal Wavell as a military commander. The despatch of an expeditionary force from Egypt to Greece in April 1941 was one of the most controversial strategic decisions of the war, and the part Wavell played in it was crucial. The account of it which Harold Raugh here gives us will undoubtedly remain for long the most authoritative account.

As a young officer, serving under Wavell's overall command in the Middle East at the beginning of the war, I, like most of my contemporaries, worshipped him as a hero. He seemed the very opposite of the Brass Hats of the First World War, whom we had been conditioned to despise. He appeared to believe in unorthodox and imaginative methods of making war, which would not involve us in heavy casualties, and the campaign against the Italians in Libya demonstrated to us that he was right to do so. For me personally, the fact that he was a cultured product of the classical education of Winchester College, of which I also had been a pupil, was an added reason for a hero-worship, which was not based on any first-hand knowledge.

The pages which follow reveal what a heavy burden Wavell had to bear in those years, juggling with inadequate resources, while constantly subjected to the 'ceaseless prodding' of his imperious political master, Winston Churchill, with whom he never established a happy relationship and whose strictures were to cast a lasting shadow over his reputation. This book firmly restores it.

Michael Carver

List of Plates

List of Maps and Figures

MAPS

FIGURE

SYMBOLS

The symbols shown below have been used to denote tactical formations on the maps in this book. Other symbols are shown in the Key to each map where necessary.

        ☐ British/Commonwealth and Allied

        ☐ Axis

        ☒ Army

Corps

Division

Brigade

Regiment (Colonel's command)

Battalion (Lieut. Colonel's command)

Armour

Infantry

Glider

Parachute

Parachute Assault

Glossary of Abbreviations and Code Names

Abbreviations – Used in Text and Source Notes

AA	Anti-Aircraft
AA & QMG	Assistant Adjutant and Quarter Master General
ABDACOM	American-British-Dutch-Australian Command
ACM	Air Chief Marshal
ADC	Aide-de-camp
ADM	Admiralty and Naval Department Papers, PRO
AE	Anthony Eden
AFV	Armoured Fighting Vehicle(s)
AG1	Adjutant General's Office, Section 1 (War Office)
AIF	Australian Imperial Force
AIR	Air Ministry Papers, PRO
AMPC	Auxiliary Military Pioneer Corps
AOC-in-C	Air Officer Commanding-in-Chief
App.	Appendix
APW	Archibald P Wavell
AQ	Army Quarterly
AWM	Australian War Memorial
BGGS	Brigadier General, General Staff
BGS	Brigadier General Staff
BL	British Library
Brig.	Brigadier
Brig.Gen.	Brigadier General
BTE	British Troops in Egypt
CAB	War Cabinet Papers, PRO
Cable	Cablegram
CAC	Churchill Archives Centre

Capt.	Captain
CAS	Chief of Air Staff
CB	Companion of the Most Honourable Order of the Bath
CIGS	Chief of the Imperial General Staff
C-in-C, ME	Commander-in-Chief, Middle East
CMG	Companion of the Most Distinguished Order of Saint Michael and Saint George
Col.	Colonel
COS	Chief(s) of Staff
CP	Connell Papers
CUP	Cambridge University Press
DAAG	Deputy Assistant Adjutant General
DAQMG	Deputy Assistant Quarter Master General
DEFE	Ministry of Defence Papers, PRO
Dept.	Department
DMO	Director of Military Operations
DSO	Distinguished Service Order
EHR	English Historical Review
EW	Eugenie, Countess Wavell
FAJ	Field Artillery Journal
FDRL	Franklin D Roosevelt Library
FM	Field Marshal
FO	Foreign Office Papers, PRO
GCB	Knight Grand Cross of the Most Honourable Order of the Bath
Gen.	General
GHQ	General Headquarters
GOC	General Officer Commanding
GOC-in-C	General Officer Commanding-in-Chief
GR	Ground Reconnaissance Aircraft
GS	General Staff
GSO 1,2,3	General Staff Officer, Grade 1, 2, or 3
HE	His (Her) Excellency
HQ	Headquarters
HMG	His (Her) Majesty's Government
HMSO	His (Her) Majesty's Stationery Office
IEA	Italian East Africa
Ind	Indian

IHR   International History Review
IJ   Infantry Journal
ILN   Illustrated London News
Inf   Infantry
IUP   Indiana University Press
IWM   Imperial War Museum

JCH   Journal of Contemporary History
JIC   Joint Intelligence Committee
JPS   Joint Planning Staff
JRA   Journal of the Royal Artillery
JRUSI   Journal of the Royal United Service Institute

KCB   Knight Commander of the Most Honourable Order of the
           Bath

LHCMA   Liddell Hart Centre for Military Archives
LRP   Long Range Patrol(s)
Lt.Col.   Lieutenant Colonel
Lt.Gen.   Lieutenant General
Ltr   Letter

MA   Military Affairs
Maj.   Major
Maj.Gen.   Major General
MC   Military Cross
ME   Middle East
MEIC   Middle East Intelligence Centre
Memo   Memorandum
MEJPS   Middle East Joint Planning Staff
MGGS   Major General, General Staff
MNBDO   Mobile Naval Base Defence Organization
MO1   Military Operations, Section 1 (War Office)
MR   Military Review
MRAF   Marshal of the Royal Air Force
MT   Motor Transport
MU   McMaster University

NA   National Archives
NAM   National Army Museum
NDUL   National Defense University Library
NLS   National Library of Scotland
NW   Northwest
NR   National Review

NY	New York
NZEF	New Zealand Expeditionary Force
OC	Officer Commanding
OKH	Oberkommando des Heeres (German Army High Command)
OSS	Office of Strategic Services
OTC	Officers Training Corps
OUP	Oxford University Press
PM	Prime Minister
PREM	Premier Papers, PRO
PRO	Public Record Office
PS	Private Secretary
PWT	Principal War Telegrams and Memoranda, 1940–1943: Middle East
RA	Royal Artillery
RAFM	Royal Air Force Museum
RE	Royal Engineers
RG	Record Group
RHL	Rhodes House Library
RMAS	Royal Military Academy Sandhurst
RN	Royal Navy
RTR	Royal Tank Regiment
SA	South African
SE	Southeast
SEAC	South East Asia Command
SIME	Security Intelligence Middle East
S of S	Secretary of State
TLG	The London Gazette
UB	University of Birmingham
USA	United States Army/United States of America
USAMHI	United States Army Military History Institute
USMA	United States Military Academy
VCIGS	Vice Chief of the Imperial General Staff
WD	War Diary
WDF	Western Desert Force
WO	War Office Papers, PRO
WSC	Winston S Churchill

Code Names

CONTINGENCY PLANS

Cordite	Proposed seizure of Rhodes (1940)
Felix	German plan to capture Gibraltar and close the Straits
Influx	Proposed attack on Sicily (1941)
Mandibles	Capture of the Dodecanese
Mongoose	Evacuation of the Nile Delta (Wavell's 'worst possible case')

Intervention in Iran – Alternative plans (1940)

Trout	One mechanised Indian division into Basra
Salmon	Preparation in Basra of a logistic base for three divisions
Herring	Three divisions to operate in Iran/Iraq (to include Trout)
Lobster	Reinforcement of Herring from Palestine

Assistance to Turkey – Alternative plans (1940)

Bear	One infantry and one armoured division to Turkey
Cheetah	Three infantry and one armoured divisions to Turkey
Leopard	Royal Air Force units to Anatolia
Lion	Force as for Cheetah but deployed to Smyrna for defence of the eastern and southern shores of the Bosporous, Sea of Marmara and the Dardanelles
Tiger	Artillery and tank units to Thrace (not to be confused with the Tiger convoy – see below)

OPERATIONS

Abstention	Commando raid on Castellorizo (February 1941)
Barbarossa	German attack on Russia (June 1941)
Battleaxe (originally Bruiser)	Offensive under Beresford-Peirse in the Western Desert to destroy all enemy forces in the area Bardia – Sollum – Halfaya – Sidi Omar – Sidi Azeiz (15–17 June 1941)
Brevity	Intended as precursor to Battleaxe to drive the Germans west of Tobruk (15–17 May 1941)

Canvas — Attack on Kismayu (Sudan) by Cunningham (February 1941)

Colorado — Defence of Crete (from 14 May 1941)

Compass — Wavell's first major offensive in the Western Desert (December 1940 – February 1941)

Demon — British withdrawal from Greece (April 1941)

Dynamo — British evacuation from Dunkirk (May 1940)

Exporter — Advance into Syria by 7th Australian Division, elements of 1st Cavalry Division, 5th Indian Brigade and Free French (June 1941). Later reinforced by Habforce and 10th Indian Division.

Marita — German occupation of Greece (April 1941)

Mercury (British – Scorcher) — German assault on Crete (May 1941)

Sea Lion — Planned German invasion of the UK (1940–41)

Sunflower — Despatch of German troops to North Africa (1941)

FORCES

Coast Force — 11th Indian Brigade for Battleaxe

Combe Force — Battlegroup based upon 11th Hussars for later stages of Compass

Creforce — Garrison of Crete before the arrival of formations evacuated from Greece (May 1941)

Force Emily — Cover for move of 4th Indian Division to the Sudan (March 1941)

Escarpment Force — 4th Indian Division and supporting elements for Battleaxe

Gazelle Force — Highly successful harrassing force of Indian, Sudanese and British troops employed against the Italians in Ethiopia (1940)

Gideon Force — Patriot force led by Wingate in Ethiopia (1940–41)

Habforce — Force based upon 1st Cavalry Division for relief of Habbaniyah, Iraq (May 1941)

Kingcol — Advance guard for Habforce

Lustre Force — Original code name for force sent to Greece under HQ 1st Australian Corps (February 1941)

Force Sabine — Revised plan for three Indian divisions to replace Herring on transfer of responsibility for Iran/Iraq from GHQ Middle East to India (February 1941)

Selby Force — Small mixed force drawn from the Mersa Matruh garrison during Compass. It was to advance along the coast road to attack the Italian base at Maktila.

Force 'T'   Naval force of six ships in support of Canvas (February 1941)

'W' Force   British and Commonwealth forces in Greece after assumption of command by Wilson (April 1941)

TERMS

Sunshields   Camouflage frames placed over tanks by the British in the Western Desert to make them look like lorries.

Tiger Cubs   Churchill's name for the tanks sent to the Middle East by Operation Tiger

Ultra   Decryption of German Enigma signal traffic

Acknowledgements

This study could not have been written without the help and encouragement of many people and institutions, and I am happy to acknowledge their considerable assistance.

My interest in Wavell, his generalship, and his Middle East campaigns was given fresh impetus and a period to germinate further while, as a serving United States Army officer, I attended graduate school at the University of California, Los Angeles, from 1986 to 1988 preparatory to serving on the faculty of the Department of History at the United States Military Academy (West Point). This study began as a doctoral dissertation under the able supervision of Professor Albion M Urdank, and I am greatly indebted to him for his professional guidance as well as to the other members of my doctoral committee: Professor Stanford J Shaw, Professor Scott L Waugh, Lieutenant Colonel John Hitchcock, and Captain Carl Cannon.

While teaching at West Point from 1988 to 1991, I was exceedingly fortunate in working for two unusually enlightened and understanding officers, Colonel Paul L Miles, Jr, and Colonel Kenneth E Hamburger. The former's interest in my research can be described accurately as avuncular, and both officers served as invaluable sources of encouragement and advice.

A number of others gave generously of their time, and in many cases their hospitality as well, in assisting me in this project. They include: Mrs. Joan Bright Astley; Mr Correlli Barnett; Lieutenant Colonel John Benson; Professor Brian Bond; Lieutenant Colonel F J Burnaby-Atkins; the late The Rt. Hon. Lord Caccia; Field Marshal The Rt. Hon. Lord Carver; Professor David G Chandler; Lady N I C Dill; the late Field Marshal The Rt. Hon. Lord Harding of Petherton; Lieutenant-General Sir Ian Jacob; The Countess of Ranfurly; and The Rt. Hon. Lord Wilson of Libya. In almost all cases I was instantly received on my research visits as an old – or new – friend, and the trust and honesty with which they imparted their recollections was simultaneously very exhilarating yet profoundly humbling. I was greatly fortunate in being able to share in their experiences of having known Field Marshal Wavell.

I am most grateful to the eminent soldier and military historian Field Marshal Lord Carver, a participant in Operation 'Compass' and numerous subsequent desert campaigns, for writing the Foreword to this study.

For permission to quote from papers in their charge, I am grateful to the following individuals: The Hon. George D Fergusson, for permission to quote from the papers of his late father, Brigadier The Lord Ballantrae (Bernard Fergusson); The Rt. Hon. The Earl Haig of Bemersyde, for permission to quote from his unpublished autobiography; Lieutenant-General Sir Arthur Norman, for permission to quote from the memoirs of his late grandfather, General Sir John Burnett-Stuart; and Mrs. Ruth Connell Robertson, for permission to quote from the papers of her late husband.

In the course of writing this study I was able to conduct research at a number of document repositories and archives, and am indebted to the following institutions to quote from documents in their collections (individuals who assisted me are listed parenthetically after their respective institution): Churchill Archives Centre, Churchill College, Cambridge (Mr. Correlli Barnett, Keeper; Elizabeth Bennett; Archivist, and staff members); Rhodes House Library, University of Oxford, Oxford (Mr. AS Bell, Librarian, and Mr. Allan Lodge, Assistant Librarian); Special Collections, University Library, University of Birmingham, Birmingham (Dr. BS Benedikz, Sub-Librarian); Franklin D Roosevelt Library, Hyde Park, New York (Dr. William Emerson, Director, and Mr. Mark Renovitch); Liddell Hart Centre for Military Archives, King's College, London (Ms. Patricia Methven, College Archivist; and Mr. Michael Page and Miss Jane Platt, Assistant Archivists); Royal Air Force Museum, Hendon, London (Mr. PG Murton, Keeper of Aviation Records); Department of Manuscripts, National Library of Scotland, Edinburgh (Mr. JF Russell and Mr. Ian MacIver); Special Collections and Archives, Rutgers University, New Brunswick, New Jersey (Mr. Edward Skipworth); Manuscripts Collections, British Library, London (Mr. RAH Smith, Assistant Keeper, and staff members); and Department of Documents, Imperial War Museum, London (Dr. Peter Thwaites). Crown copyright material in the Public Record Office is reproduced by permission of Her Majesty's Stationery Office (Dr. Helen Forde, Dr. Meryl Foster, Mrs. HE Jones, and staff members).

I also am grateful for the assistance of Colonel The Hon. WD Arbuthnott, (Colonel, The Black Watch); Mrs. Judith Blacklaw (Ministry of Defence Whitehall Library, London); Mr. John Montgomery, Librarian (Royal United Services Institute for Defence Studies, Whitehall, London); Miss Charlotte Snyder (Interlibrary Loan Office, United States Military Academy Library, West Point, New York); Mr. John E Taylor, Military Reference Branch, Textual Reference Division, and Mr. Richard Penser (National Archives, Washington, DC); Miss AJ Ward, Head; and Mr. John

Peaty (Army Historical Branch, Ministry of Defence, Whitehall, London); and staff members of the Department of Photography, Imperial War Museum, London; and the Donovan Technical Library, US Army Infantry School, Fort Benning, Georgia. I also received a great deal of assistance and photocopies of documents through the mail from numerous overseas institutions, from Australia to Zimbabwe; I have acknowledged gratefully the contributions of their staff members by listing them and their institutional affiliation in the 'Correspondence' section of the Bibliography. Any omissions are unintentional.

To attempt to achieve a balance of the human perspective with the official documents and archival material I researched for this study, I believed it essential to contact other individuals who had known Wavell or had participated in his campaigns. To contact many of these veterans now living in countries scattered across the globe, I wrote requests for information which were kindly published by the editors of the following periodicals: *British Army Review; Stand To!* (Journal of the Western Front Association); *Times Literary Supplement* (London); *Illustrated London News*; *Journal of the Society for Army Historical Research*; *Army Quarterly and Defence Journal*; *Indo-British Review – A Journal of History*; *Military Affairs*; *Legion* (Royal British Legion); *Star* (Johannesburg, South Africa); *Natal* (South Africa) *Mercury*; *Red Hackle* (Regimental Journal of The Black Watch); *Evening Post* (Wellington, New Zealand); *West Australian* (Perth); *Homefront* (South African Ex-Servicemen's League); *Reveille* (New South Wales, Australia, Returned Ex-Servicemen's League); and *Journal of the United Service Institution of India*. Indeed, the perceptions of the 'other ranks' were indispensable in evaluating Wavell's generalship and performance as Commander-in-Chief, Middle East, and I have listed in the 'Correspondence' section of the Bibliography all those who shared their impressions and reminiscences with me.

Field Marshal Lord Carver, Professor Bond, Colonel Hamburger, Colonel Robert A Doughty, and Lieutenant Colonel Dewey A Browder read relevant sections of the manuscript prior to publication, and I am grateful for their invaluable suggestions, corrections, and advice.

I admire and am most grateful for the unparalleled professionalism, sustained encouragement, and unsurpassed skill of my editor, Brigadier Bryan Watkins, and appreciate the contributions of Miss Jenny Shaw, Publishing Director, and all the others at Brassey's (UK) who helped in the editing and production of this book.

This book is rightly dedicated to my wife Si Ho. I do not always tell her how much I appreciate her patience and understanding, but I do.

While researching and writing this study, my goal has been to do everything possible to live up to the following words of Marcus Aurelius:

'if anybody shall reprove me, and shall make it apparent unto me, that in either opinion or action of mine I do err, I will most gladly retract. For it is the truth that I seek after, by which I am sure that never any man was hurt; and as sure, that he is hurt that continueth in any error, or ignorance whatsoever.'

Wavell would have approved.
West Point
16 January 1991   H.E.R, Jr.

1
Introduction

Field Marshal Earl Wavell bore a mantle of responsibility greater than that of any other British general, with the possible exception of the Chief of the Imperial General Staff, in the early years of the Second World War. He served as Commander-in-Chief, Middle East, from July 1939 to July 1941, and as Commander-in-Chief, India, from July 1941 to June 1943. During part of the latter period, he also served as Supreme Commander of the American-British-Dutch-Australian Command (ABDACOM), in the Sisyphean attempt to halt the initial Japanese onslaught against the Western Powers.

While in these positions, Wavell directly influenced every major operation in which British soldiers were engaged up to the middle of 1942 – except for the brief campaigns of 1940 in Norway and France. During the crucial period from February to July 1941 – the last six months of his tenure as Commander-in-Chief, Middle East – Wavell was directly responsible for the conduct of some eight campaigns, with three on hand at any one time and five running simultaneously in May 1941. This fact is all the more spectacular when one considers the immensity and geographical diversity of his 2,000 by 1,700-mile command, and the resources he had available with which to conduct those campaigns.

Some of Wavell's campaigns, such as the British expedition to Greece and the defence of Crete, were abject failures. Others, notably those in the Western Desert in the winter of 1940–1941 and in East Africa, were 'two of the most resounding military victories in history'.[1] These victories, in the words of one military historian and contemporary observer, 'cheered and inspired the British Empire and the neutral world at a time when Axis power seemed invincible'.[2] Indeed, one professional journal of the United States Army declared that Wavell was 'Britain's Soldier of the Hour', and that he had 'breathed new life, inspiration and confidence into the British Empire throughout the world'.[3]

In spite of these accomplishments and achievements, and his subsequent service as Viceroy of India from 1943 to 1947, Wavell is little known and largely forgotten today. 'The fact is', a former colleague recently observed, 'that, sadly enough, W. [Wavell] is now an almost forgotten commander'.[4] Although a great soldier of a nation which traditionally honours its military heroes, Wavell has suffered a curious neglect.

This historical 'oversight' can be directly attributed to five major factors.

First, Wavell's accomplishments and his tenure as Commander-in-Chief, Middle East, have been tarnished by inaccurate perceptions of his subsequent service as Commander-in-Chief, India; Supreme Commander, ABDACOM; and Viceroy of India. This apparently unwitting tendency to conflate Wavell's military accomplishments, especially in the Middle East, with his later military and political service, recurs in many post-war memoirs and documents. 'I am highly critical of [Wavell's] Viceroyalty', wrote Sir James Grigg, who served as Permanent Under-Secretary of State for War during the period Wavell was Commander-in-Chief, Middle East, 'though not so violently so as I am over the next one [Mountbatten's]. Whether it is this attitude towards Wavell as Viceroy that has led me into a slight tendency to belittle him as a soldier, I cannot tell'.[5]

Secondly, Wavell's accomplishments in the Middle East during the 'lean years' of the Second World War have been overshadowed by those of later generals who possessed a marked superiority of manpower, weapons, vehicles, and logistical resupply capabilities – as well as the all-important factor of unrestrained political support. Anthony Eden (The Rt Hon Earl of Avon), who served Churchill as Secretary of State for War and later Foreign Affairs, was keenly aware of this situation when, during an interview, he admonished those 'listeners [who] have military ambitions. I would strongly advise them against holding a high military command in the first two years of any war in the British Army,' and concluded: 'Better wait until the stuff begins to come along. Which, I am afraid, in the last two experiences was after the third year or later.'[6] Many tend, moreover, to overlook the fact that until the end of 1941, Britain was fighting against the Axis powers alone; the United States was not involved in the conflict during Wavell's Middle East tenure as Commander-in-Chief.

A third factor explaining the neglect of Wavell is the inability of historians to penetrate the shroud of obscurity surrounding his remote personality. Wavell's renowned taciturnity and stoicism have been interpreted as some sort of phlegmatic detachment from his soldiers and ongoing events. But this analysis, as will be seen, is incorrect. In many respects, his personality was self-contradictory: apparent aloofness, discomfiture and boredom, in public, contrasting sharply with wit, warmth and vivacity when in the company of his family and friends.

Fourthly, most of the senior commanders of the Second World War, on both sides of the Atlantic, took the opportunity within the first two decades after the war to present their own accounts of themselves and their actions, either in autobiographies or memoirs, or by authorising others to edit their journals or reminiscences. Many of these chronicles were written for purposes of self-justification and/or self-aggrandisement. Wavell, who was well-equipped to do so, never wrote a word to cast aspersions on his superiors or to exonerate himself of any accusation. The simple yet eloquent comment made recently by an officer who first met Wavell in the 1930s highlights this assertion: '[Wavell was] a very fine soldier who got a raw deal but never held this against his masters'.[7] No one could have served the Prime Minister, or Great Britain, more loyally or more selflessly. As a result, Wavell's reputation and accomplishments in the Middle East have fallen prey to, or have been further adumbrated by, those who have better publicised their own activities and martial achievements.

A final factor is the existence, at a minimum, of a conscious effort by others to denigrate, or at least obfuscate, Wavell's military accomplishments in the Middle East. This appears to be the method which has been, and is still being used, by the 'Churchillians',[8] in an attempt to enhance further the inviolability of their mentor, 'the greatest Englishman of them all'. Wavell, of course, was not without fault. A number of studies written about him and his Middle East campaigns have accurately shown as much, although each study remains flawed, for one or more of the reasons already cited.

Biographical sketches of Wavell began to appear towards the end of 1941, in the wake of his great victories in North Africa and Italian East Africa. However, at a time when public sentiment had been deeply stirred by those victories after a period of intense gloom, during which Britain's lone stand could only be seen by many as a forlorn hope, the early studies tended to verge, understandably, on the brink of hagiography. Yet it is a measure of the impact of Wavell's achievements upon the morale of the home front that one finds Clement Atlee, Deputy Prime Minister in Churchill's war government, writing some years later:

> People sometimes forget, in thinking of the later victory at El Alamein, how greatly Wavell's victory over the Italians raised our spirits when things everywhere were very dark.[9]

Cyril Falls, when reviewing Major General RJ Collins's admirable, if rather subjective, *Lord Wavell (1883–1941): A Military Biography*, recalls how Field Marshal Jan Smuts, that close wartime colleague of Winston Churchill and stalwart supporter of Wavell, had said in a rather similar vein:

> The early African campaigns 'were the first rays of sunlight to pierce the gloom of those early years of the war'. That is something which ought never to be forgotten of Lord Wavell.[10]

Perhaps the greatest soldier produced by Britain in this century, Field Marshal Lord Alanbrooke, in his Foreword to Robert Woollcombe's *The Campaigns of Wavell, 1939–1943*, left us in no doubt of the measure of the man:

> It is my fervent hope that the account of the campaigns of Wavell may be

extensively read and deeply studied, so that the true stature of this very great
man may be fully appreciated, and that adequate feelings of gratitude may be
engendered for the immense services he rendered to his country under conditions of appalling difficulty.[11]

Whilst the early studies contained much that was of very great value,
despite their subjectivity, they inevitably became outdated, written as they
were either very close to the events described or well before the release of a
wealth of invaluable new material under the terms of the *Public Records Act
1967*. This measure made available a host of declassified government and
military documents under what became known as 'the thirty year rule'.
Some of the most significant of these were those relating to the impact of
'Ultra' (the decryption of German signal traffic) upon the higher control of
the war – a subject which had previously been a closely guarded secret.

Sadly Ronald Lewin's study, *The Chief: Field Marshal Lord Wavell,
Commander-in-Chief and Viceroy, 1939–1947*, published in 1980, while taking full
advantage of the new material and presenting a study that was not hero-
worshipping, suffered a number of blemishes, so that it did not live up to its
publisher's claim on the dustjacket that it was 'the definitive treatment of
the subject Wavell'. Something more was clearly required if a full and fair
assessment was to be made of Wavell's achievements as a fighting commander in the first two years of the Second World War. To provide that
assessment has been the aim of this book and of the author's doctoral thesis,
upon which the book is based.

To attain that goal, primary source material has included documents
from the British Foreign Office and War Office; Ultra-based intelligence
and the minutes and correspondence of the Prime Minister; unpublished
papers and the oral reminiscences of leading British Government, Army,
Navy, and Royal Air Force and Dominion personnel; and the recollections
of private soldiers, non-commissioned officers and junior officers who served
in the Middle East during Wavell's tour of command. Army Headquarters
and unit war diaries, operation orders, and after-action reports have all
been scrutinised. To enhance the objectivity of the study, it also covers
narratives of events and perceptions from 'the other side of the hill', as
reflected in a number of monographs written by former senior officers of the
German Army and government officials under the auspices of the
Operational History (German) Section of the European Theater Historical
Division, United States Army, immediately after the end of the Second
World War. Official Histories and other published primary sources have, of
course, been used to full advantage. In no previous study of Wavell has this
whole range of sources been used in conjunction.

A multitude of secondary source material has been juxtaposed with the
primary sources described above. Much of this is in the form of contemporary articles from professional British military journals, invaluably and accurately reflecting the often ephemeral opinions and concepts of those,

including Wavell, who were involved in the modernisation and mechanisation of the British Army in the years between the Wars.

Few people today realise the immensity of the strain imposed upon Wavell as a result of the inherent responsibilities he bore, not only as military commander but also as chief diplomat and principal logistician. Yet it is impossible to maintain objectivity and balance in any assessment of Wavell's accomplishments as Commander-in-Chief, Middle East, without taking account of the omnipresent military and political exigencies and emotional pressure under which he laboured. The author has sought to keep this factor in the forefront of his mind in the process of analysis and evaluation.

In considering Wavell's achievements, this has been done within the framework of the resources available not only to him but also to his opponents. Where he suffered a defeat, the reasons for this and for his enemy's success have been analysed. His personality and attributes, in success as well as in adversity – the keys to the proper understanding of Wavell the soldier and Wavell the man – and their impact upon his performance as Commander-in-Chief, have been continuously studied and assessed. His generalship has been appraised against those standards which may be seen as the most stringent posited in the twentieth century – his own Lees Knowles Lectures on 'Generals and Generalship', delivered at Trinity College, Cambridge in 1939 – five months before he became Commander-in-Chief, Middle East.

Within this book, the chapters have been arranged chronologically, in so far as this has been possible in the light of the simultaneous conduct of numerous campaigns during 1941. At times, it has also been necessary to arrange chapters topically. The Source Notes and Bibliography have had to be kept within the bounds imposed by a normal book. However, the extensive and meticulous documentation of the doctoral thesis upon which the book is based is available to the student in the University of California's University Research Library at 405 Hilgard Avenue, Los Angeles, California 90024 USA where the dissertation is lodged. Based mainly upon a large number of unpublished primary source documents, correspondence and interviews, the 1586 endnotes alone run to 241 manuscript pages.

* * *

Wavell certainly deserves a better fate than the position of relative obscurity grudgingly conceded him by the Churchillians and to which he has been relegated by history. It is to be hoped that this study will prove that Wavell's accomplishments as Commander-in-Chief, Middle East during the stormy years of 1939 – 1941 entitle him to be seen as a general who ranks as the most farsighted and able of all the British Army commanders of the Second World War. The seeds of military preparedness and ultimate victory in the Middle East, sown and nurtured by Wavell, were later reaped by generals who took and received the lion's share of the public recognition and credit. 'He [Wavell] was unlucky, in that he was a senior commander at the start of the war, when things were not going too well: it was the younger ones who picked up the prizes nearer the end', observed an officer recently who had known Wavell well before the outbreak of the Second World War.[12]

The self-effacing Wavell never personally desired publicity, courted recognition or sought fame. His attitude towards self-promotion was very similar to that of Field Marshal Viscount Allenby, of whom Wavell himself wrote '[he] was the last man who would have cared what his biographer wrote of him, or, indeed, that his biography should have been written at all'.[13] Whatever his feelings about himself may have been, Wavell cared deeply about the health and well-being of his soldiers. Captain Alec Walkling, who served in the Middle East under Wavell's command, wrote to his wife in June 1943, describing his reaction to the film *Desert Victory*, which recorded the operations of the Eighth Army under Montgomery and had recently been released:

> One thing before I start. *Desert Victory* paid homage to the men of the Eighth Army as it was at El Alamein and afterwards – it forgot to pay homage to the thin red line which held against vastly superior armies for two years and kept them away from the Nile when mail took months, comforts were few, and numbers were still fewer. I hope and trust that they have not been forgotten.[14]

This book has been written to elucidate and evaluate the generalship of Wavell, the Commander-in-Chief of that 'thin red line' – and to ensure that he, and they, are not forgotten.

2

Born to Serve: The Years of Apprenticeship and Burgeoning Experience 1883–1918

Archibald Percival Wavell was the son and grandson of professional soldiers. His family name can be traced back to one William de Vauville of Normandy, who came to England with the Conqueror in 1066. That name became gradually anglicised over the centuries until in 1478 we find the first of eleven Wavells to become a Scholar of Winchester College. The family became closely associated with both the city and college of Winchester and a number of Wavells served as Mayors of the city in the 17th and 18th centuries.

Wavell's father, Archibald Graham Wavell, was a Major in the Norfolk Regiment when his son was born on 5 May 1883. However, in order to save his family from the privations of a tour in Burma, he 'exchanged' with an officer of the 2nd Battalion The Black Watch who was anxious to serve abroad for financial reasons. So began a family link with the Royal Highland Regiment which was to last for three generations. From his preparatory school, Summer Fields at Oxford, where he showed himself not only to be a keen games player but also to have rare powers of detachment and concentration, a natural talent for literature, and a quiet, reserved, but kindly, character marked by quite a sense of humour – all characteristics which would remain and play a significant part in his remarkable life – Wavell won a scholarship to Winchester in 1896. This was evidence enough of his marked intellectual ability.

The spartan life and scholarly atmosphere at Winchester tended to reinforce his inclination to introspection and reticence and did nothing to counter the habit of self-depreciation which he had developed at Summer Fields.

7

To Be A Soldier: From Winchester to the Outbreak of War, August 1914

Having decided to follow the family tradition of service in the Army, Wavell joined the Army Class at Winchester, despite the protests of the Headmaster, who wrote to Colonel Wavell urging him that 'this desperate step is not necessary, as I believe your son has sufficient ability to make his way in other walks of life'![1] A curious letter to a soldier! However, Wavell himself wrote later:

> I never felt any special inclination to a military career, but it would have taken more independence of character than I possessed at the time to avoid it. Nearly all my relations were in the Army. I had been brought up amongst soldiers; and my father, while professing to give me complete liberty of choice, was determined that I should be a soldier. I had no particular bent towards any other profession and I took the line of least resistance.[2]

Passing into the Royal Military College, Sandhurst in August 1900, he found that his time there would be all too brief, as the demands of the Boer War for more and more young officers had led to a dramatic shortening of the course and so to his commissioning on 8 May 1901, only three days after his 18th birthday. While at Sandhurst, Wavell had produced average results in the various fields of study although his conduct had been graded 'Exemplary'.

He joined the 2nd Battalion The Black Watch in South Africa and had his first taste of guerrilla warfare. However, the war was soon over and in 1902 he was invalided home with a shoulder broken while playing football. The Battalion moved to Ambala in India, where Wavell rejoined it in 1903. Soon they moved to the North West Frontier city of Peshawar.

Life in India in those days was all that a young officer could wish for with limitless opportunities for all forms of hunting and sporting activities and golden opportunities to learn his trade as a soldier in the frequent skirmishes on the Frontier against the wily Pathan tribesmen. It was a life that was to provide an ideal background for generations of soldiers who would later distinguish themselves as leaders and commanders in battle and Wavell was to prove no exception. However, unlike many of his contemporaries, he devoted much of his spare time to study, as his company commander in India has described, recalling that Wavell was:

> a very young officer so absorbed either in some book on military history or of the language which he was at the moment learning, as to be completely oblivious to conversations going on around him in the common sitting-room after dinner, and literally deaf even to a question addressed directly to him.[3]

Wavell's ability to concentrate intensely on a subject to the virtual exclusion of all others increased with age, as did his prodigious memory.

In 1906, he attended a transport course and was subsequently attached to the Chitral Relief Column – a new experience and one in which he served away from the Battalion for the first time. A staff attachment, to qualify him to sit for the Staff College examination, then followed. Sitting bored to tears in Divisional Headquarters in Rawalpindi, with little or nothing to do, he offered to help another officer decipher a number of telegrams which were coming in about an outbreak of trouble in the area of Peshawar. As he did so, he came upon one asking for a British subaltern officer to command the ammunition column of the Bazar Valley expedition which was about to set out to punish the Pathans for the trouble they had caused. The officer selected must have passed Higher Standard Urdu. This was too much for Wavell, who grasped the gift with both hands, as he later recorded:

> I had not only done this but had a transport course and passed HS Pushtu. I considered that there could not be a better qualified officer in Northern India. I wrote an answer that Lieutenant Wavell of The Black Watch would be selected to command the ammunition column, enciphered and despatched it, telling the hard-worked staff officer that it was a purely routine matter with which I need not trouble him. It all came out afterwards and there were some rather awkward inquiries as to who had recommended Lieutenant Wavell, but it was decided that I had shown some initiative and was undoubtedly qualified, and I was allowed to go.[4]

After the Bazar Valley operation, Wavell was given a year's leave at home during which he studied and sat for the Staff College examination. In a very competitive field, he passed in with overall marks of 85 per cent. On 22 January 1909, still only a subaltern and as much as ten years younger than many of his fellow students, he entered the 'sacred portals', very much a 'rara avis'. Rare bird or no, this course was to show many of the Directing Staff and two Commandants that here was an officer of quite exceptional ability and quality.

The period leading up to the Great War was one of great change for the British Army as the lessons of South Africa were digested and the serious defects in the Army's organisation and equipment were rectified. The most important innovation of all sprang from the report of the Esher Commission of 1904 which led to the establishment of the General Staff. Thus Wavell was at Camberley at a particularly important and interesting time.

The two Commandants at the Staff College when Wavell was there were Major General Henry Wilson and Major General William Robertson. Both would later become Field Marshals and both would be Chief of the Imperial General Staff – but they were as different from one another as chalk from cheese, and Wavell would later serve them both.

His natural skill in written self-expression and his love of military history, and his analytical mind, combined in the production of some excellent papers, one of which would lead him into a situation from which he learned his first lesson in the convolutions of military policy making.

In his second year at Camberley, Wavell was required to write a military history paper in response to an examination question: 'How far are the strategical and tactical lessons drawn from the campaigns of 1815, 1862, 1866 and 1870 confirmed or modified by the experience of the recent wars in South Africa and Manchuria?' Wavell wrote his paper, taking into consideration the politico-strategic aspects of these campaigns, since the intended reader of the examination was the Commandant, Wilson, a Francophile who was 'primarily interested in the highest levels of staff work where military and political considerations interacted'.[5]

Wavell's provocative essay was extremely well written, and Brian Bond has observed that Wavell, after assessing 'The Military Spirit' and problems of military preparedness,

> did go on to answer the question in professional terms and the modern reader, whether academic or military would surely award him a mark of 'alpha plus' for the organisation of his material, powers of critical analysis, lucidity of style and scholarly range of literary reference.[6]

The paper's first reader, however, was Lieutenant Colonel Charles Ross of the Directing Staff, who pointed out a few omissions and elaborated upon a number of Wavell's contentions. But by this time Robertson had succeeded Wilson as Staff College Commandant, and Wavell's treatise no longer possessed the viability it would have had under Wilson's tutelage.

Unexpectedly, Wavell was summoned to the new Commandant's office, a rather forbidding experience for a young subaltern. There he noticed his essay on Robertson's desk. Robertson, armed with coloured pencils, drew lines through many of Wavell's paragraphs while admonishing the student 'not to worry his head about matters which did not concern him – a budding staff officer – in fact, to keep his feet in future more firmly on the floor'.[7] Robertson had written on Wavell's essay that 'the discussions of questions of policy and political matters lead to no practical result, nor benefit of any kind to the soldier, nor is it his business'.[8] Wavell was, undoubtedly, chagrined at this unexpected rebuke, but as he was leaving the office, Robertson smiled and remarked: 'Otherwise an excellent paper, Wavell.'[9] It was, to be sure, a compliment, but it was also an important lesson on the relationship between civil authorities and the military that Wavell should have appreciated.

Wavell's two years at Camberley mark a watershed in his early military career. Passing out with a coveted 'A' grading – one of only two awarded that year – he was now a marked man. This was no mean achievement for an officer who was easily the youngest student of his year. Despite their little contretemps over his essay, Robertson would later recall 'of all the officers who came under my notice, I should consider Wavell by far the ablest'.[10] Praise indeed from a very great soldier. On Robertson's recommendation, Wavell was then selected to go to Moscow to study Russian in 1911. Early the next year he qualified as a First Class Interpreter. Not only had he done that but he had obtained permission to go on manoeuvres with the Russian Grenadier Corps – an experience which enabled him to see more of the Russian countryside and, more importantly, to study the shortcomings of the Russian officer corps. In the years that now followed, as he worked as a GSO III in the Russian Section in the War Office under his old Commandant, Henry Wilson, who was then Director of Military Operations and Intelligence, he not only wrote a handbook on the Russian Army but paid two more visits to Russia to attend the Russian Army manoeuvres. These visits gave him a golden opportunity to study the movements of a large military force in the field – something that few British officers could do, since their own army seldom deployed even as much as a single division. Wavell's reports on these manoeuvres recorded that while, in his view, the Russian soldier was first class fighting material and that he was adequately led up to battalion level, the higher command was weak and the General Staff unpractical and academic – reports that reflected the analytical nature of his mind and the breadth of his vision.[11] Little did he realise at the time that in less than four years he would see the Russian armies disintegrate on the battlefield.

While still in the War Office, Wavell was to have his first experience of the debilitating and divisive effects of a clash between government and the military. In the midst of a furious political row over the question of Home Rule for Ireland, in which a grave possibility of civil war between North and South arose, the Commander of the 3rd Cavalry Brigade, Brigadier General Hubert Gough, himself an Irishman, stationed in Ireland, on the Curragh, let it be known that he, and a number of his officers, would sooner resign than obey any orders involving the use of force against their fellow countrymen. Henry Wilson, Wavell's own Chief, was one of the schemers behind the scenes in this affair and backed Gough. For a time it looked as if a number of other officers in the Army would also support Gough and a very serious situation developed. Fortunately, cooler heads prevailed and the matter was resolved as a 'misunderstanding' although it involved the resignation of both the CIGS and the Secretary of State for War, both of whom were deemed by the Government to have exceeded their powers in their efforts to placate Gough. Wavell was appalled by the whole affair and, while having some sympathy for the plight in which Gough and his officers had found themselves, came down firmly on the need for officers to obey their orders 'whatever they were', although he considered 'that the Army was placed in a most damnable and unfair situation by the Government'.[12] Brought up, as he had been, in the strict atmosphere of a military family to whom duty, loyalty, and obedience were the first tenets of their military faith, his reaction is unsurprising. Devotion to duty and intense loyalty to his superiors were key attributes of Wavell's personality and this early experience and his reaction to it was, perhaps, a harbinger to his adamant support of the decision to send troops to Greece in 1941 – surely the most controversial episode of his whole career.

The Great War, 1914–18

Like every other ambitious soldier, Wavell was intensely anxious to go to France with the British Expeditionary Force in August 1914, fearing that the war would be over before he could get to it. However, he found himself stuck in the Operations Directorate of the War Office, first on security duties and then back in the Russian Section. Bemoaning his fate, he wrote to his sister on 12 September:

> I think I'm complete now with everything for the field, except orders to go. I'm feeling too utterly depressed and really don't care what happens [;] one will never be able to make up for having missed this last month. I wish I'd never gone near the Staff College or Russia.[13]

However, within days, the scene changed and orders for France arrived. Living from day to day and unsure of what the future might hold, Wavell became engaged on 18 September to Eugenie Quirk, the daughter of a Colonel. They had met a year earlier and had found that they had many interests in common.

Ten days later, Wavell found himself at General Headquarters in France as an acting Major and in nominal command of the nascent Intelligence Corps – most of whom were detached to subordinate formations. Hardly the sort of task that any keen soldier would relish. But Fortune soon smiled again. Early in November, the Headquarters of the 9th Infantry Brigade in 3rd Division had been badly hit and, among others, the Brigade Major had been wounded. On 16 November, Wavell took over as the new Brigade Major and, on the same day, to his great delight, an old friend from Summer Fields, Captain (later Major General Sir) K G Buchanan joined as Staff Captain.

Wavell was now in his element. He at once set about improving conditions for the troops in the trenches of the Ypres Salient where the Brigade spent the cold, dank, dismal winter of 1914–15. Unlike many of his peers, and the higher commanders and staff officers, he visited the battalions in the trenches regularly, determined to see things for himself and to be in a position to respond to their needs. Appalled by the utter futility of a number of local attacks ordered by commanders who had never taken the trouble to reconnoitre the ground, Wavell was frequently on reconnaissance in the line, always seeking to improve the layout of the brigade position, of which he kept an up-to-date large-scale map in the Headquarters.

Wavell's fine example, complete imperturbability, and calm refusal to be rattled by any situation, combined with his unsparing devotion to duty and obvious toughness, quickly inspired confidence. Buchanan would later

speak in glowing terms of his performance saying that 'as Brigade Major
... [he] earned the DSO [Distinguished Service Order] on many
occasions'.[14]

In April 1915 came a well-earned spell of home leave during which he
married Eugenie and spent a blissful two weeks on honeymoon. John
Connell believed his marriage was 'the most important factor in his
[Wavell's] life'.[15]

Months of hard fighting followed his return to France and the
trenches. On 16 June, the Brigade was committed to lead a divisional
attack on the Bellewaarde Ridge. At the end of that particularly tough
day, Wavell was making his way back to Brigade Headquarters through
a heavy German barrage when he was severely wounded, losing the sight
of his left eye. Invalided back through a base hospital, he reached
England to learn that his gallantry had been recognised by the award of
the Military Cross, one of the first to be gazetted since the institution of
that decoration.

The Battle of Bellewaarde Ridge, in which the 9th Infantry Brigade lost
73 officers out of 96 and 2,012 men out of 3,663, and other battles which
would occur later on the Western Front, undoubtedly confirmed in Wavell's
mind his conviction of the futility of massed frontal assaults by infantry
against a strongly held defensive position. Highly trained troops, employing
mobility and surprise in imaginatively planned offensive operations, would
be required to win future battles. Indeed, as late as 1933, Wavell was still
having to impress upon dogmatic military leaders the need 'therefore to
shake the last of the Flanders mud out of our minds' and to be receptive of
new ideas in order to prevent a recurrence of the catastrophes of the Great
War.[16]

After four months convalescence, and a short spell as GSO II of the 64th
Highland Division in Scotland, Wavell found himself back in France. As
GSO II (Staff Duties) he now found himself working for Brigadier General
(later General Sir) John Burnett-Stuart. Although this was not the active
post he had hoped for, he soon realised that in Burnett-Stuart he had found
a kindred spirit whom he believed to have 'probably the best and quickest
brain in the Army of his rank'.[17] That the respect was mutual is shown by
the fact that Burnett-Stuart would ask for Wavell on his staff on two future
occasions.

Promoted Major on 8 May 1916, Wavell was summoned to the office of the
second of his two former Camberley Commandants, and then CIGS, General
Sir William Robertson. There he had found that his Russian language training
and experience in the Russian Section had led to his selection by Robertson for
the post of Liaison Officer to the Russian Army of the Caucasus, commanded
by the Grand Duke Nicholas. As a local Lieutenant Colonel, Wavell made the
circuitous journey to Tiflis in 17 days, arriving in October 1916. There his
principal task was to observe and report to the War Office on all military

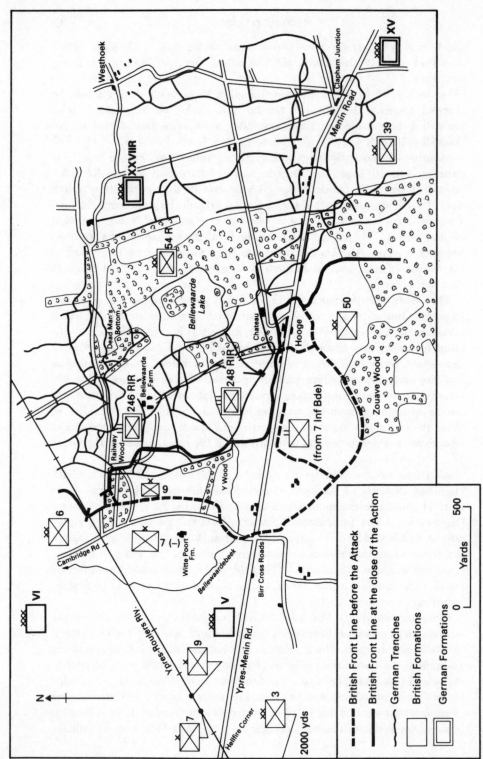

Map 1. The Battle of Bellewaarde 16 June 1915

Legend:
- British Front Line before the Attack
- British Front Line at the close of the Action
- German Trenches
- British Formations
- German Formations

0   500
Yards

Map labels:

Westhoek

XV

Clapham Junction

Menin Road

39

XXVIIR

54 R

Bellewaarde Lake

50

Chateau

Hooge

Dead Man's Bottom

246 RIR

Bellewaarde Farm

248 RIR

Zouave Wood

Railway Wood

(from 7 Inf Bde)

9

Y Wood

6

7 (–)

Witte Poort Fm.

Bellewaardebeek

Birr Cross Roads

Cambridge Rd

Ypres-Roulers Rly.

VI

V

9

Ypres-Menin Rd.

Hellfire Corner

7

3

2000 yds

N

operations, particularly those of the Turkish Army facing the Russians in the Caucasus. His reports from Tiflis would become one of the factors considered when the British plans for the campaigns in Mesopotamia and Palestine were being prepared – campaigns in which he too would later become deeply involved.

Meanwhile, careless of official prohibition, Mrs Wavell, with a determination matching that of her husband, set forth to join him in Russia, accompanied by their young son and her maid. The outbreak of the Russian Revolution in Petrograd on 15 March 1917 soon led to the replacement of the Grand Duke Nicholas by a Soldier's Council amid chaos and turmoil and to the return of the Wavells to London in June. Here they learned that Wavell had been given a brevet Lieutenant Colonelcy, thus ensuring his promotion to Colonel in four years' time and a place in the pool from which Major Generals would be selected. He was still only thirty-four.

Robertson's trust and confidence in Wavell was such that in June 1917 he was appointed as the CIGS's personal liaison officer with General (later Field Marshal Viscount) Sir Edmund Allenby, the newly appointed Commander-in-Chief of the Egyptian Expeditionary Force – a step that was to prove perhaps the most significant of his whole career until Wavell, in his turn, became the Commander-in-Chief Middle East in 1939. From Allenby, who took Wavell with him wherever he went in the operational area, Wavell learned much about the art of command in a desert theatre. He learned too about the true values of the art of surprise and deception and of the importance of a scrupulous attention to detail in operational planning, not least in the field of logistics, upon which so much of Allenby's memorable successes would depend. It was Allenby too who showed him something of the art of instilling confidence in a partly demoralised army and demonstrated to him the value of personal example – exemplified by Allenby's immediate move, on appointment, to take the unwieldy General Headquarters from the fleshpots of Cairo out into the desert where the staff and he himself, would share the discomforts and hardships suffered by the troops. The transformation of the Headquarters by Allenby from a turgid and unimpressive mass to a well-honed staff machine was yet another of the invaluable lessons Wavell absorbed and stored for the future. Wavell always held that Allenby was his mentor and it is easy to see in his own performance in command how true this was.

That he should now find himself travelling between Cairo and London as the trusted emissary of two such great soldiers was an educative experience given to few officers – made all the more significant by the intimacy of the task and the great trust which was placed in his shrewd intelligence, balanced judgement, and complete discretion. Both his masters knew that in him they had a link of outstanding competence and integrity.

Allenby's great victory in the Third Battle of Gaza showed Wavell the crucial importance in desert warfare of transport, water, and surprise –

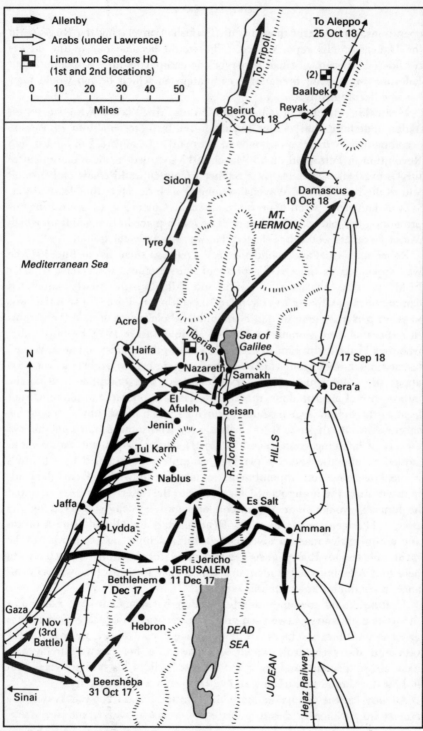

Map 2. Palestine 1917–18: Allenby's Campaigns

Allenby

Arabs (under Lawrence)

Liman von Sanders HQ
(1st and 2nd locations)

0 10 20 30 40 50
Miles

To Tripoli

To Aleppo
25 Oct 18

(2)

Baalbek

Beirut
2 Oct 18

Reyak

Sidon

Damascus
10 Oct 18

MT. HERMON

Tyre

Mediterranean Sea

Acre

N

Tiberias

Sea of Galilee

Haifa

(1)

Nazareth

Samakh

Dera'a

17 Sep 18

El Afuleh

Beisan

Jenin

Tul Karm

R. Jordan

HILLS

Nablus

Jaffa

Es Salt

Lydda

Amman

Jericho

JERUSALEM
11 Dec 17

Bethlehem
7 Dec 17

Gaza

7 Nov 17
(3rd
Battle)

Hebron

DEAD
SEA

JUDEAN

Sinai

Beersheba
31 Oct 17

Hejaz Railway

three of the primary elements in the success of his own Operation 'Compass' in 1940. He noted later, the success of Meinertzhagen's 'haversack ruse', by which the enemy was deliberately fed with false information, the lengths to which Allenby went to create dummy formations and simulated movement as part of his general deception plan, and the way in which Allenby kept up the pressure upon his beaten enemy, despite the battle-weariness of his own troops. All this, and much more, he stored in his fertile mind and would later spell out in his two-volume biography of Allenby and his definitive account of the Palestine Campaigns.[18]

* * *

After the fall of Jerusalem in December 1917, Wavell returned with his report to Robertson who, instead of sending him back to Allenby, kept him to serve as Assistant Adjutant and Quartermaster General of the British Delegation to the Supreme Allied War Council in Versailles – headed by the political and wily Henry Wilson, to whom Wavell was, of course, well known. Wavell's principal task in Versailles was to provide expert advice to both the soldiers and the politicians on the Middle East scene. He soon realised that he was caught in the toils of a deadly struggle between 'the Westerners' (Field Marshal Haig and Robertson – the proponents of priority being given to the destruction of the German armies on the Western Front) and 'the Easterners' (Lloyd George and Wilson – who sought to escape the bloodbath in the West by engaging in peripheral operations, primarily in Palestine). Connell attributes Robertson's appointment of Wavell to Versailles as a 'shrewd attempt . . . directly to influence this internal British controversy before it came out into the open in front of the other Allied delegations'.[19]

This clash of policies and personalities soon came to a head when Robertson openly opposed the Prime Minister and was relieved in consequence – by Wilson. The whole affair sickened Wavell who longed to return to active service and begged to be sent back to Palestine, despite Wilson's warning that in seeking to escape from the hub of the international direction of the war, he was in danger of doing irreparable damage to his career.

* * *

Wavell's plea was answered and he soon found himself back in Palestine, delighted to have been appointed Brigadier General, General Staff (BGGS) of Lieutenant General Sir George Barrow's newly-formed XXII Corps. Unhappily, this appointment was short lived as the demands of the Western Front for manpower, in the face of renewed German activity, began to bleed the Egyptian Expeditionary Force white – to such an extent that XXII Corps was disbanded on 29 March 1918. However, such was Wavell's reputation that he was almost immediately selected to become BGGS to Lieutenant General (later Field Marshal Lord) Sir Philip Chetwode's XX Corps. Like Allenby, Chetwode was a cavalryman and had already played a leading role in the Palestine Campaign. Wavell learned much from him and later wrote that Chetwode 'had about the best and quickest military brain [that Wavell had] ever known, an extremely good tactical eye for ground and a great gift for expressing a situation clearly and concisely, either by word or on paper'.[20] Not only did Wavell have the benefit of Chetwode's example but, as BGGS of a Corps, he saw much of Allenby. These were indeed years rich in experience for him.

Despite the depredations of the demands from Home on his army, Allenby was not one to let it lie fallow and spent the summer of 1918 in reorganising and retraining such troops as he had in preparation for what was to prove one of the most brilliant campaigns in military history. By dint of the most elaborate deception measures, which ranged from electronic warfare to the construction of no less than 15,000 dummy horses to mislead the Turks about his real deployment, he fooled the enemy completely and, with tremendous dash, advanced over 350 miles in less than six weeks, capturing more than 360 guns and 75,000 prisoners at a cost of less than 6,000 casualties. Wavell was in the thick of it all.

An armistice between the Allies and Turkey was signed on 31 October 1918. In his role as BGGS of the Corps which bore the brunt of Allenby's masterstroke, Wavell had once more demonstrated his qualities as a field soldier and as a staff officer. Not only did his Headquarters have an enviable reputation for the issue of clear, concise, and thoroughly effective orders, but he himself showed yet again that he was both farsighted and unshakeable. Constantly reconnoitring the ground over which the Corps would advance, his keen eye for ground – albeit the only one he now had – matched that of his commander. For his part in the operations, Wavell was made CMG in the following year.

*   *   *

Wavell's own summary of his Great War experience was characteristically low key. Laconically, he concluded that he:

> had had on the whole an interesting and successful war, with varied experience. I had risen from junior captain to brigadier general (brevet-lieut-colonel). Except for the loss of my eye, I had had an easy war and not very much danger or hardship. I had served in three theatres (France, Russia and the Middle East) and had travelled a good many miles. I held in all no fewer than eleven appointments . . . but all except five had been in the nature of stop gaps . . . The Western Front was a very dull, unimaginative, heavy-footed business; and I think I learnt more of the art of war in my more unorthodox wayfarings.[21]

In truth, he had had a magnificent war in which he had not only shown his true qualities as a soldier but had learned volumes from the distinguished men under whom he served but, above all, from Allenby. He emerged as one who was widely seen as a man with a great future in the Army. Level headed and discrete and personally brave, he showed a genuine and sustained concern for the well-being of his soldiers.

Two facets of his character which had emerged in the war years were to have a significant effect upon future events. The first was an inability to speak cogently and openly with those who bored or did not interest him and the second was a deep abhorrence and repugnance for the intrusion of politics on military affairs, born of his reaction to the 'Curragh Incident' in 1914 and the scheming and plotting he had witnessed during his time in Versailles in 1918, when on the staff of the Supreme War Council. As history would show, it was a combination of these two factors which would make it certain that he would fall out with his supreme political master almost from the very beginning of his tenure of command in the Middle East in 1939–1941.

Wavell's own words, at the end of his published study on *The Palestine Campaigns* perhaps provide the best summary of the thoughts that he now took forward into the years of uneasy peace which were to follow:

> A study of what well-trained troops, capable of manoeuvre, were able to accomplish may serve as a corrective to the pessimism as to the offensive power of infantry which the experience of rigid trench warfare in France engendered in the minds of some.
>
> The student of these campaigns who bears away with him the two lessons that mobility, which gives the power of surprise, should be the chief aim of the organisation of our Army, and that training, which gives the ability to manoeuvre, will restore the offensive power on the battle field which many in France believed it to have lost, will not have read them in vain.[22]

3

Journeyman Soldier and Consummate Commander 1919–1939

After a spell of leave in England, during which his second child and eldest daughter was born, Wavell returned to Cairo in February 1919 and soon became BGGS at Allenby's Advanced Headquarters in Haifa. However, Allenby's new responsibilities as High Commissioner for Egypt soon led to his relinquishing his military command and his replacement by Lieutenant General Sir Walter Congreve, the former commander of the North Force in the Egyptian Expeditionary Force. This meant the end of the close association between Allenby and Wavell which they had shared almost continuously since 1917 and which would have a lasting and immutable influence upon Wavell's further development as a soldier and a man.

Early in 1920, while still an acting Brigadier General, Wavell became the temporary Chief of the General Staff when Major General Sir Louis Bols departed to a new appointment. But the contractions of peace meant that it was inevitable that a more senior officer would appear to replace Wavell and in April 1920 he returned to England. Bemoaning his loss of Wavell's services, Congreve wrote to Henry Wilson (then CIGS):

> He is an exceptionally good staff officer – strong – quiet – sound – a great worker – and exceptional memory for details and figures, and popular too. He is worth your keeping. I don't think you can put him to any job he will not do well in. I know nothing of his power of command, but should expect it to be good . . .[1]

Regimental Duty and the War Office, 1920–26

It was natural that Wavell should then be hoping for command of a battalion but the dice were loaded heavily against him because of the large number of former brigade commanders, many of whom had two years command experience in the field, now also in the field of selection. Rather than accept a job as a GSO II instructor at the Staff College, which he

20

understandably felt was a bit too much of a come-down after his long experience as a BGGS, he now returned to regimental duty with the 2nd Battalion The Black Watch in his substantive rank of Major and Brevet Lieutenant Colonel. Although his brevet gave him seniority in the Army, it gave none in the Regiment, so that, as Connell explains, he was in 'the position of [being] about tenth or twelfth major in his regiment, with no prospect of command of a battalion in it for many years'[2]. After spending the first six months of 1921 in Germany as a company commander, his automatic promotion to Colonel (due to his brevet) put an end to his regimental soldiering. A second daughter had been born to the Wavells in July.

* * *

Then followed a period as Assistant Adjutant General (AAG) of AG1 in the War Office. It was a time of grinding hard, detailed work for Wavell dealing with the preparation of peace establishments for the post-war Army and Territorial Army. Though, on the face of it, a dreary task after the glamour of his highly responsible and active posts in Palestine, it was one in which he learned much about the administrative aspects of a modern army – knowledge that would stand him in good stead when faced by the woefully inadequate resources of the Middle East garrison in 1939.

In July 1923, Wavell found himself back with another of his old chiefs – Major General Sir John Burnett-Stuart, then Director of Military Operations and Intelligence. As GSO I of MO 1, Wavell would be his key man, responsible for Imperial Defence and Strategy – a post in which the incumbent was expected to be able to match the best brains 'in Whitehall – and elsewhere'. With the strength of the Army slashed by the 'Geddes Axe' of 1921–22, a return to the Cardwell System of linked battalions at home and abroad, and the crippling effect of the 'Ten Year Rule', which assumed no war in Europe for ten years, Wavell was faced with a formidable task. For the first time, he became embroiled in the toils of inter-service rivalry in the scramble for funds and the devastating effect that this could have on policy. Both the Army and the Royal Navy, for example, settled for fixed defences in the review of the defence of Singapore, on grounds of adequacy and economy – the price for which would be paid in 1942, to his personal chagrin.

In the aftermath of a crippling war, and in the face of such stultifying economic constraints, it was hardly surprising that the Army withdrew into its shell and the cosy security of the regimental system, absorbed with the routine of garrison duty and life in the Raj – punctuated by occasional bursts of activity on the North West Frontier of India. But Wavell refused to succumb to this mental stagnation and devoted much time and energy to reflection on his valuable and varied experience in 'the war to end all wars', seeking to distil the lessons and to share them with his fellow soldiers by writing and lecturing. At the same time, he became a voracious reader of military history and developed an extensive correspondence with other military thinkers of his day – TE Lawrence, Basil Liddell Hart, and JFC Fuller among them. In a reply to one of his letters to Lawrence, we find this significant passage:

> As for the reply to raiding techniques. As you say, it's greater mobility than the attack. This doesn't mean large drafts [of men] from the harrassed G.O.C. [General Officer Commanding]. If the Turks had put machine guns on three or four of their touring cars, & driven them on a weekly patrol over the admirable going of the desert E. of Amman & Maan, they would have put an absolute stop to our camel-parties, & so to our rebellion. It wouldn't have cost them 20 men or L20,000 . . . *rightly applied*. They scraped up cavalry & armoured trains & camel corps & block-houses against us: because they didn't think hard enough.[3]

These words must surely have been in the back of Wavell's mind in June 1940 as he played his signal role in the conception and institution of Long Range Patrols – the precursors of the Long Range Desert Group.

Brigadier Ivan Stimson has given us an illuminating example of Wavell's manner in dealing with his staff at the time which makes it easy to see why he was held in such high and affectionate regard by his juniors. Stimson tells how he first realised that Wavell:

> . . . was a great man when he was Colonel at the War Office, . . . & I (as a very junior Staff Capt.) had to explain something against *his own* suggestion & inclination. He heard me out fully, asked a few questions – and changed his mind & *told me so!* I was really surprised because such complete integrity towards any problem is (in my experience) extremely rare.[4]

But the forces of reaction were also at work in the War Office at that time and Wavell's old Staff College classmate and friend General Sir Ivo Vesey has recalled how he was button-holed by the new CIGS, General (later Field Marshal Lord) Sir George Milne to be told that Wavell must never come back to the War Office because he was a 'menace'. He and a group of other 'Angry Young Men' (Milne meant particularly JFC Fuller and Basil Liddell Hart) were pressing for speedier mechanisation of the Army – which he, the CIGS, did not like. Vesey records that this was the only occasion on which he ever heard Wavell criticised by a senior officer[5]. As we shall see, Milne would later change his tune over mechanisation.

Half-Pay and the 3rd Division, 1926–30

The appalling stagnation in post-war promotion and the superabundance of well qualified officers on the General List for an ever dwindling number of appointments meant that even the most able officers would sometimes find themselves temporarily unemployed and placed on what was euphemistically described as 'half-pay' – in fact, as they lost their allowances and the use of their soldier servant, it was effectively more like 'quarter-pay', as Wavell realised when he found himself in this situation from January to November 1926.

It almost goes without saying that Wavell put those eleven months to good use, writing and studying and pursuing his correspondence with kindred spirits. The birth of another daughter at this time helped to under-line the financial hardship suffered by the family but fortunately they were able to withdraw to General Wavell's large house in Norfolk. Even so, Wavell felt the need to earn some money and was glad to be given the chance to contribute to the *Encyclopaedia Britannica*, of which Liddell Hart was then the Military Editor and who was loud in his praise of the offerings he received, lauding Wavell's style and the clarity of his expression. It was during this time too, urged on, Liddell Hart claimed, by himself, that Wavell wrote his definitive work *The Palestine Campaigns*. This book was greeted with acclaim in the prestigious *Army Quarterly* as 'a model of what a military study of a campaign should be. It is accurate and clear. . . . His comments are shrewd and give much food for thought to those who will wish to apply the lessons to future means'.[6] No one would make better use of those lessons than Wavell himself! The post-war years saw a good deal of apathy within the ranks of the Army towards cerebral activity and even antipathy towards those who were seen to devote too much time and effort to it – needless to say, Wavell remained firmly nonconformist to that unworthy tradition.

* * *

November 1926 was to bring a most welcome new appointment for Wavell – his old master and mentor, for whom he had such high regard, 'Jock' Burnett-Stuart, had asked for him as GSO I (Chief of Staff) of his 3rd Division. It was to prove yet another invaluable and stimulating period in Wavell's career, enabling him to develop many of the ideas which he and his fellow 'Angry Young Men' had been discussing on the subject of mechanisation.

Spurred on by the Secretary of State for War, Sir John Laming Evans, Milne set up a brigade-sized force of all arms in 1927 in order to serve as a potential starting point for the mechanisation and modernisation of the whole Army. Designated the 'Experimental Mechanised Force' the brigade was concentrated at Tidworth under Colonel RJ Collins (who would later become one of Wavell's biographers). The original choice for command had been Colonel JFC Fuller who, in a characteristically pettish mood, had turned the job down on the grounds that he objected to some of the ancillary duties he would be required to perform. This change was a tragedy for, although Collins was a good friend of Wavell's, even he de-scribed him as 'the footiest foot soldier they could find'.[7] In consequence, much of the precious year available for trials and exercises was wasted in ponderous manoeuvre. It was only when Lieutenant Colonel (later General Sir) Frederick Pile, the commanding officer of a tank battalion in the Force – 3rd Battalion Royal Tank Corps – was given temporary command of the Force during a divisional exercise, that its full potential was demonstrated in a high speed encircling movement which, as Liddell Hart observed, 'virtually paralysed' the 3rd Division, even though it had the support of a cavalry brigade.[8] In the following year, the Force was resurrected and redesignated the 'Experimental Armoured Force', though the change was effectively only in name. Burnett-Stuart now set an exercise designed to restore some of the shattered morale of the dismounted infantry of the 3rd Division. In consequence, by a series of devices, he contrived what could at best be described as a 'stalemate', generating a good deal of ill-feeling among the proponents of armoured warfare who felt that they had been cheated. In November, with the results of this exercise as a partial excuse and in response to growing unrest among the opponents of mechanisation, the Force was disbanded on grounds of economy and the ostensible decision to concentrate the limited funds available on the mechanisation of infantry and cavalry units.

The 1927 and 1928 manoeuvres placed special, and unique, demands upon both Burnett-Stuart and Wavell. They were responsible for devising large exercises involving, together for the first time, infantry, mechanised infantry, armour, cavalry, artillery, and support units, each possessing different types of vehicles with varying speed capabilities and resupply requirements. Combining their intellectual resources, they designed imaginative and challenging training exercises to test new tactical concepts. The presence of Burnett-Stuart and Wavell together on Salisbury Plain has been described accurately as 'one of the most formidable concentrations of lively, original and profound military thought that had ever been put into one peace-time Headquarters'.[9]

One of the main items on the agenda of the annual Army Staff Conference in January 1929 was a discussion of the lessons from the two-year experiment of the Mechanised/Armoured Force. Collins began the discussion by providing his conclusions, emphasising the various roles that the Force was given for trial. He was followed by Wavell, who gave the perspective of the infantry division which had opposed the experimental force. Wavell addressed the vulnerability of an infantry division against an armoured force, and perceptively noted the debilitating effect that such a force, due to its speed and surprise, could inflict upon the morale of infantrymen. Keenly understanding the advantages of tanks, Wavell then ventured reasonably that 'the requirements of mobility, fire-power, and armour must always be to a certain extent conflicting. I suggest, very tentatively, that the respective value of these three might be assessed by the ratio 3: 2: 1.'[10] He also concurred with Collins that tanks would need dismounted infantry for protection, and that wireless communications should be further developed to support future armoured forces operating 'over hitherto undreamt-of distances'.[11] While these statements would be seen today as truisms, it is important to realise that in making them at that time, Wavell was showing himself to be years ahead of most of his contemporaries in his understanding of the true significance of armour in future warfare.

There is an interesting and important sidelight to Wavell's time with the 3rd Division which may give some understanding of his personal style in the years ahead when bearing the heaviest burdens of responsibility of almost any general in the Second World War.

Looking back on Wavell's performance as his GSO I, Burnett-Stuart later recalled:

> What difficulty I had to get [Wavell] to do his work. He wouldn't work if he could get someone else to do it for him – particularly me. Idle is not exactly the word for him – because he was always absorbing something – but he would always put off setting exercises for the divisional manoeuvres. The first year he got me so alarmed that they wouldn't be done that I wrote them myself – but he didn't succeed next year.[12]

While Burnett-Stuart, who had no illusions about Wavell's true potential, concluded that, rather than laziness or apathy, it was as if Wavell was saving himself for some great future opportunity, it seems as though Wavell's taciturn manner and his well-known habit of greeting people or answering questions with a monosyllabic grunt did indeed mislead many who did not know him well. We shall see, in a later chapter, that this characteristic would hopelessly flaw his relations with Winston Churchill, with devastating consequences. In his biography, Collins shrewdly quotes an anonymous officer (perhaps himself) who had almost daily contact with Wavell in the 3rd Division days and realised full well that Wavell's reserve conveyed a false impression: 'I realised after a time that though Wavell rarely appeared to be working hard, he was always thinking. He did as much in the way of seeking conclusions, correct ones, in one hour as most men did in reaching vague generalities in several'.[13] In a similar positive tone, Burnett-Stuart's aide-de-camp in the 3rd Division, a young subaltern named Francis Festing, later recalled his 'wonderful experience of being ADC [aide-de-camp] in a most brilliant Divisional HQ, with Jock [Burnett-] Stuart as the GOC and Archie Wavell as the GSO 1', and added, 'It was a liberal education for a young officer and I think I learnt more from those two brilliant soldiers than I ever have at any other period of my life'.[14] That is quite a testimony, since that young subaltern later became Field Marshal Sir Francis Festing, Chief of the Imperial General Staff from 1958 to 1961. In later life, Burnett-Stuart's criticism diminished, as he wrote: 'It was a joy to have Archie Wavell with his nimble brain, his unfailing sense of humour, and his original outlook, to work with; . . .'[15]

Wavell's experience with the mechanisation trials, when added to the ruminations about the importance of mobility which had been in his mind since his days in Palestine, served as the basis of an important article, published in the *Journal of the Royal United Services Institute* in November 1930, entitled 'The Army and the Prophets'. If evidence were needed of the brilliance of his vision and intellect, it is to be found in that article. In it he made a whole series of shrewdly prophetic statements which must have seemed revolutionary at the time and which showed how great was his almost uncanny grasp of the problems of future warfare. Emphasising that 'the aim of post-war developments was . . . to contrive [the] means of restoring to the foot soldier movement in the face of modern fire-power [rather] than to find a substitute for him as the assaulting arm on the battlefield',[16] he surveyed the views of contemporary theorists 'with no claim whatever to originality' and then postulated that 'armoured machines to fight on land must be designed for speed and fire-power rather than for armour and bulk', reminding his readers that throughout military history it has been shown that speed is often a better protection than armour.[17] He went on to emphasise the importance of wholly professional, as opposed to conscript, armies in the future – armies that would fight principally from machines, augmented by 'lightly armed highly trained soldiers' who would fight on foot in close country. His comments upon the need for rapid industrial mobilisation, the vulnerability of industrial and population centres to strategic bombing, and the importance of air-ground cooperation on the battlefield reflected the breadth of his vision and understanding. Interestingly, he made no call for rapid change but rather for evolution rather than revolution – though one suspects that this may possibly have been a tactic to outflank those reactionaries who were only too ready, as Milne had some years earlier, to brand men of vision as 'menaces'. In any case, his experience in the War Office and during the preceding three years had made him realise that to speak of the urgency of reform was to cry for the moon and could only be counterproductive.

This, then, was the man who in the summer of 1930 found himself ready for brigade command, no longer walking in the shadow of any other.

Brigade Command and Half-Pay 1930–35

In June 1930, Wavell assumed command of the 6th Infantry Brigade in the 2nd Division. His Headquarters were in Blackdown. He was curiously unsure of himself to begin with and later admitted candidly that he had 'started without much confidence in my capacity for command, and was not sure that I should make a success. I soon found to my relief that I could make up my mind and act quickly in handling my brigade, and could give orders without hesitation.[18] Collins remarked:

There is no doubt that in his brigade training Wavell really came out of his shell. The apparent lethargy on which some of his best friends had remarked when he was serving on Salisbury Plain, disappeared.[19]

In the following year, Wavell was given a new Brigade Major, Eric Dorman-Smith, who would later become a controversial figure but at this time was full of enthusiasm and energy. He soon showed that he could ably complement and support his commander's desire to train the most proficient and professional infantry force possible. Between them they were to produce new, and now legendary, training exercises designed to enhance realism and to hold the interest of the soldiers. Wavell was oblivious to the 'rat race' aspects of peacetime soldiering. Mistakes, to him, were things from which to learn and then to be avoided – indeed, an exercise in which no mistakes were observed was really no exercise at all. Attempts to impress one's superiors and oversupervision of subordinates were simply not in his book. His sole desire was to train his subordinate commanders and their soldiers to a pitch at which the blunders and chaos of the infantry battles of the Great War would never be repeated. Dorman-Smith, who, like Wavell, had been wounded and decorated in the 9th Infantry Brigade at the Battle of Bellewaarde Ridge in June 1915, was equally clear about their common aim.

The redesignation of the Brigade as the 6th (Experimental) Infantry Brigade brought fresh fuel to the fires of Wavell's enthusiasm as he and his staff planned and executed trials similar to those which he had supervised on Salisbury Plain for Burnett-Stuart. Technically, as well as tactically, the trials were important, showing as they did how transport and supporting artillery could be mechanised and how heavy weapons like mortars and anti-tank guns could be absorbed into the infantry battalion. The dead hand of reaction still existed in some corners of the Army – the Commandant of the Machine Gun School (Collins, no less!) even went so far as to call Wavell 'an unsound iconoclast' because he produced a concept for the carriage of a protected machine-gun in an armoured vehicle with a crew of only two instead of the six men required in the 'Manual'.[20] Fortunately, the idea would survive in the form of the Bren Gun Carrier.

The 6th Infantry Brigade's exercises were justifiably famous for their realism, as Wavell tried to reproduce the uncertainties and fog of war in each. The ultimate goal was 'the restoration of the foot fighter, by high training and high morale, plus high mobility and the best weapon system, to his rightful place on the battlefield'.[21] While the Brigade Commander devoted his energies to training – military, physical and mental – and the establishment of morale, his Brigade Major concentrated on armament, mobility and the organisational requirements of the trials.

During the winter of 1931–2, Wavell devised a brilliant raiding exercise for the officers and NCOs of the Brigade – something quite outside their normal span of interest and, prophetically, a first taste of thinking on

Commando lines. Equally original was his Brigade exercise for the following summer. This was given an African setting, inspired in part by *King Solomon's Mines* and involved every conceivable situation in which a battalion might find itself – it was deliberately different to 'the usual run of military training at Aldershot, to see how they would react'.[22] That exercise included a night march followed by a raid – tasks virtually unknown in the British Army between the wars. Movement and assault by night would prove key elements to his great victory in Operation 'Compass' in December 1940.

Wavell's Exercise 'Araminta' – billed on battalion notice boards as 'A Stirring Drama of Love and War, in Four Acts', was a masterpiece of innovation. The soldiers expected the unexpected and were not disappointed. Versatility and unorthodoxy were the hallmarks of the exercise – even to the point of the Brigadier and his BM bombing units in bivouac from the air with bags of flour!

Reaction was not amused. The War Office protested at the frivolity and the departures from training regulations. However, Wavell's Divisional Commander, Major General Henry Jackson, valiantly supported him and saw that no word of criticism or censure was passed down to the Brigade.

The divisional exercises which followed brigade training in the late summer of 1932 marked the apogee of Wavell's brigade command experience. His reputation as the originator of vigorous, realistic, and challenging training had given him an aura of near invincibility. Thanks to the close attention he paid to every imaginative ploy available to a commander in the field, his use of deception and surprise, of liaison officers to keep him up to the minute on battlefield information, and his careful study of all available intelligence sources, he was able to run rings round his worthy but less capable opponents. As a result, exercises due to last five days had often been wrapped up by 6th Infantry Brigade in two!

Looking back on that summer later, Wavell stressed the importance of those exercises to his own future: 'I believe it was this season probably that determined my future career, in that I was always afterwards chosen for command and never again for the staff'.[23]

Wavell loved to share his ideas and thinking with other soldiers and gave numerous lectures while he was at Blackdown – to Staff College candidates, the student body at Camberley, and to the Royal United Services Institution (RUSI). Despite his reputation for taciturnity, he was in fact a gifted speaker and lecturer. One lecture which he gave at the RUSI in February 1933 encapsulated his whole philosophy on training. Entitled 'The Training of the Army for War', it contained much which will live on as long as the British Army exists. His refreshingly down-to-earth approach as he spoke of the four principal qualities he sought to inculcate into the soldier by training – discipline, physical fitness, skill at arms, and battlecraft – made a deep impression. A highlight of that lecture was his handling of 'battlecraft', one of his most famous and challenging utterances, which is quoted today wherever battlecraft is taught:

> A well-known and enthusiastic infantry brigadier always phrases his require-
> ments for the ideal infantryman as 'athlete, sharpshooter, stalker.' I always feel
> inclined to put my demands on a lower plane and to say that the qualities of a
> successful poacher, catburglar and gunman would content me. His ideal has
> moral qualities that mine, I am afraid, would not possess; and my definition is
> deliberately meant to call attention to the value of low cunning in war.
> Certainly the knowledge and practice of battle-craft, i.e. commonsense or low
> cunning, is the weak point of the infantryman at present. We are unbuttoning
> his collar, let us also try to unbutton his mind.[24]

That lecture contained a number of priceless quotes. Of the qualities required of an officer: the 'ideal officer must be afraid of nothing – not even of a new idea'.[25] On exercises: 'However hopeless a muddle', an exercise may seem, war is always considerably worse and 'the most hopeless-looking muddle has a marvellous way of sorting itself out – both in war and in peace'.[26] Throughout, he exhibited a readiness to challenge orthodoxy and made thoughtful recommendations based upon his own well-proven, though audacious, training in his brigade. Though regarded by many in the military 'Establishment' as a heretic, the Second World War would vindicate his wisdom, time and time again.

An interesting sideline on this lecture was Wavell's apparent readiness to defer to authority rather than to tilt at windmills. Liddell Hart, who was in the audience, was dismayed to hear Wavell say that General Sir Harry Knox, an arch-conservative, who challenged one of his statements, was much more likely to be right than he, in the light of his far greater and wider experience. However, bearing in mind Wavell's tactical cunning, one might conclude that he was merely playing Knox to leg in order to avoid a confrontation, judging that the rest of his audience would draw their own conclusions. Nevertheless, Wavell came from a strict Army background and the tradition of loyalty to and respect for one's seniors may have played its part as, possibly, it did over the question of sending the expeditionary force to Greece in 1941.

Wavell's unmitigated success as commander of the 6th Infantry Brigade was recognised by his promotion to Major General on 16 October 1933, while still serving as a brigade commander. He had an inner strength, imperturbability, and resolution, and inspired his soldiers and those around him with a quiet confidence. Wavell was the epitome of the tactically and technically proficient commander, full of audacity and imagination, and not afraid to take a calculated risk when the situation warranted it. He had an excellent rapport with his subordinate commanders, officers, and soldiers. He especially liked to play golf with the subalterns in his battalions; not only did he get to know his junior officers, but through them he would have received the unvarnished truth about the attitudes of the soldiers and about life in the barracks.

*   *   *

Wavell's tour with 6th Infantry Brigade ended in January 1934. Almost unbelievably, he was again forced to go on half-pay awaiting a new appointment. As before, he put the time to good use and kept his mind fully occupied. He corrected Staff College examination papers and rewrote the Army's *Field Service Regulations (Part II)*, producing a draft which showed 'a notable advance' in tactical doctrine. Collins, who saw that draft, commented: 'It was attractive to read, alive, picturesque, and would have been far less stodgy . . . than the bowdlerised version which was all that a staid General Staff were in the end prepared to father'.[27]

Fortunately, a number of interesting short jobs turned up for Wavell as he waited for 15 long months before being selected to command the 2nd Division. In April 1934 he was one of a team reconnoitring potential routes from Haifa and Jerusalem to Baghdad – an experience which would stand him in good stead when, in 1941, he was obliged to send a relief force from Palestine to Habbaniya Air Base in Iraq after it had been attacked by insurgents. September brought a special opportunity for him to think yet again about the future possibilities of armoured warfare when he acted as Chief Umpire to his old chief and friend 'Jock' Burnett-Stuart, then General Officer Commanding-in-Chief, Southern Command, who had set an exercise for what was dubbed the 'Mobile Force'. This formation had been created by combining Britain's only Tank Brigade with the 7th Infantry Brigade. The trial was perhaps destined to fail, in large part due to the parochial and opposing ideologies of the two senior commanders of the Mobile Force on the question of the employment of armoured units.   This clash of personalities did much to spoil what would otherwise have been a very important trial but Wavell saw enough in it to give him plenty of food for thought.

Because of British suspicions over the true state of the French Army and the efficiency of its General Staff, Wavell and two other half-pay Major Generals (Marshall-Cornwall and Freyberg), with both of whom Wavell would work closely in the years ahead, were sent on a three-week course at the French Senior Officers' School. At the end of the course, they submitted a blunt and unanimous report to the War Office, inveighing against the arrogant complacency of the French Army which discouraged initiative and seemed to them to have moved not one pace forward since the end of the Great War. Marshall-Cornwall wrote tellingly that they had 'no conception of exploiting the mobility of armoured formations in tactical manoeuvre, every attack being envisaged as a head-on frontal assault . . . It was not only a reversion to the methods of 1914–1918, it was Napoleon's tactical folly at Waterloo all over again'.[28] So the total collapse of French arms will have come as no surprise to Wavell in 1940.

Divisional Command, 1935–37

Wavell's appointment to command the 2nd Division in March 1935 came, rather surprisingly, as something of a disappointment to him. He had very much hoped to become Commandant of the Imperial Defence College, for which he had been strongly recommended by General Jackson, his former Divisional Commander. However, when Wavell made this point to the CIGS in an interview, he was told that everyone (on the selection board) had thought he would prefer a divisional command.

As Bernard Fergusson, his first aide-de-camp, would observe, it was at once apparent that Wavell's contemporaries were looking to him as 'something of a prophet'. If proof of this was needed, he was soon being visited regularly by some of the most able and influential directors in the War Office, including Dill (Operations) and Brooke (Military Training), and Gort, the Commandant of the Staff College.[29]

Wavell was extremely fortunate in his Brigade Commanders – Victor Fortune (5th Brigade), who would later command the ill-fated 51st Highland Division in France in 1940; Henry Maitland Wilson (6th Brigade), who was to prove his indispensable troubleshooter in the Middle East; and Arthur Smith (4th Guards Brigade), destined to become his devoted Chief of Staff in Cairo.

Wavell was to lose three good friends in 1935–36. His father had died just before he assumed command of the Division and TE Lawrence was killed in a motorcycle accident in May 1935. Wavell went to Lawrence's funeral in a private capacity and wrote an admirable tribute to him, as he did for his old friend, mentor and master, Field Marshal Lord Allenby, in 1936. From that appreciation, it is easy to see how much the two men had in common as soldiers and how much Wavell had profited from the counsel of that very great commander.

After finishing Part II of *Field Service Regulations*, Wavell began work on *Part III: Operations – Higher Formations*. Once again, he was able to inject much of his own philosophy and personality into the draft and once again his views proved to be too strong medicine for the diehards of Whitehall. As Fergusson wrote: 'When it [*Field Service Regulations, (Part III)*] left his hand, it was readable and stimulating, with apt analogies drawn from golf, horse-racing and other spheres. Even when the dead hand of the War Office had finished with it, it was streets ahead of its predecessor.'[30]

* * *

The Army manoeuvres for 1935 were the largest in ten years and were of special significance. Involving all four British Army divisions, they were seen as something of a trial of strength between three contestants for the post of CIGS: Generals Burnett-Stuart of Southern Command (Chief Umpire), Gathorne-Hardy of Aldershot Command (Eastland), and Deverell of Eastern Command (Westland).

In the face of Wavell's warning of the dangers, Gathorne-Hardy insisted on launching the 2nd Division into an attack which would leave his left flank dangerously exposed. According to Connell, Wavell then successfully 'pulled his division out from near disaster, retreated, re-formed and withstood a strong enemy attack'.[31] At the post-exercise after-action review, or conference, Gathorne-Hardy was severely criticised for his handling of the 2nd Division, but he admitted candidly that, 'I should like it to be known that Major General Wavell formed an accurate appreciation of the situation and warned me of what was likely to happen'.[32] Needless to say, Deverell became the next CIGS. Wavell's performance throughout the 1935 training season can be best summed up by Marshall-Cornwall, who was attached to 2nd Division Headquarters during July, August and September 1935: 'Wavell was the most inspiring tactical leader we had.'[33]

A small but prophetic incident during the 1935 training season demonstrated yet again how ready Wavell was to listen to the ideas of young officers under his command and the ability he possessed to inspire creative and unconventional thinking in his subordinates. Despite having his ideas turned down by his battalion commander, a Lieutenant Fox-Davies wrote to Wavell through Fergusson, putting forward the almost unheard of proposal for a deep raid on the enemy's command and control facilities, suggesting that such an operation could wreak havoc out of all proportion to the size of force employed. Wavell replied sympathetically and the idea seemed to have been shelved. However, in the middle of another exercise in 1936, Wavell suddenly sent for Fox-Davies and told him to mount the raid that he had proposed a year earlier. The effect was devastating and, to the chagrin of Gathorne-Hardy and the umpires, it brought the exercise to a premature halt – to the delight of the soldiers who got home a day early! Small wonder that Wavell would welcome and implement the proposals for long range patrolling in the Western Desert in 1940 and David Stirling's Special Air Service, all of which would prove a nasty thorn in the side of the enemy and live on in the shape of today's SAS – the envy of every army in the world and recently the scourge of the Iraqi Scud missile crews during Operation 'Desert Storm'.

Meanwhile, Wavell continued to lecture and write. In 1935, he delivered an important address at the RUSI on 'The Higher Commander', a trenchant and pellucid lecture which would later form the basis of his historic Lees Knowles Lectures on 'Generals and Generalship' given in Cambridge in 1939. Perhaps the most important part of his RUSI lecture was the attention he paid to the question of the further education of those destined for high command, something that received little or no attention at the time other than attendance at the Imperial Defence College. What Wavell saw was a continuing process involving a great deal of personal study.

Although divisional training for the 2nd Division was somewhat attenuated in 1936 by the need to transfer equipment to the 1st Division, which was being sent to Palestine, Wavell's fertile mind led him to organise an important battlefield tour in France for the officers of the Division. Soon after he returned from this, he was offered the appointment of Director of Military Training. Sensing his unorthodoxy would be curtly rejected or, at best, that his ideas would be held in abeyance, he turned it down – rightly, in the view of Burnett-Stuart, who commented 'You are well out of it. It consists mainly of teaching several grandmothers to suck eggs'.[34]

Determined to have at least one good exercise that year, Wavell produced another masterpiece of inventiveness in Exercise 'Golden Fleece' which would rival his Exercise 'Araminta' in 6th Infantry Brigade. 'Golden Fleece' was based upon the story of Jason and the Argonauts, which was read to every soldier in the Division. As before, he devised a whole series of most instructive and stimulating engagements as 'the Fleece' changed hands and back again. Loud in its praise, *The Times* observed that the planning of such a 'dramatic, and yet not unreal' exercise 'demanded great gifts of skill and imagination. But, perhaps most of all, one came away with one's regard for the British soldier still further enhanced.'[35] Lieutenant General Sir Brian Horrocks, Brigade Major of the 5th Infantry Brigade in that exercise, would later acknowledge the debt he owed to Wavell, from whom 'I learned the value of really imaginative training'.[36]

As evidence of Wavell's readiness to seek new methods of achieving the mobility which he had long preached to be the key to success in future warfare, we find that after 'Golden Fleece' he made one of his brigades conduct a long tactical road march in buses – the first time that a formation of this size had been moved entirely by mechanical means!

As one of the few Russian-speaking officers in the Army, Wavell headed a four-man team to the Russian Army manoeuvres in the autumn of 1937. In the light of his earlier experience in Russia, he was astonished at the progress that had been made since the Revolution, as he watched a complete infantry brigade being dropped by parachute, and over 1,000 tanks passing the saluting base in the final parade. After reporting on his experience to the War Office, he gave a valuable lecture on the subject to the Imperial Defence College.

As Wavell's time with the 2nd Division came to a close in 1937, the Army's fortunes were at their nadir. After suffering even more than the other two services from the effects of the 'Ten Year Rule', as Bond has written:

> its [the British Army's] role was uncertain, its equipment mostly obsolete, and its production base almost non-existent. Perhaps worst of all was the atmosphere of pessimism and despondency which was beginning to affect even the

more progressive–minded officers and would-be reformers.[37]

Even Wavell was not immune to the effects of that pessimism and confided to one of his staff that he felt he was getting 'stale' and expected to be retired by the Selection Board in the near future.

However, a change of Prime Ministers in 1937 brought with it the appointment of the ambitious, energetic and unorthodox Leslie Hore-Belisha as Secretary of State for War. Hore-Belisha's brash reforming zeal and his extraordinary decision to appoint Liddell Hart, still Military Correspondent of *The Times*, as his senior, but unofficial, military adviser was to create an atmosphere of bitter resentment. However, Liddell Hart's high regard for Wavell made redundant any question of his being retired.

Palestine Command, 1937–38

The open conflict between Jews and Arabs in the British Mandate of Palestine had produced a situation of 'incipient revolt in main centres accompanied by lawless acts of violence, arson and sabotage' combined with 'the vigorous operations of armed bands and saboteurs'.[38] A Royal Commission had recommended the termination of the Mandate and the creation, by the partition of Palestine, of two separate states – one Jewish and one Arab.

It was against this background that Wavell was summoned to the War Office on 16 July 1937 and told that he was to succeed Lieutenant General Sir John Dill as General Officer Commanding British Troops in Palestine and Transjordan. There can be no doubt that this selection was due to the formidable reputation that Wavell had acquired both as a commander and as an intellectual soldier of exceptional ability. His immediate superior, General Sir Edmund Ironside at Eastern Command, rated him as 'one of the few officers . . . genuinely suited to high command'.[39]

Taking over on 19 August 1937, Wavell found himself serving under an old Black Watch friend, General Sir Arthur Wauchope, who had been High Commissioner and Commander-in-Chief, Palestine, since 1931. Wauchope's effectiveness had diminished, due not only to fatigue and emotional involvement in the Palestinian issue but also because it was perceived that he lacked objectivity – a quality which Wavell would maintain with total impartiality.

In a situation calling for strong measures and unorthodox tactics, Wavell was in his element and his troops soon began to produce results under his skilful direction. It was here that Wavell was to meet another unorthodox spirit, Captain Orde Wingate, who would later serve him again in other parts of the world. Unable to get an appointment as soon as he would have liked, Wingate boldly stopped Wavell's car on the road one day and climbed in, saying that he had an important proposition to put to him. He then went on to describe his plans for the formation of what he dubbed 'Special Night Squads', to be composed primarily of Jewish volunteers. Impressed by Wingate's audacity and zeal, Wavell heard him out and later approved the plan. It was a golden example of Wavell's ability to 'distinguish between valuable and worthless enthusiasm, between obsessed cranks and men driven forward by the power of irresistible ideas'.[40]

* * *

Meanwhile, as Wavell was trying to suppress a rebellion in Palestine, Hore-Belisha, in close collaboration with Liddell Hart, was developing a far-reaching programme of Army reorganisation and reform. A principal item on their agenda was the selection of a new generation of senior commanders who would be able to stand the strains of mechanised warfare, a process which would involve the culling of many of the older generals, by-products of the congestion in promotion created by the post-war reductions in the Army. To this end, Hore-Belisha invited Liddell Hart to make an analysis of the Army List and 'draw up a list of outstanding officers right down to junior ranks'.[41] An appointment of special importance at that time was that of General Officer Commanding-in-Chief, Southern Command as the incumbent was the commander-designate of the II Corps in the British Expeditionary Force in the event of war. Liddell Hart later claimed that in the summer of 1937 he told Hore-Belisha:

> that Wavell was, in my view, better than anyone else above him in the Army List (he was then a Major General), and one of the two soldiers in our Army who were potentially *great* commanders. At my urging H-B [Hore-Belisha] appointed Wavell GOC-in-C Southern Command, in face of much resistance from the CIGS and others in the War Office.[42]

The decision was a momentous one as it placed Wavell, still a Major General, over all the eligible Lieutenant Generals then serving. It was not announced until December and the intervening months would see Wavell coming within an ace of achieving even higher things as Hore-Belisha sought a replacement for the 63-year-old CIGS, Field Marshal Sir Cyril Deverell. After a good deal of uncertainty, during which Liddell Hart had put it to Hore-Belisha that the choice lay between 'Dill or Wavell – the latter the better choice if the choice was carried as far down the Army List.[43] Wavell was called back to England for an interview. Hore-Belisha had some uncertainty about him and Wavell's interview failed to impress him or the Cabinet – due largely to his apparent inability to articulate. It was therefore decided to appoint Lord Gort, then the Military Secretary, with whom Hore-Belisha would have had a good deal of contact in their daily work, and Wavell was appointed to Southern Command, the CIGS and other obstructionist members of the Army Council being summarily dismissed. The *Army Quarterly* reported that Wavell's appointment met 'with general approval in the Army'.[44]

Wavell remained in Palestine until 8 April 1938. His tenure in command may be judged a success. After the assassination of the Acting District Commissioner for Galilee in September 1937, Wavell had pressed for the establishment of military courts to handle cases of sabotage, the illegal possession of firearms, and related offences. His recommendation was approved and this measure, together with his employment of mobile columns of mechanised infantry and dismounted patrols, including the Special Night Squads, to track down and capture or kill the Arab guerrillas, illustrate Wavell's determination and adroitness in his contribution to the pacification of Palestine.

Southern Command, 1938–39

General Sir John Burnett-Stuart relinquished command of Southern Command to Wavell on 26 April 1938. Those were days of consternation and trepidation for England as the threat of war in Europe loomed and the inadequacy of the British defence forces became daily clearer for all to see. Wavell was in no doubt that as a commander designate in the British Expeditionary Force, he now had a key role in the preparation for war.

Before he had time to settle in his new command, Wavell received a letter from Major General Sir Ernest Swinton, Chichele Professor of Military Science at Oxford, who was about to retire and was looking for a replacement. He asked if Wavell would like to be considered. In his thoughtful and heartfelt reply, Wavell made it clear that if it were a matter of his personal choice, nothing would please him better but, with war so imminent that 'one has to regard oneself as almost on active service already', his duty to the Army must take priority and he must stay at his post. Should circumstances change by the time the selection fell due, he would seek release from his appointment in order to accept.[45]

Clearly Wavell had decided to make some history rather than teach it.

As the months went by, Wavell left the day-to-day running of his Headquarters very much to his Chief of Staff as he visited throughout his command, doing all he could to promote readiness and improvement and, one guesses, growing increasingly despondent over the appalling obsolescence of such things as the resources for amphibious warfare and the patent failure of the Royal Air Force to have given any thought to the close support of ground operations – a fact that was revealed in his last peacetime exercise early in 1939.

While at Southern Command, Wavell had some contact with Brigadier Bernard Montgomery, whose 9th Infantry Brigade was at Portsmouth. It is of interest to find that while this abrasive but highly competent officer was unwanted by many senior commanders as a divisional commander, it was

Wavell's influence which ultimately secured for him his command of the 3rd Division which he would command with such brilliance in France in 1940.

That much of Wavell's taciturnity, particularly in social circumstances, returned at this time but that he had not lost his magic with the troops is reflected in the recent words of a former Territorial officer whose unit Wavell visited on training in August 1938:

> [Wavell] lunched with us in our officers' mess tent. He looked what he was, strong, charming, clever. In spite of what has been written, he was on this occasion at least, talkative, amusing and witty, and, of course, as is usual, we all, however junior, were introduced to him.[46]

In February 1939, Wavell delivered his three famous Lees Knowles Lectures at Cambridge entitled 'Generals and Generalship'. Based upon his widely-studied lecture to the RUSI in 1935, they would soon receive world-wide acclaim after they had been translated into a number of languages, including German.

Connell's evaluation is incomparable and succinct:

> [The lectures] are steeped in wisdom, sanity and a profound understanding of what war is about and what men are like. The simplicity of the writing is deceptive: the lectures are the product of a lifetime's work and meditation; not a line is unconsidered. Though their immediate context is professional, and Wavell spoke out of the testing of his own experience, their application is universal. Anyone who has read these lectures and taken them to heart, though he never leads a platoon in battle, will be a better man by reason of what they have taught him.[47]

Significantly, two future German Field Marshals held the lectures in high regard. Erwin Rommel, Wavell's future opponent in the Western Desert, carried a copy of the German translation (*Feldherr*) and Wilhem Keitel, Hitler's Chief of *Oberkommando der Wehrmacht*, wrote in the year the lectures were delivered:

> In the British Army today, there is only one good general [Wavell], but he is incomparably good. The others have no proper conception of the direction of mechanised war, but this officer, from 1928 onward, has studied the subject, and he may well prove the dominant personality in any war within the next five years.[48]

* * *

The year 1939 was to prove a significant milestone in Wavell's life. In addition to the success of the Lees Knowles Lectures, and the knighthood he received in the Birthday Honours in June when he was created a Knight Commander of the Most Honourable Order of the Bath (KCB), he received what Collins had described as 'probably the surprise of his life' in the shape of a letter from the Military Secretary asking him if he would like to be considered for the appointment of General Officer Commanding-in-Chief of the newly-formed Middle East Command.[49]

With war so clearly imminent and hence the strong probability that he would soon have to assume his mobilisation appointment as Commander II Corps in the British Expeditionary Force, Wavell realised that this would be a difficult decision.

However, his abhorrence at the thought of any repetition on the Continent of the bloodbaths he had witnessed in 1915 and his natural affinity for the lands and people of the Middle East, born of years of active military experience in the area, together with his shrewd understanding of the likely significance of the new Command in any future conflict, soon helped him overcome any lingering doubts he might have had about where his duty lay. Here at last, like his great mentor Allenby, he would be able to give free rein to his views on the importance of true mobility in open warfare.

So the die was cast and on 27 July 1939, Wavell left London for Cairo, the *Daily Telegraph* observing that 'no better choice than that of Sir Archibald Wavell could have been made'.[50]

Conclusion

The years 1930–39 had seen Wavell in continuous command of troops, apart from a spell on half-pay. In that time, he had gone from strength to strength, his reputation as a brilliant and highly professional, innovative commander and trainer, who stood in the forefront of modern military thought, had gained him international recognition. However, two characteristics, which were of the very essence of the man and his deep personal integrity, remained as potential threats to his future success in command – his taciturnity, so often misunderstood by politicians, and his detestation of the unwarranted admixture of the political and military scenes, though he was the last man to deny the Clausewitzian view of war ie. that war is an extension of politics by other means. Before long, he would find that the latter would almost try his patience beyond endurance.

4

Bellicose Non-Belligerency
August 1939-June 1940

'We are fighting a crusade, . . .'
Wavell, 12 February 1940[1]

After sailing on the P. & O. liner *Comorin* from Marseilles, Wavell arrived in Cairo and took up his appointment as General Officer Commanding-in-Chief, Middle East, on 2 August 1939. His responsibilities were well defined, and awesome, having been promulgated by the Army Council on 24 July 1939.[2]

In peace, Wavell's Middle East Command consisted of Egypt, the Sudan, Palestine and Transjordan, and Cyprus, and he was responsible for the preparation of all war plans for the employment of land forces in British Somaliland, Aden, Iraq, and the shores of the Persian Gulf.

Wavell could not fulfill his charter alone, and of necessity was directed to coordinate plans with the Naval Commander-in-Chief, Mediterranean (Admiral Sir Andrew Cunningham); the Naval Commander-in-Chief, East Indies Station (Vice Admiral R Leatham); the Commander-in-Chief in India (General Sir Robert Cassels); the Inspector General, African Colonial Forces (Major General DP Dickinson); and the Air Officer Commanding-in-Chief, Middle East (Air Chief Marshal Sir William Mitchell). In addition to these military responsibilities, Wavell was also charged with maintaining 'close touch' with the leading Foreign Office representatives in the Middle East: His Majesty's Ambassadors in Egypt and Iraq; the Governor-General of the Sudan; the High Commissioner for Palestine and Transjordan; the Governors of Cyprus, Aden, and British Somaliland; and the Political Resident in the Persian Gulf. These tasks were indicative of Wavell's multifarious responsibilities, and were a portent, after the outbreak of hostilities, of his being frequently diverted by political issues when all attention should have been focused on military operations. In addition, Wavell was responsible, through the General

Commanding-in-Chief, British Troops in Egypt, for the defence of Egypt and the training of the Egyptian Army.

In war, Wavell's area of command would be extended to include all military forces in British Somaliland, Aden, Iraq, and the Persian Gulf. He was also to coordinate the actions of all land forces in his Command, and ensure the proper distribution of resources among them. In essence, Wavell was not only the Army commander for the entire Middle East, but the principal diplomat and primary logistician as well. The enormity of Wavell's assignment, as Jules Menken has observed astutely, did not 'expose him to any risk of wasting away in idleness'.[3]

The Middle East Headquarters was originally seen as a supervisory element to ensure effective planning and coordination. Initially, Wavell's staff was authorised to consist of five officers: a Brigadier, General Staff; a General Staff Officer, Grade 2; two General Staff Officers, Grade 3 (including one for Joint Planning Staff); and an Administrative Staff Officer, in addition to his aide-de-camp. As noted previously, Wavell arrived in Cairo on 2 August 1939, and along with Brigadier Arthur Smith, as Brigadier, General Staff; Major RG Thurburn, The Cameronians, Deputy Adjutant and Quarter Master General; and his aide-de-camp, Lieutenant GAF Kennard, 4th Queen's Own Hussars, established his headquarters. Two additional staff members, Major ASG Douglas, The Rifle Brigade, and Lieutenant JE Benson, The Black Watch, arrived on the following day to serve as GSO 2 and GSO 3 respectively. A six-man Joint Planning Staff was also authorised, the two Army members doubling as staff members of Wavell's Military Headquarters, Middle East. It is indicative of the ever-increasing scope and responsibilities of Wavell's Middle East Command, that the size of his Headquarters staff alone grew in fourteen months to an establishment of 1,061 officers and men, of whom over 700 were for administration.

As August 1939 continued, war seemed ever closer, and Wavell realised accurately that time was his most precious resource in familiarising himself with his new Command and in fulfilling his initial instructions from the Army Council. He immersed himself in his new position, and while en route to Cairo, wrote 'Notes for BGS, Middle East Command', in which he expounded his ideas on 'the basis of our work in the Middle East Command, and . . . its objects and importance'.[4] In this perceptive appreciation, Wavell showed that he realised that the potential enemies, Germany and Italy, held the initiative. His initial assessment, which in many aspects was remarkably prescient, was that German strategy in the West would remain defensive at the outset, and that the Germans would orientate their opening offensive towards the south-east, and might try:

> the 'grand coup,' i.e., an advance to the S E against Poland, Rumania and Greece, (bringing in Hungary and Bulgaria as Allies), which might end in seizing the Dardanelles, simultaneously with an attempt to control the

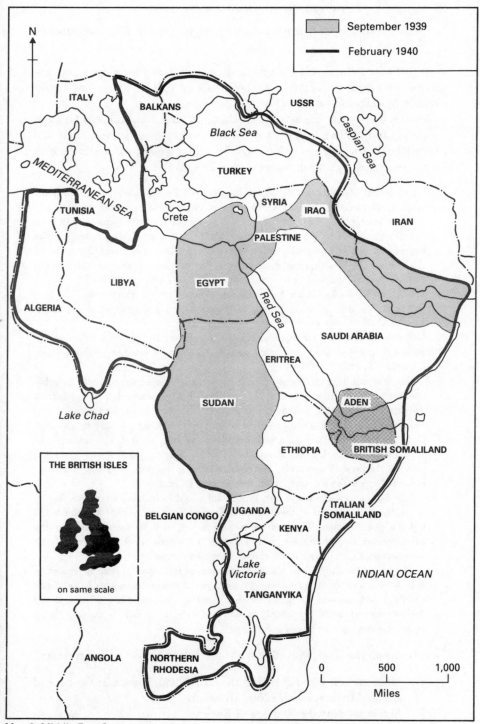

N

September 1939
February 1940

ITALY
BALKANS
USSR
Black Sea
MEDITERRANEAN SEA
TURKEY
Caspian Sea
TUNISIA
Crete
SYRIA
IRAQ
IRAN
PALESTINE
LIBYA
EGYPT
Red Sea
ALGERIA
SAUDI ARABIA
ERITREA
Lake Chad
SUDAN
ADEN
ETHIOPIA
BRITISH SOMALILAND

THE BRITISH ISLES

BELGIAN CONGO
UGANDA
ITALIAN
SOMALILAND
KENYA
Lake
Victoria
INDIAN OCEAN
on same scale
TANGANYIKA

ANGOLA
NORTHERN
RHODESIA

0   500   1,000
Miles

Map 3. Middle East Command

Mediterranean by an Italian attack on Egypt, and possibly a Spanish attack on Gibraltar.[5]

Wavell then admitted this hypothetical plan was very ambitious and unlikely to be attempted upon the outbreak of war, and that Germany would advance by stages in its quest for 'world-power'.

Correct in assessing the attack on Poland, Wavell overestimated German audacity, and believed that they would continue their attack to the Dardanelles, rather than halting after Poland was defeated and attacking France the following spring. Accordingly, he believed:

> The Eastern Mediterranean and not the Western Front, will be, from our point of view, the decisive theatre, where German plans must be countered.
>
> What concerns us first, then, is the use Germany is likely to make of Italy in her plans. It seems possible it may suit her to keep Italy neutral at the beginning; unless she really believes Italy capable of capturing Egypt or of controlling the Mediterranean. A neutral, but potentially hostile, Italy, would contain just as much of our forces, would prevent us using the Mediterranean freely, and would keep open for Germany a line of supply against the blockade, so long as we allow it. It might give Germany time to complete her plans in S E Europe with the risk of exposing her weaker partner to defeat.
>
> We must aim at placing ourselves in a sufficiently strong position in the Mediterranean to issue an ultimatum to Italy and force her to declare her intentions at once.
>
> But whether Italy is openly hostile or nominally neutral, our only possible counter to the German intention to bring S E Europe under her power is by a domination of the Mediterranean at least as complete as in the Great War *as early as possible*. If not within the first month or two of war, it may be too late. Control of the Mediterranean will speedily bring Italy to heel, will enable us to send direct aid to Greece, Rumania, Turkey, Russia; may, if swift enough, prevent Bulgaria, Yugoslavia, Spain from joining the Axis; and will enable us eventually to make a counter offensive against Germany.
>
> The last war was won in the West, and could only have been won in the West, though a success in the Mediterranean at Gallipoli might have shortened it by a year or two. The next war, as I see it, will be won or lost in the Mediterranean; and the longer it takes us to secure effective control of the Mediterranean, the harder will the winning of the war be.
>
> *The task of the Staff of the Middle East Command is therefore to plan, in conjunction with the other services, not merely the defence of Egypt and our other interests in the Middle East, but such measures of offence as will enable us and our Allies to dominate the Mediterranean at the earliest possible moment; and thereafter to take the counter offensive against Germany in Eastern and S E Europe.*[6]

To accomplish this goal, Wavell thought the following four steps necessary:

1. Make certain that Egypt and the Canal, which must be the Base of all our Mediterranean effort, are secure.
2. Action to clear the Red Sea of Enemy.

3. Action to clear Eastern Mediterranean.
4. Consideration of eventual land action in S E Europe (Thrace, Salonica, Rumania), or in Russia. [7]

Wavell's assessment, which did not take into consideration the importance of Western Europe in the later stages of the war, included the probability of conducting land operations in Greece. This analysis of the situation formed the basis of Wavell's actions from this time forward.

Because his appreciation credited the Germans with attempting to seize south-eastern Europe much earlier than they actually did, Wavell believed he had even less time to organise and prepare his Command for the anticipated onslaught than was actually to prove the case. On 3 August 1939, Wavell wrote his first demi-official situation report for the Chief of the Imperial General Staff, General the Viscount Gort. Wavell noted that the officers of his staff, with the exception of one GSO 3 from India (Major W S Cole), met for the first time that morning, and added that he hoped his authorised clerks would arrive soon. His Headquarters, along with the expected Middle East Intelligence Centre, was housed in the same building as Headquarters, British Troops in Egypt. Wavell also appreciated the immensity of his Command, which stretched some 2,000 miles from East to West and 1,700 miles from North to South. To comply with his mandate of preparing this vast area for war, Wavell knew he would have to reconnoitre much of his 3,500,000 square mile Command and coordinate his actions with officials throughout it and on its periphery. He had long understood the efficacy of air travel, and added in his letter to the CIGS:

> This is one of the first matters in which I want you to assist me. I feel that it is essential that I should have a special machine here at my disposal to take me about, with good speed and radius, and a capacity for carrying three or four passengers and some luggage. . . . It will be essential, in my command, to get about quickly and in reasonable comfort.[8]

Wavell departed on 6 August 1939 with a few of his staff officers for Aden, stopping on the way at Port Sudan, where a conference was held with the local District Commissioner and the officer designated to command the troops there when war broke out. The following day Wavell met with the Commander-in-Chief, East Indies, Air Officer Commanding Aden, and General P L Legentilhomme, commanding the French forces in French Somaliland, who flew to Aden especially for this meeting. On the 8th, Wavell's party again stopped at Port Sudan, where they saw the GSO 2, Sudan Defence Force, before returning to Cairo the next day. Wavell emphasised the trying and frustrating nature of this experience, grossly wasteful of both time and energy, to the CIGS:

> I got back late last night from Aden. It took me 44 hours flying time in an ancient Valentia to get there and back, which a modern machine could do quite

easily in less than half the time. I could have saved two whole days, besides a great deal of discomfort. It is intolerable that I should have to go about in such an ancient machine, there were times in a head wind we were doing under 70 m p h![9]

Wavell then visited Mersa Matruh and Sollum in the Western Desert on 11 August.

On 14 August 1939, Wavell wrote another letter to the CIGS, in which he again kept Gort fully apprised of his past and future activities, his perceptions of the status of his Command, and his estimate of enemy intentions. As a result of his own reconnaissances, conferences, and consultations, Wavell was constantly refining his appreciation of the situation. On that same day he wrote 'Note on Strategical Situation in Middle East by GOC-in-C., Middle East', in which he outlined his conviction that the enemy objective was 'undoubtedly the control of S E Europe', and that 'counter attack in the Mediterranean on Italy, as well as direct opposition and eventual counter attack in S E Europe, will be essential, if our enemies [sic] aims are to be thwarted'.[10] Wavell sent a copy of this appraisal not only to Gort, but also to his Royal Navy and Royal Air Force counterparts, Cunningham and Mitchell respectively, whom he was to meet for the first time in conference the following week.

Wavell spent 15 August 1939 in Alexandria, and expected to have an audience with King Farouk, but the latter was 'indisposed'. Attempting to fulfill his political responsibilities, Wavell then met British Embassy personnel, the Egyptian Minister of National Defence and Under-Secretaries of State for National Defence, and the Commander of the 2nd Egyptian Brigade. Back in Cairo on the following day, he met with the Governor General of the Sudan, followed by a briefing from the Inspector General, African Colonial Forces on 17 August.

The three Commanders-in-Chief – Wavell, Cunningham, and Mitchell – met for the first time aboard HMS *Warspite* on 18 August at Alexandria. This triumvirate formed the High Command. The Official History has commented on their command relationships and responsibilities:

> Each Commander-in-Chief was to remain responsible to his Ministry for matters affecting his own Service; jointly they would be answerable to the Chiefs of Staff [in London]. They were to take as a basis for their consultations the Chiefs of Staff's latest appreciation. Their decisions would have to be reached by discussion, since no member of the triumvirate was supreme; none was even *primus inter pares*.[11]

This command arrangement not only violated the principal of unity of command, but it also had the potential to be unwieldy and impractical. Wavell and Mitchell had their headquarters co-located in Cairo; Cunningham rightly believed in the tradition that he needed to be with his fleet and prepared to lead them at sea, and thus maintained his head-quarters at Alexandria. To ameliorate the situation, Cunningham appointed a naval officer to serve as his representative at the Cairo head-quarters. The Joint Planning Staff was also instituted and composed of high-ranking officers of the three services; it was their function to assess the feasibility of various projects and operations and plan them. They were also assisted by the Joint Intelligence Centre. In a short time Wavell, whether by virtue of the force of his personality, willingness to take the initiative repeat-edly, or acquiescence on the part of the other two, emerged as the *de facto* spokesman of the *troika*, and as such exercised the greatest influence. As unacceptable as this command disposition may be in modern terms, it was, according to General Sir William Jackson, 'a great advance on anything seen in the First World War'.[12]

At this meeting, Cunningham asked Wavell if he knew of any strategical plan for the Middle East being formulated in London; Wavell knew of none. The three Commanders-in-Chief were unanimous in noting the obvious: 'no such definite plan was known to exist beyond the fact that the general line was to hold on in the first few months of the war to see what action the enemy take'.[13] Wavell, after this meeting, notified Gort that 'it became readily apparent from our discussion that all three Services were without any detailed instructions from home as to their action in the event of war, and that there were many points which required clearing up'.[14] In the absence of updated guidance from the War Office, Wavell continued to work in accordance with his original 24 July 1939 instructions, and his own assessment of the situation. Although Wavell was incorrect in his belief that the Middle East would prove the decisive theatre of the war, there were few politicians, let alone soldiers, in July 1939 who foresaw that Hitler would eventually invade the Soviet Union and thereby change the whole balance of the war. He was certainly right in his recognition of the importance of south-east Europe to the Germans and the long-term implications that this would have for the Middle East Command.

The Joint Planning Staff met for the first time on 21 August 1939, but that event was totally overshadowed by the stunning announcement that day of the Soviet-German Non-Aggression Pact, scheduled to be signed on 23 August. On 22 August, meanwhile, Wavell flew to Jerusalem and con-ferred with the GOC, Palestine and Transjordan, and returned on the following day, to ensure that the units of British Troops in Egypt had complied with a 22 August War Office signal ordering them to assume a higher readiness posture and deploy from Cairo to forward defensive pos-itions in the Western Desert.

This confirmation of the imminence of war compelled Wavell to summar-ise his activities and concerns in a paper dated 24 August 1939, 'Notes on Strategical Situation in the Middle East', which he sent to Gort. In this appreciation, Wavell bemoaned the entire absence of any detailed and coordinated war plans, and expressed his dissatisfaction at the 'defensive mentality' which seemed to have permeated recent preparations for war and which he was endeavouring wholeheartedly to reverse. Wavell was also greatly concerned about providing assistance to Turkey and coordinating war plans with the French, Britain's staunch Mediterranean Ally. And finally, Wavell again lamented: 'GOC-in-C, Middle East must have a modern aeroplane at his disposal if he is to exercise command efficiently.'[15]

The Anglo-Polish Treaty of Mutual Assistance was signed on 25 August, after Chamberlain 'made it clear beyond all doubt that Britain's guarantee to Poland would be fulfilled by force if necessary'.[16] Wavell accelerated the pace of his meetings and preparations, conferring on 26 August with the GOC-in-C, British Troops in Egypt (BTE), his old friend Lieutenant General (later Field Marshal Lord) Henry Maitland Wilson, who had commanded the 6th Infantry Brigade while Wavell commanded the 2nd Division, and the GOC, Palestine and Transjordan, Lieutenant General (later Sir) MGH Barker. Wavell's meetings with these two officers were of the utmost importance. Once war erupted, Wavell believed it 'essential that nothing should be done which might shake the confidence and morale of the Egyptians', and he would therefore keep Headquarters, BTE, in Cairo under Wilson. He recommended Barker for command in the Western Desert.[17]

To accomplish more coordination, especially with the Allies, Wavell sent Smith, now Major General, General Staff, to Syria on 28 August 1939 to meet with the French commander. Wavell himself remained in Cairo, consulting with commanders and staff officers from the Sudan, emphasising to Major General (later General Sir) William Platt, GOC, British Troops in the Sudan, 'the value of a more mobile forward defence'.[18]

At this time, the most significant enemy threat was in the Western Desert, where it was estimated the Italians had some nine divisions in Tripoli and another five in Cyrenaica, totalling about 215,000 men. Admittedly, these Italian troops would also have to contend with about eight French divisions in Algeria, but the only British forces in the area, which had completed their deployment by 28 August, were the incomplete 7th Armoured Division between Mersa Matruh and Maaten Baggush, with the defence of the former entrusted to the Egyptian Cairo Brigade. Armoured car elements were at Sidi Barrani and Sollum, with Egyptian forces patrolling the Egyptian frontier. The 18th Infantry Brigade was in reserve at Abbassia, the newly-arrived 11th Indian Infantry Brigade was training at Fayid, and an incomplete 8th Division in Palestine was in general reserve. The French also had two understrength 'mixed' brigades in Syria.

The British deployment plan in the Western Desert was based upon a potential subsequent offensive when war was declared, in coordination with the French attacking Libya from the West. The primary objective of this plan was to 'contain as many Italian forces in eastern Libya as possible, and prevent them from being transferred to the West to oppose a French offensive', prior to conducting offensives against Bardia, Amseat, and Jarabub.[19]

Enemy forces in Italian East Africa (Italian Somaliland, Eritrea, and Abyssinia) were estimated at 225,000 troops with some 400 field and mountain guns, 200 light tanks, and 100 armoured cars. Opposing this considerable force the British had three British battalions and the twenty-company Sudan Defence Force in the Sudan and three companies of the Camel Corps in British Somaliland, augmented by a small French force in French Somaliland. In his later Despatch, Wavell summed up that the 'fighting forces in the Middle East thus included no complete formation of any kind. There were in all twenty-one battalions of infantry, but only 64 field guns. There were only 48 [anti-tank] guns and 8 [anti-aircraft] guns.'[20] It was a matter of very real concern at this time that the British, with their marked paucity of troops and resources, could not have repulsed the overwhelming Italian forces had these synchronised a massive two-pronged attack from the Western Desert and Italian East Africa and converged on the Suez Canal.

With these preparations completed, Wavell met with King Farouk on 30 August, and, on the following day, conferred with General Maxime Weygand, Commander-in-Chief of the French Forces in the Eastern Mediterranean. One of the key items raised by Weygand was the significance 'to be attached to Salonika, an importance to which the British leaders were in agreement'. This conference was crucial in that ideas and plans for Allied interoperability were exchanged. Of Wavell, Weygand later observed: 'From the first day I found him unassuming, direct, loyal, and full of intelligence and of experience, an impression that was never belied.'[21]

The German *blitzkrieg* into Poland early on 1 September 1939, and the subsequent partitioning of Poland between the Germans and Soviets appeared to confirm Wavell's earlier forecast of a German drive to southeastern Europe. War was declared on 3 September, at which time Wavell assumed operational control over the troops in Egypt, Palestine, Sudan, and Cyprus, and responsibility for military plans in British Somaliland.

Boldly poised for action with his insufficient and scanty resources, Wavell had earlier surmised that the 'jackal' Italy would not immediately enter the war, and he was correct. In fact, in May 1939, Wilson's predecessor as GOC-in-C, BTE, Lieutenant General Sir Robert Gordon-Finlayson, had observed Italian troops and remarked, 'how embarrassed the Italians are in many ways and how unlikely they are to make war in Libya on two fronts; and in any case how unlikely they are to rush into it [war] without more preparations than they have now', and concluded that 'Personally, I still feel confident that Italy will not – and really cannot seriously – attack us here *by land* as things are at the moment.'[22]

In the wake of the Fascist Foreign Minister commenting on 24 August 1939 that 'we are absolutely in no condition to wage war. The [Italian] Army is in a 'pitiful' state.'[23] On 1 September, the Italian Premier, Benito Mussolini, took up a position of 'non-belligerence', a status unrecognized in international law but, perhaps more importantly, as MacGregor Knox has suggested, 'more congenial to the dictator than that odious and degrading condition, neutrality'.[24]

The Chiefs of Staff's reaction to Italy's 'nonbelligerence' was to direct the Middle East Commanders-in-Chief not to undertake any actions which might provoke the Italians into declaring war. Given this reprieve from being required to conduct combat operations immediately, Wavell concerned himself with the internal affairs of Egypt since, unlike in the Great War when Egypt was a protectorate with a British High Commissioner, it was now an independent country, although allied to Great Britain through the Anglo-Egyptian Treaty of 1936. Egyptian internal security now became a serious dilemma, since the Egyptian Government had failed to declare that a state of war existed between Egypt and Germany, only an *état de siege*, a decision which clearly foreshadowed future difficulties.

This distasteful respite of non-provocation also gave Wavell the chance to conduct long-range planning to prepare his Command further for eventual hostilities. The day after war was declared, Wavell wrote 'Note for Long Term Policy for Middle East',[25] and sent copies to his principal subordinate commanders in Palestine and Transjordan, Egypt, the Sudan, and East Africa, requesting them to 'think out our policy and requirements some 6 months ahead, since any reinforcements of men and material that we are likely to require by that time will have to be estimated and ordered now if we are to obtain them in time'.[26] This policy was in harmony with Wavell's perceptions that the Middle East would play a signal, if not decisive, role in the outcome of the war. Wavell also brought Brigadier (later Lieutenant General Sir) Balfour Hutchison, who was serving as brigadier in charge of administration, Palestine, to his Headquarters to start planning the eventual build-up of men and matériel in Egypt.

Wavell flew to Baghdad on 12 September 1939. While returning the following day, his airplane crashed, the first of numerous aviation accidents from which Wavell would miraculously escape unscathed. Collins has written, 'even before he had been extricated from the wreck, Wavell was giving orders for a two-seater to be sent to pick him up at once. Unfortunately this machine also had trouble. A second forced landing not far short of Jerusalem [resulted].'[27] This mishap, and many subsequent air accidents, gave rise to the notion that Wavell was a 'Jonah' in an airplane; one of Wavell's staff members observed that Wavell 'had a sort of voodoo on aeroplanes'.[28]

When in Cairo, Wavell generally worked from 9:00 am to 9:00 pm, and his capacity for work seemed limitless. He conferred frequently with the British Ambassador to Egypt, Sir Miles Lampson (later Lord Killearn), and they each attended the weekly Commanders-in-Chief meetings. Lampson's early impressions of Wavell are worth recording, since they contradict much of what has been written about him:

Wavell was very much more forthcoming on this occasion and I am coming to the conclusion that when one gets to know him better he is rather a good fellow. He is the outspoken type of man one has to get to know. Certainly his comment is pretty good when he makes it though usually on the caustic side.[29]

Wavell wrote a number of offensive-orientated, seminal policies early in October 1939, and his foresight continued to bear fruit throughout his tenure in command. On 3 October, Wavell relayed to Wilson his conception of the tactics to be employed when the Italians eventually attacked, as he knew they would:

> On the Western frontier of Egypt, should the enemy seek to advance along the coast, ground is of importance only from the point of view of the morale of the Egyptians; there would be many advantages in drawing the enemy on till the length of his communications had weakened him, before making a counter stroke.[30]

This was the exact plan Wavell intended to implement after the Italians began their dilatory advance in September 1940, but was unable to do so because they halted their cautious advance much sooner than anticipated. Wavell also charged Wilson to 'make plans for the capture of Giarabub [Jarabub] Oasis and for an advance against Bardia in case our resources make these operations possible later'. This was the initial document which served as the genesis for Operation 'Compass' fourteen months later. Wilson was also given the task of reconnoitring base camps for the future accommodation of at least ten divisions.

Wavell's strategic breadth of vision became further manifest that same day, through his issuance of a 'Note on Operations against Italian East Africa'. He observed that 'these operations will certainly require the most detailed planning and preparation, and we should begin our plans and preparations at once',[31] and in a remarkably prescient statement, tentatively delineated his concept of the operation: 'I think it is quite clear that any large scale operation must be either on the line Djibuti/Harar/Addis Ababa, or the line Kassala/Asmara/Massawa, or preferably on both lines simultaneously.' Based upon Wavell's subsequent, similar guidance, Platt, with the assistance of Lieutenant General (later General Sir) Alan Cunningham's attack from the south with his East Africa Force, successfully eliminated the entire Italian East African Empire.

Another perplexing quandary which Wavell was eager to clarify was the topic of another study he wrote on 3 October 1939: 'Statement of the Relationship between HE the British Ambassador and the GOC-in-C, ME; Between the GOC-in-C, ME., and the GOC-in-C, BTE; and the Position of the British Military Mission'. Wavell was attempting to clarify his own responsibilities, and to ensure an orderly and professional conduct of all facets of military and political affairs within his Command. In defining his titular responsibilities with Wilson, for example, Wavell wrote:

While all matters of 'high policy' will be referred to the GOC-in-C, ME, other matters need not be so referred unless they would have repercussions outside Egypt. At the same time there will be many 'local' matters which the GOC-in-C, BTE may prefer to refer to GOC-in-C, ME, rather than to the War Office and he will do so at his discretion. Any questions of what constitutes 'high policy' will best be settled by personal reference.[32]

Wavell's paper also reveals the difficulty and multiplicity of his tasks.

The ostensible enigma of Italian nonbelligerency was reinforced by a War Office directive dated 14 October 1939 that the 'defensive policy will be maintained in Western Desert and this is criterion on which forces [and] administrative facilities are to be based'.[33] British policy also encouraged the formation of the Balkan Entente, since after the partition of Poland, it was highly probable the Germans would continue their sweep into south-eastern Europe, with Rumania quite possibly the next domino to fall under the treads of the *blitzkrieg*. British strategic interests in the Middle East might then be threatened. 'Herein lay the importance of Turkey and Iraq,' as Major General ISO Playfair has noted accurately, 'for their territories were capable of providing depth for the defence of the Suez Canal, the Anglo-Iranian oilfields, and the route between Basra and Palestine.'[34]

The key to the security of the entire Allied Middle East position, as the first line of defence against a German sweep from the north-west, was Turkey. General Sir Edmund Ironside, who became CIGS on 3 September 1939, following Gort's appointment as Commander-in-Chief of the British Expeditionary Force, underlined the strategic value of Turkey:

> There lies north of Syria – Turkey. The Turkish Army is a formidable body of troops. If Turkey comes in against the Germans, there is no possibility of Turkey being overrun such as there is in a country like Roumania whose army is not of high value.
>
> Our policy is therefore to develop our military strategy with Turkey, if possible, for the defence of her territory. Whether the defence of Turkey will require allied operations in Greece is a matter which can not yet be determined. Many political, naval, etc., factors are involved and the situation at the moment is too fluid for a decision to be reached. It is quite certain, however, that at the present time, when we are very definitely on the defensive, we must refuse to become involved in operations in Greece which have any aim beyond the direct defence of Turkey.[35]

Ironside's commitment to this belief was total, as he also recorded on 20 September 1939 that 'The country that cannot be overrun by the Germans is Turkey. We must bank on her and prepare an entrance into Europe behind her.'[36]

The Turks also felt threatened by the Soviet Union, and had engaged in negotiations in Moscow. However, after the breakdown of these discussions, Turkey negotiated with the Allies. In this multifaceted, Byzantine affair, the

British defensive policy towards Italy was also juxtaposed with French perceptions of a diminished German threat to the Balkans, resulting in an assessment that their earlier proposals for the defence of Salonika were no longer practical. Under these conditions, Wavell and Weygand flew to Ankara and signed the Anglo-Franco-Turkish Treaty of Mutual Assistance with Marshal Chakmak, the Turkish Chief of Staff, on 19 October 1939. Negotiations and discussions attempting to cajole Turkey into entering the war on the Allied side would demand a great deal of Wavell's attention and time throughout the remainder of his tenure in the Middle East.

Wavell realised that the Middle East would play a major role in the war, and that to do so, the land forces would have to be significantly reinforced. Towards that goal, Wavell initiated a survey for the establishment of a base for a force of fifteen divisions – some 300,000 soldiers.[37] 'To my mind,' Benson recently observed, 'one of the most important things Wavell did was to study and eventually to implement, or start implementing, the construction in Egypt and on the Canal Zone of a base to cater for at least 25 divisions.'[38]

With Italy not yet an active participant in the war, Wavell spent much of November and December 1939 working on a myriad of administrative and logistical requirements prerequisite to the establishment of the Middle East base.[39] Inventories of weapons and ammunition were conducted throughout the Command, as were additional surveys and reconnaissances. Measures for Egypt's internal security were improved and upgraded. There was a further organisation, refinement, and expansion of the Joint Planning Staff and the Middle East Intelligence Centre, and the establishment of the Balkan Intelligence Centre. Facilities for the reproduction of classified maps were created, and further preparations for receiving reinforcements were made. Indispensable signal communications were, for the first time, installed between all areas in the Middle East Command (incredibly, no Chief Signal Officer was authorised until 1940!). Planning for future offensive operations in Libya and Italian East Africa continued, and on 20 November 1939, Wavell, on his own initiative, issued guidance to the Joint Planning Staff to study the requisites for the possible defence of the oilfields in southern Iran (at that time still known as Persia). To enhance the self-sustaining character of the Middle East Command, the programmes of instruction and authorisations of a host of military schools were established, including the Intelligence, Air Force Liaison Officer, Signal, Weapon Training, Tactics, Motor Mechanics, and Motor Transport Drivers' Courses, plus the Middle East Staff College and Middle East Cookery School.[40]

In November 1939, Lieutenant Colonel (later Brigadier) Dudley Clarke was charged by the Army Council to reconnoitre a potential land route from Mombasa to Cairo to be used in the event of the Mediterranean and Red Sea being closed by a hostile Italy. After sailing on the same troopship as Lady Wavell and her three daughters, Clarke, who had been serving in

London, was startled to arrive in a Cairo which seemed oblivious to the war. 'Once inside GHQ, however,' Clarke later wrote,

> the atmosphere had changed. Waiting there to report to General Wavell, I found that no one had any illusions whatever that Italian neutrality would continue past the point where it suited Hitler to whip in Mussolini. The Commander-in-Chief had even said that all the neutral countries, with the possible exception of Switzerland, would probably be drawn in one by one before the end was reached. For the meantime care was being taken to show no sign of provocation towards Italy, but behind that facade war plans were fast developing to meet the first step of aggression in any one of the three most likely directions – the Western Desert, East Africa or the Sudan.[41]

On the following day, Clarke had luncheon with Wavell, and noted later that 'General Wavell's thoughts were directed mostly to the Balkans, and I listened to much shrewd speculation concerning the respective intentions of Hitler, Stalin and Mussolini towards that highly inflammable neighbourhood.' After Wavell's exposition, Clarke was left with the vivid impression 'of the almost limitless commitments of the Middle East Command.'

The French, notably Weygand's, eagerness to send an expedition to Salonika intensified after the signing of the Anglo-Franco-Turkish Treaty of Mutual Assistance. Perhaps blinded by the delusory impregnability of the Maginot Line, Weygand was wholeheartedly convinced, as was Wavell, that the Germans would not attack in the West, but would at the earliest opportunity continue their drive to the Balkans. The Allied neglect of military preparations in the Balkans piqued Weygand to comment that, 'We have been behaving as if we were afraid of making any noise in a sick-room filled with its patients at the point of death, whereas there are slumbering energies which we should rouse and stimulate.'[42]

The British War Cabinet, at any rate, was roused and stimulated by the apparent divergence of Allied strategy, since it was ludicrous for the British to continue to reinforce France if the French intended to transfer troops from France to the Balkans. Weygand returned to France on 3 December 1939 to discuss his proposals with General Maurice Gamelin, the French Commander-in-Chief. Knowing the British Chiefs of Staff had still not formulated their Middle East policy, Wavell requested to return to London for consultations. He arrived in London on 6 December 1939, and found that the Chiefs of Staff had concluded their review of military policy in the Middle East the day before:

> that in view of the weakness of the Allied air forces and anti-aircraft artillery it could not be said that British interests were secure against Italian attack. If Germany or Russia were to begin determined offensive operations in the Middle East, it would be necessary to provide additional land and air forces to defend our interests and to prevent the defeat of Turkey. If Italian hostility were added to German or Russian aggression, we should have to deal with the Italian fronts

before we could give any assistance to Greece or Turkey. Apart from the salutary effect of a show of force, there were therefore good reasons for building up our forces, but this ought not to be done at the expense of essential requirements in Western Europe or of the ability to defend Singapore.[43]

On 7 December 1939, Wavell conferred with Ironside, the CIGS, who noted '[Wavell] is a dour devil, but a good soldier with very great imagination. He is all for us preparing in the Middle East,' then added, 'He seems to be imbued with the firm idea that the Germans and Russians will come against the Balkans.'[44]

Wavell, as has previously been indicated, was not alone in this conviction. On 8 December 1939, he again attended conferences at the War Office. Ironside, according to Major General (later Sir) John Kennedy, who was Deputy Director of Military Operations at that time and participated in these discussions, explained that he was being pressured by the French to reinforce France, but he also thought the Middle East should be stronger than it was. With the Middle East being the centre of the British Empire, Ironside was concerned that French ambitions would result in French encroachment in that historically British sphere of influence, as well as a disjointed Allied military strategy.

Wavell did not share Ironside's concerns, and because he remained convinced the Germans would not attack in the West, but would conduct an offensive in the spring through the Balkans, the French were the only ones with the forces to halt the expected attack. To safeguard their interests in this area, Wavell continued, the British should endeavor to cut German communications through Yugoslavia and deploy troops to Thrace and Salonika. Above all, 'we should not let the Turk fall down or run out'.[45]

Kennedy recorded that,

> To this Ironside replied: '*Tout le monde est égoïste.* The Turk will see that it is to his own interest to fight against Germany and Russia.'
> Wavell answered, '*Tout le monde est égoïste,* and the Turk will see it is in his own interest to make the best terms he can.'

Ironside concluded that the predicament was that the British could not augment their forces in both France and the Middle East.

To attempt to achieve unanimity in military strategy, the British Chiefs of Staff, and Wavell, met with Gamelin, Weygand, and other senior French officers at Vincennes on 11 December 1939. Kennedy also attended this meeting, and observed that 'there was no apparent difference of opinion . . . at the meeting, . . .' and

> It was agreed that nothing should be done which might antagonise Italy, or precipitate an extension of the war to the Balkans. . . . It was [also] decided that we should make preparations and work out plans for operations in Turkey and the Balkans, so that there might be no repetition of the administrative disasters we had experienced in the previous war.

After Weygand had underscored the future probability of intervention in the Balkans, he stated that any Allied activity, to include covert diplomatic contact and the prepositioning of equipment, would help brace the Balkans against a German attack.

Wavell, according to Kennedy, 'was in full agreement with Weygand, but went further, saying that he felt it to be practically certain that we would be called upon to defend our interests in the Balkans in 1940', and therefore, 'we should start by getting the support of Turkey, and possibly by occupying Salonika'. Shortly thereafter the conference ended. Thus, over the previous six months, Wavell's staunch advocacy of a forward policy in the Balkans had become an *idée fixe*.

Wavell began the return journey to Cairo the next day, stopping in Algiers to meet with General Auguste Nogues, the French Commander-in-Chief in North Africa. Upon his arrival in Cairo, Wavell assisted his recently-arrived wife and daughters in establishing a household. For the remainder of the General's Middle East tenure, the Wavells shared Wilson's spacious house on the edge of the Gezira racecourse.

The relationship between Wavell and 'Jumbo' Wilson, who had received that appellation because of his rotundity, was in fact, a 'partnership [based upon] great mutual trust and confidence'.[46] Through two years of incredible vicissitudes, Wilson served loyally as Wavell's subordinate commander in the Western Desert, Cyrenaica, and in the Greek and Syrian campaigns. There is great truth to the current Lord Wilson of Libya's recent observation that Wavell and Wilson were 'rather like Robert E Lee and Stonewall Jackson, . . ., they complemented each other so well'.[47]

Wavell received a message on 13 January 1940 from the Chiefs of Staff which presaged the War Cabinet's announcement two days later of its Middle East military policy. Wavell's responsibilities were now to include all operational and administrative facets of all land forces in his Command, the area of which was also extended to include the Balkans, Turkey, and East Africa. The newly-formulated War Cabinet policy decreed, among other items, that only those formations currently on orders for the Middle East, which included the horsed 1st Cavalry Division and one Australian division to Palestine, and one New Zealand division to Egypt, should be sent there. Wavell was also directed to begin the establishment of base organisations in Egypt and Palestine for nine divisions, the planning for which he had initiated months earlier. It was also decided that the Turks should be induced to improve their communications and air facilities in Thrace and Western Anatolia with British technical assistance.

After reconnoitring British and French Somaliland between 8 and 13 January 1940 and coordinating plans to repulse any Italian advance into either of those two areas, Wavell returned to Cairo for a few days. He then toured Palestine and Iraq from 16 to 20 January 1940. To begin implementing his War Cabinet guidance, Wavell met Weygand on 20 January in

Beirut. Planning was started for Allied assistance to Turkey and, as preliminary measures, 'it was agreed to begin reconnaissances, by British and
French officers, of port capabilities, bases, lines of communications, and
airfields which the Turks could place at [Allied] disposal for an intervention
in Thrace'.[48] The French would provide the majority of forces in any
expedition, and would operate in Greece. The British contribution as originally conceived, was sizeable: codenamed 'Leopard' and to be composed of
air force units, the first British element was to land in Anatolia; 'Tiger', to
consist of artillery and tank regiments, was to occupy an area in Thrace.
Both British forces were to be commanded by major generals. Wavell and
Weygand arranged to meet the following month, after the initial tasks for
this project had been completed.

Smith, Wavell's Major General, General Staff, evaluated the Middle East
Command's ability to defend its increased territory against an Italian
ground attack. It was recorded, in sum, that 'Except in British Somaliland,
the situation is reasonably satisfactory.'[49] In the Western Desert, the Sudan,
Kenya, French Somaliland, and Aden, forces and defences were deemed
generally adequate, although required improvements were noted. The status was quite the opposite in British Somaliland, where

> the greater portion of the country is undefended, and the portions defended are
> only weakly held. Recommendations have been submitted . . . for the improve-
> ment of the situation; and when approved they will do something to restore our
> prestige and may act as a deterrent to the Italians from invading the country.

The War Office was given repeated assessments of the deficiencies of the
British Somaliland defences but, as will be seen, failed to heed Wavell's
admonition properly.

Inter-Allied Conferences, between not only Wavell and Weygand but
their naval and air force counterparts as well, were held in Cairo from 7–10
February 1940. The results of the previously directed reconnaissances were
examined, and additional plans for assistance to Turkey were initiated,
including:

'Bear' –   to consist of one infantry division and one armoured division.
'Cheetah' –   an expansion of 'Bear' to three infantry divisions with one armoured
                division.
'Lion' –   to consist of three infantry divisions and one armoured division,
                despatched to Smyrna for the defence of the eastern and southern
                shores of the Bosporous, the Sea of Marmara, and the Dardanelles.[50]

As the British and French continued their contingency planning for Turkish
assistance, the plans became much more grandiose and involved larger
troop formations.

Throughout the autumn and winter of 1939/1940, Wavell deftly reposit-
ioned his meagre military assets to reinforce likely enemy avenues of

approach. The headquarters of the 7th Division, for example, commanded by Major General (later General Sir) Richard N O'Connor, was moved from Palestine to Cairo and then to Mersa Matruh. Reinforcements also began to trickle into the Middle East. A second Indian infantry brigade (the 5th) arrived in Egypt on 4 October 1939, with the 2nd Battalion, Durham Light Infantry, arriving from China on 31 January 1940. The only unit to be despatched from England, the 1st Cavalry Division, composed of horsed yeomanry regiments – 'incomplete in training and equipment' – was to arrive in Palestine on 24 March 1940.

The first Dominion troops, the 4th New Zealand Brigade and additional elements of the New Zealand Division, under the command of Major General Bernard Freyberg, VC, and the 16th Infantry Brigade and headquarters of the 6th Australian Division, commanded by Major General (later Lieutenant General Sir) Iven Mackay, arrived at Ismailia on 12 February 1940. They were welcomed by Wavell, Lampson, and Anthony Eden, the British Secretary of State for the Dominions. Although all these reinforcements did total up to about 20,000 soldiers, 'they did not represent any great addition in fighting strength', because only the 5th Indian Infantry Brigade was trained and had its full authorisation of men and equipment. The other formations were only partially trained and incompletely equipped.

This was the first time Eden and Wavell had met, and they immediately developed an affinity and admiration for each other. 'I was impressed by Wavell's quiet but firm analysis of his many responsibilities', Eden recorded later, 'he made no attempt either to gloss over the shortcomings of his command or to complain about them. He just told a straightforward story. I liked him from this first meeting and our friendship was to grow very close and last until his death.'[51] Eden would return to London and serve in the War Cabinet as a staunch defender of Wavell and his plans for and conduct of operations in the Middle East.

An additional component of the War Cabinet's Middle East military policy directive of 15 January 1940 was that

> One division, which the Government of India had already offered to provide, should be made ready in India for the defence of the Anglo-Iranian oilfields. Reserves of material should be accumulated in India for a force of three divisions which might be employed in Iraq and Persia. Basra should be developed as a base port for a force of this size.[52]

To coordinate possible intervention in Iran and the operations codenamed 'Trout' (one division to Basra), 'Salmon' (base for three divisions at Basra), and 'Herring' (three divisions operating in Iran and Iraq), senior representatives of the Indian Army conferred with Wavell, Smith, Mitchell, Commander AJ Baker-Cresswell (of the Joint Planning Staff, and representing Cunningham) and others, in Cairo on 1–5 March 1940. At this conference it was decided that Force Herring would include one mechanised Indian division (Trout) of three brigades, from India; the 4th Indian Division; and a British division. Of key significance, the division of responsibility between India and the Middle East was defined as the former being responsible for the despatch of units and stores from India, with General Headquarters, Middle East, assuming responsibility as soon as the ships left Indian ports. In addition, in a 'sudden emergency', Force 'Lobster' (a force in Palestine) would be sent to Iraq. At this time, these exigencies appeared extremely remote, but, as we shall see in a later chapter, in the spring of 1941, when Wavell's resources were stretched to the limit, he was ordered to reinforce Iraq, resulting in an acrimonious exchange of telegrams between Whitehall and Cairo and a decrease in the former's confidence in Wavell.

Becoming increasingly nervous of German and Soviet intentions, Turkey requested to be informed what assistance it could expect from the Allies. Efforts were then redirected towards cooperation with the Turks and, towards that goal, Anglo-Franco-Turkish conferences were held at Aleppo on 15–21 March 1940. These talks were to be based upon the premiss of Italian neutrality, but they nearly foundered when Turkey wanted to discuss the defence of Thrace with Italy hostile. Turkey also wanted to know the French plans in North Africa, when operations were to be undertaken to neutralise or capture the Dodecanese, and a number of similar items. These queries were relayed to the Chiefs of Staff in London on 9 April 1940.

Wavell did not attend the Aleppo conferences, but from 12 to 26 March 1940 he travelled to South Africa, primarily to discuss strategy with General (later Field Marshal) Jan Christian Smuts, and to ascertain the manpower and matériel contributions South Africa could make to the Empire's war effort. After returning to Cairo, Wavell wrote to the CIGS that he had never met Smuts before, but was most impressed by him and the efforts of the South African Defence Forces.

Wavell also gave the CIGS a situation report, 'Now that we have reached what is normally regarded as the beginning of the campaigning season, and as I have recently visited all the territories under my Command which would be involved if Italy became hostile,'[53] again pointing out the ludicrousness of the policy of not 'provoking' Italy and the deleterious impact it was having on his preparations for war against that country:

> These preparations have been hampered firstly by the fact that demands for personnel or material required to meet the threat from Italy have been subject to long delays, and secondly by the restriction imposed from the Foreign Office that no action likely to annoy the Italians is to be taken. The combined result of the above has been that during the seven months since the war began, comparatively little progress has been made, and that our preparations even for defence are very far from being complete.

After assessing defensive operations, Wavell added frankly that 'Offensive operations by land against Libya on any scale would require at least six months preparation, including railway and pipeline construction.' However, Wavell's persistent forthrightness generally elicited little attention or concern from the War Office.

The complacency of the *sitzkrieg* was shattered abruptly and irrevocably on 9 April 1940 when the Germans audaciously attacked Denmark and Norway. The Military Co-ordination Committee, of which the First Lord of the Admiralty, Winston Churchill, had become the Chairman on 3 April 1940, became directly involved in directing British attempts to halt the German advances. There was no British combined command, however, with the ground force commander and the naval commander each taking orders from and directly responsible to two different officials. Churchill now superimposed himself upon this dichotomous command structure, and became obsessed with the capture of Narvik. Ironside noted:

> Winston very much interested in the Narvik affair. He wanted to divert troops there from all over the place. He is so like a child in many ways. He tires of a thing, and then wants to hear no more of it. He was mad to divert the Brigade from Narvik to Namsos and would hear of no reason. Now he is bored with the Namsos operation and is all for Narvik again. It is most extraordinary how mercurial he is.[54]

The naval commander 'urged' Major General PJ Mackesy, the local Army commander, to capture Narvik, although the latter had reported that the harbour 'was strongly held by the enemy with machine-gun posts'.[55] The Military Co-ordination Committee then sent a telegram to Mackesy urging him in the strongest terms to seize the port. Mackesy, a professional soldier of distinction, 'refused a hopeless assault from the sea in open boats on Narvik, which was defiladed by machine guns and out of reach of [supporting] naval gunfire. In military opinion such an attempt would have been 'sheer bloody murder',[56] which Churchill conceded tacitly: 'It must remain a matter of opinion whether such an assault would have succeeded. It involved . . . landings from open boats . . . under machine-gun fire.'[57] The Norwegian *débâcle* was prolonged into May, but it provided Churchill, as RW Thompson has discerned, 'with the first of his military victims in Major-General Mackesy. He was retired from the Army as soon as he reached England.'[58]

Repercussions of the Scandinavian blunder resounded to even greater heights. Amid great Parliamentary clamour and a pronounced lack of confidence in the incumbent Government, Chamberlain resigned. It was supremely ironic that Churchill, who acknowledged 'the exceptionally prominent part I had played in the use of our inadequate forces during our forlorn attempt to succour Norway',[59] was summoned to form a Government and thus became Prime Minister on 10 May 1940. Churchill immediately began consolidating the authority and responsibility for which he had yearned assiduously. All his 'past life had been but a preparation for this hour and for this trial'.[60]

The Norwegian fiasco had also demonstrated to Churchill that the existing machinery for the higher direction of the war was much too inefficient and cumbersome to meet the dynamic exigencies of modern warfare properly. To enhance the efficacy of this obsolescent system, Churchill also became, without seeking Parliament's approval but with the King's concurrence, the Minister of Defence. Churchill considered this the 'key-change': 'the supervision and direction of the Chiefs of Staff Committee by a Minister of Defence with undefined powers'.[61] He noted further,

> Thus, for the first time, the Chiefs of Staff Committee assumed its due and proper place in direct daily contact with the executive Head of the Government, and in accordance with him had full control over the conduct of the war and the armed forces.

AJP Taylor, however, observed that this 'made Churchill supreme director of the war on the military side. The three service ministers were excluded from the War Cabinet and lost their directing powers. They became little more than superior civil servants. . . .'[62]. Since Churchill ostensibly did not want to complicate further the apparatus of war, no Ministry of Defence was created. Rather, the necessary staff was provided by the Military Wing of the War Cabinet Secretariat, which had served a dual function as Secretariat of the Chiefs of Staff. This new Office of the Minister of Defence consisted of about a dozen officers, and was headed by Major General (later General Lord) HastingsIsmay, with Colonel (later General Sir) LC Hollis and Lieutenant Colonel (later Lieutenant General Sir) EIC Jacob as his chief assistants.

Churchill also replaced the Committee for Military Co-ordination with the Defence Committee, under his own chairmanship. Most of its work was accomplished in two panels: the Defence Committee (Operations) and the Defence Committee (Supply). Ismay later lauded the effects of Churchill's 'innovations' as being nothing less than 'revolutionary'. No one doubted that the Prime Minister 'exercised a personal, direct, ubiquitous and continuous supervision, not only over the formulation of military policy at every stage, but also over the conduct of military operations'.[63] Thus, supreme military and political control was vested in one man, Generalissimo Churchill, 'a superchief of a War Staff in Commission', the *de facto* Supreme Commander. Churchill's accession to this position of unparalleled power, as suggested by RW Thompson, was similar to that of King Arthur: 'He [Churchill] had plucked the sword from the stone as easily as if it were embedded in butter. It was his. He would wield it alone.'[64]

On that same day, German forces shattered the defences of the West by launching armoured assaults through Holland and Belgium, concurrently with an airborne attack on the Hague and Rotterdam.

Meanwhile, Wavell had not been idle. He continued to coordinate contingency war plans with the French. On 3 May 1940, he received guidance from the Chiefs of Staff about French plans to establish a base on Crete after the outbreak of war with Italy. The Chiefs of Staff estimated realistically that to establish and hold a base on Crete would require, as a minimum, '1 brigade of troops. 1 fighter squadron – 1 GR flight. 2 or 3 AA [anti-aircraft] batteries. Full scale of seaward defences. These forces could not (repeat not) be provided from British resources.'[65] The Chiefs of Staff added that the question of an expedition to Salonika with the French was still under examination, and that the British object 'should be to deny Crete to Italians rather than to use it ourselves', and with that goal being accomplished by sending one or two Allied infantry battalions to Crete to help 'stiffen' the local Greek garrisons, but 'Even this limited force,' noted the Chiefs of Staff, 'could not (repeat not) be provided from British resources and would have to be provided by French.'

A few days later, Wavell and Mitchell replied that the 'problem of Crete has not yet been studied here in detail', but they expected to discuss it with Weygand soon.[66]. It was agreed that Crete should, on no account, fall into Italian hands, and to help prevent such an occurrence, they recommended urging 'on Greece the importance of maintaining possession of island as otherwise Allies will be unable to support Greece on mainland', and that a battalion, in an emergency, could be flown from Palestine, but no suitable aerodromes existed to support such flights. Their main conclusion 'is one already several times emphasised i.e. that with Italy hostile we are danger-ously weak in air forces and shall suffer accordingly materially and morally'. This final prophetic statement contained the pent-up frustrations of its authors; the admonition received scant attention from the Chiefs of Staff, and 'weak air forces' were the most significant reason for the fall of Crete twelve months later.

Wavell met with Weygand in Beirut on 8 May 1940, and learned that the French general had instructions to prepare plans for the occupation of Crete and Milos in the event that hostilities with Italy appeared imminent. The authorities in London, upon notification, were satisfied with this response, and concern over the defence of Crete was temporarily allayed.[67]

The three Middle East Commanders-in-Chief, along with Air Chief Marshal Sir Arthur Longmore, met again with Weygand on 10 May 1940, and discussed Crete and other defence matters, before meeting the Turks in conference a week later.

Wavell, who first directed Wilson in October 1939 to study the possi-bilities of an offensive against Italy in the Western Desert, wrote again to Wilson on 10 May 1940: 'I want a report as early as possible,' Wavell instructed, 'on the practicability of taking offensive action against the Italian posts on the Eastern front of Libya as soon as possible after the outbreak of war.'[68] Wavell proposed the capture of the Jarabub Oasis and the post at Amseat by rapid action of the 7th Armoured Division. Typically, Wavell stated he was 'ready to accept responsibility for taking a considerable degree of risk, administrative as well as tactical', in order to attempt to gain a moral superiority over the Italians upon the outbreak of war.

The CIGS on 12 May 1940 informed Wavell of the Turks' unrelenting concern about what Allied assistance they would receive in view of threats to Balkan security. In an attempt to conciliate Turkey, British and French officers met with Turkish Army representatives at Beirut on 20 and 21 May 1940, and at Haifa from 27 May to 4 June 1940. The Turks, desiring material assistance from the Allies more than anything else, were especially frustrated when they learned that, at Dunkirk (26 May–3 June 1940), the British had lost the entire equipment of something like fourteen divisions. That incident notwithstanding, it was probably inevitable, as Lynn H Curtright has shown convincingly, that Turkey should be disappointed with the Allies, and vice versa, and would maintain its neutrality 'until the end was in sight'.[69]

As Wavell observed the steadily deteriorating situation in the West, while his Command was not at war, he was greatly concerned about the safety and sovereignty of the British Isles. He realised that there was a distinct possibility that he could be isolated from his political and military superiors in London. Wavell wrote, on 24 May 1940, a short paper known as 'The Worst Possible Case'. It was written, as Wavell recalled, 'at the time of the German breakthrough in France, when it seemed possible that things might go badly in France – as they did'.[70] Never shown to more than a very few officers, Wavell sent a copy of these notes to the CIGS:

The Worst Possible Case 24. 5. 40.

Germans obtain temporary air superiority in France. French collapse.
  BEF cut off from base and compelled to return to UK with heavy losses.
  UK in state of siege and subjected to heavy bombing attacks.
  ME cut off and attacked by Italy, supported perhaps by German air or troops.
  Egyptians and other peoples of ME frightened, unfriendly or hostile.
  We may have to maintain our position in Egypt by force, i.e. by declaring martial law and taking over the country.
  We might have anti-British rising in Iraq. Should we try and maintain position there or evacuate temporarily? Should we try to hold Basra, or ask India to do so?
  Palestine, Sudan, Kenya should be all right. We might possibly have to evacuate Somaliland. Aden must be held.

Problems at this stage

Control of Egypt and specially of all transport.
  Evacuation of women and children and if so where.

Collection of shipping and air planes.
Egyptian Army.
Whether and when to arm Jews.
Intentions of French in Syria.
Situation in India.[71]

A number of the components of 'The Worst Possible Case' were remarkably prescient, but Wavell anticipated 'The Worst Case Still':

Worst Case Still

German bombing makes UK untenable, Empire falls back to fight on line
    Canada – S. Africa – India – Malaya – Australia – NZ.
Presumably it might be difficult to hold Egypt, Palestine and Cyprus and
    we might have to fall back on Sudan and Kenya.

Problems

Keeping open Red Sea. This may mean combined attack on IEA.
    Holding of Basra?
    Evacuation of Palestine, by sea (possibility of using Akaba?) by road to
        Egypt, to Baghdad, to Basra, to Kuwait, by rail to Egypt or Iraq.
    Problem of Jews.
    Evacuation of Egypt, by sea (if Red Sea open), by rail, by river.
    4th Indian Division.
    Stores and munitions to be taken and left.
    Belgian Congo.
    Angola.

Immediate arrangements

Plan to control Egypt.
    Plan to seize all means of communication.
    Census of numbers to be evacuated and capacity of means of movement.
    Plan to transfer essential stores.

Information required

Numbers of women to be evacuated.
Quantities of transport available.
Stores to be taken and left. Time factor. [72]

Three days later, Wavell composed a much more realistic and logical assessment of the outcome of the war, based upon the availability of oil:

The Position - May 1940

1. Oil, shipping, air power, sea power are the keys to this war, and they
   are interdependent.
   Air power and naval power cannot function without oil.
   Oil, except in very limited quantities, cannot be brought to its desti-
   nation without shipping.
   Shipping requires the protection of naval power and air power.
2. We have access to practically all the world's supplies of oil.
   We have most of the shipping.
   We have naval power.
   We have potentially the greatest air power, when fully developed.

Therefore we are bound to win the war

Germany is very short of oil and has access only to very limited quantities.
   Germany's shipping is practically confined to the Baltic.
   Germany's naval power is small.
   Germany's air power is great, but is a diminishing asset.

Therefore Germany is bound to lose the war.[73]

Wavell forwarded a copy of this strategic overview to the CIGS, now
General Sir John Dill, who had replaced Ironside on 27 May 1940. In
addition to Eden, Dill would serve as Wavell's most ardent supporter, and
in many cases would shield Wavell from many of the Prime Minister's
pernicious directives and outbursts of temper.

As the full impact of the German *blitzkrieg* into the Low Countries became
appreciated in Whitehall, on 18 May 1940 the idea was mooted by
Churchill to withdraw eight battalions from the Middle East to augment the
forces in England preparing to defend against a possible invasion. As
Operation 'Dynamo', the evacuation from Dunkirk, was in progress, Dill
cabled a warning order to Wavell on 30 May 1940 that 'HMG are urgently
considering the withdrawal of eight (repeat eight) battalions from your
Command at earliest possible date.'[74] Wavell, confident that Italy was on
the verge of declaring war, was naturally reluctant to lose any of his
inadequate resources at such a crucial time.

Churchill was distressed by Wavell's evident unwillingness to support
unquestionably the demands of the home islands in this time of peril. On 7
June 1940, Wavell wrote to the CIGS, attempting to explain the impact the
withdrawal of these troops would have on the Middle East. 'The Egyptians
are frankly scared stiff at the idea of war', Wavell wrote, 'and the Prime
Minister is always asking for more troops. Removal of troops would have a
bad effect on their nerves and might give them an excuse for trying to

keep out of their obligations.'[75] Stressing the psychological aspects, Wavell added, 'If you take 8 battalions I cannot implement Lobster or afford immediate assistance to Iraq. They would undoubtedly regard this as a betrayal.'[76] After noting the probable Turkish reaction to the withdrawal of these battalions, Wavell stated he probably was short of troops for his own commitments, and recommended the replacement of the requested formations by 'lower category' units which would be suitable for internal security duties. To justify his contentions, Wavell added his ' Note for CIGS: Middle East, Situation – 6th June 1940', in which he delineated clearly his perceptions of Italy's intentions, Middle East problems, and a region-by-region analysis of the status of his defences.[77]

Although Wavell was surely concerned about his own Command, he seemed to exhibit little sympathy or understanding of the gravity of the situation and the Prime Minister's predicament. Fortunately this impasse was resolved by replacing eight Regular battalions in India with Territorial battalions, but Wavell's credibility and reputation suffered as a result of this incident in the eyes of Churchill, who wrote he was 'sorry indeed to find the virtual deadlock which local objections [had] imposed' upon the troop transfer.[78] Churchill's biographer, Martin Gilbert, has noted that 'Churchill's anger was considerable' over this incident.[79] Even before the two men met personally, Wavell's prestige was already slightly beclouded.

Adolf Hitler's unmitigated success in the West convinced Mussolini that England would fall. The Italian dictator could not control his avarice, and, according to Marshal Pietro Badoglio, the Italian Army Chief of Staff, was 'seized as it were by a frenzy of desire not to be absent from the victor's banquet'.[80] After an initial postponement, Italy declared war, from one minute after midnight, 10–11 June 1940.

Upon Italy's belated entry into the war, Wavell had about 36,000 troops, none of which were organised in complete formations, in Egypt; 9,000 in the Sudan (which had over 1,000 miles of frontier with Italian East Africa); 8,500 in Kenya (with a 700-mile common border with Italian East Africa); 1,475 in British Somaliland; 27,500 in Palestine; 2,500 in Aden; and 800 in Cyprus, for a total of about 85,775 soldiers. Against this, the Italians were able to muster about 215,000 Italian and native troops in Libya, and another 290,000 in Italian East Africa,[81] equalling about half a million troops. French forces in North Africa, Syria, and French Somaliland were effectively neutralised by governmental intransigence following the French Commander-in-Chief's declaration on 11 June 1940: 'I am obliged to say clearly that a cessation of hostilities is compulsory',[82] and the paralysis caused by subsequent negotiations, which resulted in the ignominious French armistice with the Germans on 22 June 1940.

As an illustration of the state of Wavell's forces in Egypt, it should be realised that, at this time, the 7th Armoured Division consisted of two armoured brigades each of two armoured regiments only. These were equipped mainly with light tanks, although the new cruisers were coming out slowly to increase the effectiveness of the Division. The divisional armoured car regiment (11th Hussars) was still equipped with Rolls Royce machines dating in type from the 1920s. The Support Group consisted of two motorised infantry battalions. Only in June 1940 did the additional armoured regiments arrive. Even so, one of these (3rd Hussars), had light tanks only. A valuable addition to Wavell's strength at that time was a battalion of Matilda Infantry (I) tanks (7th Royal Tank Regiment, of whom we will hear much more later). Air support for ground operations was almost non-existent.

On paper, Wavell was defeated soundly even before a shot was fired. But under his indomitable leadership, the numerically-inferior British forces would meet Mussolini's hollow challenge audaciously and draw first blood in the desert.

Conclusion

When Wavell was appointed to command in the Middle East, he was authorised five staff officers but no other facilities to prepare war plans for, and for the actual command of, all land forces in his 3,500,000 square-mile Command. His multifaceted responsibilities were not only military but proconsular as well, with Wavell also serving as primary logistician for his vast Command.

He zealously and indefatigably reconnoitred all areas of his Command and established a healthy rapport and mutually understanding relationship with local rulers and potentates, Foreign Office officials, subordinate military commanders, and Allies with whom he would have to cooperate in the event of war. He continually kept the Chief of the Imperial General Staff fully apprised of his activities, the status of forces and military preparations in his Command, and his estimates of enemy intentions. Wavell's strategic vision was focused in the Balkans, where he was convinced of the eventual necessity of intervention with Turkey as an Ally. These assessments, however, understated German intentions in the West and the precariousness of England's susceptibility to invasion after the Dunkirk evacuations. As a result of the latter, over the troop transfer issue, Wavell had unwittingly besmirched his own reputation and credibility in Churchill's eyes even before the two had met personally.

Wavell, although taciturn, was a dynamic and charismatic commander. Upon his arrival in Cairo, he shook the soldiers there out of their complacency and inculcated an ethos of the offensive into his subordinate commanders and troops. He also started planning for bold and daring offensives into the Western Desert and Italian East Africa, to be executed after the outbreak of hostilities and when the requisite resources became available.

Comprehending astutely the future significance of the Middle East, Wavell initiated planning for the establishment of a base for some 300,000 troops. This was undoubtedly one of his greatest contributions as Commander-in-Chief, Middle East; he made 'bricks without straw', and planted the seeds of future manpower and material hegemony, the harvest of which his successors would be able to reap on the road to victory.

As the size of his vast Command increased, Wavell grew in confidence, competence, and stature. He had prepared himself for four decades as an Infantry officer, and his Command for ten months, to destroy the enemies of the Crown when that course of action became necessary. His perseverance, prescience, and incomparable professionalism would now yield tremendous dividends.

5

Italy Declares War and Wavell's First Clash With Churchill, June-December 1940

'We stand firm whatever happens.'
Wavell, 17 June 1940[1]

The Middle East Command, in a state of upgraded unit alert and readiness, was more than prepared for the Italian declaration of war. After the German attack on Denmark and Norway in April 1940, it had become increasingly clear that Italy would soon enter the conflict.

On 1 May 1940, formations under the command of British Troops in Egypt were ordered to take 'unobtrusive precautionary' measures, and on the following day a covering force of the 7th Armoured Division deployed to the Western Desert. It was not possible to defend on the actual political boundary of Egypt, because there was no water at Sollum (the first town within the Egyptian boundary), for fifty miles east of Sollum (to Sidi Barrani) there was no good road, and the British forces did not possess enough transport vehicles to support adequately a large force positioned away from a base area. The centre of the British defence was positioned at Mersa Matruh, located over 200 miles west of Alexandria and about 120 miles east of the frontier with Libya, which was the terminus of the Egyptian State Railway and had remained fully garrisoned since the autumn of 1939. In addition, there was an adequate water supply at Mersa Matruh, and a metalled road, fit for motorised traffic, ran from Sidi Barrani, to the East through Mersa Matruh, all the way to Cairo. The Italians, in any attack, would thus be forced to cross a waterless, trackless expanse of desert before reaching the main British forces.

The Western Desert, the scene of numerous operations in 1940 and after, is a rough rectangle some 240 miles long and 150 miles across at its widest point. The area is bounded on the North by the Mediterranean Sea and on the East by the narrow strip of desert between the sea and the Qattara Depression and the Depression itself. The southern limits are marked by the Siwa and Jarabub Oases, and on the West by an imaginary line from El Gazala (forty miles west of Tobruk) south through the desert.

The coastal plain varies in width from about twenty-five miles near El Daba and El Alamein to less than a mile at Sollum and Maaten Baggush. On the southern edge of the coastal plain is the 'Escarpment', one of the most significant features of this area of operations, which linked the coastal plain with the Libyan Plateau, the latter rising to an average height of some 500 feet. The Escarpment is so steep in most places that only in a few passes, such as Fuka, Halfaya, and Sidi Rezegh, could all vehicles negotiate it. These passes, therefore, were to exert a significant influence on subsequent operations.

Of all the different theatres of operations in the Second World War, the Western Desert was veritably unique. German General Erwin Rommel, the so-called 'Desert Fox', who was to fight in the Western Desert from 1941 to 1943, called the desert war 'a war without hatred'; one of his subordinates, Major General Johann von Ravenstein, believed it to be 'a gentleman's war'.[2] These opinions can be attributed to the very nature of the battlefield. From the Nile Valley westwards, the country is entirely desert, with a surface alternating between areas of firm clay mixed with pebbles, to stretches of loose, fine sand. In areas where the sand has been cleared by the wind, there is an exposed rock surface. The climate is variable, with great extremes in daily and seasonal temperatures; the mean temperature in Tripoli and Benghazi hovers around 13 degrees centigrade in January and 27 degrees centigrade in July and August. Sandstorms, which occur particularly in the spring, cause the temperature to rise to over 45 degrees centigrade, and bring a finely-grained sand which 'penetrates everywhere', and, in the words of a German who fought in this theatre, 'is very annoying and inflicts great damage on weapons and equipment as well as often causing eye diseases'.[3] Water was always in short supply, and relatively no food could be procured locally; in sum, 'the main characteristic of the desert was that it produced nothing for the support of armies: every article required for life and war had to be carried there.'[4]

A new type of warfare emerged in the Western Desert. It was a war of mobility, very similar to a naval battle, because of the vast distances involved and the few recognisable routes or other distinguishing features. 'The desert war of 1940–43 . . .,' as Correlli Barnett has observed, 'was fought like a polo game on an empty arena.'[5] It was futile to try solely to control territory, for such an endeavour only exacerbated one's precarious supply position. Both sides shared the same privations, problems, and goals in this large, relatively uninhabited area. 'Men in the desert armies,' noted Roger Parkinson, 'could concentrate on the purely military aspect of warfare: the desert conflict remained largely divorced from those political or ideological influences which polluted the campaigns in Russia or in Europe. . . .'[6] In such a harsh and spartan environment, an ethos of 'kill or be killed' prevailed among the adversaries, engendering at times a more chivalrous type of war.

It was into such an exceptional area of operations that the 7th Armoured Division Headquarters and 4th Armoured Brigade moved, arriving at Mersa Matruh during the night of 12/13 May 1940. The intensive desert training, which they had begun during the last quarter of 1939 in that area, was resumed and 'certain surreptitious reconnaissances of the Italian frontier posts were carried out . . . with great discretion as there were strict orders that in no circumstances was action to be taken that might be considered provocative'.[7] Shortly afterwards, the 5th Indian Infantry Brigade was ordered to assume command of the Lines of Communications Sub-Area.

Wavell, further to augment his meagre forces, ordered O'Connor and the 7th Division Headquarters on 6 June 1940 from Palestine to report to Headquarters, British Troops in Egypt. O'Connor arrived in Cairo on 8 June, unaware of what his command was to be. At Headquarters, BTE, he was informed that he was to command all troops in the Western Desert, including a Line of Communications of nearly 200 miles. That same day Headquarters, BTE, received notification from General Headquarters, Middle East, that 'in the event of war with Italy, the Commander in the Western Desert can break the frontier wire and initiate offensive patrols and harrassing action across the frontier'.[8] After consultations with Wilson the following day, O'Connor was issued Operation Instruction No. 6, dated 9 June 1940, the salient points of which were:

> (a) Should the Italians remain on the defensive, an active policy of harassing was to be undertaken, while preparations were to be made for clearing the enemy out of Amseat and Fort Capuzzo. Thereafter the country was to be dominated as far West as possible, particular attention being paid to isolating the garrisons of Bardia and Giarabub [Jarabub].
> (b) Should the Italians assume the offensive, their advance was to be delayed by 7 Armd Div as far as possible, without risking losses, to enable reinforcements to assemble in the Naghamish Nullah position.[9]

O'Connor then arrived at Maaten Baggush late on 10 June.

Within hours of the Italian declaration of war, actual hostilities commenced. 'In fact,' Major General 'Pip' Roberts, then a major serving on the 7th Armoured Division staff, recorded later, 'the 11th Hussars were very nearly "off-side" as they captured the little frontier post of Sidi Omar before the Italians manning it knew that war had been declared.'[10] The desert silence was shattered in that skirmish, which resulted in the capture of some seventy stunned Italian soldiers. Extending their area of operations, the British captured Forts Capuzzo and Maddalena on 14 June 1940, and, two days later, a large ambush was conducted in which twenty-one Italians were killed and eighty-eight captured, including the Engineer-in-Chief of the 10th Army, who was carrying maps showing the Italian concentration ᐟ on the frontier and the plans for the defence of Bardia.

Throughout this period France remained in the death throes of defeat. On 17 June 1940, French Marshal Henri Pétain broadcast that it was necessary for France to cease fighting. Wavell was on the Gezira Golf Course when the message containing this news was brought to him, and later observed, 'I thought for a moment if there was anything I could do about it. There wasn't. So I went on with the game and was rather pleased that I did the next two holes in three and four.'[11] Wavell then returned to his office, and wrote a simple yet stirring 'Order of the Day':

> Our gallant French Allies have been overwhelmed after a desperate struggle and have been compelled to ask for terms. The British Empire will, of course, continue the struggle until victory has been won. There is no question of anything else. We shall again save Europe from tyranny as we have before. Difficult times lie ahead but will, I know, be faced with the same spirit of calm confidence in which we have faced such crises before.
>
> We stand firm whatever happens.
>
> Dictators fade away – the British Empire never dies.[12]

France signed its armistice with Germany on 22 June 1940. Even though metropolitan France had defected from the Allied cause, 'public opinion in the French colonies,' according to Eleanor Gates, 'was strongly in favour of continuing the war from the Empire'.[13] The British did everything possible to encourage the French colonial authorities to continue resistance. After slight hesitation, General Nogues in North Africa announced his intention to abide by the armistice, and his influence was significant. General Eugène Mittelhauser, who had taken Weygand's place in Syria, affirmed to Wavell on 20 June at Beirut 'his unalterable determination to continue the struggle'.[14] Wavell again flew to Beirut on 28 June to attempt to bolster the deteriorating situation, only to find that Mittelhauser, 'after much hesitation', had decided the previous morning to accept the terms of the armistice. Wavell, as he reported to the CIGS, 'tried to influence him to alter his decision but without effect'.[15]

The delicate situation in Syria raised the problem of how far the British should go in inducing individual French officers and soldiers to leave Syria and join the British. The Foreign Office urged Wavell to encourage Frenchmen to defect, and Churchill cabled Wavell to 'Do not (repeat not) therefore on any account discourage the rallying of good men to our cause upon consideration local to your own Command,'[16] but Wavell did not agree. His view was:

> that I wanted a stable and neutral Syria on my northern flank, in view of my general weakness; and that to disrupt it by removing large numbers of the best French officers would be bad policy. It might result in disorder in Syria, which I did not want, and in Vichy sending out officers definitely hostile to the

> British to replace those we had removed. I did not think the gain of a certain
> number of French officers without units was worth the risk of this.[17]

Wavell's curious and contradictory attitude towards this matter failed to take into consideration the fact that if the French in Syria adhered to the armistice with Germany, they would not be neutral, and he was much criticised over this incident by General Charles de Gaulle, leader of the Free French, and Major General (later Sir) Edward Spears, later to become Churchill's Head of the British Mission to the Free French. General Legentilhomme, however, resisted for over a month in French Somaliland until replaced by a pro-Vichy officer.

The situation facing Wavell in the Middle East after the defection of France was serious in the extreme. The large French forces were no longer available for defence against a common enemy, and all plans, which had been joint Anglo-French plans, had to be hurriedly revised and adapted to the new and unanticipated circumstances. The removal of the French threat from Tunisia permitted the Italians to shift their forces to the East and concentrate against the British in Egypt. Unruffled, Wavell continued his harassing and ambushing of Italian forces in a host of disparate locations in the Western Desert, which gave the Italians the false impression that they were opposed by overwhelming British strength.

Rather than implement a contingency plan to foster revolt among desert tribes in Libya, Wavell was better able to utilise his scant resources in the establishment of the Long Range Patrols, later renamed the Long Range Desert Group. This brought to fruition a concept Wavell had earlier called 'the motor guerrilla', a highly mobile force using surprise to gather information and harass the enemy's rear elements, reminiscent of TE Lawrence and the Arabs in the Great War. Always concerned with secrecy, Wavell required the commander of the LRP to write out his own operation orders and to show them only to Wavell himself. Starting in August 1940, the LRP wreaked havoc and material and psychological damage upon the Italians out of all proportion to their numbers. Of this period, the prominent war correspondent Alan Moorehead has written:

> If you will find greatness in General Wavell, trace it back to the summer
> months of 1940 when he was beaten on paper before he even fired a shot. He
> shut his mouth, confiding in practically no one. He put his trust in the sur-
> rounding deserts, he sent appeal after appeal to Churchill for more forces at
> once, and he held on. It required no great genius, that strategy of simply
> digging in one's toes and waiting for the enemy to come on. What did require
> brilliance was the game of bluff on which the General now deliberately
> embarked.[18]

The Long Range Patrols and conventional units of the Western Desert Force, over the summer of 1940, 'actively tormented [the Italian Army] while General Wavell's army expanded from a mere skeleton into a formidable force, still greatly inferior in numbers to its opponent'.[19] The art of deception, which he had learned so well under Allenby in Palestine, was the most potent weapon Wavell had in his arsenal in 1940. His adroit employment of his sparse troop assets served as a useful force-multiplier, emasculating, at least psychologically, the numerically-superior Italians.

To assist Wavell with his increased responsibilities, Churchill established, on Wavell's urging, a Ministerial Committee on Military Policy in the Middle East, consisting of Eden, now Secretary of State for War; Leopold Amery, Secretary of State for India; and Lord Lloyd, Secretary of State for the Colonies. Reinforcements were also needed by Wavell in order to maintain the British position in the Middle East against a possible German-Italian attack. After enumerating his troop assets in a message to Dill on 3 July 1940, Wavell emphasised that his 'essential needs are more armoured troops, more anti-tank guns, more anti-aircraft and other artillery and units to complete my improvised divisions'.[20]

British mobile units continued to do the unexpected and unpredicted throughout July. Wavell's force attacked

> not as a combined force but in small units, swiftly, irregularly and by night. It pounced on Italian outposts, blew up the captured ammunition, and ran away. It stayed an hour, a day, or a week in a position, and then disappeared.[21]

From Italian prisoners, the British learned of the exaggerated effects of their raids and patrols: 'there were two . . . three . . . five British armoured divisions operating', they exclaimed.[22] Wavell's deception had achieved his desired and calculated results, with unparalleled effectiveness. Such intensive military activity had deluded the enemy, but exacted a terrific strain on men and equipment. Two-thirds of the tanks of the Western Desert Force required repair, especially for excess track wear, and most of the other tracked vehicles were going into workshops for servicing. Brigadier (later Lieutenant General) WHE 'Strafer' Gott's Support Group remained to patrol the frontier.

The Italian forces in East Africa were not as docile as their comrades in the Western Desert and asserted themselves aggressively to fill the vacuum in the British defences caused by the collapse of France and the resultant confusion in policy and strategy. In the Sudan, which shared a 1,000-mile frontier with Italian East Africa, British forces consisted of three British battalions and the Sudan Defence Force, totalling about 9,000 soldiers. On 4 July 1940, an Italian force of 6,500 men advanced on Kassala, held by 320 men of the Sudan Defence Force and local police, and additional Italian forces crossed the border at the same time. Due to the great disparity in numbers, the Italians were able to capture Kassala, but at the high cost of forty-three dead and 114 wounded. Gallabat was also seized by the Italians the same day. (See Map 7 page 179)

After the French collapse, Wavell was obviously forced to remain on the

Plate 1   Wavell and fellow officers of the 2nd Battalion, The Black
Watch. (Ambala, India 1903).
(Reproduced by courtesy of the Colonel, The Black Watch)

Plate 2   General Sir Archibald Wavell, Commander-in-Chief, Middle
East. (Cairo, 15 August 1940).
(*Reproduced by courtesy of the Imperial War Museum(IWM)*)

Plate 3   Lieutenant General Sir Henry Maitland Wilson, General Officer Commanding-in-Chief, British Troops in Egypt. (Cairo, 15 August 1940) (*IWM*)

Plate 4   Major General Arthur Smith, Chief of Staff, Middle East Command. (Cairo, 15 August 1940) (*IWM*)

Plate 5   An armoured car passing through Italian barbed wire on the Libyan frontier (26 July 1940) (*IWM*)

Plate 6   Wavell inspecting the building of defences by British troops on Crete. (15 November 1940) (*IWM*)

Plate 7   Dummy trucks in the Western Desert: part of Wavell's deception plan for Operation 'Compass' (1 November 1940) (*IWM*)

Plate 8   Wavell with Lieutenant General Richard O'Connor, Commander XIII Corps, discussing the continuation of 'Compass' outside Bardia (4 January 1941) (*IWM*)

Plate 9   Sollum Bay, with the Escarpment in the background. (23 December 1940) (*IWM*)

Plate 10   Australian troops advancing into Bardia behind a Matilda tank of the 7th Royal Tank Regiment. (6 January 1941) (*IWM*)

Plate 11   The results of 'Compass', columns of Italian prisoners being marched to the rear, sometimes with only a single British guard. (Western Desert, 16 December 1940) (*IWM*)

Plate 12   Captured Italian artillery pieces. (Western Desert, 20 February 1941) (*IWM*)

Plate 13   A new notice in captured territory (Western Desert, 14 April 1941) (*IWM*)

strategic defensive in the Middle East. The Italian advance, relatively minor though it was, wrested Churchill's attention from a possible cross-channel invasion, and focused it on the Middle East, in particular East Africa. With total disregard and lack of understanding of the terrain, the vast distances involved, and paucity of British assets available, on 5 July 1940 Churchill, as Minister of Defence, informed his Chief Staff Officer, Ismay, of his dissatisfaction with a message received from Wavell, 'which appeared perfectly contented with the static policy which is all we have any evidences of from General Wavell'.[23] Churchill then drafted a telegram to Wavell, which included, 'We have been concerned at the apparent absence of any offensive action from Kenya against Abyssinia,' and concluded, 'I had hoped that offensive schemes prepared beforehand would have been put into immediate operation. Pray let me know your plans and when you contemplate acting.'[24] Since it had been driven off the Continent, the Middle East appeared to be the only place where the British Army could go on the offensive, and Churchill was impatient to do so. This would certainly not be the first occasion in which Churchill, apparently oblivious of actual conditions, would relentlessly prod his commanders into action, in some cases prematurely.

Eden, of necessity, became involved in this issue, and was concerned that the Italians, after seizing Kassala, would march on Khartoum. He wired Wavell on 8 July 1940 that 'any attempted Italian advance from Kassala should be met and overthrown'.[25] Attempting to reassure Eden, Wavell responded that 'GOC Sudan has no apprehension at present of any advance on Khartoum from Kassala. . . . Italian attack on Kassala was almost certainly an isolated action. . . . There was never any intention to hold Kassala if seriously attacked.'[26] Unfortunately, Wavell's forthrightness had the opposite result, as Eden reported to the War Cabinet on 11 July that Wavell had attached little importance to the Italian occupation of Kassala. On 14 July 1940, Wavell departed for a four-day inspection trip to the Sudan and Kenya to assess the situation personally. In Khartoum he also had an audience with Haile Selassie, Emperor of Ethiopia.

Upon his return to Cairo, Wavell found 'that he was now to be subjected, more and more insistently, to Churchill's unique mixture of inquisition and energetic encouragement'.[27] Indeed, Churchill was beginning to view his Middle East commander disparagingly, perceiving a lack of urgency and imagination on Wavell's part. During this time, Churchill asked other senior officers with recent Middle East experience, notably Gordon-Finlayson and Freyberg, to write their own appreciations of the Middle East *status quo*. Churchill may either have wanted as many viewpoints as possible on the Middle East situation, or he may simply have doubted the accuracy and veracity of Wavell's numerous requests for reinforcements. If Churchill was hoping for evidence to bolster his own opinion, he was sadly disappointed, especially by Freyberg's appraisal.

Freyberg, in his 'The Position in Egypt', differentiated between what he perceived to be two distinct schools of thought on defence,

> one that advocates a policy of concentrating all our military resources to safeguard the British Isles as the heart of the Empire, and the other that believes there should be no policy of defence which does not consider the defence except from the point of view of the Empire as a whole.[28]

Freyberg continued, and must have startled Churchill when he wrote:

> It is perhaps not beside the point to note that the further away one is from England the less one believes in invasion. In the Middle East itself, few responsible people, if any, regard the invasion of the United Kingdom as a serious proposition. That was my own opinion when I arrived in England a month ago, and I still look upon it as a desperate action with little chance of success.

After proclaiming the 'Defence of London School' to be 'a dangerous one', the New Zealander outlined clearly the Middle East situation:

> In the same way, people not connected with the Middle East are prone to minimise the risk there. Those of us, however, who have been stationed in the Middle East know the true picture. We have watched the position deteriorate during the last eight months until the present deplorable state has been reached. We have seen our sea communications cut off both north and south, and with France, our Ally, out of the war, we are facing single handed the large armies on either frontier.

Freyberg included 'Scale of Attack against Egypt' and other cogent topics, and concluded 'The British Army in Egypt, excellent material though it is, and excellently trained, is comparatively weak in resisting power owing to the lack of equipment and war reserves.'

Freyberg's indictment of the utter inadequacy of the Middle East's war material was confirmed that same day by the Ministerial Committee on Military Policy in the Middle East, which reported that the resources, 'both in troops and equipment, at the disposal of the Commanders-in-Chief in the Middle East are greatly inferior in numbers and quantity to the forces of the enemy in Libya and Italian East Africa', and acknowledged the precariousness of the Middle East's position after the collapse of France and deprivation of French naval control of the western Mediterranean.[29] The Committee also confirmed its 3 July 1940 pronouncement that Middle East policy must remain generally defensive, and concluded 'it is essential to assist the Commanders-in-Chief [Middle East] in that area in every way practicable and with the utmost despatch'.[30]

Wavell, on 30 July 1940, returned from a three-day reconnaissance of the Western Desert, and reported to Dill that he planned to withdraw from Sollum, since his forces there faced two complete Italian divisions plus corps troops. Attributing his forced withdrawal to lack of equipment, Wavell added unreservedly: 'We cannot continue indefinitely to fight this war without proper equipment and I hope that Middle East requirements will be delayed no longer.'[31]

'These days,' according to Eden, 'also saw the beginning of a long period of argument with the Prime Minister about General Wavell's merits . . . and so it seemed to me that I was constantly defending the reputations of men unjustly assailed.'[32] Fully supporting Wavell, Eden and Dill were extremely distressed at Churchill's incessant chastisement of the Army. The Secretary of State and CIGS, therefore, confronted Churchill and told him that 'if Wavell and his commanders continued to be singled out for criticism . . ., which we thought most unjust to them and damaging to the Army, we could not accept it and would both have to go'.[33] Churchill responded propitiatingly, and Eden recommended that Wavell, whom the Prime Minister had never met, should return to England for consultations.

Wavell departed for London on 4 August 1940, on the same day that the Italians advanced on Hargeisa, in British Somaliland, the beginning of an offensive aimed at capturing the capital and port of Berbera. Although this imbroglio was of relatively short duration and scale and involved comparatively few soldiers, the resultant British evacuation was blown well out of proportion, not only by Italian propaganda but also by Churchill. It is true that 'the somewhat hasty evacuation of this poor and dusty Cinderella of British possessions in the face of the Italian advance left a very unpleasant taste in the British mouth at the time', but a scrutiny of events reveals clearly that 'the action decided on was almost certainly the soundest if not the only one in the circumstances. It was brilliantly carried out.'[34] The most significant consequence of this incident was an act of recrimination in its immediate and emotional aftermath which also served to widen the schism in the tenuous Churchill-Wavell relationship.

The brief British Somaliland campaign was the embodiment of the British Government's fiscal indigence, interdepartmental squabbling, and irresolution. In fact, to try to mollify the impact of Wavell's Despatch on 'Operations in the Somaliland Protectorate, 1939–1940', the War Office took the highly unusual step of writing an explanatory preface to it.

The original War Office policy as put forth in the 1936 Hornby Report, was not to attempt to hold British Somaliland if attacked. On 19 December 1939, however, this policy was revoked, the Chiefs of Staff agreeing that 'the proposal to alter the defence policy of Somaliland to the defence of the territory, and in the last resort of Berbera, from the abandonment of the country in the face of Italian invasion, is approved in principle'.[35] This should have resulted in the transfer of control from the Colonial Office to the War Office, but this did not happen immediately. After reconnoitring the area from 8–13 January 1940, and deciding to place Legentilhomme in command of both British and French Somaliland in the event of war with Italy, Wavell proposed troop reinforcements for the Protectorate. It took two months to receive permission to move one battalion, and it was not until 15 May 1940 that this unit finally arrived at Berbera. Wavell later wrote exasperatedly that the delay 'in giving authority for the move was apparently due to financial discussions between the War Office and the Colonial Office, and to Foreign Office apprehension that this move might be considered provocative to Italy'.[36] The move of a second battalion, approved 'in principle' on 20 April 1940, finally took place on 12 July 1940. Although Wavell's Command received operational control of British Somaliland in January 1940, it did not receive administrative control until 1 June 1940 – only ten days before the Italian declaration of war.

France had originally provided seven battalions for the joint defence of French and British Somaliland, as compared with about three battalions from the British. The British force was obviously insufficient for such a task, as Eden reported to Churchill in June 1940 before the French collapse: 'The only aspect of hostilities in this part of the world which now troubles me is the strength of our forces in British Somaliland. . . . I feel that it is essential that we should have stronger forces in Somaliland. . . .'[37] An Indian battalion arrived to reinforce British Somaliland at the beginning of July.

The collapse of France made the situation much more problematic, and even though he had Legentilhomme's continued assurances of loyalty, Wavell realistically ordered the Middle East Joint Planning Staff to study 'In the event of the French in Somaliland following the Pétain Government, to decide if we should hold or evacuate British Somaliland.'[38] This study concluded British Somaliland 'is *not* of vital importance to us,' and recommended: 'As the retention of British Somaliland is not vital, we should begin evacuating if the French throw in their hand. We can not afford the loss of equipment which would result from a precipitate withdrawal.'[39] Wavell consequently cabled Lieutenant Colonel AR Chater, Officer Commanding Troops in British Somaliland, that day, advising him to prepare evacuation plans if the British position became untenable.

Legentilhomme's position was undermined by the civilian administration in Djibuti, and on 23 July 1940 he was replaced by a pro-Vichy general. Legentilhomme departed for Aden, eager to avoid a firing squad ordered to be prepared should the general be captured by the Italians.

The British recognised that the French downfall nullified plans for a future joint offensive to Addis Ababa, and began to study the possibility of an offensive from British Somaliland. The Italians, on the other hand, recognised astutely that the French collapse had resulted in a military vacuum in the region, and left 'British Somaliland as a ripe plum ready to fall'.[40] The Italians then launched their attack on 4 August.

Wavell arrived in London on 7 August 1940, amidst an ever-increasing crescendo of bombings by the German *Luftwaffe* endeavouring to achieve air superiority prior to the launching of a cross-Channel invasion. The plight of the British Isles was staggering; tension was mounting, since it was possible that at any moment the Army, Home Guard and civil populace might be alerted to man the beaches in order to repel foreign invaders. Despite the grimness of the outlook, Churchill had been able to unify the British behind him, to persevere during what he would later describe as their 'finest hour'. Such was the aura of circumstances in which Wavell now found himself.

On 8 August 1940, Wavell met first with Eden, then attended the meetings of the Middle East Committee and the Chiefs of Staff. Churchill and Eden also attended the latter. If there was any hope of mutual confidence, understanding, and receptive communications between Churchill and Wavell, these hopes were shattered irrevocably by their first series of meetings, starting with the 8 August Chiefs of Staff meeting. Connell has observed:

> At this supreme moment in his personal drama Churchill met, in Wavell, a man of the highest moral and intellectual stature, with a great military reputation, holding a post whose responsibilities and challenges were similar though not greater than his own, who for reasons which neither of them fully comprehended was incapable of playing the part in that drama that Churchill wished him to play.[41]

Quite simply, Churchill wanted Wavell to be the foremost of *his* generals in the field. Wavell possessed unimpeachable integrity, and would always be completely and unquestionably loyal to the Prime Minister, but he would not compromise either himself, his immutable sense of duty, or his independence of judgement, by being anyone's general. Wavell was his own man, a servant of the Sovereign, and this unstated and intangible, but perceptible friction was a further divisive factor in this relationship.

At the Chiefs of Staff meeting Wavell gave an eloquent and comprehensive exposition on the Middle East situation, which Eden thought was 'masterly and it is even more so in retrospect'.[42] Wavell made progress in that Churchill realised that 'The command in the Middle East at that time comprised an extraordinary amalgam of military, political, diplomatic, and administrative problems of extreme complexity.'[43] During this initial meeting, Wavell's reticence was obvious to all participants. This 'almost pathological taciturnity' was an additional source of irritation to Churchill, who believed this characteristic indicated a lack of the offensive spirit, lack of resolution, and lack of mental dexterity. Nothing could have been further from the truth.

It is also quite possible that Wavell's disinclination to speak was, to Churchill, furiously reminiscent of a similar situation during the Great War. Barrie Pitt has related that 'General Haig had met Lloyd George's arguments with just such a façade of impassive silence, and in his diaries published after the war, he had revealed a contempt for his political master only equalled by Lloyd George's distrust of the general.'[44] Churchill may perhaps have wondered whether Wavell's laconic behaviour indicated a similar disdain for him.

Another incident occurred during this Chiefs of Staff meeting which further marred any empathy Churchill and Wavell might have felt for each other. Brigadier John Shearer, Wavell's Director of Military Intelligence, also attended this meeting and later provided a unique and further illuminating perspective of it:

> Knowing my Chief [Wavell] as I did, I could feel the temperature rising between him and the PM [Prime Minister], whose interrogation semed to me to become increasingly curt.
> Finally, after Mr. Amery asked General Wavell to repeat his appreciation of Marshal Graziani's intentions in the Desert, I was aware that the electricity had really built up.
> My C-in-C [Commander-in-Chief] rather impatiently repeated his previous statement.
> Now the PM interjected, 'But, Commander-in-Chief, you said. . . .' In a flash, General Wavell replied, 'I did not.'
> And the relations between these two magnificent men were, at that moment, irretrievably damaged.[45]

Wavell was incensed at the unrelenting questioning and excoriating treatment he had received from Churchill, a sentiment intensified by fatigue after his harrowing plane trip to London, during which his plane had twice been attacked by German aircraft. After this fateful first meeting, Shearer recalled walking with Dill and Wavell through the streets of Westminster and the ensuing conversation: 'My Chief said that the PM had asked him down to Chequers for the weekend but he would be damned if he would risk further treatment of the kind to which he had just been subjected.' Shearer continued, 'I remember so clearly General Dill saying, "Archie, no one would deny that you have had unbearable provocation. But he is our Prime Minister. He carries an almost incredible burden. It is true you can be replaced. He cannot be. You must go to Chequers." '[46] Wavell realised that Dill was correct, and they both went to Chequers. It was unfortunate that Wavell was unwilling or unable to view the enormity of the war effort and peril to England through the eyes of Churchill; he could have achieved such an understanding without having to compromise himself or his principles.

The following night, Wavell dined at Chequers with Churchill, Eden, Dill, Admiral of the Fleet Sir Dudley Pound (the First Sea Lord), and Ismay and spent the night there. While Churchill was discussing possibilities for future offensive operations, Wavell inanely suggested Norway, to which the Prime Minister responded: 'We shall need skis for that, and we don't want to get Namsosed again. We've had enough of that.'[47] Shortly thereafter, Churchill promised Wavell he would not ask him to conduct a landing in enemy territory until the air was cleared over the place of disembarkation – a dubious pledge, considering the operations in Greece and Crete the following year. This after-dinner conference, Eden noted, 'went reasonably well, even though Churchill still kept, I thought, his reservations about Wavell. The Commander-in-Chief was not a man who could be drawn out, or one to make a special effort to please. . . .'[48] There was agreement, however, on what equipment the Middle East needed, and what could be sent from England.

On 12 August 1940, Wavell attended meetings of the Middle East Committee and Defence Committee, and a third conference with Churchill and others, the last in session, in accordance with Churchill's normal regimen, from about 10 pm to 2 am. Churchill was very concerned about Wavell's disposition of troops (Eden's consternation was expressed fully when he wrote, 'PM most anxious to move this battalion here and that battalion there.'[49]), especially the employment of West African soldiers in the Sudan rather than in Kenya, to which Wavell retorted frustratingly that the Sudan climate was unsuitable for West African troops. Wavell's answer may sound absurd, and this incident may appear trivial, but it caused Churchill to question further the competence of his Middle East commander.

The key topic of this meeting was, however, the route by which the precious reinforcements to the Middle East should be transported. The alternatives were either around the Cape of Good Hope, or through the Mediterranean, with the former option, which although longer was less risky, favoured by the First Sea Lord. Churchill believed that if he was going to denude Britain's defences at such a precarious time, the equipment and weapons must arrive in Egypt at the earliest possible moment, which would be achieved via the Mediterranean. Wavell said the increased risk of losing his supplies would not justify the gain in time of the shorter route. Finally, Churchill deferred to the Admiralty position, although a compromise was later reached, with the final decision over the route to be made as the convoy approached Gibraltar. As a result of this potentially crucial issue, Churchill perceived that Wavell's attitude indicated a lack of aggressiveness and lack of audacity, all the more distressing to Churchill fighting for national survival as the 'Battle of Britain' began.

Eden found Wavell waiting for him in his office the next morning,

> . . . clearly upset at last night's proceedings and said he thought he should have made it plain that if the Prime Minister could not approve his dispositions and had not confidence in him, he should appoint someone else. He was anxious to get back to his command if this was desired.[50]

After reviewing the situation with Wavell and Dill, Eden requested to see Churchill later that day. While waiting for his appointment, Eden received a letter from the Prime Minister, which included:

> I am favourably impressed with General Wavell in many ways, but I do not feel

in him that sense of mental vigour and resolve to overcome obstacles, which is indispensable to successful war. I find instead, tame acceptance of a variety of local circumstances in different theatres, which is leading to a lamentable lack of concentration upon the decisive point.[51]

Churchill, incredibly, also recommended further alterations to Wavell's troop dispositions. Eden replied in writing, stating that he and Dill were 'much perturbed' at Churchill's judgment of Wavell, adding 'Neither of us know of any General Officer in the Army better qualified to fill this very difficult post at this critical time.'[52] Indeed, Wavell had made excellent use of his meagre resources.

On the evening of 13 August 1940, Eden and Dill met with the Prime Minster, and the CIGS made it clear that he supported Wavell. Churchill relented, although in the ensuing conversation he opined that Wavell was 'a good average colonel and would make a good chairman of a Tory association'.[53] Irrecoverable damage had again been done to the Churchill-Wavell relationship.

Indeed, as a result of his first meetings with Wavell, Churchill wrote euphemistically that 'While not in full agreement with General Wavell's use of the resources at his disposal, I thought it best to leave him in command. I admired his fine qualities, and was impressed with the confidence so many people had in him.'[54] Wavell, much more frankly, believed Churchill 'considered my replacement by someone who was more likely to share his ideas, but could not find any good reason to do so. Winston has always disliked me personally.'[55] Perhaps such a clash of personalities was inevitable. The two men were temperamentally poles apart. Part of the temperamental difficulty, as Lord Annan has suggested penetratingly, arose from the different schools at which they were educated. Churchill had been at Harrow, and 'though he was not a distinguished member of the school, he had some qualities which are associated with Harrovians. He was a buccaneer, a man of action, and not too scrupulous about personal relations, protocol, good form, and channels of command'.[56] Wavell, in contrast, was the very typical Wykhamist: 'in military terms it meant a general who would be the very reverse of the showman that Montgomery was and very much the unassuming gentleman-like general that Wavell was'.[57] Churchill and Wavell could not have been more dissimilar.

Wavell's renowned taciturnity was a, if not the, significantly detrimental factor in his relationship with Churchill. Churchill was flamboyant, his brilliant and convincing rhetoric was inspirational, and he correlated such loquaciousness with decisiveness and audacity. 'It is hard to make anyone understand,' Jacob, who attended these conferences, recalled recently, 'how tongue-tied Wavell was, and therefore how little impression he gave of intellect and character.'[58] The impact of Wavell's taciturnity was made worse since he was very deliberate and was 'a rather slow reactor and Winston was always impatient of people who were slow to answer back'.[59]

It is quite possible, though, that Churchill himself was a contributory factor in Wavell's reticence, as suggested interestingly by Dorman-Smith:

> . . . when [Wavell] was not being stimulated by his company or surroundings or events, his busy delighted mind simply went off by itself. There was always so much to think about. . . . Pomposity bored him excessively; dullness exasperated him, life was too short for boredom. I'm sure Winston bored him. He therefore bored and perplexed Winston who only looks into a man's face to find a looking glass image of Winston there.[60]

Both Ismay and Jacob thought, as a result of Churchill's and Wavell's first meeting, that Wavell would be removed, and that 'Wavell was lucky not to be sacked then and there.'[61] Jacob encapsulated Churchill's probable opinion of Wavell at this time: 'I think Churchill did not think Wavell was more than a mediocre commander . . .,'[62] and 'I think that [Churchill] just thought [Wavell] was a rather dumb Scotsman.'[63] The mutual antipathy between Churchill and Wavell engendered by their first meeting was, unfortunately, never diminished.

Lord Boothby, who had served as Parliamentary Private Secretary to Churchill after World War I, recalled having a conversation with Lloyd George in the summer of 1940. Boothby was convinced that 'Churchill alone could save us,' to which Lloyd George responded prophetically, 'You are probably right. But it will be a one-man show. He has at least one great general – Wavell. I was not so fortunate. But, mark my words, he will get rid of Wavell.'[64]

Further conferences were held on 14 and 15 August 1940, although none were as controversial and emotional as the earlier meetings. But before Wavell's departure on 15 August, the Italian invasion of British Somaliland had already reached its climax. After advancing initially on Hargeisa on 4 August, the Italians remained idle, as they were probably concentrating their forces before resuming the offensive. On 11 August, by which time the British force had been increased to five battalions, the Italians began their main attack on the primary British defensive position at Tug Argen. Later that day, Major General (later General Sir) AR Godwin Austen, en route from Palestine to take command of a division in Kenya, assumed command of the forces in British Somaliland, ostensibly because, with reinforcements, the number of troops had increased above the level of a brigadier's command. It was not prudent to change commanders, especially in the middle of a determined enemy attack; there was little a new commander could do to turn the tide of battle.

The enemy attack continued on 12 and 13 August 1940. It was obvious to Godwin Austen, who had only one battalion in reserve, that the Italians, due to their overwhelming preponderance of artillery and manpower, would be able to isolate individual posts and soundly defeat each in turn. After repeated Italian attacks, the enemy began to infiltrate to the rear of the

British positions, and threatened to encircle the British. 'In these circumstances,' Wavell's Despatch remarked, 'General Godwin Austen came to the
conclusion that a retreat on Berbera and evacuation was the only course to
save the force from a dangerous defeat and possible annihilation.'[65] Indeed,
Godwin Austen's original instructions of 10 August directed him, among
other items, to 'take the necessary steps for withdrawal and evacuation if
necessary'.[66]

Godwin Austen cabled his recommendation for evacuation to Wilson,
who 'had no hesitation in agreeing to immediate evacuation',[67] and at 7:45
am, 15 August 1940, responded: 'Carry out evacuation of repeat evacuation
of Somaliland.'[68] Wilson who had kept Wavell in London fully informed of
the course of events in British Somaliland, cabled sixteen minutes later:
'Enemy broken through Tug Argen position with hopelessly superior forces
and firepower. Restoration of situation impossible. Have sanctioned evacuation. Hope to save 70% of force. Inform General Wavell.'[69] Wavell did in
fact receive Wilson's message, and appraised the Prime Minister of the
decision to evacuate British Somaliland, and later recalled,

> when I brought [Churchill] the news of the evacuation, I rather expected an
> outburst. But he took it very well, and said that it could not be helped, and that
> the loss of Somaliland was of little importance and that I should have the troops
> withdrawn available for more important defence.[70]

Before leaving London, Wavell cabled to Wilson at 9:55 pm:

> 1. Have had final interview with Prime Minister and start back this evening . . .
>
> 7. Evacuation of Somaliland is accepted here and there is no recrimination as to
> events here. Troops should be got away in best possible order for use elsewhere
> in Middle East.[71]

The evacuation of British Somaliland was completed by 18 August.

It was unfortunate that the British had to withdraw from British
Somaliland, and although this campaign was unsuccessful, it was not
inglorious, especially since the Italians suffered 2,052 casualties and the
expenditure of other precious resources at a cost of 260 (38 killed, 222
wounded) British casualties, with the crucial rearguard action having been
fought by Wavell's old battalion, the 2nd Battalion The Black Watch. Even
the British Chief Political Officer in East Africa, Major General Sir Philip
Mitchell, noted rather nonchalantly in his diary on 17 August 1940 that 'It
seems [the British] are now going to evacuate Somaliland after losing a
good many lives for – to my mind – no very good reason. However, if they
get all the troops away we get them back here so much to the good.'[72]

After briefing Churchill on the decision to evacuate British Somaliland,
Wavell left London on 15 August 1940. He later wrote that he had 'no
doubt that both General Godwin-Austen's recommendation and General

Wilson's decision [to evacuate British Somaliland] were correct',[73] and thought he had heard the last about this episode – but he was wrong.

When Churchill heard of the success of the evacuation and comparatively light British casualties, he became extremed agitated, believing the lower British casualty figures indicated that the withdrawal from this then strategically-useless territory had been conducted without first putting up a good fight. The Prime Minister fired a 'red hot cable' to Wavell, ordering him to suspend Godwin Austen and conduct a court of inquiry. Wavell was understandably upset at this charge of pusillanimity, and immediately cabled to Churchill refusing to hold a court of inquiry, and ending the message with 'a big butcher's bill was not necessarily evidence of good tactics'. Dill later told Wavell that 'this telegram and especially the last sentence roused Winston to greater anger than he had ever seen him in before'.[74]

Wavell probably should have acted less hastily and with better discretion; he later felt that Churchill kept 'a bad mark' against him for defending Godwin Austen. Major (later Sir) Desmond Morton, who had first met Churchill in the trenches during the Great War and later became one of his closest confidants, later described vividly Churchill's reaction when he received Wavell's telegram:

> Winston raged, but could think of nothing to say in return. Moreover, the ill-concealed satisfaction of all three Chiefs of Staff and others who saw this reply, did not do anything to mitigate his fury. And, of course, he knew in his heart that Wavell was right and that his own telegram was – to anyone but a person like Wavell – unforgiveable.[75]

Ronald Lewin has noted astutely that for Wavell, 'this episode represented the point of no return'.[76]

Churchill's lack of trust in Wavell was revealed within hours of the latter's departure from London. On 16 August 1940, Churchill drafted a 'General Directive for Commander-in-Chief Middle East', and stated 'the Cabinet approved it without amendment in accord with the Chiefs of Staff'[77] – Churchill always being careful to legitimise his actions within the legal methods of operation of the extant war machinery. This Directive was basically an operation order, containing minutely-detailed instructions, to include 'tactical employment' of the forces he had listed, down to battalion-sized elements. This clearly was not within the purview of the Prime Minister, and the Official History remarked appropriately: 'So detailed a directive from a Minister to a commander in a distant theatre was to say the least unusual.'[78] The Australian Official History elaborated further that at this time Churchill displayed one of his defects as a leader – 'his eagerness to lay down the law on details that were in the province of the man on the spot . . . his intense interest in the details of the profesion of arms was not backed by adequate schooling in the everyday problems of a military commander'.[79] Gordon Craig has equated Churchill's minutely-detailed Directive to 'the very kind of supersession of the authority of the field commander to which Hitler was prone in the last stages of the war'.[80] By implication, this Directive was a critique of Wavell's generalship, and was also indicative of Churchill's obsession to be in total control, his infatuation with minute tactical details, and assumption of omniscience in military matters. Wavell later wrote dourly: 'I carried out such parts of the directive as were practicable, and disregarded a good deal of it.'[81]

Throughout the latter half of the summer of 1940, Mussolini, greatly concerned that the war would soon end either through a negotiated peace or the success of Operation 'Sea Lion', the German invasion of England, pressed Graziani to conduct an offensive against the British, with the goal of seizing the Suez Canal. Having had no military success in the campaign against France, such an attack represented Mussolini's last remaining opportunity to establish any claim to colonial spoils at the negotiating table, which, it appeared, would convene soon.

While waiting for the expected Italian attack, Wavell did not remain idle. He reconnoitred the British defences in the Western Desert on 3 September 1940. The Joint Planning Staff, on Wavell's instruction, had completed an appreciation on 4 September considering the possibilities of a joint operation at Sollum to raid the Italian lines of communication should the Italians advance into the Western Desert. On the following day, Wavell and Wilson discussed the upcoming battle. With the Italians believing the British forces were much larger than they actually were, and in order to protect the Nile Delta, it was concluded realistically that this battle must be fought as far forward as possible. In addition, as Wavell had written as early as 3 October 1939, the British would make no serious attempt to halt the Italians until they reached the defences of Mersa Matruh. Initially, the 7th Armoured Division would only harass and delay the Italians. It would then withdraw south, later attacking the outstretched Italian lines of communication, and isolating and destroying the Italian force.

In the light of the imminent Italian offensive and while waiting for reinforcements from England, Wavell, on 11 September 1940, instructed the Joint Planning Staff to prepare for the eventual invasion of Libya. He noted realistically that 'By the end of this year, or early next year, we should, if all goes well, be in a position to take the offensive on this front.' This instruction, a refinement of Wavell's directive of 3 October 1939, represented the true starting point for Operation 'Compass'. It envisioned a four-phased operation resulting in the capture of Tobruk.[82]

The Italians had originally planned to turn the British desert flank – a contingency for which Wavell had prepared by constructing defences east of Mersa Matruh and at other locations – but in the event, the Italian brigade spearheading the assault became lost in the desert, thus postponing the actual offensive until 13 September 1940. The cautious and lethargic Italian advance was led by intricately structured divisions resembling, according to one British observer, nothing so much as 'a birthday party in the Long Valley at Aldershot'.[83] After covering the sixty-five or so miles of barren desert to Sidi Barrani – where the metalled road into Egypt begins – in four days, Graziani halted unexpectedly, after suffering some 2,000 casualties, compared to less than fifty for the British. Trying to magnify the importance of their spasmodic advance, Italian propaganda claimed that 'British resistance has been smashed' and that 'a few days after the occupation of Sidi Barrani, thanks to the skill of Italian engineers, the tramcars were running again'.[84] As Wilson wryly observed, 'the solitary mosque, police post, and a few mud huts had achieved an unexpected rise to a big city'![85]

After a few days of close and wary observation of the Italian forces, it became readily apparent to the British that their advance had halted. On 19 September 1940, after returning from another personal reconnaissance in the Western Desert, Wavell issued orders for a counterstroke to be prepared against the enemy when they reached Mersa Matruh. Wilson and O'Connor both had, to a degree, anticipated Wavell's new instructions, since not only had Wavell and Wilson discussed the upcoming battle on 5 September, but it was also obvious that the Italians were now in a vulnerable position so far into Egypt. Wavell emphasised that this proposed battle should 'be planned with a view to the enemy's complete destruction, certainly, as soon as our armoured reinforcements now on their way are in action, this should be well within our power'.[86] 'The general strategy of the battle,' Wavell continued,

> seems fairly clear, as the enemy comes up against the defences of Matruh, we should be prepared to pivot with our right on these defences and the defences of the Nagamish Nullah, and by bringing forward our left drive the enemy up against the Matruh defences and cut him off from his line of retreat westwards, our armoured troops being on the outer flank.

Considering the anticipated intentions of the enemy, this could have been an extremely effective plan. Wavell also wanted to ensure that the individual soldiers were mentally and physically prepared 'to march hard, fight hard, live hard, and go on short water rations for a period', as well as to be able to march and manoeuvre by night – proven techniques which Wavell had stressed since he was a brigade commander.

The reinforcements Wavell had been promised while in England arrived at Suez on 24 September 1940. This equipment, especially the tanks, would greatly enhance Wavell's meagre forces, and provide additional impetus for planning future offensive operations. These reinforcements were not, as Churchill probably imagined, the panacea for all Middle East equipment deficiencies and would not turn the balance of forces in Wavell's favour overnight. Eden understood that until 'Wavell knew definitely and for months ahead what [reinforcements] he was to receive, he had no chance to

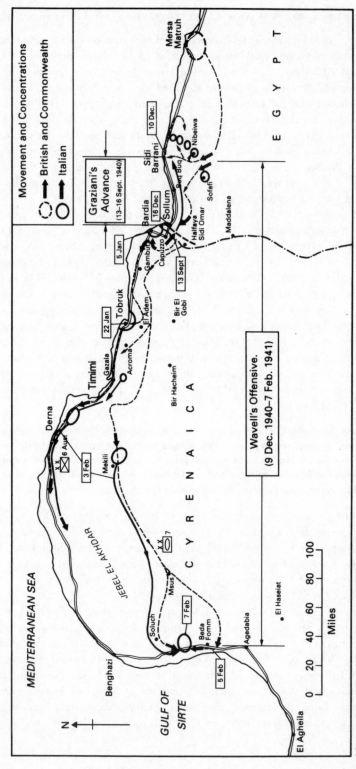

Map 4. Graziani's Advance and Wavell's Offensive 13 September 1940 – 7 February 1941

plan in advance'.[87] In this same memorandum, written on 27 September, Eden recommended that someone from the Middle East Committee should travel to Wavell's Command and assess the situation on the spot. On that same day, Germany, Italy and Japan further solidified their alliance by signing their 'Ten Year Pact'.

This was the perfect opportunity for Churchill, distrusting Wavell and believing him overly-cautious, and fervidly pushing for a British offensive – especially after the *débâcle* at Dakar – to send Eden to the Middle East, ostensibly on a fact-finding mission. Wavell's aide-de-camp, however, recognised that the 'chief object of [Eden's] mission being to "check up" on Wavell generally on behalf of the Prime Minister, who was anxious to see more action in the Middle East'.[88] Leaving England on 11 October, Eden arrived in Egypt three days later. On the second day of his visit, he received a briefing from Wavell on plans and dispositions to meet a further Italian offensive, afterwards asking the General what he would do if the Italians did not attack. Wavell had obviously thought of that, gave Eden 'one of his quiet, appraising looks', and replied that Wilson would soon arrive and answer that question fully. During these discussions Wavell and Wilson both confirmed the importance of the infantry tanks in any future offensive operations, with the result that Eden requested an extra battalion of them from the Prime Minister.

Eden wasted no time, inspecting ordnance shops and other ancillary activities, travelling to Palestine with Wavell, and flying to the Western Desert with Wilson on 21 October. Wavell gained a great deal of insight from his discussions with Eden, and a better understanding of the role of the Middle East within Churchill's overall strategic conception. Wavell forecast that the main problems facing the Middle East over the next six months would be the defence of Egypt, liquidation of Italian East Africa, support of Turkey and Greece, and other potential disturbances in Iraq, Iran, and in Syria, which could arise from enemy aggression. 'The support of Greece and Turkey,' Wavell postulated, 'is, in some ways, the most pressing of all our problems.' If there was a conflict over which of those two countries should receive British assistance, he recommended the latter.[89]

With Wavell understanding the primacy of the defence of Egypt, he continued his planning to attack the Italian forces, which had been harassed for the last month by Gott's Support Group, small combined arms columns, and the Long Range Patrols. On 20 October 1940, Wavell issued instructions to Wilson to make an attack on the stationary Italian positions in the Sofafi – Sidi Barrani – Buqbuq area: 'a short and swift [operation], lasting from four to five days at the most, and taking every advantage of the element of surprise'.[90] To cover the distances required without enemy detection, Wavell decided two night movements of about forty miles each would be conducted, followed by an attack early the next day. Wavell envisioned the attack to resemble a double envelopment, with the 4th Indian Division (commanded by Major General N Beresford-Peirse) on the right along the coast, and the reinforced 7th Armoured Division on the left attacking the Sofafi group of camps. A pincer movement would follow, cutting off the Italian Nibeiwa and Tummar camps. To maintain secrecy, Wavell concluded: 'I do not wish the contents of this note disclosed or the plans discussed with anyone except your Brigadier General Staff, General O'Connor and General Creagh.'[91] Wilson then took this plan to O'Connor, and observed that, 'Neither of us liked it', due to the extended and difficult march the 7th Armoured Division would have to conduct, and the unreliability of controlling such distant forces with the signal resources available.[92]

O'Connor believed that the key weakness of the Italian camps lay in the fact that they were out of supporting distance of each other, and by using the element of surprise audaciously, the camps could be defeated in detail. The modified general plan was initially to destroy or capture enemy forces in the Nibeiwa and Tummar camps, while the 7th Armoured Division conducted a screen operation to prevent enemy reinforcements coming from the Sofafi area and to protect the left flank of the attacking 4th Indian Division. If successful, the Armoured Division would drive northwards to the sea to sever the Italian line of retreat to the West, and the 4th Indian Division would attack the enemy camps around Sidi Barrani. After a small British column had isolated the Maktila camp, which could be crushed later, the Armoured Division would advance to Buqbuq to cut off all the Italians there from Sollum. Wilson took this revised plan to Wavell in Cairo, who approved it and directed the completion of detailed planning for this coming offensive.

After spending four fruitful days in the Western Desert, Eden returned to Cairo. Eden and Wavell planned to depart for Khartoum on 28 October 1940, but early that morning the Secretary of State was woken with the message announcing the Italian ultimatum to Greece. The Greek refusal resulted in an unprovoked Italian invasion beginning at 6:00 am that day. The immediate repercussions were that British forces were sent to defend Crete and to establish a temporary naval base: Longmore sent one air squadron, to be followed by three others before the end of November, and Wavell sent the 1st Battalion, The York and Lancaster Regiment (which had been earmarked for Malta) on 31 October, and the 2nd Battalion The Black Watch, on 17 November, in addition to other supporting units. In addition, the British Military Mission, Greece, headed by Major General MD Gambier-Parry, was established on 31 October and sent to Athens on the following day.

Eden, Wavell, and Longmore flew to Khartoum later on 28 October 1940, and conferred that evening with the South African Premier, General Jan Smuts and the principal commanders of the area. The main items on the agenda included the current disposition of forces and offensive plans for the Sudan and Kenya. In the Sudan, planning was underway for the recapture of Kassala and Gallabat, both of which had been seized by the Italians in July. Smuts mentioned sagely the importance of synchronising the attack on Kassala with those executed elsewhere, especially in Kenya. He also believed that the primary objective of the British in this region should be to clear the Italians out of the port of Kismayu – later to be known as Operation 'Canvas' – and then to concentrate their forces in order to advance on Addis Ababa in conjunction with an offensive from the Sudan. Discussions were reconvened the following morning, during which the tentative offensive against Kismayu in January 1941 was addressed, as well as a subsequent major offensive to start about August 1941. The Ethiopian Emperor, Haile Selassie, also participated in some of these conferences.

Due to the exigencies involved with the Italian invasion of Greece, Wavell returned to Cairo, while Eden inspected units and garrisons in East Africa before returning to Cairo on 1 November 1940. Wilson and O'Connor had completed the detailed planning and preparations for 'Compass' during Wavell's absence, and on 2 November Wavell issued a confirmatory note to Wilson, his only formal written directive for this offensive. Wavell wrote that he was cognisant of the risks involved in such an operation, but was fully prepared to accept them:

> In everything but numbers, we are superior to the enemy. We are more highly trained, we have better equipment. We know the ground and are better accustomed to desert conditions. Above all, we have stouter hearts and greater traditions and are fighting in a worthier cause.[93]

Wavell's directed dissipation of forces to assist Greece had the potential of compromising the success, and even the execution, of 'Compass'. Rather than jeopardise his plans, Wavell made Eden aware of them, and the Secretary of State approved them and promised his full support. In that vein Eden cabled to Churchill on 1 November that:

> We should presently be in a position to undertake certain offensive operations which, if successful, may have far-reaching effect on course of the war as a whole. It would surely be bad strategy to allow ourselves to be diverted from this task and unwise to employ our forces in fragments in a theatre of war where they cannot be decisive.[94]

Eden continued that he was anxious to return to London to 'put before you in detail at the earliest date the positions and plans which have been worked out here',[95] referring to 'Compass', the plans for which Wavell would trust to be relayed to Churchill only via Eden. Wavell had not intended to disclose his plans at such an early date, but he 'realised Winston's sanguine temperament and desire to have at least one finger in any military pie'.[96]

Churchill, failing to understand Eden's intent and unaware of the plans for 'Compass', wanted Eden, because of the Greek situation, to remain in the Middle East for another week. Eden continued to press his case, sending two messages to the Prime Minister on 3 November 1940. The first included that the 'Commanders-in-Chief were strongly of the opinion that . . . the security of Egypt is most urgent commitment, and must take precedence of attempts to prevent Greece being over-run,'[97] and Eden later stated adamantly that 'My anxiety is lest by dividing our limited resources we risk failure in both theatres.'[98] The Chiefs of Staff in London, undoubtedly on Churchill's exhortation, decided on the following day that Greece now became the overriding priority, to receive the greatest material and moral support, which was available only from Egypt, at the earliest opportunity. Eden, still in Egypt, acknowledged on 5 November that he and Wavell understood that reinforcements to Greece would involve additional risks in the Western Desert, but 'that these risks must be faced in view of political commitments'.[99] Thus, at an early stage, political considerations overrode military factors in despatching assistance to Greece. It was also fortunate for Churchill that Eden was in the Middle East when the Greek invasion occurred, and Eden was directed to stay there an additional week, thus giving the Prime Minister the chance to develop a pro-Greek policy in London without Eden's personal opposition.

Departing finally from Cairo on 6 November 1940, Eden arrived in London two days later. Of this first week after the Greeks were attacked, Churchill later wrote:

> Our correspondence during this period was thus on both sides based upon misunderstanding. Wavell and the Secretary of State thought that for the sake of giving ineffectual aid to Greece we were pressing them to dissipate the forces they were gathering for an offensive in the Western Desert. We, on the other hand, not crediting them with offensive intentions, objected to their standing idle or trifling at such a crucial moment.[100]

This statement reveals not so much Churchill's 'misunderstanding' of the situation, but his total underestimation of the initiative and abilities of the 'mediocre commander' in the Middle East. Churchill's mistrust of Wavell was allayed temporarily when, on 8 November, Eden described the plans for 'Compass', to the Prime Minister, who was so delighted that, as he later admitted, he 'purred like six cats'.[101] Ismay added, 'That is putting it mildly. He was rapturously happy.'[102] Wavell's plans were immediately sanctioned by the Chiefs of Staff and the War Cabinet, and 'Compass' became the top priority operation.

With the threat of an invasion of England significantly reduced, Churchill was able to turn his attentions to Wavell's forthcoming attack. Impatient, eager to know the details of 'Compass', and wanting to influence its execution, Churchill bombarded Wavell with messages requesting more information, especially as to the timing of the offensive. In one of these many messages, Churchill, in admonishing Wavell to hasten his offensive, believed the success of 'Compass' might 'determine action of Turkey and Jugoslavia', and that 'One may indeed see possibility of centre of gravity in Middle East shifting suddenly from Egypt to the Balkans, and from Cairo to Constantinople.'[103] Wavell refused steadfastly to provide more than the basic information, concerned about secrecy and the prevalence of Italian spies in Egypt, but even more so about losing control of the operation to the possessive Churchill in London. In addition, Wavell did not want Churchill to place unduly positive hopes on this operation, which had been designed as a raid.

Originally, it had been planned to launch 'Compass' at the end of November, but the drain of resources for Greece required a postponement until the first week of December. During November, the enemy was further deceived by the Long Range Patrols, which incessantly attacked Italian outposts and airstrips, and conducted raids deep inside enemy territory, diverting Graziani's attention from Wavell's true intentions and giving the impression of simultaneous appearances at places 600 miles apart.

But this was not the only technique Wavell employed to deceive the enemy. He later wrote cryptically,

> I attempted, through certain channels known to my Intelligence, to convey to the enemy the impression that my forces in the Western Desert had been seriously weakened by the sending of reinforcements to Greece and that further withdrawals were contemplated.[104]

Through Security Intelligence Middle East (SIME), a part of the Middle East Intelligence Centre (MEIC), Wavell was able to funnel deceptive information through double agents and other operatives whose function was to pass such disinformation to the enemy.

Simultaneously, the double agent network was spreading information on a massive British troop buildup on the Italian right flank in the desert. Italian reconnaissance airplanes produced photographs that confirmed these stories, but these 'reinforcements' were actually dummy tanks made of inflatable rubber, heavy field guns composed of logs on supports with a length of drain pipe fitted to the end of each containing chemicals that produced realistic flashes, and lastly a platoon of natives who drove their camels and horses across the dunes dragging wooden frame devices behind them which stirred up the desert dust and from a distance gave the appearance of a moving motorised column. These highly effective ruses were almost a carbon copy of the ploys implemented so superbly by Allenby, in which Wavell had played a part in conceiving and executing, and which had permitted the Egyptian Expeditionary Force to break through the Turkish positions in the Jordan Valley in September 1918.

Essential logistical and administrative preparations were also completed during this period, in accordance with Wavell's conviction that 'administration . . . is the real crux of generalship'.[105] In 1940, Field Marshal Lord Carver was the Staff Captain (Q) on the 7th Armoured Division staff, and wrote recently:

> The only way the plan ['Compass'] could be made possible was to establish a field supply depot, holding several days' requirements, forward of the area where the division was concentrated, in spite of the risk that, if its existence were detected by Italian air reconnaissance, it could give away our offensive intentions. Planning the contents and layout, as well as actual supervision of its establishment, was very much my concern, and on 11 November [1940] I began to form the depot 25 miles west of the Siwa track. I was therefore brought into the secret at an early stage.[106]

The 4th Indian Division also established a similar forward field supply depot.

'Training Exercise No. 1,' which was conducted on 25/26 November 1940 near Mersa Matruh, was in fact a rehearsal for 'Compass'. Camps representing the enemy Nibeiwa and Tummar camps were marked out to scale on the ground, although this fact was known to only the few aware of the upcoming operation. The soldiers thought this to be a routine training exercise, with an intimation that a further exercise would be held at a later date. This exercise was productive, especially in terms of learning lessons about the moonlight approach march and improving the techniques of attacking an enemy camp in the desert. After this exercise, in which live ammunition was used, an after-action review was conducted by the senior and leading participants. Based upon their review of the exercise and analysis of the most recent aerial photographs, alterations were made to the original plan and embodied in a pamphlet entitled 'A Method of Attack on an Entrenched Camp in the Desert', which was distributed to the units to use as a training guide in preparation for 'Training Exercise No. 2'. The United States Military Attaché, Major (later Brigadier General) Bonner F Fellers, attended 'Training Exercise No. 1' at the invitation of Wilson, and commented that Wavell and O'Connor, each in unarmed aircraft, observed the exercise from the air. Fellers thought this was rather bold, especially since the exercise was conducted 'within eighty miles of the enemy, whose air force outnumbers that of the British at a ratio of possibly seven to one. Yet at no time was an enemy plane sighted.'[107] 'The British position in the Western Desert', Fellers concluded, 'is strong. They need more air power and motor transport. Morale is high; training is progressing; fresh troops and new equipment are arriving. An offensive may be expected.'[108]

On 28 November 1940, perhaps as a result of the first corps training exercise, perceptions of the efficacy of his deception plans, or an increase in his self-confidence and possession of 'a spirit of adventure, a touch of the gambler' – moral qualities the possession of which Wavell claimed marked the 'really great commander as distinguished from the ordinary general'[109] –

Wavell issued a directive to Wilson urging a full and bold exploitation of the expected enemy defeat in 'Compass'. Stressing the tactical and administrative requirements of such an exploitation, Wavell desired to 'make certain that if a big opportunity occurs we are prepared morally, mentally and administratively, to use it to the fullest'.[110] This was certainly a noble goal but as O'Connor related accurately, 'It was impossible with such short notice for the dumps to be increased, as all that could be done was to think out arrangements for bringing up supplies as quickly as possible after the battle had started.'[111]

Amidst the continuing fusillade of badgering telegrams from Churchill, Wavell oversaw the completion of all preparations for 'Compass'. Concerned not only with the tactical and operational levels of warfare in the Western Desert, Wavell was also preoccupied with the overall and intricate strategy of his vast Middle East Command. Wavell's strategy was that once the Italian threat to Egypt was removed, he would turn his attention to eliminating the Duke of Aosta's Italian Army in East Africa. As a step towards implementing that strategy, on 2 December 1940 Wavell met in Cairo with Platt and Lieutenant General Alan Cunningham (brother of the Naval Commander-in-Chief, Mediterranean), commanders in the Sudan and East Africa, respectively. In addition to prescribing policy for those areas, Wavell intended Kassala to be recaptured early in 1941, but that operation could not be conducted without reinforcements. One infantry division would be required to supplement Platt's forces, and Wavell stated that, dependent upon the success of the forthcoming desert offensive and the availability of shipping, he would withdraw the 4th Indian Division from O'Connor's Western Desert Force and send it to the Sudan. This proposed withdrawal of a whole division, involving half of O'Connor's Corps, would, if executed, have a significant impact upon the progress and results of 'Compass'. Wilson was made privy to this scheme; O'Connor was not.

On 4 December 1940 the final conference for 'Compass' was held, presided over by Wavell. After an introduction and other remarks, O'Connor 'explained the stages of this limited three-day operation which, starting with an assault on the Italian armed camps of Nibeiwa and East and West Tummar at dawn on 9 December, would in all probability end with the capture of Sidi Barani'.[112] After the final details were coordinated, Wilson, on Wavell's instigation, issued an operation order to O'Connor on 5 December. This was the only written order to emanate from Headquarters, BTE, for 'Compass', and confirmed the proceedings of the previous day's conference: 'The plans which you have drawn up and which you described . . . are approved.'[113] This order also noted

6. The first Australian Bde Gp is due in Western Desert Force on 12 Dec. 6 Aust. Div. should complete its concentration there by about end of Dec. But in the event of relief of formations taking part in the operations being urgently required, everything will be done to speed up this programme.[114]

The withdrawal of the 4th Indian Division was thus implied to O'Connor in veiled terms.

On the afternoon of Saturday, 7 December 1940, Wavell and his family visited the races at Gezira. 'This they often did,' observed Peter Coats, then Wavell's aide-de-camp, 'but as quietly and unobtrusively as possible, simply walking over from the C-in-C's house, which looked over the race course. This time they arrived in a fleet of cars, with flags flying, and Press photographers were welcomed.'[115] That same evening, Wavell held an unusually flamboyant dinner party at the Cairo Turf Club for fifteen or twenty of his senior commanders, including the Australians and New Zealanders. Throughout that weekend Wavell was observed by local society enjoying himself and engaging in lavish entertainment.

While Wavell appeared to be frivolously enjoying himself, the desert sands were witnessing the stealthy movement of the Western Desert Force to their rendezvous positions. The unsuspecting enemy verged on being encompassed.

Conclusion

Upon the Italian declaration of war on 10 June 1940, Wavell had about 36,000 soldiers spread throughout his vast 3,500,000-square mile Middle East Command, as opposed to about 215,000 Italians in Libya and another 290,000 enemy soldiers in Italian East Africa. This balance of power was shifted further in favour of the Axis forces after the defection of France later that same month.

In the face of seemingly insurmountable obstacles, Wavell attacked immediately to gain a moral superiority over his adversaries. He maintained this psychological dominance through the adroit employment of the Long Range Patrols and other mobile elements as combat multipliers to deceive the enemy into believing they were confronted by a much larger force than they actually were. Throughout the summer months, Wavell continued to request material and manpower reinforcements, and to build up the administrative and logistical base for the Middle East.

Wavell travelled to London in August 1940 and met the Prime Minister for the first time. Attempts at mutual empathy, trust and understanding were frustrated throughout this series of meetings. Wavell's almost impenetrable taciturnity was a key source of this friction, as Churchill thought it implied, however erroneously, a lack of mental agility and lack of audacity. Wavell, on the other hand, was severely distressed by the curt interrogations to which the Prime Minister subjected him, and by Churchill's attempts to usurp the prerogatives of the military commander in the field. Any hope of reconciliation between them was shattered by Wavell's response to Churchill's charge of faint-heartedness over the evacuation of

British Somaliland, that 'a big butcher's bill was not necessarily evidence of good tactics'.

Wavell initiated the planning for an offensive against the Italians even before Graziani's cautious September offensive. Wavell's guidance through Wilson was revised by O'Connor, whose tactical plan was eventually utilised in Operation 'Compass'. The Italians were effectively deceived by Wavell's false information, spread by double agents, and by an amalgam of other ruses and ploys, very similar to those employed successfully by Allenby in Palestine in 1918. In addition, an inherent element of Wavell's planning for 'Compass' was the maintenance of the highest degree of security and secrecy to prevent the compromise of the plan.

The unprovoked Italian invasion of Greece forced new demands upon Wavell's paltry resources, and almost jeopardised the preparations for 'Compass'. Churchill became obsessed with providing the maximum possible assistance to Greece and harboured chimerical visions of an invincible 'Balkan bloc'.

Undaunted, Wavell continued supervising the planning of the operational, administrative, and logistical aspects of his forthcoming offensive, which was to succeed far beyond all expectations.

6

Operation 'Compass', December 1940–February 1941

'These achievements will always be remembered.'
Wavell, 14 February 1941[1]

On the morning of 9 December 1940, Wavell summoned the seven or eight accredited Middle East war correspondents to meet him in his office at 9:00 am. Alexander Clifford recalled that such a 'summons was quite unprecedented',[2] and the correspondents speculated as to its import.

At the appointed hour, Wavell, in his shirt sleeves and leaning back against his desk, and 'for the first time in [correspondent Alan Moorehead's] knowledge of him, he was smiling slightly',[3] explained quietly:

> Gentlemen, I have asked you to come here this morning to let you know that we have attacked in the Western Desert. This is not an offensive and I do not think you ought to describe it as an offensive as yet. You might call it an important raid. The attack was made early this morning and I had word an hour ago that the first of the Italian camps had fallen. I cannot tell you at this moment how far we are going to go – it depends on what supplies and provisions we capture and what petrol we are able to find.[4]

After answering a few questions, Wavell asked the assembled group if they had had any hints of the impending operation. None of them had; Clifford marvelled that 'there can be no higher tribute to Wavell's security than this, for Cairo is a place where no secret is a secret for longer than a few hours, and it is a war correspondent's job to know them all'.[5] Wavell was complimented by the Egyptian Prime Minister later that day for being the first to keep a secret in Cairo. Wavell's deception had been executed flawlessly.

During the few days before the start of 'Compass', while Wavell ensured that Cairo society and the press saw him indulging in high-visibility functions, the Western Desert Force had been a hub of activity. After receiving Wilson's written order on 5 December, O'Connor issued his own operation order to his subordinate commanders on that same day. The forces under O'Connor's command were:

7th Armoured Division	General O'Moore Creagh
4th Indian Division	General Beresford-Peirse
16th Infantry Brigade (attached to 4th Indian Division)	Brigadier Lomax
7th Battalion, Royal Tank Regiment (Infantry tanks)	Lieutenant Colonel Jerram
Matruh Garrison Force (brigade group made up from the Matruh Garrison)	Brigadier Selby

The total force consisted of about 31,000 men, 120 guns, 275 tanks, and 60 armoured cars – against an estimated total Italian strength, situated within the Egyptian border, of some 80,000 soldiers, with 250 guns and 120 tanks.

One of the most crucial yet intricate and delicate aspects of 'Compass' was the preliminary movement of some seventy-five miles through open desert for the majority of the troops. The entire Western Desert Force was either mechanised or motorised, which greatly facilitated movement. Although the march times and actual distances varied by unit, both divisions were at their first rendezvous point by the evening of 7 December 1940, when most units were issued the orders showing that 'Training Exercise No. 2' would, in fact, be an actual attack on the Italian camps. Security had been preserved so well that even the junior officers on O'Connor's own Western Desert Force staff had been unaware of the impending offensive, as one of those former officers recently recalled: 'We didn't know – the junior staff officers – until late in the night of the 7th [December 1940] that this was to be the real thing.'[6]

Both divisions conducted the second phase of the approach march during the daylight hours of 8 December, a day which, according to O'Connor, 'dawned with poor visibility, which fortunately for us tended to increase as the day went on'.[7] Remarkably, the movement involving hundreds of vehicles was not detected by the enemy, even though an Italian reconnaissance aircraft was observed flying overhead at about noon. By 5:00 pm, formations had reached their pre-designated rally points, and O'Connor's advanced Headquarters, in order better to control the final stage of the approach march and the impending battle, moved forward to a location, quickly dubbed 'Piccadilly Circus'. This was near the Escarpment and about fifty miles west of the main Mersa Matruh-Siwa road. Wilson, meanwhile, established his headquarters at Maaten Baggush.

The last phase of the approach march was conducted under a moonlit sky, with all units arriving undetected in their assembly areas, within striking distance of the enemy, by 1:00 am, 9 December 1940. To help conceal the noise of this movement, British planes bombed the Italian camps simultaneously, and flew over the area throughout the night. These sorties had a dual purpose, in that they also kept the Italian pilots grounded, thus prohibiting them from conducting reconnaissance flights. The Royal Navy also provided a monitor and gunboats which bombarded Sidi Barrani and Maktila. Less than four hours later, in the bitter cold, a battalion of the 4th Indian Division opened fire on the Nibeiwa camp from the East, thus diverting the Italians' attention there. After an hour of desultory firing, a deceptive silence again reigned in the Desert until 7:15 am, when the seventy-two guns of the divisional artillery began an intense bombardment, again from the East. Shortly thereafter the infantry ('I') tanks of the 7th Royal Tank Regiment struck the northwest corner of the Nibeiwa camp, surprising the defenders and avoiding a frontal attack. They were followed by assaulting infantry from the 11th Indian Infantry Brigade. By 8:25 am Nibeiwa had fallen, with over twenty Italian medium tanks and some 2,000 Italian soldiers being captured. That afternoon, following an artillery preparation, the 4th Indian Division captured the Tummar camps, and was directed to push on towards Sidi Barrani.

The 7th Armoured Division had effectively screened the left flank of the 4th Indian Division, had captured Azzizaya, and was fully astride the Sidi Barrani-Buqbuq road. 'Selby Force', which had a few days earlier emplaced a brigade of dummy tanks in the desert, attempted audaciously to prevent the enemy's escape from Maktila, but was unable to do so because of darkness and bad terrain.

During the first day of 'Compass', Wavell remained in Cairo, although he was kept fully informed of the progress of operations by Wilson, and he kept Dill in London apprised in a similar timely and accurate manner. That evening, before the attack on Sidi Barrani was to start the following morning, Wavell wrote and issued an inspiring 'Special Order of the Day':

> The result of the fighting in the Western Desert will be one of the decisive events of the war. A signal and crushing defeat of the Italian forces will have an incalculable effect not only on the military situation everywhere, but on the future of freedom and civilisation throughout the world. It may shorten the war by very many months. It must be the firm determination of every man to do everything that in him lies without thought of self to win this decisive victory.
>
> In everything but numbers, we are superior to the enemy. We are more highly trained, we shoot straighter, we have better equipment. Above all, we have stouter hearts and greater traditions and are fighting a worthier cause. The Italians entered the war treacherously and without reason because they expected a cheap and easy victory. Let us show them their mistake by inflicting on them a stern and costly defeat. . . .
>
> We have waited long in the Middle East; when our chance comes let us strike hard. The harder blows we strike against the servants of tyranny and selfish lust of power, the sooner we shall bring peace and freedom back to the world and be able to return to our own free peaceful homes.[8]

Flushed with an indomitable spirit of victory, the Western Desert Force

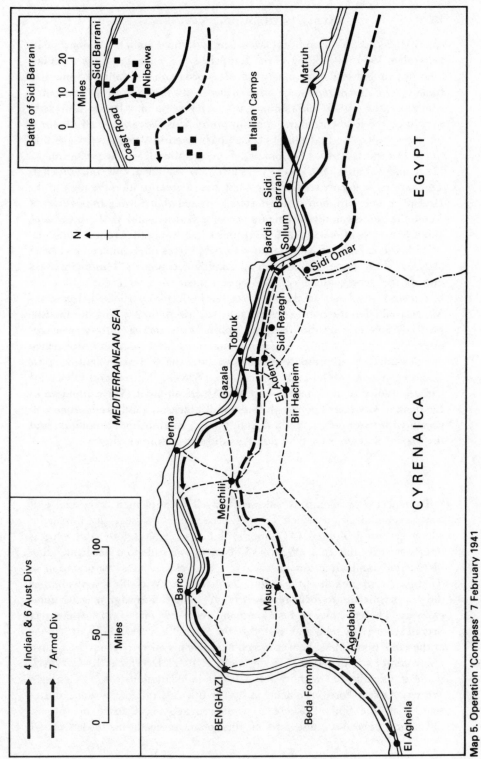

Map 5. Operation 'Compass' 7 February 1941

4 Indian & 6 Aust Divs

7 Armd Div

Miles
0   50   100

MEDITERRANEAN SEA

N

BENGHAZI

Barce

Derna

Gazala

Tobruk

Mechili

El Adem

Sidi Rezegh

Bir Hacheim

Beda Fomm

Msus

Agedabia

El Agheila

Bardia

Sollum

Sidi Omar

Sidi Barrani

Matruh

EGYPT

CYRENAICA

Battle of Sidi Barrani

Miles
0   10   20

Coast Road

Sidi Barrani

Nibeiwa

■ Italian Camps

captured Sidi Barrani and destroyed two additional Italian divisions on 10 December 1940, and Selby Force compelled the surrender of two Italian divisions caught in the open between Mersa Matruh and Sidi Barrani. The backbone of Italian resistance was crushed, with the Western Desert Force continuing the pursuit and mopping up the few remaining Italian pockets of resistance the following day. The capture of Sidi Barrani for all practical purposes ended the first phase of 'Compass', and in three days of fighting (9–11 December 1940), O'Connor's Force captured 38,300 prisoners, 73 tanks, and 422 guns, at a cost of 133 killed, 387 wounded, and eight missing. The number of enemy soldiers captured was so great that on the night of 10 December one battalion headquarters reported that it was impossible to count the unexpectedly large number of prisoners, and that 'there were about five acres of officers and two hundred acres of other ranks'.[9]

With the capture of Sidi Barrani, the objectives of 'Compass' had been achieved. The operation had been an unmitigated success. This victory was due to the synergistic effect of Wavell's insistence on ensuring secrecy throughout all phases of the operation and effective battlefield deception, which resulted in the enemy being totally surprised; the farsighted establishment of forward logistic resupply points; outstanding inter-service co-operation; the dynamic leadership qualities and tactical proficiency demonstrated by subordinate commanders and the aggressive fighting spirit exhibited by the soldiers. Of special note, Wavell, Wilson, and O'Connor had all studied at the Staff College the American Civil War campaigns of Lieutenant General Thomas J 'Stonewall' Jackson, and were thus well versed with ruses, feints, 'hit and run' tactics, a campaign of mobility, and the maxim that superiority of numbers did not guarantee victory.

* * *

The success of 'Compass' allowed Wavell to implement a crucial and controversial decision which he had been contemplating, the impact of which certainly blunted O'Connor's ability to exploit fully and expeditiously the 'five-day raid'. Whereas O'Connor was able to concentrate all of his energies and attention on the Western Desert and a continuation of 'Compass' and pursuit of the demoralised Italians, Wavell's responsibilities did not permit him to focus his one eye on a single campaign or geographical area. The enormity of his Command required him to plan and direct overall strategy therein, and to engage the enemy in several different regions at the same time. Thus, he was forced to juggle his meagre resources against many competing demands. On the night of 10/11 December 1940, Wavell made the decision to withdraw the 4th Indian Division from O'Connor's Western Desert Force, replacing it by the 6th Australian Division, and to send it to the Sudan, where it would engage in offensive operations. O'Connor, who was unaware of this plan, received his order on 11

December, 'a most unwelcome piece of news, namely that the 4th Ind. Div. was to be withdrawn as early as possible for service in the Sudan'.[10]

Referring to this troop withdrawal, Churchill recorded with apparent surprise that 'General Wavell took on his own direct initiative a wise and daring decision.'[11] Compton MacKenzie was convinced that

> The decision of General Wavell on that December night to withdraw the 4th Indian Division from the triumph of Sidi Barrani and send it to wage an offensive campaign in East Africa must rank with any major military decisions which have set the course of history. Such a decision required imagination, faith, and a plenitude of moral courage.[12]

A dissection of this decision reveals that, made when it was, it was not a master stroke of generalship, but was the result of Wavell's failure to realise the full potential of 'Compass' and the necessity of exploiting fully the victory there, coupled with his submission to political pressure, which resulted in an uncharacteristic mental inflexibility which did not permit him to alter the plans he had made.

When Wavell visited Churchill in London in August 1940, the Prime Minister had dispensed conflicting guidance about the importance to be placed on East Africa and the Sudan. At their conferences in Khartoum on 28/29 October 1940, Wavell took the lead in discussions with Eden and Smuts on future offensive operations in East Africa and the Sudan, and the three agreed upon the projected plans. Wavell was also astutely aware, according to Smuts's son,

> of the feeling of nervousness, not only in Kenya but also in Rhodesia and even in South Africa, that the forces in East Africa were not sufficiently strong to prevent an Italian invasion of Kenya and the countries farther south, and my father frequently impressed on [Wavell] the danger of reducing the forces in East Africa.[13]

Wavell acknowledged this judgement in his relevant Despatch.

One of the offensives decided upon at the Khartoum conference was Operation 'Canvas', the planned capture of Kismayu in Italian Somaliland, to be executed in January 1941. When the local commander, Cunningham, submitted that that offensive would have to be postponed until about May 1941, Smuts expressed his chagrin directly to London. Churchill responded by demanding a full account of the reasons for the delay, and Dill cabled Wavell on 26 November 1940 that,

> We have received telegram from General Smuts expressing disappointment that offensive operations on any scale must be postponed till May, particularly after the reinforcements he has provided. In view of general deterioration of Italian morale which has been reported from many quarters, it is highly desirable that every effort should be made to hit them wherever and whenever we can. In these circumstances hope at your early conference with commanders you will be able to arrange to carry out operations in East Africa as originally intended.[14]

On 2 December 1940, Wavell showed his recognition of the political necessity to mount such offensives in East Africa, even if they did not fully justify
the expenditure in resources and effort:

> 1. Kismayu operation is not very satisfactory in that it uses up much transport
> [,] troops [,] and time for somewhat inadequate results. But Smuts is anxious
> for it and there is no other direction in this theatre from which quicker results
> can be obtained. For political reasons in South Africa it must be mounted so as
> to make it a success, even if it is slow.[15]

Six days later Wavell informed Dill of his intention, 'if situation in Western
Desert permits, to withdraw 4 Indian Division towards end of this month
and send it to Sudan for Kassala operation', and that he attached considerable importance to the recapture of Kassala 'for moral effect on progress of
rebellion and since freeing of railway will greatly ease administrative difficulties in Sudan'.[16] The following day – the first day of 'Compass' – even
before Sidi Barrani had been attacked, Wavell cabled to Platt and detailed
the tentative schedule of the transfer of the 4th Indian Division to the
Sudan, 'subject to outcome of present operations in Middle East',[17] even
though the evidence points to Wavell having already made up his mind
about this decision. Thus Wavell yielded to political pressure by continuing
with projected plans for an offensive in the Sudan.

Wavell admitted tacitly to O'Connor in 1945 that nothing but a defeat in
'Compass' would have changed his mind about transferring the 4th Indian
Division to the Sudan or interrupted his overall strategic plans:

> I am not quite sure whether you ever realised the necessity for the withdrawal
> of the 4th [Indian] Division immediately after Sidi Barrani. It was a matter of
> shipping; a convoy had come into Suez, and I could use some of the returning
> ships to carry part of the Division to Port Sudan, the only means by which I
> could get the Division complete in the Sudan *by the time I had fixed as the latest
> favourable date for attacking the Italians*. I could not hold up the ships, and if I lost
> the opportunity I did not think I could have attacked from the Sudan that
> winter. The people at home were, coincidentally, rather nervous about the
> Sudan. With my limited resources, I had to decide whether to remain entirely
> on the defensive in the Sudan for some time to come, or to accept the delay in
> the pursuit in the Western Desert, while the Australian Division relieved the
> Indian. My decision was a difficult one, but I am sure it was right.[18]

O'Connor believed that Wavell had not anticipated the extent of the success
of 'Compass', otherwise he would have considered seriously using the 4th
Indian Division to develop the situation in the Western Desert further.
Brigadier JAL Caunter, who commanded the 7th Armoured Division temporarily during the opening stages of 'Compass', was equally convinced that
the lack of preparations to send the 6th Australian Division forward 'prove
conclusively that the victory was not expected'.[19]

Other military historians, notably Field Marshal Lord Carver and

Brigadier CN Barclay, contend that 'Compass' had been planned as a limited offensive, and its 'success would ensure that Wavell's main base in Egypt was made secure, while he dealt with the Italians in East Africa. . . . it is unlikely that it [the withdrawal of the 4th Indian Division] made any significant difference to the campaign.'[20] This formation transfer did make a significant difference in that the lines of communication and administrative resources, already stretched to the limit, were, according to O'Connor,

> further complicated by the large number of prisoners captured, now amount- ing to 20,000, who had all to be fed, watered, and guarded, and eventually brought back to Matruh. At the moment, however, there was no transport under my command available for ferrying purposes, and transport was required simultaneously for carrying back the 4 Ind. Div. and the prisoners, and for carrying forward the 6 Aus. Div. The situation, without a relief pend- ing, from the administrative point of view, was extremely difficult, and with the relief doubly so.[21]

Carver reinforced recently O'Connor's opinion by recording that by 14 December 1940, 'Logistic problems now loomed larger than ever. . . . Wavell's decision to withdraw 4th Indian Division from the desert and send it to the Sudan, . . ., added to the transport crisis.'[22] It was, as noted succinctly by Wilson, 'A first-class administrative problem.'[23] In addition, from the tactical perspective, the withdrawal of the 4th Indian Division on the third day of 'Compass' meant, as O'Connor later recalled, 'that the whole impetus of our pursuit would vanish and the enemy would be alerted and it would be no longer possible to surprise him, in fact we were back to rather below square one'.[24]

Of the utmost consideration is Wavell's notion of a 'matter of shipping' in withdrawing the 4th Indian Division when he did. On 12 December 1940, the 4th Indian Division disengaged itself from contact with the Italians, and spent the remainder of the day removing enemy minefields near Sidi Barrani. The Division prepared slowly and methodically to withdraw, arriving at Naghamish Nullah by 14 December. By 20 December it was redeployed at Amiriya and Mena – approximately one hundred-fifty and sixty miles, respectively, from Suez. It was not until about 28 December, that the 7th Indian Infantry Brigade – only one of three infantry brigades of the 4th Indian Division – boarded ships and convoyed to Port Sudan, landing there on 2 January 1941. The 5th Indian Infantry Brigade did not use any marine shipping, but moved overland by rail and Nile steamer, and reached Khartoum on 9 January. The last of the three brigades, the 11th, travelled on a different convoy from the 7th, sailing from Port Said on 1 January and arriving at Port Sudan five days later. The Division's service support elements generally arrived in the Sudan by the end of January 1941. Wavell's emphasis on the urgency of withdrawing the 4th Indian Division to meet priority shipping schedules, in light of the above information, is not convincing.

What is known, however, is that Wavell was under pressure from Smuts, Churchill, and Dill to launch an offensive in the Sudan and East Africa as soon as possible, before the rainy season started in February. In addition, with the Mediterranean Sea routes virtually closed, Wavell was highly concerned about the possibility of the Italians blocking the vital Red Sea, through which he received his reinforcements from India and the United Kingdom. The evidence suggests that Wavell, knowing that Churchill was determined to send the maximum assistance to Greece, had decided, regardless of the outcome of 'Compass', to send the 4th Indian Division to the Sudan. There it was likely to make a significant contribution to a successful operation, and could not be diverted easily and prematurely to Greece by the Prime Minister, as it could have been had it remained in North Africa.

This episode also shows that not only was Wavell beginning to confront multiple priority tasks on a large scale with extremely limited resources and having to shift troops accordingly, but he was also succumbing to political pressure. Fortunately, Wavell's decision proved to be correct, at least in the long term and from the perspective of the operations in the Sudan and East Africa. Even though the rationale behind (and some of the potential results of) this decision will remain problematic, one is left with the distinct impression that Wavell should have and could have deferred the decision to transfer the 4th Indian Division for at least another week and so could have exploited fully the success of 'Compass'. Even Carver conceded, in addressing the delay in the continuation of the offensive caused by the untimely withdrawal of the 4th Indian Division, that 'It is just possible, however, that the delay of about ten days could have been critical.'[25] The last word on this decision belongs rightly to the commander on the ground, O'Connor, who stated 'There is no doubt, however, that the loss of the 4th Ind. Div. lost us three weeks or more, since 6 Aus. Div. was not ready for Bardia for a full month', and then lamented, 'And what a lot we could have done with 4 Ind. Div. & a fleeing enemy.'[26]

*   *   *

Churchill was naturally ecstatic when he was informed of the initial successes of 'Compass'. He delivered a rousing statement to the House of Commons on 10 December 1940, followed two days later by an even more stirring pronouncement, in which he remarked that the success of these operations 'reflects the highest credit upon Sir Archibald Wavell, Sir [Henry] Maitland Wilson, the staff officers who planned this exceedingly complicated operation, and the troops who performed the remarkable feats of endurance and daring which accomplished it'.[27] On 13 December, Churchill signalled his 'heartfelt congratulations' to Wavell, and exhorted Wavell that 'pursuit will hold the first place in your thoughts. It is at the moment when the victor is most exhausted that the greatest forfeit can be exacted from the vanquished.' Near the end of this message, Churchill added metaphorically that 'It looks as if these people were corn, ripe for the sickle.'[28] Wavell's natural reaction to such praise from the Prime Minister was to cable back and ensure that he knew the success of 'Compass' was mainly due to the planning of Wilson and O'Connor, careful training over an extended period, and the units involved.

Wavell visited Wilson's headquarters in the Western Desert on 12 December 1940 to assess the situation for himself, and discussed plans for the second phase of the operation with Wilson and O'Connor. He returned to the Desert two days later and held a conference at O'Connor's head-quarters where he outlined his plans for the capture of Bardia to Wilson, O'Connor, and Major General (later Lieutenant General Sir) Iven Mackay, commander of the 6th Australian Division (which consisted of the 16th, 17th, and 19th Australian Infantry Brigades), which, as we have seen, was in the process of deploying to the Western Desert to replace the 4th Indian Division. Wavell kept control of the operations throughout 'Compass' and decided the extent of advance in each phase of the campaign, as demonstrated by this conference. In the light of the sudden collapse of Italian resistance at Sidi Barrani, it was thought that Bardia might also be abandoned by the Italians. In view of this possibility, Wavell ordered the 19th Australian Infantry Brigade to be prepared to embark at Alexandria and move by sea to occupy Bardia, if abandoned. At the same time, Wavell issued directives for the punctual forward deployment of the remainder of the 6th Australian Division to the Bardia area.

The successes in North Africa put Churchill in a much more charitable frame of mind and allayed temporarily his suspicions of lethargy and indecisiveness in the Middle East Commander-in-Chief. On 18 December 1940, after agreeing enthusiastically on Bardia as the Western Desert Force's next objective, the Prime Minister cabled additional encouragement to Wavell: 'St. Matthew, Chapter 7, Verse 7.' ['Ask, and it will be given you; seek, and you will find; knock, and it will be opened to you.'], to which Wavell responded:

> St. James, Chapter 1, Verse 17, first part. ['Every good endowment and every perfect gift is from above, coming down from the Father of lights with whom there is no variation or shadow due to change.'] More aircraft are our immediate need and these you are providing. Additional anti-aircraft also much required.[29]

A heavy naval and air bombardment failed to induce the Italian garrison of some four divisions, together with tanks and artillery, to surrender or evacuate the Bardia fortress. On 19 December 1940, while the 7th Armoured Division protected its left flank, the 16th Australian Infantry Brigade marched forward to continue the encirclement of Bardia.

Subsequent days were spent reconnoitring the intricate defences of Bardia's seventeen-mile perimeter, and in light of the transport shortages exacerbated by the 4th Indian Division's withdrawal, in ferrying needed supplies, ammunition, and the remaining two Australian infantry brigades to the forward area, and in opening the port of Sollum. 'Meanwhile, transport is my chief anxiety', Wavell admitted to the CIGS, 'these desert operations at such distances are throwing very heavy strain on all vehicles.'[30] After again visiting the Western Desert on 20 December, Wavell emphasised: 'Transport situation still very strained owing to great distances and difficulties of conditions. Large percentage of vehicles out of action awaiting repair.'[31]

O'Connor was always pleased to see the Commander-in-Chief, Middle East. Illuminating Wavell's character and personality, O'Connor chronicled subsequently that,

> It would be impossible to say what great pleasure and assistance [Wavell's] visits gave to me, and also to all other Commanders and Units, which he visited. He listened patiently to all our difficulties, and made notes of everything, and I always received a wire from him on his return to Cairo, regarding which of my many demands he was able to supply. I felt the greatest confidence in him, and knew that he would support me to the full in any bold action. Inaction was what he could not do with. All my instructions emanated from him, . . .[32]

With great efficacy, Wavell was implementing his own adage that 'What troops and subordinate commanders appreciate is that a general should be constantly in personal contact with them, and not see everything simply through the eyes of his staff.'[33].

On 20 December 1940, the Middle East Joint Planning Staff prepared a study entitled 'Advance into Libya' to consider what near-term policy should govern British operations in Libya after the capture of Bardia. Maintenance was considered to be the determining factor in the continuation of the advance. After a thorough assessment, the study concluded there were four possible courses of action at that time:

A. Remain at Bardia and consolidate.
B. A land advance to capture Tobruk.
C. To capture Tobruk immediately by a combined operation.
D. To capture Benghazi in the immediate future.[34]

The study concluded that options A and B were the only viable courses of action and the only ones worth considering in relation to the general policy current in the Middle East theatre of war, and recommended that the policy should be:

> To capture Tobruk, provided that it can be accomplished within the next few weeks. If this is not possible, we should consolidate a position covering Bardia.

In either event, we must aim at standing on the defensive in Libya in the Spring, in order to release the maximum forces to act more decisively in Eastern Europe, should the need or opportunity arise.[35]

While the Joint Planning Staff was concerned with the eventuality of despatching forces to the Balkans, it had totally discounted the possibility of capturing Benghazi as being beyond the capabilities of Wavell's force, even though the impossible would become a reality only six weeks later.

The three Commanders-in-Chief met in Cairo on 28 December 1940 and agreed that the advance into Libya should have priority over all other operations, at least up to the capture of Tobruk. At the same time, in the Western Desert, Mackay, with guidance from Wavell and O'Connor and the results of aerial photographs and night reconnaissance patrols, had devised his plan for the capture of Bardia. Unlike the capture of Nibeiwa camp, the planned assault on Bardia had already lost the important element of surprise. Whereas the Italian camps seized earlier were not well fortified and were out of supporting distance from each other, the same was not true of Bardia. At Bardia, the perimeter consisted of concrete posts, containing machine-guns and anti-tanks guns, protected by wire and anti-tank ditches, spaced at seven hundred-yard intervals along the entire seventeen-mile perimeter. A second line of support posts was found about five hundred yards behind the first, with a continuous anti-tank ditch and wire obstacle encompassing the entire perimeter.

These defences were reminiscent of Great War trenches, and Mackay believed that the capture of the fortress would require 'operations approaching those in France during 1916-18'.[36] Artillery would obviously play an important role in their destruction and in the suppression of the enemy. It was also realised, based upon earlier experience, that the combined effect of shock, firepower, armour, and mobility of the 'I' tanks would be crucial to success. The plan of attack was for one infantry battalion of the 16th Australian Infantry Brigade to attack at a specified point located approximately at the centre of a sector – which had been determined by the terrain, depth of defences, and the fact that a successful breakthrough in this area would isolate the enemy artillery. While this bridgehead was being held, engineers would fill in the anti-tank ditch, cut the wire, and clear a passage through the mines. A full-scale replica of the obstacle had been constructed behind the British lines and repeated rehearsals had shown that the ditch could be filled in half an hour. With an additional time allowance of thirty minutes, dawn would just be breaking as the 'I' tanks charged into the perimeter, followed by two additional infantry battalions, which would then sweep to the southeast. The 17th Australian Infantry Brigade would pierce the perimeter south of the original penetration, and also drive south-east to contain the Italian forces manning the strongest defences there. Demonstrations against other parts of the perimeter would be conducted simultaneously in the North by the 7th Armoured Division, positioned there with its Support Group to block the Bardia garrison's escape route, and in the South by additional Australian units. The entire attack would be supported by a massive concentration of artillery, on a scale similar to that employed in a number of 1917 and 1918 battles.

On 28 December 1940, Mackay decided that the attack would start at 5:30 am on 2 January 1941. To confer with commanders, visit the soldiers, and ensure all preparations for the assault on Bardia had been finalised, Wavell spent 29/30 December in the Western Desert. On the 30th, (and it is unknown whether Wavell influenced this decision), Mackay postponed the attack by twenty-four hours, to ensure that more artillery ammunition was brought forward to the guns supporting the attack.

As part of the preparation for the attack by XIII Corps – as the Western Desert Force had been redesignated on 1 January 1941 – Royal Air Force squadrons bombed Bardia, dropping 20,000 pounds of ordnance on the night of 1 January, and 30,000 pounds the following night, while Royal Navy gunboats shelled targets during daylight on 2 January. Throughout the night of 2/3 January, heavily-laden Australian infantrymen with bayonets fixed, about to be blooded for the first time in this war, advanced stealthily. At 6:00 am on 3 January, engineers exploded bangalore torpedoes to blow gaps in the wire, and the attack began.

In sum, the initial infantry attack and the passage of the 'I' tanks through the perimeter, according to O'Connor, went 'without a hitch',[37] as did the attack of the remainder of the 16th Australian Infantry Brigade, which had captured most of its objectives, many weapons, and about 8,000 prisoners by 8:30 am. Offshore, the battleships *Warspite*, *Valiant*, and *Barham* threw additional steel into the fray with their fifteen-inch guns. The Italians soon began surrendering and, after two days of mopping-up, the entire garrison surrendered, yielding a bag of some 45,000 prisoners, 130 tanks, and 488 guns, although the bombastic Italian garrison commander, Lieutenant General 'Electric Whiskers' Bergonzoli, so named because of his long, wiry blue-grey beard, eluded capture. Commonwealth casualties were under 500. After the capture of Bardia on 5 January 1941, Italian radio reported that the garrison had been attacked by 250,000 men and 1,000 aircraft.

Even before the Bardia operation had been completed, Wavell 'had decided that an attack on Tobruk was justified on both operational and administrative grounds', and towards that goal the 7th Armoured Division was moving to cut off Tobruk from the West.[38]

* * *

On 5 January 1941, appreciating that Tobruk, too, would soon be taken, Wavell stated in a note to his Chief of Staff that his ultimate objective was Benghazi. But the spectre of British intervention in Greece had again risen to the forefront of policy in London through Enigma decrypts, or 'Ultra' information, as it has become known. During the latter half of December 1940, Enigma decrypts revealed a great deal of information on German Army concentrations in southern Rumania. As intercepted information became more detailed, especially about completion of Rumanian airfields and the allocation of German Air Force units to them, it appeared, in one interpretation at least, that Germany was on the verge of intervening to assist Italian forces in Greece and Albania, or, alternatively, that 'the object of her new moves was only to intimidate Greece, Yugoslavia and Bulgaria before advancing through Turkey to the Middle East'.[39] The British, however, were unable to ascertain the true reason for the concentration of German units in Rumania until March 1941. With Britain's Mediterranean and Imperial position possibly at stake, Churchill was grasping for any straw. The only option seemingly available was the establishment of a 'Balkan bloc' to halt the Germans, the success of which, in Churchill's opinion, would redress his abysmal Great War failure at Gallipoli.

On 5 January 1941, as the capture of Bardia was being completed, new intelligence was received which suggested that the Germans might attack Greece, Yugoslavia, and Bulgaria as early as 15 January. The following day, Churchill cabled to Wavell a message which included 'Time is short. I cannot believe Hitler will not intervene soon', and a warning that he would soon be sending the General a long appeal 'about purging rearward services'.[40] With the euphoria of the initial victories of 'Compass' having worn off, and disturbed by prospects of Germany invading the Balkans, Churchill sent his promised message bemoaning the 'tooth-to-tail' ratio of combat strength versus support units on 7 January: 'You have well over 350,000 troops on your ration strength and the number of units which are fighting or capable of fighting appears to me disproportionately small.'[41] Of course Churchill had to be concerned about war economy and utilising the maximum resources available to the utmost, but on this and other occasions, he failed to understand the requirements of modern, mechanised warfare. 'He [Churchill] was brought up in the days when small bodies of adventurous and ardent men could defeat much greater numbers', recalled Jacob, and that,

> Weapons then were limited to rifles, bayonets and sabres, though more deadly ones were beginning to emerge. He tended to think that, even in the modern age, determined men with rifles and bayonets were all that was wanted to withstand attack.[42]

Wavell was convinced that the Prime Minister's knowledge of equipping troops was based upon his Boer War experiences, when each soldier was issued with little more than a rifle; in addition, 'Winston's tactical ideas,' he reflected, 'had to some extent crystallised at the South African war.'[43]

Germany's ominous activities in Rumania gave Churchill occasion on 6 January 1941 to survey the world situation and write an appreciation on the war as a whole. In it he envisioned Benghazi as the ultimate objective of Wavell's 'Army of the Nile', with a projection for its capture in March 1941. Wavell's successes in North Africa up to that time, and the expected German attack on the Balkans, were the keystones of the Prime Minister's estimate. 'It is quite clear to me', noted Churchill, 'that supporting Greece must have priority after the western flank of Egypt has been made secure.'[44] The Defence Committee discussed the Balkan situation on 7, 8, and 9 January. During the 8 January meeting, Eden, now again Secretary of State for Foreign Affairs, stressed the importance of despatching aid to Greece as a means of influencing Turkey to take the lead in forming a 'Balkan bloc'. 'It was of the utmost importance, from the political point of view', decided the Defence Committee, 'that we should do everything possible, by hook or by crook, to send at once the fullest support within our power to Greece.'[45]

On 8 January 1941 the Chiefs of Staff, charged with assessing what assistance could be sent to Greece, first wired to Longmore for his views, perhaps because air support was urgently required. Longmore was naturally reluctant to impede Wavell's advance, but on the next day he was instructed that 'for political reasons, priority must now be given to Greece. . . . Absence of British help might put Greece out of the war, keep Turkey out and cause most serious political consequences both here and in America.'[46] The decision to aid Greece was made firmly by the Chiefs of Staff on 10 January: 'assistance to Greece must now take priority over all operations in the Middle East once Tobruk is taken, because help for the Greeks must, in the first instance at least, come almost entirely from you'.[47] The despatch of forces to Greece was authorised, up to the following limits:

Army:
1 squadron of Infantry tanks
1 regiment of cruiser tanks
2 field artillery regiments
2 anti-tank regiments
2 heavy anti-aircraft regiments
2 light anti-aircraft regiments
2 medium regiments, Royal Artillery
Air:
3 Hurricane squadrons
2 Blenheim IV squadrons

plus all equipment and personnel required to maintain these units. Wavell and Longmore were both dismayed by the directed dispersal of their forces while the momentum of 'Compass' was again being maintained and the investment of Tobruk was taking place. The German concentration was a move in a war of nerves, responded Wavell, that was designed to induce the British to halt the Libyan offensive and disperse their forces.[48] This was a reasonable assessment from Wavell, who would not receive Ultra information for another two months.[49] On the same day, the *Luftwaffe* announced dramatically its presence on Sicily by bombing and severely damaging the aircraft carrier *Illustrious* near Malta, which effectively meant the loss of Britain's essential air support in the Mediterranean.

Even though Wavell had been adamantly opposed to sending forces to Greece and dissipating his paltry resources ever since the Italian attack of 28 October 1940, it was his professional responsibility to initiate contingency planning for such an eventuality. As early as 30 October 1940, the Middle East Joint Planning Staff produced a paper on 'Immediate Assistance to Greece and Turkey', in which the basic policy promulgated was to and ensure the security in depth of British bases in Egypt by maintaining the integrity of Turkey. Assistance to Greece, this study concluded, 'should not therefore prejudice our ultimate ability to assist Turkey'.[50] The Middle East, remaining in a vacuum over the course to follow regarding Greece, completed another brief Joint Planning Staff Paper on 17 December 1940, entitled 'Assistance to Greece and Turkey in April, 1941'. This paper, forecasting that logistical, maintenance and communications factors would limit British assistance to Greece and Turkey, recommended preliminary reconnaissances and railway and aerodrome construction, and in April 1941 'provide all possible material help to Greece and Turkey'.[51] The timing of the completion of this paper indicates that it was thought possible to complete first the annihilation of Italian forces in North Africa, then divert all necessary forces to the Balkans. The policy of the Middle East towards the Balkans was further refined and amplified in another J P S paper produced on 4 January 1941, which stated:

> The basis of our policy of assistance to Greece and Turkey *in the Spring of 1941* must be:-
> (a) to secure our sea communications in the Aegean and the Eastern Mediterranean.
> (b) to prevent a German advance against Egypt and Iraq through Turkey.
> (c) to be in a position to undertake air operations against South-Eastern Europe, Italy and the Roumanian oil organisation.
> (d) to be in a position to support Greece, Turkey and Yugoslavia in operations against Germany.[52]

The type of assistance the Middle East intended to despatch to Greece or Turkey, if necessary, was to consist primarily of air forces and 'specialist army units' – field artillery, anti-tank, and anti-aircraft elements.

The perceptions of those in London and in Cairo towards German intentions in the Balkans and assistance to Greece were significantly divergent, only made worse by the Middle East military commanders not being recipients of Ultra information. On the morning of 8 January 1941, Wavell met for the first time US Army Colonel (later Major General) William J Donovan, ostensibly on a fact-finding mission on behalf of US Secretary of the Navy, Frank Knox. In an overview of the Middle East strategical situation, Wavell told Donovan that he thought the Germans, who had constructed strong defences in Rumania to protect their sources of oil, were using Bulgaria as a buffer state. The Germans would, according to Wavell, try to keep the Balkans quiet and consolidate in the South-East, thus avoiding operations on two fronts. This helps account for Wavell's and Longmore's reaction of disbelief and chagrin, and after the latter received the Chief of Air Staff's 9 January wire giving Greece priority over all other military operations, the Middle East Joint Planning Staff met and amended JPS Paper No. 34, 'Assistance to Greece and Turkey in April, 1941', to read 'With our present resources we can give no direct assistance to Greece and Turkey.'[53]

The Prime Minister quickly overrode Wavell's and Longmore's protests, telling them curtly that 'We expect and require prompt and active compliance with our decisions for which we bear full responsibility', and to proceed with an earlier directive of the Chiefs of Staff to visit Athens to confer with Greek leaders and ascertain the support they required.[54]

Churchill's fervour in desiring the maximum assistance for Greece is especially ironic since, on 10 January 1941, he told Harry Hopkins, President Franklin D Roosevelt's personal emissary, that he realised any British expedition to Greece would be ill-fated. Hopkins reported that Churchill:

> thinks Greece is lost – although he is now reinforcing the Greeks – and weakening his African Army – he believes Hitler will permit Mussolini to go only so far downhill – and is now preparing for the attack which must bring its inevitable result. He knows this will be a blow to British prestige and is obviously considering ways and means of preparing the British public for it. He realizes it will have a profound and disappointing effect in America as well. Churchill, too, thinks Turkey will stay put and probably be in the war when Germany moves through Bulgaria. This Churchill thinks will be the route.[55]

This unusual penetration of Churchill's façade reveals that he pressured his service advisers and commanders to approve, or at least acquiesce in, sending eventually a sizeable British force to Greece, cognisant that the result would be débâcle.

Wavell flew to Athens on 13 January 1941 (Longmore followed on 15 January), and had courtesy calls with King George II and the Prime Minister, General John Metaxas, that evening. Substantive discussions started the following day and continued on 15 January, with Wavell, Metaxas, and the Greek Army Commander-in-Chief, General Alexander Papagos, the leading participants. In sum, the hopes of the Greeks had been raised unduly high, not only by Wavell's victories in North Africa but also by previous political exchanges between London and Athens. Papagos stated that in view of Yugoslavia's neutrality, the German attack would probably be directed against Eastern Macedonia, and to reinforce the area the Greeks needed nine British divisions with air support immediately. Wavell replied that he did not have such forces at his disposal, and had been able to win the battles in North Africa with only two divisions. He added that, in view of his commitments in Cyrenaica and East Africa, he could send two or three divisions, although it would take time to concentrate them at the ports of embarkation and a further two months for their transport.

On 15 January 1941, Metaxas asked Wavell for equipment to fight against the Italians in Albania. At this point Wavell, perhaps wanting to ensure Greek participation in the war, offered, for immediate despatch to Greece, one combined anti-aircraft and anti-tank regiment. Metaxas refused the offer. A long discussion on Salonika followed, during which Wavell stated that the despatch of even a small British force to Salonika would convince the Turkish and Yugoslav Governments of British determination to assist Greece, which in turn might persuade the Turks and Yugoslavs to abandon their neutrality and join the Allies in forming a 'Balkan bloc'. Metaxas took the opposite view, 'that despatch of these troops, while not sufficient to ensure safety of Salonika, would provoke Germany to attack'.[56] Only if the British could land sufficient numbers of troops to act offensively as well as defensively, continued Metaxas, should they land any troops at all. In the meantime, it was desired that the British should prepare to land such a force at Salonika in the future. At this point the talks ended, having failed, as Martin van Creveld has suggested, because 'They took place in an atmosphere of intense political mistrust': the Greeks suspecting the British of trying to involve them in a war against Germany, and the British concerned that the Greeks would attempt to make a separate peace with Italy.[57] Throughout these discussions, Wavell, who was well known for his unfailing loyalty, presented the British position as if it was his own, even though he had been personally opposed to it. Leaving Athens on 17 January, Wavell landed *en route* in Crete and held discussions with the local commander before returning to Cairo that evening.

Wavell later recollected that when Metaxas refused his offer of limited, albeit immediate, troop assistance, he was rather relieved because 'if that offer had been accepted I should have had to stop my advance at Tobruk; I could not have gone on any farther'.[58]

With Wavell temporarily distracted in Athens, Wilson and O'Connor continued preparations for the capture of Tobruk. Stockpiles of ammunition and petrol were established and numerous night reconnaissance patrols were conducted, to determine the depth and composition of Tobruk's defences. O'Connor was anxious for this attack to begin, because it was believed that fresh Italian divisions were landing at Tripoli, and he was concerned about any further denuding of his Corps, which had already provided transport, labour, and anti-aircraft units, to assist the Greeks.

* * *

During the preparation phase of the attack on Tobruk, the normal quiet and machine-like efficiency of O'Connor and the XIII Corps was interrupted by conflicting guidance from his superiors in his chain of command. Wavell, on occasion, had bypassed Wilson, O'Connor's immediate superior, and had given guidance on plans and proposals directly to O'Connor. Before departing for Athens, Wavell had held a conference at General Headquarters in Cairo to discuss the continuation of the advance. At this conference, attended by Wavell, Longmore, O'Connor, and Brigadier A Galloway, Wilson's Brigadier, General Staff, Wavell agreed to the occupation of Mechili after Tobruk's capture. The following day, O'Connor met with Wavell, and was asked to study an appreciation that Wavell had written on the possibility of a raid on Benghazi. O'Connor returned to his own headquarters, 'delighted to think there was a possibility of an attempt of some sort [of an advance on Benghazi] being made'.[59]

After returning to the Western Desert, O'Connor debriefed Wilson on the proceedings of the meetings he had attended in Cairo, and told him of Wavell's ideas about Benghazi, adding that he hoped Wavell could be persuaded to permit a full-scale advance to be conducted rather than just a raid. Shortly thereafter, O'Connor received messages from Headquarters, British Troops in Egypt, stating no arrangements were being made for any type of advance on Benghazi and that such a project was not being proceeded with. This information directly contradicted the guidance he had received from Wavell. Frustrated, anxious to continue the offensive, beset with a stomach ailment, and in receipt of conflicting instructions from Wavell and Wilson, O'Connor wrote to Galloway that:

> I have tried very hard to serve two masters. It is far from being an easy job,. . . . and also find that it adds to my anxieties that my activities should be the cause of difficulties or friction between the C in C [Wavell] and the GOC in C [Wilson]. I feel therefore that I cannot continue without protest and in a system which I believe to be unsound and have therefore written to the C in C asking if he can spare the time to come down to see me. If he finds he is able to do so, I propose to ask him to relieve me of my Command as I am quite sure General Wilson is as unhappy as I am in the present situation. . . . [60]

Shortly thereafter, Wavell and Galloway flew to see O'Connor in the Western Desert. As a result of their visit, it was decided that an advance on Benghazi, in O'Connor's words, 'was to be worked out on any basis which I thought would succeed, and that in future I should work directly under GHQ . . .'[61] Of this command arrangement, Field Marshal Lord Harding, who as a Brigadier became O'Connor's Brigadier, General Staff, in December 1940, recently reflected that 'I think it was awful, it was rotten. I think it caused great problems. O'Connor should have been placed under the direct command of Wavell.'[62]

This episode depicts a facet of Wavell's generalship in which it was easier for him to maintain the *status quo* in terms of the chain of command, even if it was a potentially unwieldy command structure – as it proved to be – rather than offend anyone, especially Wilson. Yet Wavell circumvented the centre link in this chain of command, and communicated directly with O'Connor, to Wilson's distress and resultant conflicting orders. Wavell might have followed one of two possible courses of action: he could either have followed the extant chain of command, or simplified it by eliminating the middle link. The latter course of action, to which he had eventually to revert, would have been preferred.

Preparations for the capture of Tobruk had continued. Its perimeter was twice as long as that of Bardia, but the garrison was thought to be only half as large, thus raising British hopes for a relatively quick success. The general plan for the assault was almost identical to that for Bardia. Originally planned for 20 January 1941, the attack had to be postponed due to severe sandstorms, but was finally launched at 5:30 am on the following day. Carried out with great dash, in the tradition of their forebears in the 1st Australian Imperial Force of the Great War, the Australians' attack was highly successful. By dusk, one-third of the defended area was in British hands.

Fighting continued throughout the night, and the Australians entered the town without resistance on the morning of 22 January 1941. All fighting ceased that afternoon. Italian prisoners of war numbered almost 27,000, with 236 large-calibre guns and 87 tanks also captured. XIII Corps' casualties numbered slightly over 400, of whom 355 were Australian. Among the spoils at Tobruk were stockpiles of enough tinned food to last the Italian garrison two months; 10,000 tons of water; intact refrigeration and distillation plants; 4,000 tons of coal; and a power station. Within two days, the harbour, which had received only slight damage, had been swept of mines and was ready to receive supply ships. The second phase of Wavell's offensive had ended on a high note.

Revised intelligence appreciations made in London during this period showed that Whitehall had been too hasty in warning earlier that a German advance in the Balkans was imminent. Because of the Greeks' refusal of the British offer of aid – with Churchill observing that it was no good trying to 'force little dogs to eat mutton'[63] – coupled with these updated intelligence estimates, the Chiefs of Staff now instructed Wavell, on 21 January 1941, that not only was the capture of Benghazi and the seizure of the Dodecanese of the greatest importance, but that he should also create a strategic reserve for the purpose of assisting Turkey or Greece within the following two months.

Neither Wavell nor O'Connor needed cajoling to continue the advance.

O'Connor, described by Creagh as being 'as keen as a terrier after a rat',[64] after the capture of Tobruk, saw the chance for a rapid advance to Benghazi and a decisive victory. By the evening of 22 January 1941 elements of the 7th Armoured Division were already nearing Derna and Mechili.

The XIII Corps was now approaching an area vastly different in character from the Western Desert. This region was dominated by the Jebel Akhdar, an upland area rising to heights of 2,500 feet. Possessing fertile soil and the recipient of adequate rainfall, it was an important area for Italian colonisation. From the military point of view, the terrain of the Jebel Akhdar made the area ideal for the defence.

O'Connor was now determined to defeat the enemy in detail, with the 6th Australian Division applying pressure on Derna while the 7th Armoured Division closed in and engaged Italian tanks at Mechili. Hindered by fuel shortages, the 7th Armoured Division arrived at Mechili on the morning of 27 January 1941 only to find, to its disappointment, that the enemy had slipped away the night before. While awaiting supplies, plans were made by Wavell and O'Connor for the advance to continue on 12 February.

* * *

Wavell flew to Nairobi on 28 January 1941, and discussed and approved Cunningham's plans for an offensive into Italian Somaliland. The Commander-in-Chief also met with Platt and encouraged him to press on with his advance into Eritrea. After visiting units and reconnoitring the terrain in Eritrea and Kenya, Wavell returned to Cairo on 1 February.

During Wavell's absence, the Joint Planning Staff in London examined British strategy in the Balkans and Eastern Mediterranean in the light of discussions that were taking place with Turkey. While maintaining the strategic primacy of securing the Benghazi area and the capture of the Dodecanese, the Joint Planning Staff recommended, 'since Turkey is of the greater strategic value we must not lock up such forces in Greece as are considered essential for the support of Turkey'.[65] The British Balkan policy, under Churchill's impassioned direction, continued to vacillate; Robin Higham has observed metaphorically but accurately that 'The Prime Minister in London kept changing his mind about the objectives like a puppy in a fire-hydrant factory.'[66] The support of Greece was now secondary to assisting Turkey.

This policy revision prompted Dill to wire Wavell asking for the projected date for the capture of Benghazi, to which the reply given, in Wavell's absence, was 'about end of February, but this may be optimistic'.[67] Armed with this data, the Prime Minister, in the process of trying to persuade the Turks to take the lead in forming the 'Balkan bloc' after the rebuff from the Greeks, minuted to the Chiefs of Staff Committee on 31 January 1941 that,

We must not overlook the decision we have conveyed to General Wavell that once Tobruk was taken the Greek-Turkish situation must have priority. The advance to Benghazi is most desirable, and has been emphasised in later telegrams. Nevertheless, only Forces which do not conflict with European needs can be employed. As the forecast is now that Benghazi cannot be captured till the end of February, it is necessary that this should be impressed upon General Wavell. For instance, the Air support promised to Turkey cannot be delayed until then. It may, however, be possible to reconcile both objectives.[68]

Churchill had been willing to permit Wavell to exceed his earlier instructions, provided there was no conflict with attempts to form a 'Balkan bloc' against Germany.

Accelerating his pressure on the Turks, Churchill wired on his own initiative to the Turkish President later that day – apparently believing full War Cabinet approval was unnecessary – offering to send him immediately ten squadrons of fighter and bomber aircraft (which were basically non-existent in the Middle East) and one hundred anti-aircraft guns, and requesting an alliance between Great Britain and Turkey. This message was repeated to Wavell on 1 February 1941, and was followed up by directions from the Chiefs of Staff declaring that the highest priority must now be given to countering German infiltration into Bulgaria, and,

> Advantage of going on to Benghazi and thus securing Egypt and the fleet base in the Eastern Mediterranean are fully realised, provided that it can be done without prejudice to European interests. Its capture as soon as possible is, therefore, of the highest priority.[69]

Explicit in that directive is the understanding that once Benghazi was seized, Egypt would be secure.

* * *

In the Western Desert, the enemy began to withdraw from Derna on 30 January 1941. O'Connor, concerned rightly that the enemy would be able to slip away undefeated, held a conference the following evening and put forth his plans to move quickly to intercept the fleeing Italians. This plan was approved by Wavell late on 1 February, and a hastily-organised element called 'Combe Force' (named after its commander, Lieutenant Colonel J F B Combe and consisting of his own 11th Hussars, field, anti-tank and light anti-aircraft artillery and 2nd Rifle Brigade) struck out for Msus at about 7:00 am on 3 February, followed shortly thereafter by formations of the 7th Armoured Division. O'Connor's plan was for the 6th Australian Division to continue pressing the Italian 60th Division westwards from Derna along the coast road, while the Armoured Division would occupy Msus and be prepared to move on Soluch or Agedabia, as required.

Wavell himself flew to Cyrenaica on 4 February to assess the situation, at which time 'the decision was made to take the bold course and try to cut off the Italians south of Benghazi'.[70] Combe Force occupied Msus that day, having travelled over rugged and unreconnoitred terrain, and the Armoured Division arrived a few miles east of Msus early on 5 February.

Creagh sent forward two detachments that morning, one to drive, via Antelat, straight to the coast, with orders to interdict the Benghazi-Tripoli road north of Agedabia, and to be followed by the 4th Armoured Brigade. The second detachment was to continue in a northerly direction and occupy Soluch. That afternoon, the vanguard of the retreating Italian 10th Army, 'driving unconcernedly without taking any particular precautions to the East and South',[71] numbering some 5,000 men, including civilians, drove into the British positioned at Sidi Saleh, about ten miles south-west of Beda Fomm. After a sharp engagement, during which the 4th Armoured Brigade arrived at the rear of the enemy column, many Italians surrendered, after making half-hearted attempts to break through the hastily-established British defences.

Much more severe fighting occurred throughout 6 February, with the Italians attempting unsuccessfully to breach the British blocking position – the mainstay of which were the 29 cruiser tanks of the 4th Armoured Brigade – and losing 84 tanks in the process. Reinforced by the 7th Armoured Brigade, the British repelled at least nine vigorous enemy attacks that night. The 6th Australian Division had been pressuring the Italians from the East and then the North, so that the Italian force huddled into a congested mass of vehicles some 20 miles long. After a final forward surge by 30 Italian tanks at dawn on 7 February had failed, Bergonzoli surrendered unconditionally.

The Battle of Beda Fomm had been an incredible victory. After travelling a vast distance over appalling going, remarkably quickly, the British, outnumbered by at least four-to-one in cruiser tanks and numerically greatly inferior in personnel, concluded the destruction of the Italian 10th Army and captured about 20,000 more enemy soldiers, 120 tanks, and 190 guns. O'Connor signalled to Wavell on 7 February 1941: 'Fox killed in the open. . . .'[72] O'Connor, in a typical understatement, observed 'I think this may be termed a complete victory, as none of the enemy escaped.'[73]

In a broadcast address made on 9 February 1941, Churchill lauded the military commanders of the Middle East, stating that 'Wavell, Commander-in-Chief of all the Armies of the Middle East, has proved himself a master of war, sage, painstaking, daring and tireless.'[74] Commenting upon Operation 'Compass', the Prime Minister opined that it 'will long be studied as a model of the military art'.[75] A contemporary War Office publication, however, made some differing comments upon O'Connor's and Creagh's leadership, within the context of Churchill's aforementioned address:

Neither General O'Connor, the Corps Commander who directed and inspired the advance from Barrani to Benghazi, nor General Creagh, commander of the armoured force, thought of the battle in that light, for it had broken every text-book rule, and violated every staff college precept. Its rules had been dictated by the exigencies of the moment: to the purist it may not have been a perfect battle; to the less well informed observer it was an inspiring example of the triumph of resource, audacity, staying power, and above all individual courage.[76]

O'Connor wanted to exploit the victory and wasted no time in pushing westwards towards Tripoli. The 11th Hussars reached Agedabia the night of 6 February 1941, and were at El Agheila the following night, with patrols out some forty or fifty miles along the coast road to Sirte. 'No resistance whatever was encountered', recalled O'Connor, 'but a few prisoners were picked up along the coast. Other than that, of the enemy there was no sign.'[77] Since he had accomplished his mission of capturing Benghazi, O'Connor thought that he would need permission to advance to Tripoli, so he sent Dorman-Smith, Wavell's former Brigade Major and now a brigadier serving frequently as Wavell's personal liaison officer with O'Connor, to Wavell's Headquarters in Cairo to seek such permission. After a tortuous 570-mile drive, Dorman-Smith reached Cairo early in the morning of 12 February, and met Wavell later that morning. Dorman-Smith found that the maps of the Western Desert, formerly on the Commander-in-Chief's office walls, had been replaced by maps of Greece and the Balkans. Wavell, in welcoming Dorman-Smith, declared, 'You find me busy with my spring campaign.'[78]

* * *

On 8 February 1941, a new Greek Government asked the British Government to re-open discussions about the size of the force that the British could send to Greece if the Germans entered Bulgaria. Churchill, after the Greek rebuff of the previous month and his inability to persuade the Turks to form a Balkan alliance, perceived this as a sign of encourage-ment and, with alacrity, attempted to persuade the British Government to underwrite his desired policy. On 10 February, the Defence Committee (Operations) – chaired by Churchill – met and dismissed perfunctorily the argument to continue the advance in Libya to Tripoli. According to the meeting minutes, 'The Prime Minister thought',

it would be wrong to abandon the Greeks, who were putting up a magnificent fight, and who were prepared to fight the Germans, so that we could later help Turkey, who was shirking her responsibilities, and taking no action to prevent the Germans establishing themselves in a threatening position in Bulgaria.[79]

'There was considerable further discussion', but Churchill, typically, was able to impose his dominant personality on the group, and it was 'generally expressed that it was essential for us to come to the assistance of the Greeks, if they would have us.'[80] Although no decisions were taken at the meeting, the Chiefs of Staff were directed to study the various courses of action and to prepare instructions to the Middle East Commanders-in-Chief, 'on the assumption that our policy would be':

(i) That no serious operation should be undertaken beyond Benghazi, which should be held as a secure flank for Egypt.

(ii) That we should shift the largest possible force from Egypt to the European continent, to assist the Greeks against a probable German attack through Bulgaria.

(iii) That certain special steps should be taken forthwith to enable our plans to be concerted with the Greeks.[81]

On the following day, in response to a cable from the British Military Mission in Athens, Wavell, indicating his willingness to comply with related directives, stated that his available reserves to send immediately to either Greece or Turkey consisted of one armoured brigade group and the New Zealand Division, of only two brigades. In the middle of March he could send another armoured brigade group, the New Zealand Division complete, and an Australian division of two brigades. This latter division, in Wavell's estimation, could be complete by mid-April, with a second Australian division available by the end of that month.

The Defence Committee (Operations) met again on 11 February 1941, and amended and authorised the despatch of a telegram, which Wavell received early the following day and included:

> We should have been content with making a safe flank for Egypt at Tobruk, and we told you that thereafter Greece and/or Turkey must have priority, but that if you could get to Benghazi easily and without prejudice to European calls, so much the better. We are delighted that you have got this prize three weeks ahead of expectation, but this does not alter, indeed it rather confirms, our previous directive, namely, that your major effort must now be to aid Greece and/or Turkey. This rules out any serious effort against Tripoli, although minor demonstrations thitherwards would be a useful feint. You should therefore make yourself secure at Benghazi and concentrate all available forces in the Delta in preparation for movement to Europe.[82]

'Compass' had been halted; there would be no advance to Tripoli.

* * *

The failure of the British to exploit fully the complete victory at Beda Fomm by an advance to Tripoli and the elimination of the Italian forces in Libya, is one of the most controversial, and in some quarters lamented, decisions of the Second World War. Its roots, however, can be traced back to the very successes of the opening phase of 'Compass' and the capture of Sidi Barrani, the reverberations of which reached all the way to Berlin. On 10 December 1940, Adolf Hitler reversed an earlier decision and ordered *Luftwaffe* formations

> to operate as soon as possible from the South of Italy, for a limited time. Their most important task is to attack the British Navy in Alexandria but also in the Suez Canal . . . and in the Straits between Sicily and the north coast of Africa, owing to the critical situation in the Mediterranean.[83]

Wavell's offensive persuaded the vacillating Spanish dictator, General Francisco Franco, to refuse to collaborate with Hitler, who abandoned Operation 'Felix', the plan for the capture of Gibraltar, on 11 December. Hitler, more convinced than ever that Great Britain was further from defeat or surrender than ever before, decided to turn on the Soviet Union. 'Undertaking Marita', the codename for Hitler's Directive No. 20, was issued on 13 December and outlined the plan for the occupation of Greece. Directive No. 21, for 'Case Barbarossa' – the invasion of the Soviet Union – was issued only five days later. Both of these operations were interrelated, in that the Balkans, the German southern flank in the projected offensive against the Soviet Union, had first to be secured.

It was only after the fall of Bardia that Hitler decided, on 11 January 1941, that 'for strategic, political and psychological reasons, the Mediterranean situation, where Britain is employing superior forces against our ally, requires German assistance'.[84] The German 5th Light Division (Motorised) was authorised for despatch on 21 January, and later augmented by a Panzer division. The force was programmed to arrive in North Africa in mid-February.

Throughout this period, Churchill remained fixated with attempts to establish a 'Balkan bloc', and the death of Greek Prime Minister Metaxas on 29 January 1941 bolstered Churchill's aspirations for such an alliance. This confused the Anglo-Greek and Anglo-Turkish relationships even more, and precluded Wavell from concentrating his forces for a single offensive operation.

After the war Wavell wrote:

> As for the advance to Tripoli, Italian opposition could be discounted as small and likely to be easily overcome, and nothing was at this time known of the despatch of German forces to Africa; but even so our own resources were not equal to the task. Our armoured vehicles were worn out by an advance of 500 miles; we had not enough mechanised transport to maintain even a small force for an advance of another 500 miles to Tripoli; and both in the air and on the sea we were still numerically inferior to the Italians alone, without any German reinforcement. It would have been an intolerable strain on the Navy to maintain a military and air force at Tripoli when even Benghazi could not be used as a port for lack of AA artillery and other resources.[85]

This passage coincides with what Wavell told Julian Amery in the spring of 1941, in that, on balance, Wavell had not thought that he could have driven the Italians out of North Africa, due to the great strain on vehicles and shortage of petrol.

An analysis of Wavell's perceptions of the viability of continuing the advance to Tripoli indicates that he had an unrealistic appreciation of conditions at the 'front'; underestimated the number of vehicles available to transport a force to Tripoli; misunderstood the operational status and abilities of the Royal Air Force and Royal Navy; and failed to consider the high state of readiness, training, and morale of the soldiers of the XIII Corps. In essence, Wavell stressed all of the difficulties of advancing to Tripoli without properly emphasising its advantages; he was mentally prepared to send an expeditionary force to the Balkans.

Wavell's comment that 'our own resources were not equal to the task' of advancing to Tripoli is certainly open to challenge. While it is true that after the Battle of Beda Fomm, only 12 cruiser tanks and 40 light tanks were still battleworthy, a redistribution of assets took place, with the 3rd Hussars receiving all the serviceable light tanks, and the 6th Royal Tank Regiment being re-equipped with captured Italian M13 medium tanks, of which about 60 had been captured with only a few hundred miles on their odometers. In addition, O'Connor was scheduled to receive, in the near future, two fresh regiments from the recently-arrived 2nd Armoured Division, which would have given him four armoured regiments with which to continue the advance.

The 6th Australian Division had not been in severe fighting since Tobruk, and on 2 February 1941 it was only a little more than ten per cent understrength. Immediately after the Battle of Beda Fomm, one of its brigades was mounted in captured trucks and 'was all ready on the road waiting for the order to advance.'[86] O'Connor was confident that this composite force could have been in Tripoli in thirty-six hours.[87] Wavell, on the other hand, not having visited the scene of operations since 4 February, was not as familiar as he should have been with the status of captured equipment, unit preparations for a continuance of the advance, and the morale of the soldiers. Or, perhaps, he did not seriously consider an advance to Tripoli, being aware of Churchill's probable intentions in the Balkans.

Longmore later wrote in his autobiography that at this time the increasing gravity of the situation in Greece was calling for the early despatch of air reinforcements to that theatre, resulting in a decrease in the number of air squadrons in Cyrenaica. 'It was therefore with some relief to me that the decision was made not to continue the advance towards Tripoli. I was fairly sure', he continued, 'that the *Luftwaffe* was arriving in Tripoli and would be playing havoc with our recently captured ports and lines of communication, which were quite long enough already.'[88]

These comments, though, are tainted with information that Longmore learned after the event. It was not until after London had made the decision to halt the advance at Benghazi that Headquarters No. 202 Group (which had controlled all Royal Air Force formations in the Western Desert), Nos. 45 and 113 (Bomber) Squadrons, No. 274 (Fighter) Squadron, No. 208 (Army Cooperation) Squadron, and other RAF elements, were withdrawn from the Western Desert, all before the end of February 1941. Additional squadrons were sent from Egypt to Greece in March 1941. Longmore also wrote that 'The German air offensive in Libya began to build up towards the end of February', and coupled with the German air activity of the following few months, the *Luftwaffe* could not have made it impossible to maintain a military presence at or near Tripoli.[89] Thus, the claim of the Royal Air Force's inability to support the advance to Tripoli, and the myth of the *Luftwaffe's* marked preponderance of forces and capability to annihilate any British force marching to Tripoli, can be discounted. The German Air Force would have been overextended, attempting simultaneously to protect the sea routes across the Mediterranean Sea; mine the ports of Tripoli, Benghazi, Tobruk, Sollum, and the Suez Canal; contain Malta; and provide support to ground units. 'But', O'Connor observed, 'bombing has never forced good troops to withdraw from an area.'[90]

From the naval perspective, supplying the Army by sea through Benghazi, according to Cunningham, 'was a problem indeed'.[91] The decision to go on the defensive at Benghazi, and the requirement to send air force squadrons and anti-aircraft units to Greece almost immediately meant that the harbour at Benghazi was left relatively unprotected from attack from seaward or from the air. The Germans also started planting magnetic mines in Benghazi harbour on 13 February 1941, although this did not prevent the Royal Navy from sailing a convoy there the following day. Despite the problems, Cunningham's attitude at the time was, however, very different from Longmore's. After learning of the halting of the Western Desert offensive, Cunningham wrote that he was 'most bitterly disappointed at the turn this Libyan campaign has taken', and continued 'I don't know the reason. I know it was not due to any naval shortcomings (we had just landed 2,500 tons of petrol and over 3,000 tons of other stores at Benghazi and had doubled the amount we had guaranteed to land daily at Tobruk).'[92] Although a difficult proposition, the Navy could have supplied the Army in an advance to Tripoli. The eminent naval historian Captain Stephen Roskill, was convinced that 'the right strategy was for O'Connor to drive straight for Tripoli after the battle of Beda Fomm'.[93]

Longmore and Cunningham were naturally very concerned about shepherding their resources, but it is quite probable that their respective services sustained more loss by their engagement in the Balkans than they would have supporting the Army at Tripoli. During the six months' campaign in Greece (November 1940-April 1941) the RAF lost 209 aircraft. From 1 January 1941 to 30 April 1941, total RAF losses throughout the

Middle East, including those sustained in Greece, numbered 345 aircraft. The Royal Navy, in supplying the Army in the Western Desert, lost the following ships:

- Minesweeper *Huntley* (Derna, 31 January 1941)
- South African whaler *Southern Floe* (Tobruk, 11 February 1941)
- *Ouse* (Tobruk, 20 February 1941)
- Monitor *Terror* (Benghazi/Derna, 22/23 February 1941)
- Destroyer *Dainty* (Tobruk, 24 February 1941)

During the Battle for Crete alone (22 April-1 June 1941), which followed the unsuccessful land campaign in Greece, three cruisers and eight destroyers were sunk, two battleships were damaged, one aircraft carrier was damaged and taken out of service, five cruisers were seriously damaged, and seven destroyers damaged to varying degrees. The maintenance of the Army, if it had advanced to Tripoli, would not have been as burdensome to the Royal Air Force and Royal Navy as was the support of the Greek campaign.

O'Connor was not alone in his conviction that an element from XIII Corps could 'have got to [Tripoli] without difficulty, & that they could have maintained themselves'.[94] On the night of 7 February 1941, Wilson sent a signal to Wavell recommending that a light column be sent, at least to Sirte, to clear the Italians out of North Africa, and 'if opportunity offered', to Tripoli.[95] Wavell's personal liaison officer, Dorman-Smith, adamantly maintained that,

> Considering that we had two strong fleets in being at either end of the Mediterranean either able to reach Tripoli and moreover the Italian 10th Army had ceased to exist, added to the fact that the Supreme Command [in Whitehall] had not even made up its mind when or where the Middle East forces to be concentrated in the Delta were to go to Europe, it is fair to hold that these decisions [embodied in Churchill's 12 February 1941 cablegram] constitute the biggest strategical blunder in Britain's history.[96]

He also believed that 'It was like having a lovely checkmate before one's eyes and then deliberately declining in favour of some lesser move which loses you the game.'[97]

On 10 February 1941, Wavell sent a tepid message to Whitehall, which stated:

1. Extent of Italian defeat at Benghazi makes it seem possible that Tripoli might yield to small force if despatched without delay, repeat undue delay. Am working out commitment involved, but hesitate to advance further in view of Balkan situation, unless you think capture of Tripoli might have favourable effect on attitude of French North Africa.

2. Further advance will also involve naval and air commitments and we are already far stretched. Navy would hate having to feed us at Tripoli and air

force to protect us. On other hand, possession of this coast might be useful to both.

3. Will make plans for capture of Sirte, which must be first step. Meanwhile, cable me most immediate your views as to effect on Weygand and war situation generally. Will probably go to Cyrenaica to discuss matter with Wilson 12th or 13th February.[98]

Wavell failed to grasp the situation on the Cyrenaican front quickly enough, but when he finally did, he hesitated. Preoccupied with Churchill's pressure pertaining to the Balkans, Wavell did not exhibit the 'spirit of adventure' or the 'touch of the gambler'. Any inkling he had of the potential success of advancing to Tripoli was irrevocably shattered by the 12 February 1941 order to halt from the Prime Minister.

Unknown to Wavell, as early as 26 January 1941, Amery, Secretary of State for India, had urged Churchill to permit Wavell to advance to Tripoli in order to keep the Sicily Channel open and relieve the pressure on Malta. On 3 February, Amery, after pointing out to Dill the advantages of advancing not only to Benghazi but all the way to Tripoli, wrote an exceptionally cogent, detailed, and prescient paper on that topic. Stressing the element of surprise, he also advocated using naval vessels not only to transport troops rapidly in order to outflank the enemy, but also to support the proposed motorised advance. Futhermore, arriving at Tripoli at the earliest opportunity would also have preempted the Germans from establishing a foothold on the North African coast. Amery concluded correctly that:

> My argument is that the advance to Tripoli should not be considered merely as the exploiting of Wavell's success in North Africa, but as the key to any future operations on a serious scale against Sicily, Sardinia, or in the Balkans. It might be the Open Sesame of the whole war and as an operation of surprise might completely disorganise the enemy's plans.[99]

Connell wrote 'There is no evidence that this document ever received the careful and detailed study, either by the Chiefs of Staff or by the War Cabinet, which it merited.'[100] The Chiefs of Staff did in fact receive Amery's study, and instructed the Joint Planning Staff in London to examine its possibilities. The Joint Planning Staff, however, was also imbued with the idea of assisting Greece and Turkey, and framed its considerations within that context. Even further away from the Cyrenaican front than Wavell, the London Joint Planners had an even less realistic understanding of the status and capabilities of O'Connor's XIII Corps, and concluded dogmatically on 8 February 1941 that:

> While agreeing with Mr. Amery that the possession of Tripoli would be of some strategic value to us, we think that, in view of the large operational and administrative commitment that its capture and maintenance would involve, we should adhere to our present strategic policy.[101]

Jacob, who served as Military Assistant Secretary to the War Cabinet, admitted recently that 'although there were obvious attractions of going to Tripoli, it was never seriously considered. . . .'[102]

This episode is again illustrative of Churchill's influence over the decision-making process in London. As described earlier, after becoming Prime Minister, Churchill also assumed the portfolio of Minister of Defence. Churchill's motives are open to interpretation, and Dorman-Smith suggested that:

> It seems to have been thought that had he [Churchill] been PM in 1914/15 he'd have both initiated the Dardanelles operations and carried it to success which impelled him to grasp direct control of both political and military operations by making himself Minister of Defence and then taking into his 'Operational System' both the Joint Planners and the Joint Intelligence Staff while issuing orders and directives to the Service Chiefs of Staff (individually or in committee via Ismay). His inner Cabinet, his 'cronies circle,' his relegation of the Service Ministers to the outer circle and his degrading of the Service Chiefs of Staff to the position of operators of policy rather than makers of policy in the military field, in effect his assumption of Cromwellian-dictatorship powers all seem to stem from his 1914/15 trauma.[103]

Historian Robert Rhodes James's dissection of Churchill's role in the Dardanelles project, which Churchill pushed 'forward with vigour, overruling or ignoring the doubts and criticisms of his Service advisers',[104] is strikingly similar to the method of operations employed by the Prime Minister in the Second World War. By February 1941, the machinery for the higher direction of the war operated in the manner described by David Day:

> Decision-making on the war was increasingly concentrated in the smaller War Cabinet Defence Committee (Operations) over which Churchill held practically undisputed sway. The War Cabinet then tended to rubber-stamp decisions already reached in the Defence Committee.[105]

It is, perhaps, significant that Major General John Kennedy, Director of Military Operations in the War Office, also favoured unequivocally an advance to Tripoli. He believed that:

> The biggest mistake was committed by Wavell when he did not insist on sending at least a small force in a bold attempt to seize this great prize [Tripoli]. The diversion of such a force would not have affected his ability to operate in Greece.[106]

While Wavell hesitated over permitting O'Connor to advance to Tripoli, the Middle East Joint Planning Staff was preparing a study on the same topic. Major General Sir Francis de Guingand was a major serving on the Middle East Joint Planning Staff at that time, and later recalled that after Tobruk and Benghazi were seized and 'after a pause of a week or two', an adequate force could have advanced and captured Tripoli.[107] A contemporary of de Guingand's on the MEJPS, Major (later Major General) David Belchem, was the staff officer responsible for collecting the data and making the calculations of serviceable tanks and other vehicles, the logistical tonnage lift required from Benghazi, the vehicle capacity, fuel availability, and other similar factors. He concluded:

> The answer was positive: It could have been done. If British forces had reached Tripoli by the end of February the war in North Africa might well have ended, even though it was a matter of calculated risk as far as the Royal Navy and RAF were concerned.[108]

When asked almost three decades after the event if the British could have advanced successfully to Tripoli, Belchem responded 'I say categorically YES.'[109] After thoroughly and objectively assessing the advantages and disadvantages of naval, Army, and air aspects of continuing the advance to Tripoli, the Middle East JPS – composed of officers from all three services – concluded:

> . . . that only the employment of a small force is possible, and that there should be NO delay. The situation as it is at present holds out a chance that a small but powerfully armed force might produce decisive results, provided that the operation can be staged before the enemy forces can be re-equipped and before German air forces have time to establish themselves.[110]

The J P S prepared this study during the period in which Wavell was wavering over advancing to Tripoli. The study was published on 11 February 1941; the order from London to halt the offensive was received the following day, and thus spared Wavell the responsibility of deciding to continue the advance.

The senior officers of the XIII Corps and members of the Middle East Joint Planning Staff were not the only ones who favoured the advance to Tripoli. Often overlooked, a number of the Other Ranks involved believed that that course of action was possible and realistic. 'I think we should have advanced after Beda Fomm', recently recalled Ernest Mason, who served in the Royal Artillery of the 7th Armoured Division during 'Compass',

> because the Italian Army were beaten and we had captured 9/10 of them and all their equipment and our men were in good spirits and morale was very high. Yes, there were supply problems but now we had more of everything, vehicles, petrol, and food, in fact we had used a lot of Italian vehicles to get to Beda Fomm. My Regiment had some very large Fiat trucks twice as big as our own, which we put to good use carrying more stores and water, . . . I say a great chance was missed to finish the campaign in that area.[111]

RJ Mathews, who served in the 7th Medium Regiment, Royal Artillery, also believed that the advance to Tripoli was possible,[112] as did George Rose, another former Gunner of the 7th Armoured Division, who observed:

I do think we could have gone straight through to Tripoli, as we had no opposition, as the Italians had no heart in the war, as they were surrendering in the thousands. Even now I do not know why we stopped at Benghazi.[113]

Numerous other sources confirm the comments of these former soldiers pertaining to the lack of opposition by the Italians. These include the American Consul in Tunis, who reported on 10 February 1941 that the remainder of Italian troops in Tripoli had given up all idea of resisting a British advance, and that it was believed that Tripolitania was being evacuated.

The Germans, the first detachment of which, under the command of Rommel, landed at Tripoli on 12 February 1941, were similarly astounded that the British had not advanced. 'If Wavell had now continued his advance into Tripolitania', Rommel wrote, 'no resistance worthy of the name could have been mounted against him – so well had his superbly planned offensive succeeded.'[114] *Generalmajor* FW von Mellenthin, who participated in the Balkan campaign before being assigned to Rommel's staff in June 1941, believed that the British decision to halt the advance and send troops to Greece 'only managed to deprive Wavell of an excellent opportunity of getting to Tripoli'[115]. And after becoming a prisoner of war in April 1941, O'Connor recorded:

Having had the opportunity of speaking to several German and Italian Officers on passing through Tripoli, all asked why we did not go on to Tripoli, as they said there was nothing to stop us. Such Italian Units as there were, were in a state of complete confusion and demoralisation.[116]

Two other distinguished soldiers who participated in 'Compass', Field Marshals Harding and Carver, recently expressed more moderate opinions on this subject. 'I have no doubt' that the British could have advanced to Tripoli, observed Harding, 'since the opposition was negligible, but if we could have maintained it is another matter.'[117] Carver also believed that a small force of armoured cars could have made it to Tripoli, but stressed that such a force could not have been maintained there either logistically or in terms of air support.[118] It was also within this context that Carver deprecated the untimely withdrawal of the 4th Indian Division and its resulting delay to operations in December 1940:

If victory at Beda Fomm had been achieved ten days earlier, and if then Wavell had permitted an advance to Tripoli, O'Connor might have been able to get a light force there before the first ships bringing Rommel's 5th Light Panzer Division had arrived, which it did on 12 February 1941.[119]

Whether or not an element of O'Connor's XIII Corps could have advanced to Tripoli and could have been sustained there, will remain a matter for speculation. When asked that question recently, Lieutenant Colonel John Benson, who as a captain served on O'Connor's staff from October

1940 to March 1941, responded: 'Ask yourself a converse question: If you had asked on 8 December 1940 "was the Western Desert Force capable of capturing 130,000 Italian prisoners, 800 guns, and 400 tanks", the answer would be "no".'[120] The Western Desert Force defied all odds and accomplished the impossible. As Benson's unquestionably accurate response, as well as the evidence presented, suggests, Wavell's perception of the viability of advancing to Tripoli was at fault. His resources, as shown, were equal to the task. Wilson, O'Connor, Dorman-Smith, and other senior officers, plus many of the enlisted soldiers, were confident in their ability to advance to Tripoli. The only question was in the ability of the Royal Air Force and Royal Navy to support such a task force, and this sustenance could have been provided and maintained as long as there was no significant diversion of forces.

It would have been a calculated risk to continue the advance, and for years after the event O'Connor brooded over his lack of foresight and failure to grasp audaciously an unparalleled opportunity. He lamented the fact that he was the only person who could have implemented such a move, and wrote 'I blame myself for not going on, & telling GHQ I had done so.'[121] Similarly, Wavell, undoubtedly due to his physical and psychological distance from the Cyrenaican front at the time and his preoccupation, as a result of Churchill's incessant exhortations, with the possibility of sending significant forces somewhere in the Balkans, discounted the potential 'Open Sesame' of the war. A 'window of opportunity' was open from 7 to 11 February 1941, during which a British force could have seized Tripoli, but it was shut irrevocably by Churchill's 12 February telegram prohibiting a further advance in North Africa.

While the success of 'Compass' was spectacular, due in large measure to Wavell's leadership, Wavell's inability to press Whitehall for permission to advance to Tripoli, or his failure to present Tripoli to the Prime Minister as a *fait accompli*, reflects on his performance. Wavell believed that 'the mark of the really great commander as distinguished from the ordinary general' was possession of 'a spirit of adventure, a touch of the gambler'.[122] Wavell certainly demonstrated those qualities during the planning and opening phases of 'Compass', but he hesitated and lost the opportunity to advance to Tripoli.

The entire complexion of the North African campaign was altered unmistakably on that fateful day of 12 February 1941 with the arrival of German troops in Libya.

Conclusion

'The entire campaign ['Compass']', commented one United States Army military journal perceptively, 'was nothing short of miraculous.'[123] During the two months from 7 December 1940 to 7 February 1941, Wavell's 'Army of the Nile' advanced over 500 miles. It totally destroyed the Italian 10th Army of nine-and-a-half divisions and captured some 130,000 prisoners, 400 tanks, and 1,290 guns, at a cost of only 500 British and Dominion soldiers killed, 1,373 wounded, and 55 missing. Throughout 'Compass', the British never employed a force of more than two divisions, or about 31,000 men. In addition, and perhaps of even greater significance, revived confidence in the British cause, as a result of 'Compass', facilitated the passage of Lend-Lease legislation in the United States House of Representatives on 8 February 1941.

Some historians debate whether to call Operation 'Compass' 'Wavell's Offensive' or 'O'Connor's Offensive'. Wavell was always more than generous in ensuring that his subordinates received the proper recognition for their successes. At the strategic level, Wavell was responsible for the plan's initiation and concept, and for the overall direction of the offensive, whereas O'Connor, as a subordinate of Wavell's, was properly responsible for its detailed planning and its execution at the operational level of war. With success being said to have a hundred fathers and failure being an orphan, there is little doubt that had 'Compass' not been successful, O'Connor would have received little more than a footnote in history, and the *débâcle* would have been condemned forever as 'Wavell's Offensive'.

With very few exceptions, Wavell's generalship throughout 'Compass' was outstanding. He continually oversaw the direction of the offensive, and personally visited the commanders and soldiers on a frequent basis. Whenever possible, generally in conjunction with his visits to the battle 'front', he reconnoitred the terrain and areas of operations. He planned the extent of the different phases of 'Compass', and personally issued his commander's guidance before a significant attack, such as the attacks on Bardia and Tobruk. He then gave his subordinate commanders the authority and responsibility, and full support, to accomplish those objectives. When success was achieved, he ensured that his subordinate commanders and units received the recognition commensurate with their contribution.

Wavell, however, underestimated the potential of 'Compass', adhered rigidly to his earlier plan, and withdrew prematurely the 4th Indian Division for transfer to the Sudan. This action did not permit O'Connor to exploit the attack's success and continue the offensive against the shocked and demoralised Italian forces. In addition, the chain of command in the Western Desert, from Wavell through Wilson to O'Connor, was unnecessarily cumbrous and unwieldy. It should have been simplified by eliminating the middle link before 'Compass' began, but due to Wavell's complacency, this was not done. Only when the friction of personalities impeded the effectiveness of this chain of command did Wavell enact the requisite simplification.

Churchill's obsession with the Balkans and vacillating strategic priorities hindered Wavell's ability to direct 'Compass' properly. Distracted by the

Prime Minister's relentless pressure and fusillade of often-contradictory cables, Wavell did not appreciate adequately the capabilities of O'Connor's XIII Corps, and so did not allow O'Connor to continue the advance to Tripoli.

It is no exaggeration to note, as chronicled by a contemporary source, that after the Norwegian fiasco and the *débâcle* at Dunkirk, 'Nothing since the beginning of World War II, a year ago last September, has boosted British morale or given them greater courage to fight on as has this brilliant Libyan campaign.'[124]

7

Greek Diversion, February–April 1941

> '. . .; it was a series of misfortunes.'
> Wavell, 1 August 1941.[1]

The spectacular successes of Operation 'Compass' propelled Wavell over-night from a position of relative obscurity to a pinnacle of prestige and public adulation with typical headlines in the press during this period reading 'Wavell's Wave Sweeps Over Libya'; 'Wavell: Warrior of the Desert'; and 'Wavell: Hero of North Africa'. His portrait was featured on the cover of the *Illustrated London News* of the 15 February 1941 and was captioned 'A master of war'.[2]

When delivered in 1939, Wavell's lectures on 'Generals and Generalship' had been heard by only a few dozen students. In the wake of his Libyan victories, these three lectures were republished in *The Times* newspaper on 17, 18, and 19 February 1941. In introducing these articles, *The Times*, unaware of the controversies over the withdrawal of the 4th Indian Division on the third day of 'Compass', the friction in the chain of command in the Western Desert, or the advance to Tripoli, stated that Wavell's 'latest exploits prove him to be gifted in high degree with the imaginative daring which is the hallmark of the great commander who reaches that higher and rarified atmosphere wherein so many others cannot easily breathe', and that 'Now the lectures are given to the world after he has put his precepts into practice and in the process gained the victory in a campaign of outstanding brilliance.'[3] Wavell's lectures received an overwhelmingly positive response, and on 20 February *The Times* announced that they would be reprinted in a booklet which would be available on 25 February. However, on 24 February the first printing, due to mail requests, had been exhausted! This booklet was reprinted four times by 6 March, with one reader observing that he had 'never read anything on generalship as illuminating as the articles published in your columns this week from the pen of the victor of Libya'.[4]

In the United States, Wavell was given the appellation of 'Britain's Soldier of the Hour', and considered to be 'a brilliant commander,' a 'soldier's soldier', 'a beloved and trusted leader, [who has] breathed new life, inspiration and confidence into the British Empire throughout the world'.[5] In the light of later Allied victories and the eventual successful outcome of the war, it is difficult to appreciate fully the extent of Wavell's fame within the early months of 1941. Thrust into the limelight, Wavell – the 'one-eyed Desert Fox' – retained his modesty. On 9 February 1941, for example, while listening to one of the Prime Minister's radio broadcasts, Wavell, knowing he was going to receive numerous compliments, excused himself from the room and 'hid behind a doorway', returning only when the broadcast was over.[6]

In addition to public recognition, Wavell was rewarded tangibly for his signal role in 'Compass'. On 5 March 1941, along with Cunningham and Longmore, he was elevated to the Most Honourable Order of the Bath, becoming a Knight Grand Cross (GCB), and O'Connor was knighted in that Order (KCB). The highest class of the Most Excellent Order of the British Empire (GBE) was conferred upon Wilson, and the commanders of the three divisions which had participated in 'Compass' – Beresford-Peirse (4th Indian Division), Creagh (7th Armoured Division), and Mackay (6th Australian Division) – were the recipients of knighthoods (KBE) in that same Order.

But by the middle of February 1941, the foundation of Wavell's newly-found fame was already on the verge of crumbling, although this was unknown to him at the time, and would be imperceptible to the public at large for many months. The advent of Rommel in North Africa on 12 February was a significant factor in the shifting sands of Wavell's fortunes, but even more crucial was the Churchill Government's decision to despatch an expeditionary force to Europe, since it was Wavell's responsibility to execute the Government's policy. The decision-making process in sending a force to Greece, the eventual destination, and Wavell's role therein, has been one of the greatest conundrums of the Second World War.

It should be recalled that at the conclusion of 'Compass', a major command reorganisation took place among the British forces in North Africa. After Tobruk had fallen, Wavell realised that it was imperative to create a new command, Cyrenaica Command, not only to replace the former Italian civil administration there but also because it had become impossible for Headquarters, British Troops in Egypt, both to command troops in Egypt and to control operations at such a vast distance. Accordingly, on 4 February, Wilson became Military Governor and Commander-in-Chief in Cyrenaica with Headquarters at Barce.

At the time of Wavell's receipt of the Prime Minister's order of 12 February 1941, to make his Command 'secure at Benghazi and concentrate all available forces in the Delta in preparation for movement to Europe', the forces that Wavell had available in the Middle East, and their status of readiness, were:

In Western Desert –

7th Armoured Division (on the verge of being withdrawn for reconstitution and complete overhaul)
6th Australian Division (seasoned by 'Compass')

In Egypt –

2nd Armoured Division (arrived January 1941; short of two regiments; mechanical problems)
6th British Division (in process of formation; no artillery or supporting arms)
New Zealand Division (fully trained and equipped)
Polish Brigade Group (not fully equipped)

In Palestine –

7th Australian Division (no training as a division; not fully equipped)
9th Australian Division (short of one brigade and one battalion; only partially trained; very short of equipment)
1st Cavalry Division (composed of horsed Yeomanry regiments)

In Eritrea –

4th Indian Division
5th Indian Division (both engaged in front of Keren)

In East Africa –

1st South African Division
11th African Division
12th African Division (all about to begin operations against Kismayu)

The need to withdraw and refit the 7th Armoured Division, and the new requirement for the Balkans, compelled Wavell to make significant and far-reaching alterations to his order of battle.

On 15 February 1941, the I Australian Corps, commanded by Lieutenant General (later Field Marshal) Sir Thomas Blamey, replaced XIII Corps, 'the staff of which was dispersed – a reckless step for an army with no other corps staff that had conducted a successful campaign'.[7] O'Connor complained to Wavell's Chief of Staff that he 'thought they were making a great mistake in breaking up a fairly well trained Corps Staff, as it had required months of training and experience to raise it to a reasonable standard of efficiency'.[8] The shortage of staff officers supposedly necessitated this step. Still suffering from stomach problems, O'Connor returned to Cairo on 17 February and assumed command of British Troops in Egypt.

The British decision to despatch a large force to Greece in 1941 marks the beginning of one of the most perplexing episodes of the entire war, especially when one considers the plethora of contradictory opinions and evidence regarding the political and military feasibility of such an operation and its eventual outcome. No less confusing is Churchill's dominant role in this incident, especially since he had apprised Harry Hopkins on 10 January 1941 of the futility of assisting Greece,[9] had cabled Wavell on 26 January that 'We must expect a series of very heavy disastrous blows in the Balkans, and possibly a general submission to German aims,'[10] and, as late as 3 February, had predicted gloomily to the War Cabinet that 'Last year's history in NW Europe is likely . . . to repeat itself this year in SE Europe.'[11] Wavell's function and culpability in this circumstance is even more obscure, because, up to the first week of February 1941, he had adamantly opposed any major commitment to Greece. Despite his earlier misgivings, Wavell's attitude then changed from loyal acquiescence and obedient compliance to outspoken advocacy. It is the primary purpose of this chapter to unravel this enigma.

It was originally believed, especially since the campaign ended so disastrously, that Wavell had been forced by his political and military superiors to send a force to Greece against his will. Wavell himself consistently denied this speculation, acknowledging, as early as 31 October 1942, that he 'never questioned the wisdom of the decision to support Greece and have always expressed myself in full agreement with the policy'.[12] But because of his tremendous popularity and reputation, people were reluctant to believe in his complicity in such a *débâcle*. Wavell's position is even more puzzling because he admitted supporting the decision on Greece, when informed military opinion, such as General Jacob, believed that 'Wavell must have been crazy to advocate the campaign on *military* grounds',[13] and General Sir (later Field Marshal Lord) Alan Brooke, Commander-in-Chief, Home Forces at the time and Dill's successor as Chief of the Imperial General Staff, later wrote: 'I have, however, always considered from the very start, that our participation in the operations in Greece was a definite strategic blunder.'[14]

There are a number of other historiographical arguments, in addition to that of Wavell being compelled to mount the operation, that seek to explain why he was 'in full agreement' with such an obviously forlorn hope. Most historians, however, unable or unwilling to solve this dilemma, merely circumvent the issue and note only in general terms that 'In the event, Wavell loyally mustered a mixed . . . army . . . and sent it to Greece.'[15] Others, such as General Sir William Jackson, have attempted to rationalise the reason for Wavell's *volte face* by suggesting that '. . . Wavell had cleared his mind by writing a new appreciation of the situation. His reasoning led him to reverse his previous position on the Greek venture.'[16] In his biography of Wavell, which was heavily-censored by the Field Marshal's family, Connell noted cryptically that 'Wavell certainly did not have to be persuaded against his will. The problem, as he saw it, was that of finding the means to implement the choice he had already made between two sets of difficulties.'[17] Robin Higham, on the other hand, has attributed the 'puzzling metamorphosis in Wavell's policy towards Greece'[18] to a premeditated deception plan in which Wavell 'believed that he could make a gallant gesture at almost no risk at all',[19] because it seemed that the Germans would attack and defeat Greece in early March, before Wavell could transport many troops there. Although intriguing, Higham's thesis runs contrary to Wavell's unimpeachable personal and professional ethics, and fails to take into consideration Wavell's strategic plans for and the interrelationships of the North African, Greek, and East African campaigns, and facts hitherto undisclosed.

In solving this historical riddle, one must identify, analyse, and delineate, in chronological order, the evolution of Wavell's attitude towards the provision of assistance to Greece. The formulation and development of his philosophy occurred with varying intensity throughout four clearly identifiable phases:

I. 31 July 1939–27 October 1940
II. 28 October 1940–11 February 1941
III. 12–19 February 1941
IV. 19 February–6 April 1941

These phases correspond to significant events in the Middle East, none of which were of Wavell's choosing.

Wavell, as demonstrated clearly in Chapter 4, believed as early as 31 July 1939, while en route to assume his new command in Cairo, that the initial German advance would be orientated towards 'the S E against Poland, Rumania and Greece, (bringing in Hungary and Bulgaria as Allies), which might end in seizing the Dardanelles, . . .'[20] He was correct in forecasting the German attack on Poland, but the Germans failed to maintain their momentum, and halted their advance after Poland was subjugated. The following spring, the Germans launched a new offensive against the West, rather than towards the Balkans, as a continuation of their 1939 operation, and by doing so failed to realise Wavell's prognostication, at least in regard to his timetable of projected German plans. In that same appreciation, Wavell declared that the task of the Middle East Command was to plan for (and eventually to conduct) offensive operations to dominate the Mediterranean, *'and thereafter to take the counter offensive against Germany in Eastern and S E Europe'*.[21]

The importance of Turkey as a bulwark of the British Middle East position was reinforced by Wavell throughout the autumn of 1939. Wavell was a signatory of the 17 October 1939 Anglo-Franco-Turkish Treaty of Mutual Assistance, and when he attended an Anglo-French conference at Vincennes on 11 December 1939, he not only agreed with Weygand's proposal to make plans for Allied operations in Turkey and the Balkans, but also argued vehemently that 'we would be called upon to defend our interests in the Balkans in 1940', and therefore, 'we should start by getting the support of Turkey, and possibly by occupying Salonika'.[22] During the latter half of 1939, Wavell had become a stalwart proponent of a forward policy in the Balkans.

Additional inter-Allied conferences were held in January, February, and

March 1940 to continue planning for Allied assistance to Turkey and to monitor the progress of such preparations as were already being made. Wavell's fervour for an expedition to the Balkans lapsed temporarily into ambivalence as a result of the German attack on Scandinavia in April 1940 and the onslaught against France in the following month, with the exception of meetings to plan for the possible occupation of Crete. Wavell's diminished interest in the Balkans at that time is reflected directly in an appreciation which originated from his Headquarters on 8 June 1940 and which stated, in part, that 'On the whole, politically, it would appear that Germany today has less reason to invade the Balkans than at any time during the war.'[23] Attempts by the Allies to conciliate Turkish demands for material assistance were frustrated by the British evacuation from Dunkirk and loss of invaluable equipment.

With the Italian declaration of war on 11 June 1940, Wavell's visions of operations in the Balkans receded even further into the background. After that time, Wavell was concerned not only with a potential Italian advance on the Suez Canal, but he was also preoccupied with harassing the enemy and, after September, with the plans and preparations for his own offensive, Operation 'Compass'.

The Italian attack on Greece on 28 October 1940, which serves as the beginning of the second phase of this paradigm, came at an extremely inopportune time for Wavell. With a marked paucity of manpower and material resources, even the slightest diversion of forces had the potential to postpone or even cancel Wavell's impending offensive in the Western Desert. At a meeting held within hours of the Italian attack, Wavell was naturally reluctant to disperse any of his assets, and when the question was posed of providing anti-aircraft guns to Crete, Wavell responded hesitatingly that he 'would look into the AA question and see if anything could be made available', but if anything was sent, 'it would, of course, weaken our Egypt defences'.[24] After being informed of the 'Compass' plans, Eden shared Wavell's opinion, as recorded previously, that 'It would surely be bad strategy to allow ourselves to be diverted from this task and unwise to employ our forces in fragments in a theatre of war where they cannot be decisive.'[25] Wavell then remained unwavering in his conviction not to send forces to Crete, and did so reluctantly only after being directed to do so, after admonishing Whitehall that 'if we allow the Greek and Cretan commitments to grow any further at the expense of Egypt, we shall risk our whole position here'.[26] While forecasting, at the end of November, possible developments in the Middle East for the upcoming six months, Wavell, in his four-page appreciation, devoted only two sentences to Crete (and none to Greece), the second of which was: 'It is hoped to avoid further commitments here [Crete] unless the situation in Greece undergoes radical change.'[27]

Although contingency plans were prepared for possible assistance to Greece, the execution of 'Compass' continued to dominate Wavell's thoughts and actions throughout December 1940 and January 1941. As noted in the previous chapter, Wavell – who was not a recipient of Ultra intelligence until March 1941 – was exceedingly sceptical when told by the Chiefs of Staff on 10 January that 'assistance to Greece must now take priority over all operations in the Middle East once Tobruk is taken'.[28] It was due only to explicit instructions from the Prime Minister that Wavell, with no little anxiety, flew to Athens on 13 January to offer equipment to the Greeks. Throughout these discussions, Wavell loyally supported the British Government's policy, although personally opposed to it. To Wavell's relief, the Greeks declined the British offer, and he returned to Cairo on 17 January. During the following three weeks, Tobruk was captured and the advance continued, although Wavell was instructed by the Chiefs of Staff on 21 January to prepare a strategic reserve for the purpose of assisting Turkey or Greece within the following two months.

Wavell's attitude towards assisting the Balkans remained equivocal until 12 February 1941, when he received from the Prime Minister an order that his 'major effort must now be to aid Greece and/or Turkey. This rules out any serious effort against Tripoli, . . . concentrate all available forces [which Churchill envisioned as at least four divisions, including one armoured division] in the Delta in preparation for movement to Europe.'[29] That same message stated that Eden and Dill would be leaving England that day and arriving in Cairo on 14 or 15 February to give Wavell 'the very best chance of concerting all possible measures, both diplomatic and military, against the Germans in the Balkans'.[30] Dill had attempted to persuade the Prime Minister to send Kennedy, the Director of Military Operations, to Cairo in his stead, but without avail. The CIGS, as he later related, also informed Churchill that, in his view:

> All the troops in the Middle East are fully employed, and that none are available for Greece. The Prime Minister lost his temper with me. I could see the blood coming up his great neck and his eyes began to flash. He said: 'What you need out there is a Court Martial and a firing squad. Wavell has 300,000 men, etc., etc.'[31]

Dill believed he should have said, 'whom do you want to shoot exactly? but I did not think of it till afterwards'.[32] Dill and Kennedy both believed that 'the British Government was now trying to force an unsound policy down Wavell's throat, and down the throats of the Greeks and Turks', and that any British force sent to the continent of Europe was 'certain to be annihilated or driven out again.'[33]

It did, in fact, appear that Churchill was forcing upon Wavell the requirement to assist in the Balkans, as he had been since October 1940. However, during the period 12 to 19 February 1941, while Eden and Dill were in transit to Cairo, a remarkable transformation took place in Wavell's attitude. Even though Eden and Dill had been instructed by Churchill to insist upon Wavell carrying out an offensive in the Balkans, such coercion was not needed.[34]

A key factor in Wavell's decision to countenance sending forces to the Continent can be found, quite simply, in the fact that he had been ordered to halt the North African offensive and to prepare to send forces to Greece or Turkey. Being a good soldier, it was Wavell's duty to obey all lawful orders and support loyally his political and military superiors. Wavell demonstrated these traits throughout his career, just as when the possibility existed in mid-January 1941 that he would have to send technical troops to Salonika; he protested emphatically against such a move, but added dutifully, 'If Greeks now accept troops proposed and War Cabinet orders their dispatch, I shall, of course, send utmost available, . . .'[35] De Guingand has suggested critically that 'Surely a commander as fine as Wavell is supposed to have been, would have firmly told the Prime Minister that if he wished to proceed with the Greek expedition against his advice, he would resign his command.'[36] But de Guingand's rhetoric fails to take reality into account. Wavell's resignation, coming from the Empire's leading soldier and a rival in popularity to the Prime Minister himself, would have done nothing but undermine the British war effort. After Wavell had needlessly sacrificed himself, a commander would have inevitably been found who would have executed the Government's policy. Wavell's resignation, therefore, would not have been a viable option, even if he had been opposed to sending a force to the Balkans.

After being opposed to British assistance to Greece for so many months, Wavell's change of heart was so sudden and so complete that a number of his closest associates and friends were unaware of it, and continued to believe that Wavell did not personally favour the despatch of a British force. Bernard Fergusson (later Lord Ballantrae) suggested that:

> . . . as a matter of history, he [Wavell] was against that intervention to begin with; was persuaded, almost ordered, to agree with it; loyally addressed his mind to his orders; and when his political and military superiors got cold feet over it, his own retained the warmth which he had loyally injected into them.[37]

With greater insight and accuracy John Benson believed that Wavell:

> . . . did *not* want to go to Greece. However he knew he was in a unique position – he knew it would be a crisis if he refused to go and he knew that at all costs, if we were to pull through this war, there must be unity as between the military and political. He therefore weighed up all factors, [and decided] that he would go to Greece. Furthermore that it was no use doing it unwillingly or with a bad grace. He would have said to himself, there is no point in getting myself sacked, as I seem to be doing a satisfactory job at present. So I shall go flat out to do everything I can to make Greece a success. I hope it will come off but I have my doubts but no one, not even my family or my Chief of Staff will know that I have any serious doubts. I believe he realised that he had to think himself into this position, which he did with great success and afterwards, when the expedi-

tion was a failure – and this is where I always thought him to be such a great and selfless man – he never tried to blame anyone else. That is my belief and I cannot say more.[38]

An analysis of the facts, however, reveals incontrovertibly that Wavell, after slight hesitation, did want to send a British force to Greece. Prevented from continuing the advance in Libya, the order to prepare to send a force to Greece or Turkey rekindled Wavell's earlier ardour for such a project. Wavell, a soldier, has been criticised roundly for his advocacy of it, especially since it was believed that political considerations overshadowed the military feasibility of the operation.

De Guingand observed simply that 'our strategy in Greece can be looked upon as a test case respecting the relationship between the political and the military factors'.[39] 'All the service advice given on the problem', noted Kennedy with equal simplicity, 'had been coloured by political considerations – a very dangerous procedure.'[40] These two soldiers failed to take into consideration the exigencies of modern warfare in an era of relatively high-speed communications, among other factors. 'In war', moreover, as Jacob has observed, 'there are few problems that have no political content.'[41] Military strategy is indeed inextricable from politics, and in the decision to go to Greece, the two were closely related, with political considerations at least impinging on if not overriding the military aspects of the decision. This was a conundrum studied by the eminent Prussian military theorist Carl von Clausewitz, who concluded that:

> Subordinating the political point of view to the military would be absurd, for it is policy that has created war. Policy is the guiding intelligence and war only the instrument, not vice versa. No other possibility exists, then, than to subordinate the military point of view to the political.[42]

Of the utmost importance was the guarantee that Great Britain had made to Greece on 13 April 1939 – six days after the Italian invasion of Albania and thirteen days after a guarantee had been pledged to Poland. Great Britain was duty-bound to honour its pledge to Greece, although the amount of assistance necessary to satisfy this obligation was debatable. This guarantee had originally been an Anglo-French pledge, but after the defection of France, Great Britain was forced to shoulder this responsibility by herself. 'From the political point of view', Wavell wrote later:

> . . . we secured obvious advantages. By supporting our ally Greece, we encouraged others to resist, for instance, Turkey and Yugoslavia. It would help to convince the USA and the rest of the world that we meant to fight it out to the end, and would raise our prestige.[43]

The importance of public opinion in the United States cannot be overestimated, since even though the Lend-Lease Bill had been passed in the House of Representatives, it was expected to face opposition in the Senate, which it also had to pass before being signed into law by the President.

It is interesting to note that Wavell's dilemma at this time was similar to the one he faced in 1910, when, it will be remembered, he wrote a military history paper in his second year at the Staff College. Wavell wrote his paper in accordance with the philosophy of the incumbent Commandant, Henry Wilson, who was 'primarily interested in the highest levels of staff work where military and political considerations interacted'.[44] But before Wavell's essay was evaluated completely, Wilson was replaced by 'Wully' Robertson, who read the paper and, possessing a different opinion of the relationship between political and military factors, adjured Wavell that 'The discussion of questions of policy and political matters leads to no practical result, nor benefit of any kind to the soldier, nor is it his business.'[45] The Great War would later show Robertson (then C I G S) that, at 'the highest levels', political and military considerations are interrelated.

Eden considered the political point of view to be synonymous with the ethical line of approach, and stated forcefully that 'Britain has never regarded her treaties as scraps of paper: her word remains her bond. If therefore Greece called on Britain for help, the latter was ethically bound to send all the help she could spare.'[46] He also stressed that if Great Britain failed to live up to its guarantee to Greece, the affect on public opinion, especially in the United States, 'must be deplorable'.[47]

As alluded to earlier, the American envoy Donovan exerted a considerable amount of influence on Wavell, which helps to account for Wavell's rapid change of attitude after 12 February 1941 in favour of assistance to Greece. In addition to their first meeting on 8 January 1941, Donovan dined with Wavell on 12 January, before Wavell departed for Athens the next morning. Wavell and Donovan were both staying at the British Legation in Athens on 15 January, and they had dinner together that evening as well as a meeting the following night, and an interview early in the morning of 17 January, prior to Wavell's return to Cairo.[48] A more substantial meeting was held on 8 February, during which Donovan gave Wavell and Longmore his impressions of the Middle East situation, based upon what he had seen to date in his Mediterranean mission. Donovan's British Army escort officer, Colonel (later Brigadier) Vivian Dykes, attended this meeting and recorded:

> [Donovan] put over very well his idea of looking at the Mediterranean not as an east-west corridor, but as a no-man's land between two opposing fronts. The north-south conception seemed to strike Wavell very forcibly, and he was clearly impressed by [Donovan's] insistence on the need for keeping a foothold in the Balkans.[49]

Two days later Donovan again met with Wavell, 'who was apparently most cordial and told him [Donovan] that he had given them all a great mental stimulus in GHQ by his fresh way of looking at the problem'.[50]

Donovan thus influenced Wavell to favour aid to Greece not only by stressing the importance of American public opinion, but also by reinforcing Wavell's commitment to a forward defensive posture in the Balkans. 'Critics of Wavell', Lord Wilson observed in 1989,

> . . . have ignored the immense strategic importance of the northern part of the Middle East. Looking further ahead, control of Iraq and Syria would have given Hitler access to the Russian oilfields in the Caucasus by the backdoor instead of having to fight at Stalingrad.[51]

Wavell wrote later that 'it was worth while to take considerable risks to maintain a hold on the northern shores of the Eastern Mediterranean'.[52] From the military point of view, Wavell was convinced that he needed to fight the enemy as far forward as possible.

Even though omniscient hindsight has revealed that Rommel landed at Tripoli on 12 February 1941, this was not immediately known in Cairo or London. Although Whitehall had received, as early as 9 February, via Ultra, intimations of the movement of convoys between Naples and Tripoli carrying German troops, this information was discounted and, on 15 February, the convoys and increased German transport aircraft flights were thought to be associated with the evacuation from North Africa. The first confirmation of the arrival of German troops in Libya occurred when a British patrol made contact with German armoured cars at El Agheila on 22 February, and when an aerial reconnaissance plane sighted '8-wheeled armoured cars, almost certainly German and very probably manned by Germans'.[53] (It was not until 9 March 1941 that the commander of the 'German Africa Corps' was identified even tentatively as 'Generalleutnant Rommel'). It was a fateful day, as will be seen, for the fortunes of Wavell and his Middle East Command.

During this period, Wavell was, as he later wrote, 'working almost entirely in the dark as to the possibility of German formations being sent to Libya, and on the whole the balance of our information was against any such troops having been sent or being on their way to Libya'.[54] Wavell predicted realistically that German troops would be sent eventually, and estimated that it would be at least two months after their landing at Tripoli before they could undertake a 'serious offensive' against Cyrenaica. Accordingly, he believed there would be no significant threat to British forces there before May at the earliest,[55] and that it would therefore be safe to position only skeletal forces – one armoured brigade and the partially trained and equipped 9th Australian Division – to secure the 'western flank' at Benghazi. In taking this calculated risk, Wavell believed that the Italian East African Empire would be liquidated before or by May, and he would be able to withdraw at least one experienced Indian division from that theatre to reinforce the troops in Cyrenaica.

On 12 February 1941, Wavell had discussions with the visiting Australian Prime Minister RG Menzies about the general proposal to offer a force to

Greece, and the General informed Churchill he hoped to be 'able to improve on [the available reserve situation] especially if Australian Government will give me certain latitude as regards use of their troops. I have already spoken to Menzies about this and he was very ready to agree to what I suggest.'[56] This episode is illustrative of one of the other difficult and complex demands forced upon Wavell as the commander of a multi-national force, one which none of his successors would have to face as part of their military responsibilities. The Dominion contingents, particularly those from Australia and New Zealand (commanded by Blamey and Freyberg, respectively), each had a charter outlining the authority and responsibility of its commander, how the force could be employed, and in the case of the former,

> (a) The Force to be recognised as an Australian force under its own Commander, who will have a direct responsibility to the Commonwealth Government with the right to communicate direct with that Government. No part of the Force to be detached or employed apart from the Force without his consent.
>
> Questions of policy regarding the employment of the Force to be decided by the United Kingdom and Commonwealth Governments, in consultation; except that, in an emergency, the Commander of the Force may, at his discretion, take a decision on such a question, informing the Commonwealth Government that he is so doing.[57]

The details of the controversy surrounding Commonwealth, or Dominion, consultation in the decision-making process of the Greek campaign are outside the purview of this study.

Wavell decided that the force he would send to Greece would be composed of the 1st Armoured Brigade; the New Zealand Division; Headquarters, I Australian Corps; the 6th and 7th Australian Divisions; and the Independent Polish Brigade Group, known collectively as 'Lustre Force'. Christopher Buckley noted accurately that 'Wavell had to perform some intricate jugglery to produce even the modest contingent to which we had pledged ourselves for Greece.'[58] The last two units were still incomplete in equipment and were scheduled to be transported to Greece during the last phases of the movement. On 17 February 1941, Wavell told Freyberg that the New Zealand Division was to be the advance guard of an 'Imperial force' to be sent to Greece. Thus Wavell had determined to send a force there while Eden and Dill were still on their way to Cairo. The exact operational details were still undecided, although it appears that Wavell had decided it was more feasible to defend along the Aliakhmon Line rather than attempt to safeguard Salonika, because he told Freyberg that the New Zealanders would:

> . . . disembark at Piraeus or Volos, thence moving by road and rail to take up a line which he [Wavell] understood had already been dug along the mountains of Macedonia. The Australians were to take over this line and the NZ Div. was

to go into Force Reserve ready to operate north should there be any threat from
Monastir.[59]

Freyberg was later criticised for not questioning Wavell's directive, but he
afterwards stated:

> The decision to go to Greece was taken on a level we could not touch. . . . I was
> never in a position to make a well informed and responsible judgment. . . .
> Wavell told me our Government agreed. . . . Wavell had established the right
> to deal direct with the New Zealand Government [thought Freyberg erroneous-
> ly], without letting me know what was happening. . . . we should have cabled
> them.[60]

There is no contemporary evidence that Freyberg had any qualms about
Wavell's directive for the New Zealand Division to be sent to Greece.

Also on 17 February 1941, Wavell committed to paper his thoughts
regarding the courses of action available pertaining to the deployment of a
force to Greece. This candid appreciation reveals Wavell's innermost quan-
daries and hesitations over this project. One is struck with the impression
that writing this paper provided Wavell with the opportunity to argue with
himself the pros and cons of this crucial decision, and by the time this drill
had been completed, Wavell had exorcised any vestiges of self-doubt, as
suggested by Benson's explanation on page 139, Wavell introduced his
paper by observing that:

> The problem of our intervention in the Balkans is a most complicated one since
> many political as well as military factors are involved, and the time and space
> calculation is a very delicate one. Owing to the political hesitations of our Greek
> and Turkish allies, to say nothing of the Yugo-Slavs, we have been placed in a
> most difficult situation.[61]

Wavell continued that, 'Apart from purely military objectives, the entry of
our troops into the Balkan theatre would have as its object to keep Greece in
the field, to encourage Turkey to fulfill her treaty obligations to us, and
Yugoslavia to resist German domination.'[62] While recognising the insepara-
bility of the political and military factors in arriving at a decision, Wavell
deduced that three possible courses of action existed:

  ▷ A very bold and dangerous line of action – the attempt to secure
      Salonika.
  ▷ A compromise line of action – to send to Greece, or make prep-
      arations to send to Greece, sufficient forces to assist them to hold
      the Aliakhmon line, or
  ▷ A negative line of action – to resign ourselves to the probable loss of
      any footing or influence in the Balkan Peninsula.[63]

Wavell possessed no illusions as to the difficulties of sending a force to

Greece and of the considerable risk which would have to be taken, and advocated realistically the 'compromise line of action'.

Wavell's Director of Military Intelligence, Brigadier Shearer, had misgivings over the feasibility of this proposed operation, which he included in an appreciation entitled 'German Intentions in South-East Europe and in North Africa', also written on 17 February 1941. He was not, however, as vociferously opposed to this expedition as he later wanted people to believe, as de Guingand recognised when he observed that 'The DMI, Brigadier Shearer, did produce a paper drawing attention to the great dangers of this campaign in view of the German resources and methods.'[64] The gist of Shearer's analysis, presupposing that the British would land at Salonika, was that the Germans had devised 'a clever and opportune plan' to force the British to dissipate their forces, which would prevent the British from clearing the Axis forces out of North Africa and, 'to cause a dispersion of [British] forces with the object of delivering us in Macedonia a military blow that will greatly weaken our forces and our prestige in the Near and Middle East'.[65] Once the British force in North Africa was weakened, posited Shearer, the Germans would attack from Libya with the ultimate goal of seizing the Suez Canal. Shearer did concede, however, that:

> If, therefore, we are to undertake the support of Greece at all at the present stage, I suggest our only chance is to try and secure their consent to a landing at Pyraeus [sic] with an advanced base at Volos. This might catch Germany in two minds and enable us to reach the Aliakmon [sic] position before she decided finally to risk Turkish intervention and the deterioration of her situation vis-à-vis Yugoslavia by attempting an invasion of Northern Greece.[66]

Later, in a row with Fergusson about the campaign, in which he threatened to sue him for libel, Shearer failed to mention that he had believed the effort to hold the Aliakhmon Line – the plan eventually adopted – had a chance of success.

On the morning of 18 February 1941, Wavell explained to Blamey the composition of 'Lustre Force' and its role in the probable operations in Greece. Blamey responded that, in accordance with his charter, the plan for intervention in Greece would have to be referred to Australia. Wavell allayed some of Blamey's misgivings, however, by stating that 'he had discussed the possibility of such an operation with the Prime Minister of Australia',[67] Menzies, on 12 February. After this conference Blamey told his Brigadier General Staff (later Lieutenant General Sir) Sydney Rowell, that 'he didn't like the prospect',[68] but apparently did nothing else for the time being to inform his superiors of his trepidation. Other accounts emphasise Blamey's later vehement complaints that 'the Greek expedition hadn't a dog's chance from the start . . . The Greek plan was a bad one and our plan to support them was equally bad',[69] but, as David Horner has pointed out, if Blamey had really felt that way at the time, 'then surely he would have made his views known to someone in the Australian government'.[70]

The Eden-Dill party, which included RCS Stevenson, Eden's Principal Private Secretary; Pierson Dixon, Southern Department, Foreign Office; and Brigadier AWS Mallaby, DDMO(O), the War Office, had, as noted earlier, begun its trip to Cairo on 12 February 1941. The journey was delayed by bad weather, and while weather-bound at Plymouth on 13 February, Dixon prepared a report in which he argued 'that we ought not to send help to Greece, but to reserve it for the use of the Turks. [He] also suggested that we ought to profit by the good going and push on to Tripoli.'[71] As might be expected, Dixon's report was not well received.

Eden had been given 'sealed orders' by the Prime Minister before he departed England, with an injunction that he could not open them until he had left England. Accordingly, Eden opened his instructions on 15 February in Gibraltar. Written by Churchill, this 'Note for the Foreign Secretary' declared that 'the Foreign Secretary will represent His Majesty's Government in all matters diplomatic and military'. It stated further:

> His principal object will be the sending of speedy succour to Greece. For this purpose he will initiate any action as he may think necessary with the C-in-C of the Middle East, with the Egyptian Government and with the Governments of Greece, Yugoslavia and Turkey.[72]

Interestingly, Dill was designated as the mission's military adviser, and a number of detailed instructions were included, again usurping the authority and prerogative of Wavell, the theatre military commander. Eden was tasked, among other items, to ascertain 'the minimum garrison that can hold the western frontier of Libya', and of the greatest significance, he was charged with 'The formation in the Delta of the strongest and best equipped force in divisional or brigade organisations which can be despatched to Greece at the earliest moment.' Churchill summed up Eden's responsibilities as to 'gather together all the threads, and propose continuously the best solutions for our difficulties, and not to be deterred from acting upon his own authority if the urgency is too great to allow reference home'. Eden was thus given by Churchill plenary powers, a veritable *carte blanche*, in coordinating and ensuring British assistance to Greece. By doing so, the Prime Minister also deftly distanced himself from the decision he had already made, that of intervening in Greece, knowing that his zealous underling would spare no efforts in negotiating and finalising all arrangements for British aid to the Balkans. Churchill's directive also reinforces strongly the impression that the decision to assist Greece had previously been made by Churchill, with the formal approval of the Cabinet, prior to the departure of the Eden-Dill mission. In fact, in April 1941 Dill wrote accurately that 'the general policy had been settled before the S of S [Secretary of State, Eden] left London, . . .'[73]

Late on 18 February, Eden cabled Wavell with a summary of his instructions from the Prime Minister, and charged the General to 'examine military implications of policy in preparation for discussion on my arrival in Cairo'.[74] Thus possessing explicit knowledge of Eden's mission and undoubtedly influenced by it, Wavell wrote a revised appreciation of the situation, partly in response to Shearer's 17 February assessment of 'German Intentions in South-East Europe and in North Africa'. Wavell's 19 February appreciation gained a fair degree of notoriety since it was headed by one of Wavell's favourite quotations (from General Wolfe): 'War is an option of difficulties.' Wavell began by conceding partially to Shearer's argument:

> 1. I quite agree that by sending a force into the Balkans, and especially by attempting to cover Salonika, we shall be taking considerable risks. We are risking failure and a military defeat, we shall be exposing a considerable portion of our force to the dangers of an unhealthy climate, we are becoming involved in a commitment which may cause us a considerable wastage of shipping that we can so ill afford, and we shall have to weaken our power in Cyrenaica to resist an enemy counter attack.[75]

He then elaborated upon the favourable aspects of assisting Greece:

> 2. On the other hand, if we are successful in saving Salonika, we shall put new heart into Greece and into the other Balkan peoples, Turkey and Yugoslavia; we may administer a military check to the Germans and force them to fight on a front where they hope to attain their aims by peaceful penetration and threats. We are making it much more difficult for them. . . .[76]

The deleterious impact on British prestige if no action was taken was then addressed, as were the prospective difficulties faced by the Germans if they would attack. Wavell then refuted Shearer's contentions about the Germans attempting to lure the British into the Balkans and the risk of a German/ Italian counterattack in Cyrenaica. 'To sum up', he concluded:

> . . . we have a difficult choice, but I think we are more likely to be playing the enemy's game by remaining inactive than by taking action in the Balkans. Provided that conversations with the Greeks show that there is a good chance of establishing a front against the Germans with our assistance, I think we should take it.[77]

With his eyes open to the dangers involved, and after receiving an appreciation from his senior intelligence officer – although neither the Middle East Joint nor Army planners were asked to study the feasibility of the project – Wavell understood clearly the necessity for British assistance to Greece.

That same afternoon Wavell had a long talk with his old friend and colleague, Lieutenant General Sir James Marshall-Cornwall, then serving as Head of the British Liaison Staff to Turkey. Marshall-Cornwall later wrote that:

> Wavell then told me, obviously with a heavy heart, that he had decided to send the expeditionary force to Greece. I was horrified and said I was sure that it was

a gamble which could only lead to military disaster. Archie replied slowly, 'Possibly, but strategy is only the handmaid of policy, and here political considerations must come first. The policy of our Government is to build up a Balkan front.'[78]

Donovan, meanwhile, on the verge of completing his Mediterranean mission, was involved in writing an after-action report on the activities and results of his fact-finding tour. Dykes took a draft copy of this report to Wavell in the evening of 19 February 1941, at which time, as Dykes recorded,

> Wavell showed me a paper [undoubtedly the paper Wavell had written earlier that day] from which it was clear that he had made up his mind to leap in as soon as possible . . ., fearing otherwise that we should be forestalled. He showed the same paper to [Donovan], who dined with him alone that night. I think his judgment had been considerably influenced by [Donovan's] advocacy, as it was a very finely balanced question to decide.[79]

There seems to be little doubt that Donovan's persistent pro-intervention posture, as a representative of the United States, influenced significantly Wavell's decision to send a force to Greece.

Later in the evening of 19 February 1941, Eden and Dill arrived belatedly in Cairo, in Wavell's words 'five valuable days being lost at a critical time'.[80] Both Eden and Dill knew that Wavell had been opposed personally to intervention in Greece, and were apprehensive as to the type of reception they would receive from him. When Wavell met them upon their arrival, he remarked dourly, 'You have been a long time coming.'[81] Eden later remembered that,

> We felt this reproach rather unjust and murmured our explanation. He nodded and then came the comment: 'As you were so long I felt I had to get started, and I have begun the concentration for a move of troops to Greece.' Dill and I exchanged a glance, relieved that Wavell's mind was apparently in tune with our instructions.[82]

Thus, as has been demonstrated, from 12–19 February 1941 Wavell's attitude over intervention in Greece evolved, due to a myriad of factors, from adamant opposition to loyal advocacy.

When Churchill halted Wavell's North African advance on 12 February, the Prime Minister had no clear cut idea as to where in the Balkans Wavell was to send his expedition. Churchill intentionally sent Eden and Dill to the Middle East to develop the politico-military basis for a Balkan strategy. In addition, during this crucial period, His Majesty's Government's leading diplomatic and Army advisers were thousands of miles away from Whitehall, thus permitting Churchill further to consolidate his authority by assuming temporarily the portfolio of Foreign Secretary and eliminating the considered and honest criticisms of the Chief of the Imperial General Staff.

The arrival of Eden and Dill in Cairo also served as a harbinger of the tremendous and ever-increasing pressures and burdens which would fall on Wavell's shoulders from that time forward until the end of his command. The decision to intervene in Greece served as the catalyst for the fall of a series of metaphorical dominoes, which not only added to Wavell's responsibilities, but triggered from London a terse and anxious barrage of demanding cablegrams which were, on many occasions, out of touch with a realistic appreciation of conditions and the situation in the Middle East. Before Greece, Wavell was the master of his destiny, in command of events; after the decision was made to intervene there, events were to command Wavell and force him into the unenviable position of being compelled to react against external threats and enemies.

Even though Eden and Dill arrived in Cairo late on 19 February 1941, they still met with Donovan that evening. Donovan, strongly in favour of forming a Balkan front and sending aid to Greece, emphasised, in addition to Great Britain's moral responsibility, the strategic necessity of keeping the Mediterranean lines of communication open. The American envoy also stressed the importance of establishing a bridgehead in Europe and upsetting the plans of the Germans.

The following day, Donovan completed his trip report, encapsulating his views and conclusions, and besought the President to 'tender his good offices in their forming a Balkan barrier against Germany, so organized that the benefits of the Lease and Loan Bill would be of real value.'[83] Donovan was convinced, as he had been for weeks, that the Balkans offered perhaps the only place for a defeat of the Germans, and for that reason the British must retain a foothold there and form a Balkan alliance with Greece, Turkey, and Yugoslavia.[84]

Eden and Dill met with the three Middle East Commanders-in-Chief on the morning of 20 February to discuss the question of intervention in Greece. No minutes were kept of this discussion, although Eden recorded in his diary that 'There was agreement upon utmost help to Greece at earliest possible moment.'[85] Another meeting was held that night; those present included Lampson, Smith, the Heads of the British Liaison Staff to Turkey and the British Military Mission to Greece. Eden highlighted the decision made at the morning conference, stating that contact should be made with the Greek Government at the earliest opportunity. The decision made meant that there would be little or nothing to spare for the Turks. At this meeting it was 'unanimously agreed that it would be fatal for us to divide our effort, and that we must for the present concentrate on giving assistance to Greece'.[86]

Donovan met with Dill alone in the evening of the same day and had a long discussion about Balkan policy. Dykes was convinced Donovan 'put a good deal of stiffening into Dill in the course of it'.[87] The American's ardent rhetoric, in addition to the views expressed at the earlier conferences, convinced the pro-Turkish Dill that there was a fair military chance of holding a line in northern Greece successfully if action was taken at the earliest opportunity. 'I have concluded', Dill cabled to London on 21 February, 'that our only chance of preventing the Balkans being devoured piecemeal is to go to Greece with all that we can find as soon as it can be done. The risks are admittedly considerable but inaction in my view would be fatal.'[88]

On 21 February, additional meetings were held with Eden and Dill and the three Commanders-in-Chief. There was still concern over the approach to be taken with the Turks, and the discussions generally confirmed the idea that the best course of action would be to persuade the Turks to declare war on Germany, and then provide the maximum assistance to Greece.

Dill later wrote that the conferences on 20 and 21 February 1941 provided 'an opportunity . . . of condeming [sic] the project as unsound for military reasons'.[89] This comment indicates that, as the senior uniformed official and the mission's 'military adviser', if Dill had permitted one of the three Middle East Commanders-in-Chief to 'condemn' the project in contravention of his own opinion, which it appears they could have, he would have divested himself of that position and abrogated his responsibility as decision-maker for the Army and the mission's military adviser. Dill summarised 'The Military Appreciation of the Possibility of Sending Forces to Greece', and recorded that while 'the risks . . . were clearly seen', unanimous agreement was reached to make an offer to the Greeks to send forces at once if the Greek Government would accept them and if 'a sound military plan could be agreed upon with the Greeks as to the line to be held'.[90]

After these two days of meetings, Dixon chronicled that 'the Commanders-in-Chief showed themselves surprisingly enthusiastic for an expedition to Greece'.[91] Eden wired to London on 21 February 1941 that 'We are agreed we should do everything in our power to bring the fullest measure of help to Greeks at earliest possible moment.' In the same message the Foreign Secretary informed Churchill that:

> Cyrenaica will be garrisoned by one of the less trained and equipped Australian divisions, Indian motor brigade at present under training and one armoured brigade group which represents all remaining at present of 7th Armoured Division. You will remember that this armoured division was never at full strength.[92]

Looking ahead, this message was of singular importance, since it confirms that Churchill was in fact aware of the strength and state of forces which would garrison the 'western flank' of Cyrenaica.

With Churchill's subterfuge – the Eden-Dill mission – successfully in operation and supporting strongly, with the unanimity of the three Middle East Commanders-in-Chief in Cairo over intervention in Greece, his own ardour, perhaps expectedly, began to wane. On 20 February, Churchill told the War Cabinet he thought that it 'was unlikely that it would be possible for a large British force to get [to Greece] before the Germans'.[93] The next day, Churchill sent a message to Eden, which crossed with the aforementioned cable from Cairo, stating emphatically: 'Do not consider yourselves obligated to a Greek enterprise if in your hearts you feel it will only be another Norwegian fiasco. If no good plan can be made, please say so.'[94] But the next, and concluding, sentence contradicted this admonition and offered encouragement: 'But of course you know how valuable success would be.'

After the receipt of the Prime Minister's telegram, Eden despatched to London on 21 February 1941 the final version of a message which had been drafted the night before. It included:

> 3. As regards general prospects of a Greek campaign, it is, of course, a gamble to send forces to the mainland of Europe to fight Germans at this time. No one can give a guarantee of success, *but when we discussed this matter in London we were prepared to run the risk of failure, thinking it is better to suffer with the Greeks than to make no attempt to help them.* That is the conviction we all hold here. Moreover, though campaign is a daring venture, we are not without hope that it might succeed to the extent of halting the Germans before they overrun all Greece.[95]

Eden thus informed Churchill of the risk involved in intervention, but also reminded him of previous discussions in London in which the Prime Minister and Foreign Secretary 'were prepared to run the risk of failure'.

The decision to assist Greece had been deferred ostensibly until the British could confer with the Greeks. To achieve that goal, a British delegation flew from Cairo to Athens on 22 February 1941. The group consisted of Eden, Dill, Wavell, Longmore, and a number of staff officers, including de Guingand. The two planes stopped to refuel at El Adem, where the party met Wilson, who had been directed by Wavell the night before to meet them there, since in all probability Wilson would be designated to command any force sent to Greece.

Since the meetings were to be held under the most secret conditions, Dill and Wavell were dressed in unusual raiment: Dill, who had no mufti, wore a mackintosh and a black hat, and Wavell wore a brown lounge suit. After their arrival in Athens, the party was driven to the Royal Palace at Tatoi. Before tea, Wavell was alone with Sir Michael Palairet, the British Minister in Athens and an unfailing advocate of British assistance to Greece; Harold Caccia (now Lord Caccia), First Secretary at the British Legation; and Colonel Jasper Blunt, the British Military Attaché. The informal conversations among that group, which have hitherto been undisclosed, are of indispensable significance in solving the riddle of why Wavell favoured intervention in Greece.

Palairet initially briefed Wavell that after the death of Metaxas the political situation in Athens had changed, and that the King – King George

of the Hellenes – would actually make the decision to accept or refuse
British aid. It would be Wavell's responsibility to persuade the King to
accept such British assistance. Wavell was well known even in Athens
(which he had visited in January 1941) for his taciturnity, and as Lord
Caccia has recently recalled, Palairet's briefing:

> . . . triggered it, and [Wavell] held forth, and said, well, he'd have to remind us
> that the situation in Greece was not unlike that in North Africa; that is to say
> the Qattara Depression constrained the area of operations possible for an
> enemy force coming to attack. And therefore the question was not really how
> many divisions could [the enemy] deploy, but if they could all be brought into
> action at once; but what was possible in the narrow strip of land – in the case of
> Greece between the mountains and the sea [and the mountains themselves] as
> in the Western Desert between the Qattara Depression and the sea. And
> therefore you had to look at that rather than the totality of reserves on either
> side.[96]

Caccia was convinced that it was unlikely that Wavell would have spoken
with such vigour if he had not totally believed in what he was saying.[97] De
Guingand later stated, in relation to Wavell's expression of the possibilities
of success of British intervention in Greece, that 'to this day I cannot see
any sound military reason for Wavell acting as he did';[98] Belchem wondered
'whether [Wavell] needed his head examined'.[99]

Wavell was fully aware of the friendly and opposing troop densities and
dispositions: Italy had the equivalent of over thirty divisions in Albania;
Bulgaria, who might collaborate with the Axis, had fourteen divisions, of
which three-quarters were mobilised at the time (although these forces
would probably be occupied guarding the Turkish and Yugoslav frontiers);
and Germany had twenty divisions in Rumania. The mountainous terrain
of northern Greece would canalise an attacking enemy, as Wavell had
alluded, and Papagos estimated that the Germans could deploy a maximum
of eight divisions only in their initial onslaught. After an analysis of possible
defensive positions, it was realised that the Aliakhmon Line, a naturally
strong position about seventy miles long which ran along the line of hills
west of the Vardar River and in part followed the Aliakhmon River, offered
the best chance of success against an attack. The Metaxas and Strimon
Lines, both covering Salonika, were discounted because Yugoslavia could
not be counted upon as an ally.

At the second of the four meetings held at Tatoi on 22 February 1941, it
was decided that the Greeks would withdraw units from Thrace and
Macedonia, so that 'when the withdrawal was complete, the Greeks would
have 35 battalions [the equivalent of almost four divisions] on the Aliakhmon
line, plus one division (motorised) at Larissa, and possibly one more in
reserve'.[100] Thus, with almost five, maybe six, Greek divisions, potentially
joined by three British (Dominion) divisions, an armoured brigade, and a

separate brigade – or a total of almost nine or ten divisions – in a highly
defensible position (Papagos estimated that this line could be held with a
minimum of five well-equipped divisions), it would have been militarily
feasible for this force to defend successfully against a canalised German
force of up to eight divisions. This was the point Wavell was emphasising
during his discussion with Palairet, Caccia, and Blunt.

At the fourth meeting held late that night Wavell stated that, considering
the uncertainty of the attitudes of the Yugoslavs and the Turks, the only
sound course of action – from a military point of view – was that the
Anglo-Greek force should establish itself in as great strength and as soon as
possible on the Aliakhmon Line. This confirmed what Wavell had earlier
written in his notes at the conference:

> Line to be held depends largely on Yugoslav attitude. If Germans attack,
> offensive operations in Albania must stop. We must therefore establish a line
> behind which Albanian front can withdraw. If Y.S. [Yugoslavs] do not play,
> Aliakhmon is only possible line and all troops in E. Macedonia must be
> withdrawn to it.[101]

It was recognised that the main danger to the Aliakhmon Line was its
exposed left flank in the event of the Germans invading Yugoslavia advancing towards the Monastir Gap, a natural avenue of approach into northern
Greece. But earlier that day Wavell had told the group, that included
Caccia, that the Yugoslavs (who had sixteen infantry divisions, reminiscent
of the Serbs who had conducted a remarkably brave defence of Belgrade in
the First World War), would at least delay any invader in their mountainous terrain. Wavell also based his plan on promised air reinforcements
which would come to the Middle East via Malta and the recently-
established Takoradi route; these replacements failed to materialise.

On 22 February 1941, the die was cast with the Greeks, to intervene and
attempt to assist them in saving their homeland against an expected
German attack. On the same day, the British, for the first time, encountered
a German patrol in Libya. Seen in juxtaposition, these were ominous signs.

The mission and the three Commanders-in-Chief returned to Cairo on 23
February; de Guingand was tasked by Wavell to stay behind 'and carry out
a reconnaissance of the Aliakhmon position with the Greeks'.[102] Before
leaving Athens, Eden wired Churchill that 'We are all convinced that we
have chosen the right course and, as the eleventh hour has already struck,
felt sure that you would not wish us to delay for detailed reference home.
The risks are great, but there is a chance of success.'[103]

The results of the Tatoi meetings, as relayed to London by Eden, and his
recommendation to 'do everything in our power to bring the fullest
measure of help to Greeks at earliest moment', were scheduled to be discussed by the War Cabinet on 24 February 1941. At that meeting, Churchill
stressed that Wavell 'was in favour of the operation, although he was

inclined to understatement, and so far had always promised less than he had performed, and was a man who wished to be better than his word';[104] the fact that Dill had also endorsed the expedition, according to the Prime Minister, should also carry great weight.

The Chiefs of Staff had also 'considered very earnestly', from the military point of view, whether it was 'correct to endorse' Eden's offer to the Greeks. Pound, Portal, and Haining stressed initially – shifting the onus of responsibility to their colleagues in Cairo – that:

> It goes without saying that the expedition must be a gamble, but our representatives on the spot, after conference with the Greeks, and full examination of the Greek plan, evidently think there is a reasonable prospect of successfully holding up a German advance. We feel that we must accept their opinion.[105]

After assessing the advantages and disadvantages of intervention in Greece, this report also noted the political aspects of the proposal, with the Chiefs of Staff concluding that:

> The possible military advantages to be derived from going to the help of Greece are considerable, though their achievement is doubtful and the risks of failure are serious, the disadvantages of leaving Greece to her fate will be certain and far reaching. Even the complete failure of an honourable attempt to help Greece need not be disastrous to our future ability to defeat Germany. A weighty consideration in favour of going to Greece is to make the Germans fight for what they want instead of obtaining it by default. On balance we think that the enterprise should go forward.[106]

Menzies, who attended the meeting, was shocked at the lack of discussion at the session where this momentous endorsement of Eden's recommendation was purportedly made. The Australian Prime Minister recorded Churchill's role in opening the discussion, casting great light on the normal *modus operandi* of the War Cabinet:

> 'You have read your file, gentlemen . . . The arguments are clear on each side. *I favour the project.*' And then around the table, nobody more than three or four sentences. Does this denote the great clarity and directness of mind in *all* these ministers, or has Winston taken *charge* of them, as the one man whom the public regard as indispensable. There may be a good deal in this business of *building yourself up* with the public by base acts so that you can really control a Cabinet.[107]

This was Menzies's first experience of the War Cabinet, and according to Day, 'it not only confirmed his view of Churchill as the virtual dictator, but left him as well with a mostly poor opinion of Churchill's colleagues.'[108] Even though Menzies had doubts about going to Greece, he voted for the proposal. Armed with the mandate he needed, Churchill cabled to Eden that 'Decision was unanimous in the sense you desire, . . . Therefore while being under no illusions, we all send you the order "Full Steam Ahead."'[109]

Churchill sent this message even though the Vice Chief of the Imperial General Staff had been apprised that day by the War Office's Director of Military Intelligence that 'we must be prepared to face the loss of all forces sent to Greece'.[110] It is highly probable that the Prime Minister received the same information.

It seems extraordinary that at no time throughout these deliberations did the inadequacy of the air support available for an expeditionary force for Greece become a major issue. Nor, apparently, did the withdrawal of air squadrons from the Western Desert, with all the subsequent effect this would have upon Wavell's ability to guard his western flank, ever arise. Yet, as the story of the coming months will show, British weakness in the air would prove a major factor in the disasters which would follow in Greece, Crete and Cyrenaica – a weakness which Wavell himself would identify later and would cost Longmore his appointment. Only on 6 March did Eden even mention the subject in any of his signals to Churchill. But even that rather feeble prod should have alerted the Chiefs of Staff to the grave danger.

While Eden and Dill travelled to meet with the Turks, Wavell was free to continue the planning and execution of the movement of forces to Greece and other operations. The offensives in Italian East Africa were progressing exceedingly well and the 6th (British) Division was training to conduct Operation 'Cordite' (the seizure of Rhodes), but a commando raid on the Dodecanese island of Castellorizo (Operation 'Abstention') on the night of 24 February 1941 met with failure.

Eden and Dill were unable to persuade the Turks, who had concluded a non-aggression pact with Bulgaria on 17 February 1941, to declare war on Germany, but they did receive Turkish acquiescence in the despatch of British troops to Greece. A discouraging situation was made even worse on 1 March when the Germans crossed the Danube and entered Bulgaria, and the Bulgarian President decided to adhere to the Tripartite Pact.

After their discussions with the Turks, Eden and Dill returned to Athens on 2 March, only to discover that Papagos had not withdrawn Greek troops from Macedonia to the Aliakhmon Line as promised. This confusing episode has been attributed to Papagos's misunderstanding that the decision to withdraw depended on definite news of Yugoslavia's position; Wavell believed that Papagos believed the redeployment of troops 'to be impossible in view of German entry into Bulgaria, since the troops might be attacked while in the process of withdrawal'.[111] Rumours of a renewed Italian offensive in Albania prevented Papagos from removing troops from that front. It appears that the Greek general, who had initially been reluctant to leave Salonika unprotected, now felt that the threat to the important port was so great that he would not leave it vulnerable.

In any event, Eden summoned Wavell back to Athens for renewed talks with the Greeks. Before leaving Cairo, Wavell assessed the enemy's capabilities and potential courses of action. In his cable to the War Office, in which he again enumerated the composition of the force garrisoning Cyrenaica, Wavell forecast that 'Eventually two German Divisions might be employed in a large-scale attack. . . . Shipping risks, difficulty of communications, and the approach of hot weather make it unlikely that such an attack could develop before the end of the summer.'[112]

Due to the urgency of the situation, since the first body of combat troops was scheduled to depart Egypt on 5 March 1941, three days of excruciating talks were held with the Greeks from 2 to 4 March, which, according to Eden, 'at times resembled the haggling of an oriental bazaar'.[113] Wavell, accompanied by Wilson, both travelling incognito (Wilson stayed at the British Legation under the assumed name of 'Mr. Watt'; his son was known as 'Mr. Watson'), attended meetings on 3 and 4 March. In the discussions which Wavell attended, he stated adamantly that only the defence of the Aliakhmon Line held forth a reasonable chance of success, given the uncertainty of Yugoslavia's position. Dill and Papagos, however, dominated the proceedings, and when it appeared an impasse to the resolution of the problem had been encountered, Dill stated 'that the matter must be referred to the Secretary of State'.[114] The following evening Eden – described by some as mercurial and 'highly strung' – accepted a compromise solution, which was the Greek offer of two divisions and twenty-three battalions and one motorised division to concentrate on the Aliakhmon Line. 'The military risks were throughout seen', recorded Dill the following month,

> . . . and given full weight. Nevertheless, opinion was at the outset unanimous that we should aid Greece by the despatch of forces, and the military authorities concerned were all agreed that even in the altered circumstances of the second visit to Athens the risks must be accepted and the plan had still a reasonable chance of success.[115]

Dill then signed an agreement with Papagos to ensure there would not be another 'misunderstanding'.

Churchill appears to have had doubts about the Greek enterprise, or at least gave the impression of such, even before he was informed of the Greek failure to withdraw to the Aliakhmon Line. On 1 March 1941, the Prime Minister informed Eden that while he was prepared to continue to support the project as long as it had a chance of success, Eden 'should ensure an escape clause for Britain in the case of the expedition facing certain defeat'.[116] Whitehall did not receive word from Eden of the altered situation in Greece until 5 March.

On that same day, Churchill considered abandoning the Greeks, telling the War Cabinet that 'we would liberate them [the Greeks] from any undertaking which they had given to us'.[117] The War Cabinet debated the decision, and on the following day the Prime Minister advised Eden that 'We do not see any reasons for expecting success except that, of course, we attach great weight to opinions of Dill and Wavell', and since cooler heads had prevailed at the War Cabinet meeting, the message included this passage:

> Loss of Greece and Balkans by no means a major catastrophe for us provided Turkey remains honest neutral. We could take 'Mandibles' [capture of the Dodecanese Islands] and consider plans for 'Influx' [attack on Sicily] or 'Tripoli.' We are advised from many quarters that our ignominious ejection from Greece would do us more harm in Spain and Vichy than the fact of submission of Balkans which with our scanty forces alone we have never been expected to prevent.[118]

During this period of ironic Government intransigence, the Eden-Dill mission members and the three Middle East Commanders-in-Chief met to consider the ramifications of Churchill's latest message. They were apparently under pressure to provide more convincing evidence of the prospects for success of the project to Whitehall. Longmore foresaw problems when the Germans discovered that troops were being shipped to Greece, and Cunningham, while concurring with Longmore 'that the decision taken at Athens was the only possible one',[119] observed that the naval situation had deteriorated over the last ten days. Wavell, who had also explained earlier to Blamey and Freyberg the additional risks involved, according to the minutes of this meeting:

> . . . remained of the opinion that provided we could get our forces into Greece, there was a good prospect of a successful encounter with the Germans. The results of success would be incalculable and might alter the whole aspect of the war.[120]

After re-examining the entire issue during that meeting, Eden cabled to Churchill that 'We are unanimously agreed that, despite the heavy commitments and grave risks which are undoubtedly involved, especially in view of our limited naval and air resources, the right decision was taken in Athens.'[121]

Connell has related the amusing incident during this stress-filled period when Eden, in the midst of a late night telegram-writing session, awakened Dill and Wavell to listen to his reasoned compositions. The weary soldiers fell asleep.[122] The following morning, Wavell walked into Longmore's office with a Lewis Carroll parody which ended: 'and Alice said – It's generals I want, not dormice.' 'A proof, if one was needed', Eden later wrote, 'that Wavell's sense of humour (and his balance) were proof to almost any strain.'[123]

General Smuts, the South African Prime Minister, had arranged as early as 28 February 1941 to travel to Cairo to discuss Middle East strategy with Eden, Dill, and Wavell. He arrived in Cairo on the afternoon of 6 March, and met with them all that evening. Smuts admitted that the British were faced with 'a grave dilemma, but ... it was too late to retreat', and emphasised that he saw 'the gravest objections to our backing out' and that 'there was a good chance of ultimate success'.[124] Smuts cabled to Churchill the following morning his adamant opinion that it was imperative for Britain to support this new front with all its strength, and 'Black as the prospect looks here at the moment, I think that it is still possible to transform this apparently promising situation for the Germans into disaster for them and from this front pave the way to victory.'[125] As encouraging as Smuts's message was, in all probability its effect was little more than to validate a decision that Churchill knew would be made – and broaden the base for subsequent blame.

Churchill had earlier informed Eden that the War Cabinet would defer making its final decision until the Secretary of State was able to review the situation and consider a revised recommendation. As noted previously, the Cairo group again endorsed its earlier decision, with the result that the War Cabinet in London approved the expedition to Greece on 7 March 1941; it could hardly have done anything different, since the first combat troops were scheduled to arrive in Greece the following day. The Prime Minister relayed to Eden that 'Cabinet decided to authorise you to proceed with the operation, and by doing so Cabinet accepts for itself the fullest responsibility.'[126] Churchill advised the American President, Roosevelt, of this decision on 10 March:

> Although it was no doubt tempting to try to push on from Benghazi to Tripoli, and we may still use considerable forces in this direction, we have felt it our duty to stand with the Greeks who have declared to us their resolve, even alone, to resist the German invader. Our Generals Wavell and Dill, who have accompanied Mr. Eden to Cairo, after heart-searching discussions with us, believe we have a good fighting chance. We are therefore sending the greater part of the Army of the Nile to Greece, and are reinforcing to the utmost possible in the air.[127]

In one month the Prime Minister's loyal and dedicated envoys had, through a series of unforeseen trials and tribulations, brought his project to fruition. Through most of the process, Churchill had tried to have it both ways: he was intent on British intervention in Greece, yet endeavoured increasingly to distance himself from the disastrous result he knew was inevitable. From the arrival of Eden and Dill in Cairo on 19 February 1941, Wavell was an unswerving advocate of assistance to Greece, not only out of loyalty to his political and military superiors and their policy, but also because he was genuinely convinced such intervention would succeed.

The chronicle of British military operations in Greece has been narrated in many sources, and only an outline of events is necessary here. Attempts to stiffen the resolve of the Yugoslavs and Turks continued throughout March 1941 as elements of 'Lustre' Force concentrated in Greece. On 25 March, the Yugoslav Government signed a pact of allegiance with the Axis, but less than forty-eight hours later a spontaneous *coup d'état* led by the armed forces overthrew the Yugoslav Government and King Peter assumed power in place of the Regent Prince Paul. Churchill noted with satisfaction that 'Here at last was one tangible result of our desperate efforts to form an Allied front in the Balkans and prevent all falling piecemeal into Hitler's power.'[128] But this 'tangible result' increased the precariousness of the British position in Greece. When Papagos had learned earlier of Yugoslav discontent, he refused a British offer of transport vehicles to help move his troops to the Aliakhmon Line. He believed the Yugoslav coup to be a vindication of the wisdom of his policy, and he hoped that his divisions which remained on the Bulgarian border would eventually link up with Yugoslav forces.

Hitler's reaction, however, was much more violent and impulsive; he declared he would 'destroy Yugoslavia as a military power and sovereign state'. Towards that end, Directive No. 25 was produced and issued to the three German armed services within twenty-four hours of the military revolt in Yugoslavia. But before the Germans could launch their land offensive, the first shots of the Balkan campaign were fired at sea.

The Germans had been pressuring the Italian Admiralty to strike the highly vulnerable British convoys transporting troops and supplies to Greece. The British interception on 25 March 1941 of German Air Force Enigma signals revealed that the Italian Navy was planning a large-scale operation. Cunningham altered convoy courses and set sail in the *Warspite* with his battlefleet after dark on 27 March. On the following day, the Battle of Matapan, 'the first important operation in the Mediterranean to be based on Sigint [signal intelligence]',[129] took place. In sum, as a result of this action, the Italian Navy lost three heavy cruisers, two large destroyers, and 2,400 officers and men, against the British loss of one aircraft with crew. Of even greater significance, this battle psychologically and physically impaired the Italian fleet to such an extent that the British fleet and convoys in the Eastern Mediterranean were never again threatened by surface attack.

As 'Lustre' Force was continuing its concentration in Greece, 'the situation in Cyrenaica,' Wavell later recorded with typical understatement, 'gave me increasing cause for anxiety'.[130] The German ability to conduct an offensive had been severely underestimated by numerous sources, in Cairo and in London, and on 24 March 1941 a reinforced German reconnaissance unit seized El Agheila. (This German attack will be examined in detail in Chapter 9.) After a short pause, Rommel continued his offensive a week later, and by the evening of 2 April was north of Agedabia. The British had planned to counterattack at that stage with their armoured forces, but due to a shortage of reinforcements it was decided to withdraw gradually and delay the enemy. Sensing his adversary's weakness, Rommel pressed his attack with the utmost audacity and forced the British back, reeling in confusion. The ease with which the Germans tore through the British defences in Cyrenaica was apparently one of the many factors in the anti-British *coup d'état* which took place in Iraq on 3 April – another incredible burden which Wavell would soon have to shoulder.

As these calamitous events were occurring in Cyrenaica, Wilson officially assumed command of the redesignated 'W' Force in Greece on 5 April 1941. He observed candidly that 'The prospect was not too cheerful and one envied the Commander who had a firm base from which to fight a campaign; ours might be described as flimsy.'[131] One reason for Wilson's comment was that shortly before assuming command he had been informed by Wavell that, due to the emergency in North Africa, the 7th Australian Division was being withdrawn from 'Lustre' and the shipment of the Polish Brigade was postponed indefinitely.

Early on 6 April 1941, Eden, in Cairo, having had a lengthy discussion with Wavell a few hours before, advised Churchill that 'The general conclusion to which we have all come is that the Italo-German effort in Cyrenaica is a major diversion well timed to precede the German attack in the Balkans.'[132] Rommel's unanticipated and impetuous attack was certainly not coordinated with any other advance, even though the Germans declared war on Yugoslavia and Greece at 5:45 am on 6 April and began their Balkan *blitzkrieg*.

Ultra intelligence, although still in an embryonic and rudimentary state, was an important factor in the British conduct of the campaign. Wavell first received Ultra on 14 March 1941, and to accelerate its timeliness of transmission, signal links were established with British Army Headquarters in Greece. It was from this source that Wilson learned on 5 April (the day he had assumed command) of the impending outbreak of hostilities scheduled for the following morning: 'GAF [German Air Force] units Arad area have instructions indicating start hostilities nought five three nought [0530] hours GMT April six.'[133] The repeated withdrawals Wilson was forced to make 'appear to have been extremely well-timed as a result of the Enigma appreciations that were being sent to him'.[134]

On 6 April, the 1st Armoured Brigade and the New Zealand Division were on the Aliakhmon Line, while the 6th Australian Division was still arriving. The Greek 12th and 20th Divisions – part of 'W' Force – were also in the line, but the third division which had been part of the Greek Central Macedonian Army, the 19th, had been transferred to Macedonia. It had become apparent to Wilson by 8 April through Ultra and other means, that Yugoslav resistance in the south was collapsing quickly and exposing the left flank of 'W' Force's position. He was obliged to shift his troops accordingly to protect the exposed sector. First contact was made with the Germans on 9 April, and three days later it was learned that the German 40th Corps had advanced through the Monastir Gap and was boldly employing tanks in what had been considered unsuitable terrain.

As the crisis continued in the Western Desert, Wavell first visited the front in Greece. He stayed at Wilson's Headquarters on the night of 11 April 1941 – the Germans had made their expected attack on the Aliakhmon Line earlier that day – and met with Blamey on the 12th. On 12 April, Wavell, in agreement with Blamey and Freyberg, made the momentous and gallant decision to reinstitute the Anzac Corps, reviving for another generation a legacy of unparalleled dedication and courage in combat from the Great War. Wavell also discussed the need for a further withdrawal with Wilson and Blamey. To prevent 'W' Force from being outflanked, and in the face of the disintegration of the Greek 12th and 20th Divisions, together with the inability of the Greeks to withdraw from Albania and the reported capitulation of numerous Yugoslav forces, the decision was made to continue to withdraw, this time to the Thermopylae Line.

Before Wavell left Athens on 13 April 1941, he discussed with de Guingand, the only readily-available member of the Middle East Joint Planning Staff, the possibility of evacuation, but admonished him 'upon pain of death' to mention this topic to a selected group only.[135] The following day the JPS completed its plans for evacuation; on 15 April, Wavell, Longmore, and Cunningham held a conference in which they 'were forced to the conclusion that the only possible course was to withdraw the British troops from Greece'.[136] The subject of evacuation was broached by Papagos – his army crumbling under the weight of the massive German onslaught – on the 16th by suggesting that the time had come for the Imperial forces to consider evacuating Greece in order to spare the devastation of the country. Wavell immediately relayed this new development to London, with Churchill responding that:

> We cannot remain in Greece against wish of Greek Commander-in-Chief and thus expose country to devastation. Wilson or Palairet should obtain endorsement by Greek Government of Papagos' request. Consequent upon this assent evacuation should proceed without, however, prejudicing any withdrawal to Thermopylae position in co-operation with the Greek Army. In the meantime all your proposed preparations for evacuation should proceed, and you will naturally try to save as much material as possible.[137]

As the British force continued its withdrawal to the Thermopylae Line, a committee of the Middle East Joint Planning Staff was formed and was sent, under Rear Admiral (later Vice Admiral) HT Baillie-Grohman, to Athens on 17 April.

Wavell again flew to Athens on 19 April, and found himself in a chaotic situation which had become even more confused since his last visit of only six days before. The Greek Prime Minister had committed suicide on the eighteenth. After arriving in Greece, Wavell met with Wilson and three other senior officers to discuss the question of evacuation. The available

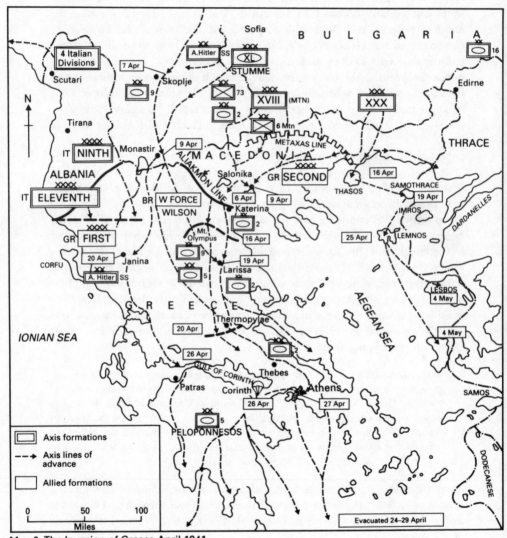

Map 6. The Invasion of Greece April 1941

courses of action were obvious: either to fight it out or to evacuate. After a
thorough assessment of the 'military pros and cons', the inevitable decision
was made, and Wavell gave out clear guidance on the priority of embarkation. 'The feeling was', the conference minutes record glumly, 'that we
would be lucky if we embarked 30 per cent of the Force. This was
accepted.'[138] Later that day, Wavell and Wilson met with the Greek King
and Papagos, but the decision to evacuate was held in abeyance until a new
Greek Prime Minister could be selected and form a government.

Late that night, Wavell drove himself to Blamey's Headquarters, and
after a long and fatiguing drive, finally arrived there at about 2:00 am on
the 20th. John Hetherington described the scene:

> Wavell and Blamey were sitting in the back of Wavell's car discussing the
> evacuation plans and studying a map in the light of an electric flash-lamp.
> Heavy rain thudded on the roof of the car, like a depressing obbligato to the
> words of the two men.[139]

After his discussion with the Australian general, Wavell returned to Athens,
arriving there at dawn. As 'W' Force completed its consolidation on the
Thermopylae Line and beach reconnaissance parties completed their tasks
on 20 April 1941, Wavell had further talks with King George of Greece.
Wavell, according to one observer, 'looked tired. And well he might, . . .,
considering the vastness of the Middle East Command. A lesser man than
Archie Wavell would have broken down long ago under the strain of
fighting four campaigns simultaneously.'[140] But Wavell was very robust,
with remarkable powers of resilience. Finally the King, obviously with a
heavy heart, agreed to the evacuation. Wavell immediately instructed
Wilson that, in view of the German Air Force's overwhelming superiority,
Piraeus and other ports could not be used for the re-embarkation, which
would have to be made from open beaches on as wide a front as possible.
Wavell then returned to Cairo the following day.

On 22 April 1941, Wavell advised Churchill that: 'Consider time has
come to prepare public in official communiqué for impending Greek collapse', and included a suggested draft version of such an announcement.[141]
In Greece, the general British withdrawal to the designated beaches began
on the night of 22/23 April, with a New Zealand brigade group serving as
the covering force. Operation 'Demon' – the British evacuation from Greece
– began the following night, and continued for five nights. The operation's
definite success was marred by two incidents: at Nauplion, on the night of
26/27 April, some 1,700 soldiers could not be picked up, since a burning
ship blocked the channel; and on the night of 28/29 April, at Kalamata,
where a confusing situation had developed, in which the senior officer at the
port had failed to establish local security, the Germans attacked. The Royal
Navy was informed that the quays were mined, and this resulted in some
8,000 troops being left behind. In all the 'Lustre' convoys, 58,364 British

soldiers were transported to Greece, with about 4,200 having been shipped earlier. Of that number, 50,732 (including a very small number of Greeks and Yugoslavs) were re-embarked, about 27,000 of which were landed in Crete and the remainder returned to Egypt. All guns, transport, and equipment, other than individual kit, were lost.

Thus ended the Greek campaign. The Prime Minister, on 1 May 1941, congratulated Wavell upon the successful evacuation, adding 'we have paid our debt of honour with far less loss than I feared.'[142] There were numerous recriminations and criticisms after this campaign, and even though it was subsequently observed that British intervention in Greece may have delayed the German invasion of the Soviet Union by up to six weeks, such hindsight cannot be used to rationalise the defeat.

As early as 17 December 1941, Dill wrote that,

> . . . as regards the Greek campaign, I would remind you that although we may have suffered a tactical defeat, the strategic gains to our cause in this campaign were immense, and may well prove to have been decisive.
>
> By our action, the offensive against Russia was delayed by five weeks. Who can yet assess what this delay may have cost the Germans?[143]

The New Zealand Prime Minister, Peter Fraser, appreciated the dilemma the British had faced when he observed that 'They [the critics] will agree that we took the only course open to us, and that any decision to the contrary would have involved dishonour.'[144]

Even though it appeared that the British Army in Greece suffered a defeat – in actuality 'W' Force withdrew as required in accordance with the Ultra intelligence it received – the soldiers were not demoralised, nor did they lose confidence in themselves or their leaders. One officer serving with the Australian forces in Greece expressed the sentiments of many soldiers when he recorded that:

> As events turned out, every man who left Greece is still confident in his own mind that he is as good as his opposite number-that-was, and also sure in his own mind that we could have held and smashed the Hun but the chance to do so was never given us. Half an army cannot fight a full army, and no army is a full army without close air support.[145]

'From a military point of view the expedition to Greece', Wavell later wrote,

> . . . was by no means the hopeless and quixotic affair that it has appeared in the light of what happened. Actually, the plan on which it was originally conceived had a very good chance of success. But certain actions taken, or rather not taken, by the Greeks, after the plan had been agreed, the events in Yugoslavia, and our weakness in the air, led to our being turned out so speedily.[146]

Wavell, in the ensuing months, would find his meagre resources, even more depleted as a result of the Greek *débâcle*, being required for more demanding campaigns in the centre as well as on the periphery of his enormous

Command. Truly, at this later time more than any other, Wavell would be required, in the words of one of his subordinate officers, 'to make his own bricks without either straw or moulds and design his own structure on a slipping bog.'[147]

Conclusion

The decision to intervene in Greece in 1941 is one of the most controversial topics in the military history of the Second World War; Correlli Barnett believed that decision 'seem[ed] one of the biggest and most important mysteries of the war.'[148]

Wavell, shortly after becoming Commander-in-Chief, Middle East, fore-saw the German strategy, including a massive, initial offensive through Poland and continuing towards south-eastern Europe with the ultimate objectives of seizure of the Dardanelles and the domination of the Mediterranean. Wavell's conviction waned after the Germans failed to attack the Balkans in the spring of 1940, although he remained a firm advocate of the necessity for a forward defence policy on the northern shores of the Eastern Mediterranean.

After the Italian invasion of Greece on 28 October 1940, Wavell was fervently against assistance to Greece, primarily because any dispersion of his weak forces would annul his plans for Operation 'Compass', a large-scale 'raid' against the Italians in the Western Desert. Remaining opposed personally to such aid to Greece, Wavell, strictly out of obedience and loyalty, represented his Government in Athens in mid-January 1941 in offering assistance to the Greeks.

The period 12 to 19 February 1941 witnessed a remarkable and complete transformation in Wavell's attitude towards intervention. First, on 12 February, he was ordered to halt further offensive operations in North Africa, to make his Command secure at Benghazi and to 'concentrate all available forces in the Delta in preparation for movement to Europe'. As a soldier, it was Wavell's duty to obey all lawful orders; resignation in protest, as suggested by de Guingand, was certainly not a viable option at this stage in the war. In addition, Wavell's unfailing loyalty to his political and military superiors and their policies made any thought of disobedience personally repugnant.

However, as has been demonstrated, he believed honestly and sincerely that intervention in Greece 'was not really such a forlorn hope from the military point of view as it may seem from its results'.[149] Wavell, as well as intelligence sources in Cairo and London, underestimated the ability of the Germans to launch an offensive in Libya, and believed that Rommel could not attack before May 1941. Based upon that assumption, Wavell believed it would be safe to leave a small covering force to protect the western flank of Cyrenaica and Benghazi, and upon the successful conclusion of the East

African campaign, at least one battle-hardened Indian division could be withdrawn from that area of operations and sent to reinforce the units in Cyrenaica, before the expected German attack.

Wavell knew that any Anglo-Greek force would be outnumbered numerically, but he understood that the rugged terrain of northern Greece would restrict and channel the movement of German armoured forces into the region. The terrain would serve as a force multiplier for the defence and would thus bring the combat potential of the forces involved in any engagement closer to parity. In addition, Wavell overestimated the tenacity and fighting abilities of the Yugoslavs. Furthermore, his planning relied upon the receipt of projected air reinforcements which, in the event, did not reach the Middle East in a timely manner or in the quantities scheduled. But a military operation cannot be planned and executed on the basis of promised reinforcements or hypothetical assumptions. In view of Wavell's adamant insistence on assisting Greece and advocating the project's feasibility in military terms, one must conclude that it was an error of judgement (which Wavell admitted explicitly to Harding at Barce on 3 April 1941, when he said that he should have sent less to Greece[150]).

Wavell, rightly, took the moral and political aspects of intervention in Greece into consideration when he decided to support the venture, and realised that *noblesse oblige* also required intervention. He was undoubtedly influenced by Donovan, and was made further aware of the importance of American public opinion and the significance of the Lend-Lease Bill. It is highly probable that these factors at least swayed, if not overrode, Wavell's military judgement.

By the time Eden and Dill arrived in Cairo on 19 February 1941, Wavell wholeheartedly supported assistance to Greece. He did so due to a multitude of factors: obedience; loyalty; cognisance of Britain's moral and legal guarantee to Greece; and his perceptions of the military considerations described above. He remained a staunch supporter of the Greek diversion, even after it was discovered that the Greeks had failed to withdraw to the Aliakhmon Line. At and past this point, Wavell was dogmatic and inflexible in his advocacy of forming a Balkan alliance. Another facet of Wavell's personality, his acquiescence of 'fate', was certainly responsible, at least in part, for his uncharacteristic rigidity in this situation.

The question of responsibility and liability looms large over the calamitous results of the British imbroglio in Greece. 'Well, [the responsibility] must point to Winston in the last resort', suggested Jacob recently, 'because, after all, he was running the war. He could have, if he'd wanted to, he could have said "I'm not going to send anybody to Greece, even if the soldiers had said that's what we ought to do".'[151] As truthful as Jacob's assertion is, it is much too simplistic.

The War Cabinet and Chiefs of Staff could certainly have vetoed all proposals to send assistance to Greece, but as has been shown, these bodies generally did little more than serve as ciphers to give the perception of a legitimate, democratic process in endorsing the Prime Minister's proposals. Eden could unquestionably have prevented the campaign, but armed with ego-inflating plenary powers, he wholeheartedly wished to consummate the Balkan front he knew his mentor, Churchill, desired, in order to vindicate his own Great War failure at Gallipoli and in order to establish a foothold on the continent of Europe. Furthermore, Eden wished to boost his own reputation and political prospects. Dill might have been able to halt the project, but this is doubtful. He had been berated and criticised so many times by the Prime Minister, that he may not have possessed the fortitude to resist Churchill's omnipresent pressure. Blamey and Freyberg, had they protested vigorously and in a timely manner to their respective governments, might have been able to prevent the despatch of troops to Greece. Wavell might have been able to influence the continuation of attempts to form a Balkan front, but since Dill had been told by Churchill to pressure Wavell into compliance, if necessary, his real input into the decision was limited – although Churchill exaggerated the reliance placed upon Wavell's opinions. The other two Middle East Commanders-in-Chief, Cunningham and Longmore, might also have been able to influence the project, but they tended to defer to Wavell's lead and decisions.

There is no doubt that Churchill harboured grand illusions of forming a 'Balkan bloc', and sought indefatigably to achieve that goal while attempting simultaneously to distance himself from the defeat he knew to be inevitable. As a subterfuge, the Prime Minister sent Eden and Dill to the Middle East, but throughout this period, it was Churchill's silent hand on the rudder which steered the course unswervingly to inevitable military defeat in Greece.

8

Italian East Africa, January–May 1941

'. . . *a swift and brilliant campaign*. . . .'
Wavell, 1 August 1941[1]

Wavell's offensive operations to reconquer Italian East Africa, conducted thousands of miles from Cairo, resulted in roughly one million square miles of colonial territory being wrested from Mussolini's 'New Rome' and another quarter of a million enemy soldiers and their equipment being permanently withdrawn from the war. This highly successful campaign culminated in the capture of Addis Ababa on 6 April 1941 and the surrender of the Duke of Aosta, Viceroy of Ethiopia and Supreme Commander of all armed forces in Italian East Africa, at Amba Alagi on 19 May 1941. These events and the entire campaign itself were, however, overshadowed by the concurrent disastrous activities in North Africa, Greece, Crete, and Iraq.

Italian East Africa consisted of Italy's old colonies of Somalia (Italian Somaliland) and Eritrea and of Ethiopia (formerly known as Abyssinia), which had been subjugated by the Italian Army in May 1936. The Italian Empire in East Africa possessed numerous strategic features, one being its immense size. Ethiopia alone was 900 miles long and 750 miles wide, which is larger than the combined area of Italy and France. Additionally, the Italian forces in Ethiopia were a quiescent threat to the garrisons in Uganda and Kenya – British colonies to the South – as well as to South Africa. Italian Somaliland, to the East, harboured Italian troops who could easily attack Kenya along the coast. Bordering Ethiopia on the North and situated on the Red Sea, Eritrea functioned as the supply depot of Ethiopia and Italian Somaliland. It could also serve as the assembly area for a massive Italian attack on the Sudan and Egypt from the South, possibly synchronised and concurrent with a direct easterly assault from Libya, Italy's other colony in North Africa.

The reconquest of Italian East Africa was one of the fundamental and original tenets of Wavell's strategic concept for the Middle East, and it is appropriate to review Wavell's policies and attitude in relation to that area.

In the analysis which Wavell wrote on 31 July 1939 while en route to Cairo to assume his new Command, of the four requisites to defend, and eventually to dominate, the Mediterranean and to take the counteroffensive against Germany in Eastern and south-eastern Europe, the mission of taking action to clear the Red Sea of the enemy was listed second only in importance to the security of Egypt and the Suez Canal. After arriving in Cairo on 2 August 1939, Wavell visited Port Sudan on the 6th (while on his way to Aden) and French Somaliland the following day. He was in Port Sudan again on 8 August while returning to Cairo.

On 14 August 1939, Wavell issued guidance to the Middle East Joint Planning Committee (the forerunner of the Middle East Joint Planning Staff) to study immediately, among other items, 'The action necessary to ensure effective control of the Red Sea at the earliest moment.'[2]. Ten days later, Wavell wrote down and sent to the C I G S his impressions of his first three weeks in command in the Middle East, and lamented 'the almost entire absence of any detailed and co-ordinated war plans' and the prevalence of a debilitating 'defensive mentality' in all areas of his Command. As for Italian East Africa, Wavell observed accurately that:

> In the Sudan, Aden, Somaliland and Kenya, the attitude towards Italian East Africa has up to date been that of purely passive defence. In British Somaliland, it has been, and apparently still may be, a policy of pure scuttle. In the Sudan, so far as I have been able to ascertain, the attitude is an exaggeratedly defensive one.[3]

Wavell added that he hoped this attitude would evolve to one orientated towards active defence, and eventually to an ethos of the offensive in that region.

As Wavell's strategic philosophy gestated and his knowledge of his vast Command grew, he was able to formulate more detailed plans for the recapture of Italian East Africa. He understood the intricacies of such a campaign, which would entail detailed planning and preparation, and these he directed his staff to begin at once. As noted previously, Wavell's general guidance to his staff included his concept of the operation: 'I think it is quite clear that any large scale operation must either be on the line Djibuti/ Harar/Addis Ababa, or the line Kassala/Asmara/ Massawa, or preferably on both lines simultaneously.'[4] This concept served as the basis for the eventual British domination of the area.

Wavell reconnoitred British and French Somaliland in January 1940, in which month the defence of East Africa was added formally to his responsibilities. With comparatively few reinforcements, Wavell concluded, it would be possible to hold both British and French Somaliland against any future Italian attack, and that, 'if Italy entered the war, we should eventually attack the Italian forces in Abyssinia, when sufficient troops become available'.[5] He travelled to South Africa in March 1940, and in the light of deteriorating relations with Italy, discussed with Smuts his tentative plans for action in East Africa and British Somaliland in the event of war.

Italy declared war, with effect from one minute past midnight on the night of 10/11 June 1940, at which time British forces numbered about 9,000 in the Sudan, 8,500 in Kenya, and 1,475 in British Somaliland – against an estimated 290,000 enemy troops in Italian East Africa. The Italians stationed there were much more aggressive than those stationed in Libya, and their attacks on Kassala on 4 July 1940 and on Gallabat two days later have already been described. In the wake of these acts of Italian aggression, Wavell left Cairo on 14 July for a four-day trip to the Sudan and Kenya to assess the situation for himself. He also met the Emperor of Ethiopia, Haile Selassie, in Khartoum.

Shortly after his arrival in the Middle East, in August 1939, Wavell had instructed his staff to study the possibility of fomenting covertly a rebellion which the Italians had never been able to suppress in the western Ethiopian province of Gojjam. A friend of Emperor Haile Selassie, with some fifteen years' experience of Ethiopia, Colonel (later Brigadier) DA Sandford, arrived in Cairo the following month to direct the project. Hindered by the British policy of restricting activities which might provoke the Italians, only slight progress was made in fulfilling Wavell's goal. The Italian declaration of war, however, removed these fetters, and a small military mission, No. 101, was established under Sandford's command to travel to Ethiopia to advise and coordinate the efforts of the local tribal chiefs.

On 3 August 1940, less than one month after Kassala was attacked and only one day before the Italians launched their assault on British Somaliland, Wavell's Operations Section produced a paper entitled 'Operations Against Italian East Africa'. Realistically appraising Wavell's troop and equipment shortages, this study recommended, among other courses of action, the staging of a limited offensive in the Kassala area and an advance on Kismayu, the latter appearing to be feasible in January/February 1941. Since a large-scale offensive was not possible at that time, 'the policy should therefore be', the report concluded, 'to maintain pressure from as many directions as possible, thus forcing the Italians to use up their resources'.[6] One method the British intended to employ to force the Italians to dissipate their resources was to further indigenous unrest. To that end Sandford crossed the frontier into Ethiopia on 12 August to 'stimulate the first phase of the revolt – the isolation of outlying Italian garrisons by small patriot parties'.[7] The Italian campaign in British Somaliland began on 4 August, and although the outnumbered British fought gallantly, they were forced to evacuate the colony, completing their withdrawal fourteen days later.

While Mission 101 assessed the rebel situation in Ethiopia, another officer was selected and posted to Cairo to assist Sandford. At a meeting of the Middle East Committee in July 1940, LS Amery had suggested to the Vice Chief of the Imperial General Staff that 'a certain Captain OC Wingate'[8] would be the ideal man to lead insurgent forces in Ethiopia. Wingate was well qualified for such an appointment, having served in the Sudan Defence Force from 1927 to 1933, qualified as an interpreter in Arabic, and had proven himself as a highly effective and unorthodox guerrilla leader in Palestine from 1937 to 1939. Wavell, who remembered Wingate from Palestine, accepted the suggestion of the latter's assignment enthusiastically but, concerned about his pro-Zionist obsession, added the proviso that Wingate could never, for any reason, return to Palestine. Arriving in Cairo on 17 October 1940, Wingate was assigned temporarily as a staff officer at General Headquarters.

In his 20 October 1940 forecast of British strategy in the Middle East during the winter of 1940/1941, Wavell wrote that forces in the Sudan and Kenya were sufficient at that time for defensive purposes only, and that activities to spread the rebellion inside Ethiopia would greatly assist either defensive or offensive operations. British strategy during that period, Wavell calculated, should be to:

> . . . take such action in the Sudan and Kenya as will gradually weaken the Italian position in Italian East Africa, remove any threat to the Sudan and Kenya, lessen [the] danger to our communications in the Red Sea, and increase the revolt within Abyssinia to an extent that [it] will occupy the whole of the Italian effort.[9]

The conferences held in Khartoum on 28 and 29 October 1940 between Eden, Smuts, and Wavell, with Haile Selassie as a participant in some of the discussions, have already been described. The key results of these meetings were these: General Platt, commanding troops in the Sudan, stated that he was planning an operation to drive the Italians out of Gallabat in mid-November, thus opening the Ethiopian frontier to sub-sequent infiltrations and larger offensives. He also intended to attack the Kassala region, thereby gaining control of the entrances to the Eritrean plateau and enabling the British to recover the use of the important railway loop and aerodrome at Kassala. Smuts noted the importance of conducting simultaneous operations elsewhere, especially in Kenya, and stated that the primary objective of British strategy should be first to clear the port of Kismayu and then concentrate forces to advance on Addis Ababa in conjunction with an offensive from the Sudan. Eden wanted the offensive operations to begin as soon as practicable, definitely before the rains in March 1941, and his provisional timetable suggested the attack on Gallabat be made in early November and on Kassala and Kismayu in early January 1941. 'There was general agreement with this view', recorded the minutes of the meeting, 'subject to it being found practicable to mount the offensive against Kismayu by that date.'[10]

Eden's vision for the start of the offensive by conventional forces into Italian East Africa coincided with the guidance Wavell had given earlier to

Platt. The 5th Indian Division, commanded by Major General (later Lieutenant General Sir) LM Heath, arrived in the Sudan in September 1940. After a period of reorganisation, the Division consisted of the 9th, 10th, and 29th Indian Infantry brigades. On 16 October 1940 'Gazelle Force' – composed of Skinner's Horse, a dashing mechanised Indian cavalry regiment; the 1st Machine-gun Regiment of the Sudan Defence Force; and units of the Royal Artillery, Royal Horse Artillery, and supporting arms and services – under the command of Colonel (later General Sir) Frank Messervy, was established. The mission of Gazelle Force was very similar to that of the Long Range Patrols in the Western Desert: to harass incessantly and intimidate the Italian forces, to keep them off balance, and to create the false impression that the Italians faced a British force much larger than it actually was. 'Terrify the enemy. Make his life absolute hell!', Messervy told his officers, adding 'I want it to be so that they [the Italians] are afraid to move by day or sleep by night, so that they think more of protecting themselves than trying to probe for our weak points. They must become completely defensively minded.'[11] The superb performance of Gazelle Force, coupled with the deliberate act of addressing the Division in all official correspondance as 'Five' instead of '5th', resulted in Italian Intelligence reporting that there were 'five Indian Divisions' in the sector occupied by the 5th Indian Division.[12]

In accordance with Wavell's earlier directives and the decisions made at the Khartoum conference on 28 October 1940, the attacks on Gallabat and Metemma were scheduled for early the following month. After a night deployment, the 10th Indian Infantry Brigade, with B Squadron of the 6th Royal Tank Regiment attached, commanded by a relatively unknown officer, Brigadier (later Field Marshal Viscount) W J Slim, launched their assault on Gallabat early in the morning of 6 November 1940. As Wavell recorded euphemistically, the attack was 'not as successful as had been hoped'.[13] Mechanical failures plagued the British tanks, and an intense Italian aerial bombardment demoralised a British battalion, causing a number of panic-ridden soldiers to flee the battlefield. Although the fort at Gallabat was captured early on the sixth, Slim 'took counsel of his fears' and withdrew his brigade to less exposed ground the following afternoon, at a high cost of forty-two killed and 125 wounded. 'The hard fact remains', in the words of the British Official History, 'that General Platt's operation at Gallabat, carried out early in November, failed in its object.'[14] Slim, in addition, received serious wounds, 'four large bullets from an Italian aeroplane which put him out of action for some time'.[15]

British military activity during the remainder of November 1940 was limited to operations of Gazelle Force, which continued to torment the Italians. Messervy's mobile force operated from the Gash Delta against Italian outposts in the vicinity of Kassala. Situated on the Ethiopian plateau, the region is dominated by a series of hilly ranges, 2,000–3,000 feet high, separated by wide valleys. 'The country around Kassala', wrote Platt metaphorically,

> . . . can be compared with a sea studded with islands. The desert is the sea, the jebels [mountains] the islands, rising steep and rocky from the desert plain. West of Kassala the jebels are few and unimportant. Eastwards they increase in numbers and size until the foothills are reached. North and South are scattered jebels of considerable tactical importance. The desert is, on the whole, good going for MT [motor transport] of all types.[16]

Receiving an average annual rainfall of thirteen inches, the Gash Delta area tends to be highly malarial from July to October.

The coastal region of Eastern Ethiopia consists of a belt of sandy plains, usually covered by low scrub, stretching inland from ten to twenty miles. Beyond this area rise mountain ranges, where it is generally very hot and humid. The terrain of Eritrea is equally varied, although a large plateau covers most of the area. Near the coastal plain, this plateau rises abruptly to a general elevation of some 6,000 feet, with the highest hills over 10,000 feet high. Although gradually dropping towards the west, this rugged terrain, described by one Italian as 'a tormented landscape like a stormy sea moved by the wrath of God',[17] would serve as a significant barrier to any invader. This same tableland stretches into Northern Ethiopia, where the mountains and gorges serve as formidable obstacles to an attacking force and give a marked advantage to the defender.

The topography of Kenya, where General Cunningham's East Africa Force would operate during part of this campaign, was also daunting. Kenya and Italian East Africa shared a common border almost 1,200-miles long which stretched from Lake Rudolf to the Indian Ocean. Bush and semi-desert followed its entire length except near Moyale, where a rocky but green escarpment existed. A barrier of almost impenetrable desert nearly 300-miles wide spread like an impassable cordon between the border and the rich farmlands of Central Kenya. The scarcity of water made potential military operations in the area even more tenuous, as did the high temperatures which, for month on end, never dropped below 100 degrees Fahrenheit during the day.

Wavell had attempted to coordinate offensive operations against Italian East Africa with Operation 'Compass', his attack in the Western Desert. The setback at Gallabat, however, and Cunningham's assessment that, due primarily to inadequacy of forces, mainly supporting arms, and the shortage of water, the operation to capture Kismayu would have to be postponed until the rains were over in May 1941, prevented this from occurring. In reporting the latter development to Dill on 23 November 1940, Wavell stated that he was reconsidering his plans and would hold a conference before the end of the month to discuss strategy for the following six months.[18] Smuts received a copy of Wavell's cable and, concerned not only that the brigade South Africa was sending to Kenya would remain idle over the winter months but also with the impact that the postponement of the operation would have on his own precarious political position, expressed his consternation and disappointment to Churchill.

Churchill addressed the issue at the Defence Committee meeting of 25 November 1940, inquiring why the projected offensive against Kismayu – Operation 'Canvas' – would have to be postponed until May, 'strongly criticiz[ing] the Cairo Commander' in the process.[19] Dill reported the contents of Wavell's telegram of 23 November. However, as Churchill, who was chafing with anxiety over the start of 'Compass', later wrote, 'We were none of us satisfied with this, and the Committee invited the Chiefs of Staff to call for a full explanation of the matter from General Wavell, and to report further to the Prime Minister.'[20] Churchill's actions in this situation reflect clearly the influence Smuts was able to exert over him, since as early as August 1940, during Wavell's visit to London, 'he [Churchill] had urged on me', Wavell later recorded, 'the policy of reducing troops to an absolute minimum in Kenya and he continued to suggest that a proportion of the troops in East Africa could more usefully be employed elsewhere'.[21]

On the eve of 'Compass', Wavell held a conference in Cairo on 2 December 1940, to discuss future strategy in East Africa. With Wilson, Platt, Cunningham, and others in attendance, one of the main items to consider was the attack on Kismayu. The South African liaison officer, Colonel Frank Theron, again propounded Smuts's view of the urgency of capturing the important Italian port of Kismayu, but Cunningham felt there was insufficient time to prepare for and launch this attack. Wavell, too, was opposed to the offensive at this time, not wanting additional forces to operate in the unhealthy coastal region.

After discussions and input from his staff officers, Wavell laid down his general policy for future operations in East Africa. Preparations were to be made for the recapture of Kassala in the Sudan, the attack to be conducted early in 1941, if the necessary reinforcements could be made available from Egypt. 'For these purposes', Platt later wrote, 'he [Wavell] ear-marked the 4th Indian Division who were to make the initial assault on Sidi Barrani. Their transfer to the Sudan would naturally depend on success in the desert.'[22] Wavell also directed that pressure be maintained in the Gallabat area, and that all possible means be used to further the rebellion in Ethiopia. In the southern area of Kenya, an advance to the frontier on the line Kolbio-Dif was to be made as soon as possible, and in the North, west of Moyale, the enemy would be harassed by mobile patrols. The advance on Kismayu was postponed until May or June 1941, after the rainy season.

As we know, the Western Desert offensive, Operation 'Compass', gained complete surprise over the Italians when it was initiated early in the morning of 9 December 1940. The rapid success of the attack far exceeded all expectations, and permitted Wavell on the night of 10/11 December to make the controversial decision to withdraw the 4th Indian Division and send it to the Sudan to form part of Platt's force in the projected recapture of Kassala and further operations.

Confident of the eventual demise of the Italian Army in Libya, Churchill advised Wavell on 17 December 1940 that after 'Compass' had run its course, 'The Sudan is of prime importance, and eminently desirable.'[23] As the full results of 'Compass' became more apparent, Smuts recommended to Churchill on 8 January 1941 that it would be opportune to consider the liquidation of the 'Abyssinian situation', and emphasised Wavell's tentative plan to conduct a simultaneous two-pronged attack on Ethiopia from the North and from Kenya.[24] But as the 4th Indian Division was being transported to the Sudan, the apparition of Wavell being forced to halt the North African offensive and send considerable forces to Greece rose to the forefront of concerns.

The echoes of the crushing Italian defeat in Libya, coupled with the vigorous activities of Gazelle Force and Mission 101, reverberated all the way up the Nile Valley and caused the Italians to forestall the expected British attack by evacuating Kassala precipitately on 18 January 1941. It was originally thought that 'Force Emily' – the 4th Indian Division – would arrive in the Sudan in time for Platt to launch his offensive in March 1941, but Wavell was not satisfied with that late date, and directed Platt to accelerate his planning and preparations. Eventually 9 February 1941 was selected. This date was put forward to 19 January when there were indications that Italian determination was waning, but the unexpected Italian withdrawal from Kassala completely altered Wavell's timetable. Like a bloodhound on a scent, Wavell ordered Platt to pursue the fleeing Italians rapidly, and realising the unique opportunity which now presented itself, he travelled to East Africa to assess the situation in person.

Wavell first visited Platt in the Sudan, and instructed him to continue the pursuit audaciously and press on to Asmara, using the forces assembling at Port Sudan to advance along the Red Sea coast and into the hills in the direction of Asmara. A South African staff officer on his way from Pretoria to Cairo stopped at Nairobi on 26 January 1941 just as Cunningham had received a signal informing him of Wavell's impending visit. Cunningham then wrote a letter to Wavell which he handed to this staff officer for hand delivery. The letter stated, in part:

> I am proposing to make an attempt at the capture of [Kismayu] round about February 12th. The finding of water at [Hagadera] has released just enough transport to make it possible, and I am hoping that the enemy morale is sufficiently shaken to make up for my lack of resources. . . .[25]

Connell has pointed out accurately that Churchill's subsequent claims that 'under the strong pressure from home Wavell eventually decided to make the effort [to capture Kismayu] before the rains', and that Wavell 'animated the Kenya Command' are patently false.[26] It was Cunningham, as written above, who proposed the early execution of Operation 'Canvas', while Wavell wholeheartedly supported the initiative of his aggressive subordinate.

Wavell arrived in Kenya two days later, and after discussions with Cunningham about the operation to capture Kismayu, informed the Commander-in-Chief, East Indies – since the assistance of the Royal Navy was essential – that the attack would take place on 10 February 1941. Then on the 29th Wavell visited the Headquarters of the 1st South African Division, commanded by Major General (later Lieutenant General) George Brink. In the vicinity of Dukance 'General Wavell studied the surrounding country, showing great interest in the problems facing the South Africans, the most pressing of which were still shortage of water and lack of roads.'[27] Wavell returned to Cairo on 1 February 1941, and informed Dill of the results of his trip, operations in progress, and the fact that he had approved Cunningham's proposal for advancing the execution of 'Canvas'. He also added that he had given instructions 'to both Platt and Cunningham for maximum effort they can make against Italian East Africa during next two months'.[28]

The first fortnight of February 1941 was arguably the most crucial period of Wavell's command in the Middle East. In the Western Desert, 'Compass' reached its climax with the Battle of Beda Fomm, 6–7 February. On the 10th, the War Cabinet ruled out any possibility of the continuation of the advance to Tripoli. On 12 February – the same day that Rommel landed in Libya – Wavell received confirmation of the War Cabinet's decision, and was directed to give first priority to his efforts to assist Greece and/or Turkey.

The decisions made in London had the potential to jeopardise Wavell's plans for action in Italian East Africa, especially if they would have been decided upon only a short time earlier. The British cause gained momentum when Emperor Haile Selassie on 20 January 1941, following the Italian withdrawal from Kassala, crossed the frontier from the Sudan into Ethiopia. Sandford, in the meantime, was promoted to brigadier and became Political and Military Adviser to the Emperor. Wingate, who had arrived in Khartoum on 6 November 1940, became commander of patriot forces in the Gojjam. These forces were shortly thereafter formed into 'Gideon Force' and significantly aided the British in isolating and harassing Italian outposts.

Cunningham's plan was for the 11th African Division (commanded by Major General HEdeR Wetherall), supported by the 12th African Division (commanded by Major General (later General Sir) AR Godwin-Austen) and the Royal Navy's six-ship 'Force T' (commanded by Captain (later Admiral Sir) JHH Edelsten), to capture Kismayu. This attack began on 11 February 1941. After a great deal of severe fighting, the enemy began to evacuate the port city during the evening of the 13th. Kismayu (which still had 25 ships in its harbour and was eventually to yield a boon of 222,000 gallons of petrol and half that amount in aviation fuel) was entered by elements of the 12th African Division on 14 February, six days ahead of schedule.

At this point Wavell, in receipt of the War Cabinet's directive dated 12 February 1941 ordering him to halt the Libyan offensive and send all available troops from the Middle East to the Balkans, had to make the crucial decision to continue the offensive operations against Italian East Africa or to withdraw units from that theatre to replace those which would be despatched to Greece. Wavell's decision to continue the offensive warrants further comment.

Wavell's earlier decision to withdraw the 4th Indian Division from the Western Desert has been analysed in detail in Chapter 6. We have seen that the evidence is compelling that, at the very least, he should have delayed the transfer of the division for one week before sending it to the Sudan. Similarly, one may question his expenditure of vast resources to dismember the enormous Italian East African Empire, especially with the Royal Navy blockading the Italian ports in Somaliland and after the capture of the port of Kismayu. With the Italian Navy emasculated, it was extremely difficult for Italy to resupply its forces in Italian East Africa, and a potential course of action for Wavell could have been, as one South African veteran of this campaign recently suggested, to have 'starved them out'.[29] But having already completed the withdrawal of the 4th Indian Division from the Western Desert to the Sudan, and in the euphoria of the aftermath of the spectacular successes of 'Compass', Wavell had no inkling of the imminent German presence in North Africa, and continued with his plans to reconquer Italian East Africa. Wavell had told Platt to confine his operations to the occupation of Eritrea and not to advance south from there into Ethiopia. He told Cunningham that after the capture of Kismayu, he should advance to Mogadishu.

By mid-February 1941, after the occupation of Kassala, Platt's forces continued the offensive and captured Agordat on 1 February and Barentu the next day. Leaving the plain, British forces were confronted by 'a sudden wall of razor edges, pure rock at the top',[30] a series of steep mountains and deep gorges which marked a line of Italian fortresses guarding Keren and the route to Asmara and Massawa. The 4th Indian Division, believing it was opposed to Italian soldiers of the same low quality that it had encountered during the initial phase of 'Compass', assaulted the massif on 3 February. After six days of ferocious attacks and counterattacks, the British had to admit temporary failure, and the momentum of Platt's advance ground to a halt as the 5th Indian Division was transported forward to assist the 4th when the attack would be resumed.

In the south, after the capture of Kismayu, Cunningham's forces advanced towards Mogadishu, the capital of Italian Somaliland, with light-ning speed, one brigade reaching that objective unopposed on 25 February 1941, having advanced 235 miles in three days. A pause was made at Mogadishu so that the port could be cleared of mines, and supplies could be brought forward to support the continuation of the advance. A huge quan-tity of supplies, including 350,000 gallons of motor fuel and 80,000 gallons of aviation fuel, was also found at Mogadishu.

Eden and Dill, it will be recalled, had arrived in Cairo on 19 February 1941 to concert 'all possible measures, both diplomatic and military, against the Germans in the Balkans'.[31] From that time forward, until Churchill's emissaries departed Cairo on 7 April 1941, Wavell's time and energies were generally devoted to implementing the Government policy of assisting the Greeks. After 6 April, when the Germans launched their simultaneous assaults on Greece and Yugoslavia, Wavell's full attention was focused in the Balkans, and then the Western Desert, Crete, Iraq, and Syria. After providing the initial vision, impetus, and required resources, Wavell was only able to give periodic strategic guidance to his two able subordinates, Platt and Cunningham, who executed adroitly their respective facets of the overall offensive in accordance with the Commander-in-Chief's intent.

On 1 March 1941, Wavell reported to the Prime Minister that the Italians were evacuating Italian Somaliland, to which Churchill quipped: 'At present we seem to have swapped Somalilands with the enemy.'[32] The apparent dichotomy was soon rectified, however. On 16 March, after a preliminary naval bombardment, a task force of two Punjab battalions and the two-company 1401/1402 (Aden) Companies, Auxiliary Military Pioneer Corps Group, conducted an amphibious landing at Berbera, British Somaliland. Due to a misunderstanding on the part of the recently appointed Aden Strike Force commander, the Arab Pioneers, although unarmed, were ordered to assist the Punjabis in assaulting the entrenched Italians. Captain SHJ Harrison, who was commanding the 1401/1402 AMPC Group during the attack, observed recently:

> The sun was just peeping above the eastern skyline [;] we came under rifle fire from various points in the enemy defence line, when to our utter amazement we saw the Italian enemy leaping out of their trenches, and racing toward trans-port vehicles formed up in column, they clambered aboard, the vehicles started up and the entire enemy column, high-tailed, in a great cloud of yellowish grey dust, southwards, on the main highway to Hargeisha and the Somaliland/ Abyssinian border.[33]

Four days later, an advance element from the 1st South African Infantry Brigade Group travelled from Hargeisa to Berbera and made contact with Aden Force. After travelling by truck an incredible 825 miles in ten days, starting at Brava (85 miles south of Mogadishu), the main body of the Brigade Group arrived in Jijiga.

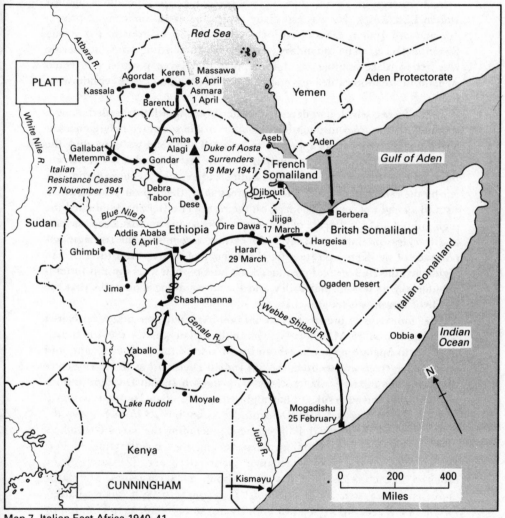

Map 7. Italian East Africa 1940–41

The first British contact with German troops in North Africa occurred on 22 February 1941. The aggressive German patrolling of the skeletal British positions in Libya – denuded by the requirement to aid Greece – seemed to serve as a harbinger of an impending enemy counteroffensive. Apprehensive, Wavell realised that he was in urgent need of troops to form a fresh reserve in Egypt, and had to reconsider the operations against Italian East Africa. He was especially concerned about the combat-proven 4th and 5th Indian Divisions which were held up in front of the strong Keren defences. The quandary, as Wavell phrased it, was 'to decide whether to make another effort to capture the Keren position and reach Asmara or to adopt a defensive attitude in Eritrea and begin withdrawing troops'.[34]

Platt's forces, which had departed earlier from Agordat, travelled along a gradually rising road through open, slightly rolling country before encountering unexpectedly what appeared to be a tall and solid wall guarding the plateau on which Keren was situated. For the last few miles before Keren, the road runs through the narrow Ascidira Valley, which is bounded on the left by the escarpment itself, and by a great spur, the highest peak of which rises to a height of some 6,000 feet, on the right. The Italians dominated the high ground and key terrain of this region of imposing massifs, deep ravines, and trackless mountains. Many years earlier, recognising the strategic importance of the Keren position for the defence of Asmara and the Eritrean highlands, the Italians had positioned the bulk of their forces in this formidable terrain. It was in that valley and the surrounding mountains that the Battle of Keren was fought.

After four days of preparatory aerial bombardment, the attack on Keren was resumed on 15 March 1941. The outline plan was for the 4th Indian Division to operate on the north and west side of the road to Keren, and once the left flank was secured, the 5th Indian Division was to attack east of the road. The fighting was ferocious, with the 4th Indian Division's attack meeting with mixed results. That night, the 5th Indian Division attacked, and one brigade seized Fort Dologorodoc, standing 1,475 feet above the valley. Some of the finest Italian regiments, including the Savoy Grenadiers and the Alpini, were defending the pass, and they counterattacked Fort Dologorodoc no less than seven times between 18 and 22 March, being repulsed on each occasion with a total of some 5,000 casualties. The Battle of Keren was a struggle of attrition; 'It is going to be a bloody battle', forecast Platt accurately, 'against both enemy and ground. It will be won by the side which lasts longest.'[35]

Typically, the Prime Minister was anxious for another battlefield victory, and after Wavell had informed the War Office on 20 March of the limited progress at Keren and added that 'the enemy has been counter-attacking fiercely and repeatedly and shows no immediate signs of cracking', Churchill's rejoinder was that 'I presume you have considered whether there are any reinforcements which can be sent to give you mastery at Keren.'[36] Churchill should unquestionably have known the status of forces in the Middle East, especially since the fourth flight of 'Lustre' had just left Egypt the day before, bound for Athens.

There were, of course, no reinforcements for the Middle East. As noted earlier, with indications of a German offensive in Libya and the need for British reinforcements to deter such aggression, Wavell was highly concerned with the apparent stalemate at Keren, although he possessed 'hope that enemy resistance will crack under pressure'.[37] Accordingly, Wavell flew to Keren, not only to show his concern about the battle to his subordinate commanders and soldiers, but also to ascertain if there was a better tactical plan which could be used to break the deadlock and guarantee British victory. On 25 March, just as the final assault began, Wavell and Platt went as far forward as they could. Wavell later wrote:

> As soon as I had a good look at the position, I said to Platt that it looked to me as if the way through was straight up the main road, neglecting the high peaks to north and south. He replied that this was his plan, and it succeeded. I wonder whether it would have come off if he had tried it earlier instead of his attempts on the peaks to right and left.[38]

The attack was successful. Early on 27 March, Keren – the gateway to Asmara and Massawa – was in British hands. This signal victory was not lightly won, and during the fifty-three day battle the British suffered 536 soldiers killed and 3,229 wounded, compared with some 3,000 combat deaths alone for the Italians. The success at Keren also allowed Wavell, on 27 March, to order the first brigade group of the 4th Indian Division (which would soon be followed by the remainder of the Division), to move to Port Sudan for redeployment to North Africa. 'In terms of the large forces engaged', wrote one veteran of the East African campaign, 'the stubborn fighting, the duration of the battle and the heavy casualties on both sides, it [the Battle of Keren] must rank as great so far as men continue to settle their differences in this primitive manner.'[39] This battle made such an impression upon Wavell, and so significant did he believe it to be, that when he received the dignity of an Earldom in 1947 he assumed the title of a second Viscountcy, Keren of Eritrea.

The winding road from Keren to Asmara was suited ideally to the conduct of delaying actions by the Italians, but the British retained the initiative and pursued their goal doggedly. Asmara was abandoned by the Italians on 1 April 1941, and Platt's forces continued to Massawa. Despite being given an ultimatum to surrender on 5 April, Rear Admiral Bonetti, commanding the Italian forces at Massawa, refused to do so. A British infantry attack on 8 April was opposed resolutely by the Italians, but a simultaneous tank thrust penetrated the Italian perimeter, resulting in the Italians surrendering that afternoon. The capture of the port of Massawa signalled the end of all organised opposition in Eritrea and the successful attainment of the strategic object of the East African campaign: the removal of the threat to shipping through the Red Sea. On 11 April, President Roosevelt declared that the Red Sea and the Gulf of Aden were no longer a combat zone within the meaning of the American Neutrality Act, which meant that American vessels could now carry war supplies to the beleaguered Middle East by this route.

Shortly after the fall of Keren, the Duke of Aosta realised that hopes of any further resistance would have to be centred on the near impregnable Amba Alagi, an 11,186-foot-high peak, honeycombed with fighting positions, gun pits and storage areas and protected by a number of fortified hills. Wavell had meanwhile permitted Cunningham, advancing from the south, to capture Addis Ababa. The city fell on 6 April 1941 (with the Emperor re-entering his capital on 5 May), but its capture received scant attention or recognition since the Germans had invaded Greece and Yugoslavia on the same day. At that time British forces were rapidly retreating in the face of Rommel's onslaught in Cyrenaica, and Wavell's policy 'was that no major operations should be undertaken in Eritrea and Northern Ethiopia which would interfere with the withdrawal of troops to the Middle East'.[40] Although the main body of the remaining Italian troops was no longer a threat to the Sudan, and had little chance of launching an offensive to regain Eritrea, its presence was a source of potential problems and had to be eliminated.

Wavell also urgently needed the South African Division and its transport in Egypt, and ordered Cunningham to advance north to secure the main road to Massawa and Port Sudan, to facilitate the movement of troops to those ports for embarkation and transport north. Amba Alagi blocked this route, and as the northern half of the huge British pincer, the 5th Indian Division, approached the Italian stronghold from the north, Cunningham's forces marched on this objective from the south.

The main attack by the 5th Indian Division to capture Amba Alagi began on 4 May 1941. After initial progress, the leading battalion of the 1st South African Brigade – from Cunningham's force – arrived in the area on 10 May and completed the encirclement of the Italian redoubt. The Indians resumed their attack on the 13th and, assisted by the South Africans on the following day, forced the Italians to abandon a number of key positions. As the net closed around Amba Alagi, the Duke of Aosta realised he would eventually be defeated. Concerned about the recovery of the wounded and stories of atrocities committed by patriot forces, he began negotiations for an armistice on 16 May. In sum, the Italians agreed to surrender unconditionally provided that they were granted the 'honours of war', in which they would be permitted to march past a reviewing stand and give and receive a salute before laying down their arms. On 19 May, the Duke of Aosta and some 5,000 of his soldiers marched past a British guard of honour, were disarmed, and then surrendered formally. This novel episode ended the main operations of the East African campaign, although pockets of resistance kept two African divisions occupied throughout the summer and until the last Italians surrendered on 27 November 1941.

Conclusion

'The presiding genius of the campaign,' stated Michael Glover,

> was Wavell. He was the man who saw the need for the operations, realized the possibility of overwhelming success and fed in just enough resources to enable it to succeed. He did this in the teeth of the opposition of Churchill who, most of the time, opposed undertaking it, hoping that Italian East Africa would waste away if ignored and blockaded.[41]

Disregarding distractions and competing demands, Wavell never lost sight of the primary objective of the campaign: opening the Red Sea to American shipping. The Indian Official History recognised Wavell's signal contribution to the unmitigated success of this campaign by noting that 'by his [Wavell's] perseverance and ability he ensured British victory in this region'.[42]

Wavell's own description of the East African campaign is much more balanced:

> The ultimate pattern of the conquest was a pincer movement on the largest scale, through Eritrea and Somaliland converging on Amba Alagi, combined with a direct thrust through Western Abyssinia by the patriot forces. It looks Teutonic in conception and execution; but, . . ., this result was not foreseen in the original plan but arose gradually through the development of events. It was in fact an improvisation after the British fashion of war rather than a set piece in the German manner.[43]

Although overshadowed by the simultaneous disastrous events in Libya, Greece, Iraq, and Crete, Wavell conquered Italian East Africa 'on two fronts with an economy and flexibility of force that ought to rank as a feat of spontaneous exploitation unsurpassed in war'.[44]

9

Breach of the Western Flank, April 1941

'As things proved, I took too great a risk here, . . .'
Wavell, 1 August 1941[1]

The period April to July 1941, during which the German offensives in the Western Desert and the Balkans were launched with their full fury, and the results of German infiltration, brought revolt to the peripheries of the enormous Middle East Command, was clearly the most demanding and stressful for Wavell. The requirement to send troops to Greece had forced him to halt his North African offensive, to denude his Command's western flank in Libya, and had occupied the majority of his time and energies from February to April 1941. While five divisions were being employed in the offensive operations to reconquer Italian East Africa, Rommel took advantage of the British vulnerability and his probing actions turned into a full-scale counteroffensive. These German operations forced Wavell onto the strategic defensive in the North African area of operations for the remainder of his tenure in the Middle East. The incessant pressure upon him and his grossly inadequate resources was at its peak in May 1941, when he had five campaigns on his hands; this prompted one distinguished military historian to comment that 'It is doubtful whether any commander-in-chief has borne greater responsibilities than those of Lord Wavell in the month of May 1941.'[2]

The beginnings of the unexpected German counterattack have been mentioned previously. When it became apparent, on 31 March 1941, that Rommel's audacious probing actions had become a determined attack and that it was on the verge of shattering the 'western flank', British forces in Cyrenaica (commanded by Lieutenant General (later Sir) Philip Neame, VC, since 27 February 1941) consisted of:

▷ 2nd Armoured Division (minus 1st Armoured Brigade Group in Greece), commanded by Major General MD Gambier-Parry, and

deployed on the frontier of Cyrenaica about thirty miles northeast of El Agheila:
- 3rd Armoured Brigade:
  - 3rd Hussars (35 light tanks)
  - 5th Royal Tank Regiment (25-A13 Cruiser tanks)
  - 6th Royal Tank Regiment (1 squadron only of 15-M13 Italian tanks)
- King's Dragoon Guards (about 40 armoured cars)
- Support Group

▷ 9th Australian Division, commanded by Major General (later Lieutenant General Sir) Leslie Morshead:
- 5 infantry battalions and 51st Regiment, Royal Artillery, sited on the Tocra-Er Regima escarpment, blocking the roads from Benghazi to the east
- 3 infantry battalions, 'untrained, unequipped, and with no MT at Tobruk. They were more of a commitment than an asset.'[3]

▷ 3rd Indian Motor Brigade, at El Adem

Of this polyglot and ill-equipped force, Neame wrote during the second half of April 1941, while in a prisoner of war camp in Italy, that 'I suppose this was not [even] the equivalent of one fifth of the minimum force that I considered the minimum necessary' for the defence of Cyrenaica.[4]

Wavell, preoccupied with assisting Greece, later wrote that he:

> . . . never realised until [he] went out [to Cyrenaica] in the middle of March the deplorable state of the tanks of the 2nd [Armoured] Division. Only 50% of them were runners, and the organisation of the Italian M.13 tanks was still quite incomplete. Both in Cyrenaica and in Greece, the 2nd Division tanks broke down immediately they were asked to move under active service conditions; they were in fact completely worn out before they ever left England.[5]

Neame continually bemoaned the shortcomings of his Command, and requested reinforcements – which were non-existent – on numerous occasions; Morshead, similarly, pointed out deficiencies in his Division's armaments in a memorandum dated 17 March 1941 intended for, but never delivered to, Neame, since it was presented orally to Dill and Wavell the same day. 'No one at home can ever understand', a subaltern then serving in Cyrenaica wrote candidly, 'the pitiably weak army we had then. One armoured brigade, half equipped and just out from England – a new untried Australian Division not even half equipped with rifles and a few more machine guns and hardly any transport', and three artillery regiments.[6] Against this 'pitiably weak' force, Rommel was able to field the German 5th Light Division (the 5th Panzer Regiment of which was equipped with 120 tanks, of which 60 were medium tanks, Panzer IIIs and IVs), and the Italian Ariete (with 80 tanks) and Brescia Divisions.

After Dill and Wavell met with Neame and Morshead on 17 March, Wavell was extremely concerned about Neame's pessimistic attitude, faulty tactical dispositions, and the alarming state of the vehicles in the 2nd Armoured Division. 'I came back anxious and depressed from this visit', Wavell later recorded, 'but there was nothing much I could do about it. The movement to Greece was in full swing and I had nothing left in the bag. But I had forebodings and my confidence in Neame was shaken.'[7] This visit also gave Wavell, who had always been keen to reconnoitre personally the terrain of any potential area of operations, an opportunity to do so, of which he had been deprived due to the hectic requirements of the Eden-Dill visit. Wavell later recognised the significance of this oversight when he wrote:

> I think my first error was that I never went out and looked at the ground for myself till too late. Eden and Dill arrived immediately after the Benghazi battle, and kept me fully occupied, and I never had time to go out till, I think, about the middle of March, and it was rather too late. I remember that I got from a report from Jumbo Wilson an entirely erroneous idea of the escarpment south of Benghazi; I imagined that it was an escarpment similar to that running east from Sollum, with only a very few passages fit for vehicles. I therefore imagined that if we had a mobile force on the escarpment, holding those passages, it would be impossible for an enemy to advance across the open plain below towards Benghazi; and what I had continually in mind for the defence of Benghazi was a mobile force operating on the escarpment and able to attack the flank or rear of any force which attempted to move on Benghazi. When I actually went out and saw the escarpment, I realised that it could be ascended almost anywhere and was no protection. The second topographical feature which I failed to realise was the Salt Marshes near Agheila. If I had gone out there and seen for myself what a formidable barrier they could be made [sic], I think I should certainly have insisted on our pushing our force down to those marshes, whatever the supply difficulties were. As it was, we stopped short of them, and allowed the Germans passage through them.[8]

Thus, Wavell's inaccurate perceptions of the Cyrenaican area of operations, caused by his inability to reconnoitre the terrain there earlier, resulted in his initial underestimation of the forces required to secure the western flank and in his misunderstanding of the nature of the battle which might have to be fought there.

After Wavell's eye-opening visit to Cyrenaica Command on 17 March 1941 (and the information he was able to glean from the rudimentary Ultra intelligence he started receiving only three days before), he realised that he needed to issue specific mission guidance to Neame. To supplement the oral instructions given to Neame during the visit, Wavell dictated a memorandum on 19 March which informed Neame that 'Your present task is to defend Cyrenaica against possible enemy counter attack.' The essence of these instructions was that,

> The safeguarding of your forces from a serious reverse and the infliction of

losses and ultimate defeat on the enemy are of much greater importance than the retention of ground. The reoccupation of Benghasi by the enemy, though it would have considerable propaganda and prestige value, would be of little military importance, and it is certainly not worth while risking defeat to retain it.[9]

Wavell thus realised that the token British force in Cyrenaica would be outnumbered by the Germans, and the only viable course of action, if attacked, was for Neame to conduct a delaying action, trading space for time. It appears that these instructions were temporarily lost en route, with Neame receiving them on 26 March. This delay did not, however, hinder Neame's planning and preparations, since he had earlier issued his own instructions, based upon Wavell's oral guidance of 17 March, and they required no amendment.

Wavell became even more concerned about the security of Cyrenaica after reading an Ultra message on 19 March 1941 stating that all leave had been stopped suddenly for German Air Force units in Africa and that detailed orders were awaited. On the following day, Wavell learned, again via Ultra, that German aircraft were planning to conduct a photographic reconnaissance mission over the forward British area. He reported to the War Office that the 'Situation on Cyrenaica frontier is causing me some anxiety as growing enemy strength may indicate early forward movement. If our advanced troops are driven from present positions there is no good covering position south of Benghazi as country is dead level plain', and concluded that German administrative and logistical problems should preclude anything but a limited advance by the enemy.[10]

Whitehall, according to Hinsley, 'did not dissent from this conclusion'.[11] MI 14, the section of Military Intelligence at the War Office responsible for studying Germany and German-occupied Europe, produced an appreciation which stated relatively accurately that 'Parts, if not the whole, of a [German] light armoured division and possibly units of a second armoured division are believed to be in Tripolitania but the present force could be increased to a total of 5–7 divisions although the rate of reinforcement is likely to be slow.' The assessment basically coincided with Wavell's analysis of the possibility of a German attack in Libya, and went so far as to note that the 'information available tends to show that the Germans fear an attack from Cyrenaica'.[12] Wavell and the intelligence community in London both estimated with a fair degree of accuracy the possible courses of action open to an understrength, unacclimatised German force, but neither of them knew or understood Rommel.

The MI 14 appreciation referred to above stated that Rommel had returned to Berlin, but speculated erroneously that his visit 'may be connected with the report that the experiences of the German troops in Tripolitania have been unsatisfactory'.[13] In fact Rommel, who had come to the conclusion as early as 1 March 1941 that the size of the British covering force in Libya was greatly exaggerated and had no large-scale offensive intentions, and eight days later proclaimed in a draft letter to Berlin that his first objective 'will be the reconquest of Cyrenaica; my second, Northern Egypt and the Suez Canal',[14] desired aggressively to attack the British at the earliest opportunity. He, therefore, optimistically sent his ambitious campaign plans to Berlin.

Rommel's grandiose ideas, however, conflicted with the proposal made by the OKH on 17 March 1941 and approved by Hitler for a much more limited counteroffensive which was little more than a defensive policy for North Africa. Prior to flying to Berlin on 19 March, Rommel instructed that, in his absence, plans should be developed for an operation to seize the eastern outlet of the El Agheila defile on 24 March. The following day, at OKH Headquarters in Berlin, Rommel explained to Field Marshal Walter von Brauchitsch (Commander-in-Chief of the German Army) and Colonel General Franz Halder (Chief of the German Army General Staff) his conviction that British forces in North Africa were significantly fewer than the OKH's estimate of four to eight divisions, that the British were not preparing an offensive, and that the Cyrenaican frontier was only lightly held by Wavell's forces. A compromise was reached in which Brauchitsch and Halder authorised Rommel, after the arrival of the 15th Panzer Division in May 1941, to conduct a limited offensive to recover the area around Agedabia. Later, if the manpower and supply situation warranted, an 'attack toward Benghazi and even Tobruk' could be made.[15]

Disgruntled and 'not very happy', the impetuous Rommel returned to Libya on 23 March 1941. During his absence, a number of British radio transmissions and other intelligence indicated clearly that the British were withdrawing key units from the Mersa Brega area and were leaving only 'strong rearguards' there.[16] He directed the attack on the El Agheila defile to proceed as planned, and the German 3rd Reconnaissance Battalion, with little opposition, occupied the old fort, water points, and airfield at El Agheila early on 24 March. The British patrol there withdrew quickly, and this significant position, considered 'the gateway between Tripolitania and Cyrenaica', was in German possession. Rommel boldly decided to exploit this unexpected windfall quickly, and a short pause ensued while the main bodies of the German and Italian units deployed forward.

In Cairo, Brigadier Shearer, Wavell's Director of Military Intelligence, produced a paper on that same day which concluded that:

> The enemy can concentrate forces for a counter offensive against Cyrenaica with maintenance for 30 days dumped forward as follows:
>
> One Italian Motorised Div.
>   and one German Colonial Armd Div.   by 16 April, 1941.
>
> Additional   "   "   "   "   by 14 May, 1941.
>
> Additional Italian Division
> (Armoured or Lorried Infantry)   by 24 May, 1941.[17]

The British estimate was based upon orthodox logistical requirements, and also stated that if the British were able to retain the port of Benghazi, continuation of a German advance would, at a minimum, be exceedingly difficult. The British were unable to fathom the ease with which Rommel, within a fortnight, would be able not only to capture Benghazi but would also boldly continue his counteroffensive over the open desert.

The following day, the Middle East Joint Planning Staff also considered the 'Immediate Policy on Cyrenaica.' While emphasising the logistical difficulties any potential German attack would encounter, this estimate conceded a local German numerical superiority within the following two or three weeks, 'but against this', the analysis continued, 'should be set his lack of experience in desert conditions'.[18] The guiding policy for the Middle East, according to the paper, was to hold as far forward in Cyrenaica as resources permitted. One of the final recommendations made by the Joint Planning Staff (which, stated bluntly, was what turned out to be the inevitable), was that 'Our policy hitherto has been to accept risks in Cyrenaica in order to assist Greece, but the stage has now been reached when, by continuing this policy, we court disaster in both.'[19]

When Churchill learned of this German advance, he expressed his concern on 26 March 1941, observing 'It is their habit to push on whenever they are not resisted. I presume you are only waiting for the tortoise to stick his head out far enough before chopping it off. It seems extremely important to give them an early taste of our quality.'[20] But this was only one of a number of important tasks Wavell was attempting to direct simultaneously. After returning from a visit to Sudan and Eritrea on 27 March, he responded candidly to the Prime Minister, admitting 'to having taken considerable risk in Cyrenaica after capture of Benghazi in order to provide maximum support for Greece'.[21] After relating the status of his units in North Africa and noting that steps to reinforce Cyrenaica were in hand, Wavell accurately forecast that the next month or two would be 'anxious'. As it turned out, the events which were unfolding at the time and in the following fortnight, would require Wavell to summon his innermost reserves of professionalism, perseverance, imperturbability, and competence.

In the meantime, on 25 March 1941, the Yugoslav Government signed a pact of allegiance with the Axis Powers. Two days later, after Wavell's return from the Sudan and Eritrea, a spontaneous and bloodless *coup d'état*, led by the armed forces, overthrew the pro-Axis Yugoslav Government. Also on 27 March, the British success at Keren permitted Wavell to order the first elements of the 4th Indian Division to move to Port Sudan for redeployment to buttress Neame's weak Cyrenaica Command. Admiral Cunningham's stalwart battlefleet soundly trounced the Italians at the Battle of Cape Matapan (as we have already seen) on the 28th, and the 3rd Indian Motor Brigade arrived at El Adem the next day to reinforce the western flank. London's eyes, however, remained fixed firmly on the Balkans, with British hopes for a Balkan bloc raised considerably by the pro-Allied Yugoslav revolt.

Wavell continued to view the situation in Cyrenaica with trepidation. On 30 March, he signalled Neame with reports of large German forces landing at Tripoli, but added that he did not believe 'that he [the Germans] can make any big effort for at least another month'.[22] Wavell also informed Neame that his task for the following two months would be to prevent the enemy 'from crossing the 150 miles between Agheila and Benghazi without heavy loss to your armoured and mobile troops',[23] and that no additional reinforcements would be available during that period. Neame responded the next day that he was quite clear as to his mission.

Rommel renewed his offensive early on 31 March, a few hours after Neame had sent that signal. One German column, according to Neame, advanced from El Agheila, and the second from a position some fifteen miles south,[24] with an immediate objective of the weak British position at Mersa Brega, the right flank of the eight-mile-long front held by the Support Group. On the left flank there was about a five-mile gap which was impassable to tanks, and beyond this the 3rd Armoured Brigade was echeloned to the North-East. The German ground attack was initially cautious and was resisted by the Support Group, the commander of which requested at about 1730 hours that the 3rd Armoured Brigade should attack the German right flank. Gambier-Parry, however, responded that there would be 'insufficient time to get them into action from their present position before dark'.[25] 'It would have been better', Wavell wrote with hindsight:

> . . . if the 3rd Armoured Brigade had made an immediate counter-attack, their tanks would then at least have done some damage to the enemy before breaking down, as most of them did in the withdrawal. But Gambier-Parry was quite right in carrying out his instructions to withdraw to the escarpment above Benghazi if heavily attacked.[26]

After further German attacks, the Support Group and 3rd Armoured Brigade withdrew under the shroud of darkness to a pre-planned phase line about twenty miles in front of Agedabia.

Although there was a lull in the ground fighting in the Western Desert on 1 April 1941, the 3rd Armoured Brigade continued its withdrawal to Agedabia. As a result of aerial and ground reconnaissances conducted that day, Rommel realised that the British were withdrawing. 'It was a chance I could not resist', he wrote later, 'and I gave orders for Agedabia to be attacked and taken, in spite of the fact that our instructions were not to undertake any such operation before the end of May.'[27] The aggressive German advance the next morning cut off a number of the British units, and the Support Group then moved some thirty miles to a position north of

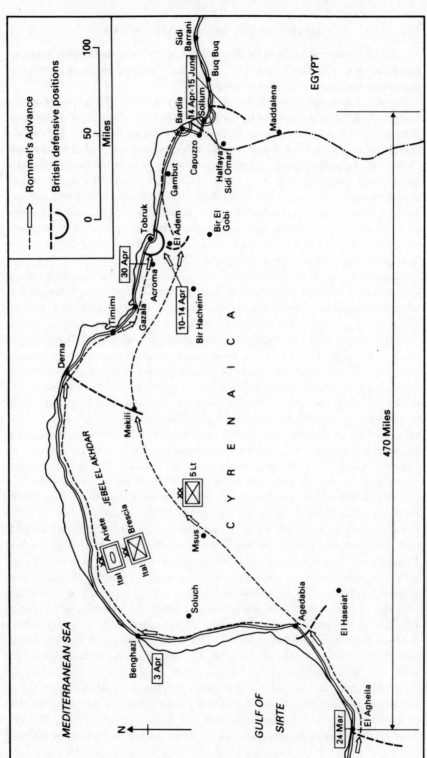

MEDITERRANEAN SEA

N

GULF OF
SIRTE

EGYPT

Rommel's Advance

British defensive positions

Miles

0   50   100

JEBEL EL AKHDAR

CYRENAICA

Benghazi

3 Apr

Soluch

Agedabia

El Haseiat

El Agheila

24 Mar

470 Miles

Derna

Timimi

Gazala

Acroma

30 Apr

Tobruk

El Adem

10-14 Apr

Bir Hacheim

Mekili

Msus

5 Lt

Ariete
Ital

Brescia
Ital

Gambut

Bir El
Gobi

Capuzzo

Bardia

Sollum

14 Apr-15 June

Halfaya
Sidi Omar

Buq Buq

Sidi
Barrani

Maddalena

Map 8. Rommel's first offensive 24 March-15 June 1941

Agedabia. Neame attempted ineffectively to control the battle from his main headquarters, a difficult task even if he had had his full complement of signallers and communications equipment.

Wavell informed London on 2 April 1941 that 'Forward troops in Cyrenaica are being attacked by German Colonial armoured division', and that the losses were not serious. Wavell was, however, concerned about the poor mechanical state of the armoured vehicles, and noted that he had told Neame to keep his scanty forces intact, 'even if it involves considerable withdrawal, possibly even from Benghazi'.[28] The Prime Minister's prompt rejoinder was that it would be 'most desireable to chop the German advance against Cyrenaica. Any rebuff to the Germans would have far-reaching prestige effects.' While he sanctioned the delaying operation in progress, Churchill remonstrated strongly that 'any serious withdrawal from Benghazi would appear most melancholy'.[29]

Meanwhile, in the Western Desert, Neame – still in his static head-quarters well over a hundred miles from the scene of action – attempted to keep the withdrawal under his personal control. His directions to Gambier-Parry were generally in consonance with Wavell's guidance of 19 March 1941 to ensure that the Support Group protected the Agedabia-Benghazi road, while the armoured force took up 'a position on the flank towards Antelat, with the object of discovering the direction of the enemy's advance, which may be North towards Benghasi or possibly North-East across the desert towards Tobruk'.[30] Neame, however, directed Gambier-Parry to be prepared to move the Armoured Brigade towards Sceleidima, about thirty miles north of Antelat, but more importantly, at a location where the escarpment rises steeply and the terrain is broken with deep ravines. In Gambier-Parry's acknowledgement, which took almost two hours in trans-mission, he requested to retain personal control of his armour assets, and advised that he might have to evacuate his positions that night. As a result, he questioned Neame's directive which would have required him to with-draw the two main elements of his Division – the 3rd Armoured Brigade and the Support Group (which was to continue to cover the road to Benghazi) – in two separate groups not within supporting distance of each other. It was preferable, in his view, 'to avoid a course of action that involved splitting his force and so risking defeat in detail, even though keeping the Support Group and armoured brigade together might result in uncovering the coast road to Benghazi'.[31] Gambier-Parry reported further that his division had been reduced to 22 cruiser tanks and 25 light tanks, and that he expected one tank to break down from mechanical failure for every ten miles travelled.

Wavell, due to his lack of confidence in Neame's ability to react to Rommel's counter-offensive and conduct a delaying operation properly, flew to Headquarters Cyrenaica Command on the afternoon of 2 April 1941. Shortly before Wavell's arrival, Neame received Gambier-Parry's message referred to above. Neame was about to accede to Gambier-Parry's requests, but Wavell intervened quickly, ordering that the coast road to Benghazi should continue to be blocked for as long as possible. From this point onwards, events, both on the battlefield and in the command element, become increasingly confused and confusing, especially during the following day. Disconcerting is Wavell's assumption, albeit for a short time, of personal command of the battle and his contradiction of Neame's orders and his emphasis on blocking the road to Benghazi, the latter in apparent contravention of his own directive of 19 March 1941. The British Official History observed that:

> This emphasis on Benghazi is interesting, because the basis of General Wavell's previous instructions was that the armoured troops were to be conserved as much as possible, and that there was to be no hesitation in giving up ground – including even Benghazi. The explanation appears to be that General Wavell was thinking as usual as much of the enemy's difficulties as of his own. He did not believe that the enemy was ready for an ambitious operation; yet General Rommel had taken the offensive, and must therefore be presumed to have in view a quickly obtainable objective. This could only be Benghazi, which he ought not to be allowed to have for the asking.[32]

The Australian Official History, however, explained Wavell's decisions and actions in this incident in a more pragmatic manner:

> Now that Gambier-Parry's force was too small to split, Wavell ordered the whole division to withdraw by this route [while blocking the road to Benghazi]. Perhaps he thought that if (as Gambier-Parry stated) the armoured division was likely to lose one tank out of its small force in each ten miles of movement, little advantage was to be gained by expending it in long withdrawals out of contact; . . .[33]

and it would have been most advantageous to use this force to delay the enemy on the Agedabia-Benghazi road. It is quite probable that Wavell believed Rommel's forces would exhaust themselves and outrun their lines of communication after capturing Benghazi, and would remain at that port until resupplied and augmented with additional forces.

Brigadier (later Field Marshal Lord) Harding, who had served as O'Connor's Brigadier General Staff in Western Desert Force, was then serving Neame in the same capacity. Harding was distressed at Neame's inability to control the battle effectively, and 'took an opportunity to talk to Wavell personally and beg him to send O'Connor back to replace Neame'.[34] That action, combined with Wavell's observation that 'In the battle, he [Neame] seemed to me never to have any idea whatever where his troops were, or to make any particular effort to find out',[35] caused Wavell to send a message to his Chief of Staff in Cairo, who in turn contacted O'Connor and told him to fly out to Cyrenaica Command Headquarters at the earliest opportunity. O'Connor, with his unparalleled experience of desert warfare and knowledge of the area of operations, would 'advise' on the situation. Those instructions were, however, superseded a few hours later by another message from Wavell stating that O'Connor would take over command from Neame. 'This meant that the situation was really serious', O'Connor wrote less than a month later, 'and that just what I had feared might happen, was in fact happening. I cannot pretend I was happy at the thought of taking over Command in the middle of a battle, which was already lost.'[36]

The 3rd of April was, from Wavell's viewpoint, 'the unfortunate day of these operations'.[37] This extraordinarily tense and chaotic situation was not so much the result of hostile action, but was due primarily to an erroneous report of enemy activity. As the Support Group continued to cover the left flank of the 9th Australian Division in their withdrawal to Regima, the 3rd Armoured Brigade proceeded to Msus, its primary petrol and supply dump, reported to be the objective of a German column. When the officer-in-charge of the Msus logistical depot received the report that the enemy was approaching, he ordered that the fuel be destroyed immediately. The report turned out to be false, and the lack of petrol was to curtail the activities of the British tanks severely. Benghazi was also evacuated on 3 April.

O'Connor, accompanied by the recently promoted Brigadier Combe (who had commanded the 11th Hussars and 'Combe Force' during Operation 'Compass'), arrived at Barce at about 1500 hours on 3 April 1941. Wavell briefed O'Connor as to the activities of the past few days, including the period when he took over control of operations from Neame. 'As a result of these orders', O'Connor wrote shortly afterwards, 'the situation seemed most confused.' Wavell, according to Neame, still believed that the enemy could not advance beyond Benghazi: 'The Chief [Wavell] was still doubtful of the enemy's intentions', O'Connor observed retrospectively,

> ... and continued to hope that his [Rommel's] ultimate objective was not further east than Benghazi, but I think the wish was father to the hope.
>
> It seemed to me the situation was definitely more serious than the Chief believed, and that one of the most important things to do was to get our defences organised much further east than the Benghazi area.[38]

O'Connor, as noted earlier, was extremely reluctant to assume command under such dire conditions, and stressed to Wavell that he did not know the units then in Cyrenaica Command, and believed that Wavell was misjudging Neame. Accordingly, O'Connor asked Wavell to retain Neame in command, with O'Connor to remain with and 'advise' Neame until the situation stabilised. Wavell agreed to O'Connor's proposition, and returned to Cairo; the latter, however, came to regret his decision, believing this 'to be the worst proposal he [O'Connor] had ever made'.[39]

The rapidity of Rommel's advance certainly affected Wavell, but

Churchill's claim that 'I seem to remember Eden saying that Wavell had "aged ten years in the night"'[40] after the initial German attack, appears to be little more than a calumnious aspersion. O'Connor later wrote less critically that Wavell, on the afternoon of 3 April 1941, looked 'worn and rather depressed, but he soon cheered up a bit . . .'[41] Harding, however, who was with Wavell throughout 2 and 3 April, believed that 'he [Wavell] inspired me with complete confidence that all would work out well really without doing much about it and that again was typical of the man'.[42] While this episode did not have as detrimental an impact upon Wavell's self-confidence and performance as Churchill would have one believe, the decision to keep O'Connor at Headquarters of Cyrenaica Command to 'advise' Neame violated the principle of unity of command and was not typical of Wavell's sound judgement. Wavell was, according to Benson, at fault for 'this bad arrangement'.[43]

Realising the seriousness of Rommel's offensive and the potential for a further advance into Egypt itself, Wavell, upon his return to Cairo, withdrew the 7th Australian Division from 'Lustre' Force and the incomplete 6th British Division from participation in the proposed operation to seize the Dodecanese. To exacerbate Wavell's problems, on 3 April 1941 the pro-Axis Rashid Ali el Gailani seized power in Iraq by overthrowing the pro-British Regent. This crisis could not have come at a more inopportune time for Wavell, who had veritably no resources to spare to intervene in this situation.

As the British forces retreated precipitately in the face of the reinvigorated German offensive, it became obvious to Rommel through aerial reconnaissance that his forces would have to converge on Mechili if they hoped to intercept a considerable portion of the British force. On 6 April, O'Connor realised, however, that the exposed British left flank could be protected from encirclement only by a general withdrawal, and in Neame's absence, he ordered that mission to be executed. Late that night, during the ensuing confusion, O'Connor, Neame, and Combe lost their way in the desert, inadvertently drove into a German battalion, and were captured. This was a bitter blow to the British in general and Wavell in particular; de Guingand, who delivered this information to Wavell on the 7th, stated sympathetically that 'The news of the capture of both Neame and O'Connor came as a real shock to the C-in-C [Wavell], and I have never seen him so moved.'[44] After receiving this dreary news, Wavell went back to his quarters.

The 9th Australian Division conducted its withdrawal from Tocra via Barce, Derna, and Tmimi, and by the night of 7 April 1941 it, along with 2nd Armoured Division's Support Group, was deployed in positions some fifteen miles west of Tobruk. The 9th Division's 24th Infantry Brigade, joined recently by a brigade of the 7th Australian Division which had been diverted from transfer to Greece, was in Tobruk preparing defensive positions. The following morning, the remnants of the 2nd Armoured Division, the 3rd Indian Motor Brigade, and other small units tried, unsuccessfully, to break out of Mechili. Gambier-Parry and some 3,000 of his soldiers suffered the same ill-fortune as O'Connor and Neame and went into the German 'bag'.

The decision to hold Tobruk was made at a Commanders-in-Chiefs' meeting, also attended by Eden and Dill, held on Palm Sunday, 6 April 1941, only a few hours after it had been learned that the Germans had launched their lightning attack on Yugoslavia and Greece. At this sombre and tense meeting, the pros and cons of holding Tobruk, and other alternatives, were examined exhaustively. The Army had cached a large amount of supplies at Tobruk, and was reluctant to lose such an important logistical stockpile; both the Royal Navy and Royal Air Force were in agreement that it was essential to keep the enemy, particularly the German Air Force, as far away from Alexandria as possible, and holding Tobruk would be a means of doing so. Admiral Cunningham also stated his conviction that the Royal Navy could resupply Tobruk from the sea.[45] 'After the problem had been discussed from each service point of view', wrote de Guingand, a staff officer present at the meeting,

> Wavell was asked to give his views. I admired him tremendously at that moment. He had a very heavy load to carry but he looked calm and collected, and said that in his view we must hold Tobruk, and that he considered that this was possible. One could feel the sense of relief that this decision produced, and the other Commanders-in-Chief agreed, . . .[46]

This incident again illustrated Wavell's paramount position of influence among his Royal Navy and Royal Air Force counterparts, and the fact that he was responsible for the crucial decision to maintain Tobruk. In addition, Tobruk would remain a thorn in the side of Rommel's line of advance, for the retention of that port by the British added another 700 miles to Rommel's already extended line of communications.

On 8 April 1941, Wavell flew to Tobruk to ensure the implementation of the decision to hold that key location. He took with him Major General (later Lieutenant General Sir) John Lavarack, the commander of the 7th Australian Division, whom he had appointed to succeed the captured Neame as commander of Cyrenaica Command. During the ensuing conference there with Harding, in temporary command at Tobruk, from whom he received an updated situation report, and other senior officers, 'he [Wavell] asked me', wrote Harding,

> if I thought we could hold it [Tobruk] to which I replied 'Yes Sir, provided Rommel does not wheel up a mass of heavy tanks and the Royal Navy can maintain supplies'. In response he said 'Well if you think you can hold it, you had better hold it. Give me your millboard and a sheet of foolscap.' He then wrote out a directive to hold Tobruk in his large round handwriting on one side

of the sheet of foolscap [actually three sheets], handed it to me to read, asked if I was satisfied and then said 'Show it to General Lavarack' who expressed his satisfaction whereupon, without saying any more Wavell left. Again I felt complete confidence in the future. It was certainly an uncanny knack he [Wavell] had of inspiring confidence without really doing very much to produce it.[47]

These instructions, in addition to appointing Lavarack formally to the command of all troops in Cyrenaica, directed him to hold the enemy's advance at Tobruk for about two months, to give time for the assembly of forces for the defence of Egypt. Wavell also realistically charged Lavarack with the preparation of evacuation plans from Tobruk, should they become necessary, and to maintain as mobile a defence as possible to hinder the enemy's ability to concentrate his forces.

On the return flight to Cairo, Wavell's plane, due to mechanical problems, made a forced landing west of Sollum. During the evening a patrol approached and Wavell, apprehensive that the group was German, sought refuge in a neaby wadi and burned a number of sensitive documents he was carrying. Fortunately, the group turned out to be Sudanese, and Wavell was taken to Sollum. During his absence, General Headquarters in Cairo had called Tobruk enquiring frantically about the overdue Commander-in-Chief's whereabouts, and Harding had sent out search parties. Shortly thereafter, at about midnight, Harding received a telephone call from Wavell himself, who 'replied that he was alright, they had been forced to land at Sollum and would I send a Lizzie (Lysander aircraft) for him in the morning' to take him to Cairo. According to Harding, Wavell was 'the most phlegmatic and near imperturbable senior commander I ever knew and I have worked closely with quite a few'.[48]

The Germans, regardless of casualties sustained and logistical difficulties, continued to press their attack vigorously. Rommel feverishly made preparations to assault Tobruk before the British had time to reorganise and prepare their defences, and was able to invest the British 'fortress' on 11 April 1941. That day Wavell travelled to Greece, and shortly after his return to Cairo on the thirteenth – Easter Sunday – the Germans resolutely assaulted the southern defences of the twenty-eight mile Tobruk perimeter. By noon on the following day, the German attack had been soundly repulsed.

The Germans had also been able to continue their advance past Tobruk and towards Bardia, a situation which, combined with the earlier capture of Neame and O'Connor, necessitated a change in the British organisation and chain of command. With effect from 14 April 1941, the Western Desert Force was reconstituted under the command of Beresford-Peirse, who had commanded the 4th Indian Division. After successfully defeating the German attack on Tobruk, Lavarack was disappointed to have to return to the command of the 7th Australian Division, now at Mersa Matruh, while

Morshead became commander of the Tobruk fortress, directly responsible to Wavell.

With the exception of a half-hearted Italian attack on Tobruk on 16 April 1941, there was a temporary lull in the fighting in the Western Desert as Rommel planned intently for a subsequent assault on Tobruk and diligently trained his troops and shepherded his resources to accomplish that goal. In Greece, however, the war raged, as the British force continued its withdrawal to the Thermopylae Line in anticipation of its imminent evacuation from the Greek shores. There were ominous signs from London, in the form of a more demanding bombardment of minutely-detailed telegrams, which placed Wavell increasingly on the defensive from that sphere as well.

This apparent stabilisation of the front in North Africa prompted Churchill to write an inspiring directive entitled 'The War in the Mediterranean' on 14 April 1941, which was sent to Wavell two days later. The gist of these instructions was that the German lines of communication across the Mediterranean and from Tripoli to El Agheila must be subject to incessant harassment and interdiction. After stressing the significance of Tobruk, Churchill declared that 'It is above all necessary that General Wavell should regain Unit ascendancy over the enemy and destroy his small raiding parties, instead of our being harassed and hunted by them.'[49] While conceding that the directive 'breathed a splendid spirit of courage, defiance, and initiative', Kennedy, Director of Military Operations at the War Office, opined that it,

> . . . was cast almost in the form of an Operation Order by a Commander-in-Chief; and it included unsound and impracticable propositions which could only be dismissed after hours and days of unprofitable work by busy and responsible men who would have been better employed in getting on with their jobs.[50]

This order again reflects not only Churchill's ardent desire to be in total control of military operations, but also reveals implicitly Churchill's increasing distrust of Wavell's ability to allocate properly his resources to stem the tide of Axis aggression. Churchill's myopic directive failed to address the deteriorating Greek situation, which was Wavell's foremost priority and concern. Two days later, the Chiefs of Staff attempted to reconcile Wavell's multiple priorities by issuing clarified guidance: 'victory in Libya counts first, evacuation of troops from Greece second, Tobruk shipping, unless indispensible to victory, must be fitted in as convenient. Iraq can be ignored and Crete can be worked up later.'[51] 'But no mere directive could erase Wavell's colossal burden', Roger Parkinson observed realistically, 'dealing as he had to with operations in Greece, Libya, Crete, Iraq – officially still in the Indian command area – Kenya, Somaliland, the Sudan, Abyssinia and Syria, . . .'[52]

Although given official permission to 'ignore' Iraq, Wavell had earlier

taken into consideration the potential of enemy infiltration into or occupation of Iraq and Persia. Memoranda had been exchanged between Wavell
and General (later Field Marshal) Sir Claude Auchinleck, who had become
Commander-in-Chief, India, in February 1941, over the responsibility for
the despatch, maintenance, and reinforcement of any force sent to the area.
Contingency plans for 'Trout', 'Salmon', and 'Herring' were replaced by
plans for Force 'Sabine' to consist of three divisions. On 8 March Wavell
and Auchinleck agreed, and the Chiefs of Staff concurred, that if any
military operations occurred in Iraq, they would be controlled initially by
India. Shortly after the Rashid Ali coup of 2 April 1941, the Chiefs of Staff
asked Wavell what forces he could send to Iraq; Wavell had responded on 7
April that all he could do in an extreme emergency was transport one
British battalion from Palestine to Iraq: 'Any other action is impossible with
existing forces.' Considering that Wavell's forces were already stretched to
the limit in Italian East Africa and attempting to blunt German offensives
in the Western Desert and the Balkans, 'The Chiefs of Staff', Compton
MacKenzie observed with acerbity, 'might have known this without waiting
for Wavell's reply.[53]

In response to a request from Churchill, the Viceroy of India stated that
the Commander-in-Chief, India, could divert to Basra one brigade which
was scheduled to sail from Karachi to Singapore on 10 April 1941. This
offer was readily accepted by the British Government, and on the 10th
Wavell quite rightly told London that he was fully engaged in Cyrenaica
and could not even spare one battalion for Iraq, with the best course of
action being firm diplomacy and Royal Air Force support. As the assets for
'Sabine' were being provided by India, Wavell persevered in attempting to
stabilise the tenuous Middle East situation, and was undoubtedly relieved
when he was advised by the Chiefs of Staff in the aforementioned 18 April
telegram: 'Don't worry about Iraq for the present. It looks like going
smoothly.'

Wavell would later be forced to assist in the intervention in Iraq, but the
initial phase of this imbroglio clearly had far-reaching consequences for
him. Churchill, apparently oblivious of the dimensions of the burdens
Wavell was shouldering and unwilling to understand the precariousness of
the British position in the Middle East, attributed Wavell's reluctance
further to dissipate his forces to indecisiveness, lethargy, and an unwillingness to take risks. Auchinleck, on the other hand, was praised for his
alacrity and promptness in dealing with this situation. Hence, while
Wavell's reputation, in the opinion of the Prime Minister, was sinking
steadily, the positive attitude displayed and the decisive actions taken by
Auchinleck in this episode earned him Churchill's attention and admiration.

Indeed, on about 19 April 1941, Churchill recommended that Auchinleck
should be transferred to the Middle East as second-in-command to Wavell.
Dill was adamantly against this move, believing that Auchinleck was doing

invaluable work in India. Dill had also told Wavell earlier that if anything should happen to him, he would recommend that Auchinleck succeed him in the Middle East. If Auchinleck was sent to Egypt at this time, it would certainly appear to Wavell that he was on the verge of being superseded, with a resultant dimunition in his self-confidence and perhaps in his performance. The CIGS believed that Auchinleck, 'though a fine General with great force of character, is not a super-man. Wavell has a better brain than Auchinleck, and is more versed in the conduct of military operations under modern conditions.'[54] Dill continued to defend Wavell:

> I realise fully the difficult position in which Wavell finds himself. I realise the mistake he and I have made, i.e., underestimating the forces which the Germans could concentrate and maintain in Cyrenaica. I realise too that he has many balls on which to keep his one eye; but when he has to go to Greece, for example, he has a very able Chief Staff Officer in General Arthur Smith, who is perfectly capable of acting in his name. Moreover, I think it is important to remember that Wavell is not in fact commanding in the field. He is much more, with the other C.'s-in-C., a deputy Chief of Staff for the Near and Middle East area.[55]

Dill recommended to the Prime Minister, in summing up, that 'the minute you lose confidence in Wavell, or should anything happen to him, Auchinleck should at once succeed him'.[56] They were prophetic words.

Wavell, as in the case of Iraq, had similarly foreseen the importance of Crete. It will be recalled that well over a month before the Italian declaration of war in June 1940, Wavell received information about French plans to establish a base on Crete after the expected outbreak of war, but at that early date even the one or two Allied infantry battalions it was proposed to send there 'could not (repeat not) be provided from British resources and would have to be provided by French'.[57] The Italian attack on Greece in October 1940 increased the strategic importance of Crete to such a high degree that Wavell sent two battalions, and a temporary naval base was established on the island. Those forces were augmented periodically by additional support units, but the overall shortage of manpower and material resources, and more pressing requirements for their utilisation, continually hindered Wavell's ability to reinforce Crete significantly and prepare its defences adequately. The Chiefs of Staff, it will be seen, were totally unrealistic in ambiguously advising Wavell on 18 April 1941 that 'Crete can be worked up later.'

Wavell flew to Greece on 19 April to discuss and coordinate the British evacuation. On the day before his departure, Wavell informed Churchill that 'In this desert warfare it is armoured strength that counts, especially armour with speed and range, and this is where I am so weak.'[58] Wavell cabled fuller and more detailed appreciations to Dill also on the 18th, and estimated that the Germans had at least 150 tanks in Cyrenaica, most of

Plate 14   'Sugar for his horse'. From a series of photographs entitled 'A Day with General Sir Archibald Wavell, Commander-in-Chief, Middle East Forces' (Cairo, 18 February 1941) (*IWM*)

Plate 15   Another photograph from 'A Day with General Sir Archibald Wavell . . .': 'After his morning ride, he reads the morning paper before breakfast'. (Cairo, 18 February 1941) (*IWM*)

Plate 16   Mr Anthony Eden (Foreign Secretary); General Sir John Dill (CIGS); Admiral Sir Andrew Cunningham; Air Chief Marshal Sir Arthur Longmore; Wavell. (Cairo, 11 March 1941) (*IWM*)

Plate 17   At the Cairo 'War Council', 11 March 1941: Smith; Dill; Wavell; and Eden (*IWM*)

Plate 18   Overlooking the Nile. Australian camera men filming Wavell (Cairo, 11 March 1941) (*IWM*)

Plate 19   With Lady Wavell and Sir John Dill (Cairo, 18 February 1941) (*IWM*)

Plate 20   Lieutenant General Sir Thomas Blamey, commanding 1st Australian Corps, and Eden. (Cairo, 11 March 1941) (*IWM*)

Plate 21   Greece, 21 April 1941. British vehicles passing Greek transport, including ox wagons, on a narrow mountain road (*IWM*)

Plate 22   Lieutenant General Alan Cunningham and General Jan Smuts monitor progress of the East African campaign (Kenya, 21 March 1941) (*IWM*)

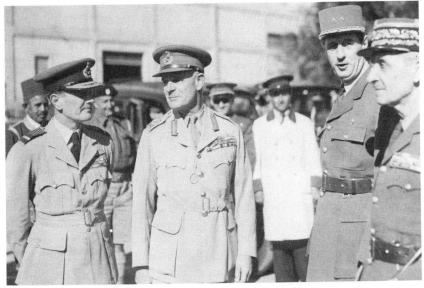

Plate 23   Longmore, Wavell, and General Catroux meet General Charles de Gaulle on his arrival in Cairo. (1 April 1941) (*IWM*)

Plate 24   Wavell at an observation post at Merdjayoun, personally
             directing operations during the Syrian campaign. (26 June
             1941) (*IWM*)

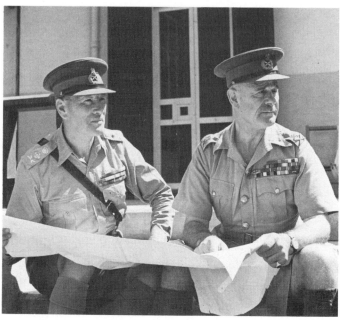

Plate 25   General Sir Claude Auchinleck and Wavell discuss future
             operations (Cairo, 8 September 1941) (*IWM*)

Plate 26   Wavell and General Wauchope, flanked by pipers of The Black Watch. Personal staff members NGA Noble, AJ Wavell, DH Walker, JC Monteith, and FJ Burnaby-Atkins. (New Delhi 1946) (*Reproduced by courtesy of Lieutenant Colonel FJ Burnaby-Atkins*)

Plate 27   Lord and Lady Wavell greet Lady Pamela Mountbatten. Looking on are Captain FJ Burnaby-Atkins and Wentworth Beaumont (New Delhi, 22 March 1947).(*Reproduced by courtesy of Lieutenant Colonel FJ Burnaby-Atkins*)

Plate 28   Wavell, as Colonel of The Black Watch, visiting the 1st
             Battalion. He is speaking to CSM Faltergill, Captain FJ
             Burnaby-Atkins and the Commanding Officer, Lieutenant
             Colonel Bernard Fergusson, look on. (Vogelsang, West
             Germany, June 1949).
             (*Reproduced by courtesy of Lieutenant Colonel FJ Burnaby-Atkins*)

Plate 29   Lord and Lady Wavell visit the 2nd Battalion, The Black
             Watch. (Karachi, 23 March 1947). (*Reproduced by courtesy of
             Lieutenant Colonel John Benson*)

them in the Bardia-Sollum area, and it was highly likely that they were preparing to advance into Egypt. This German armoured phalanx greatly outnumbered the British tank assets, and the force ratio was made potentially even worse when a newly-arrived German unit was tentatively identified as an armoured division (containing over 400 tanks) rather than as a colonial armoured division as expected. Even though outnumbered, at Wavell's direction, planning was initiated on 19 April for a limited counterattack, to be known as Operation 'Battleaxe', against the Germans.

Churchill seems to have been shocked into reality by the combination of Wavell's telegrams about his own and the estimated German tank strengths and Ultra revelations of the imminent arrival at Tripoli of the 15th Panzer Division,[59] to which Wavell had referred obliquely. The Prime Minister persuaded the reluctant Chiefs of Staff to agree to the reinforcement of the Middle East – via the Mediterranean – 'with tanks with all speed and at all costs'[60] on 21 April 1941. Five days later a convoy of six fast merchant ships, codenamed Operation 'Tiger', left England. On 22 April, Churchill advised Wavell that 'I have been working hard for you in the last few days, and you will, I am sure, be glad to know that we are sending 307 of our best tanks through the Mediterranean, hoping they will reach you around May 10,'[61] but the Prime Minister imagined fancifully that these tanks would be the panacea to all Wavell's equipment and personnel shortages in the Middle East: 'If this consignment gets through the hazards of the passage, . . ., the boot will be on the other leg and no German should remain in Cyrenaica by the end of the month of June.'[62]

The period of the British evacuation from Greece, 23–29 April 1941, provided little respite for Wavell. To maximise the number of naval sorties and soldiers that could be recovered from Greece, it was necessary for Crete to serve as the 'receptacle' for the soldiers evacuated. The defence of Crete then became a major task, made all the more urgent in the knowledge that that island could serve as a forward staging area for further German infiltration or even intervention in Iraq or the Levant States. In addition, since the Ploesti oilfields were within bombing range of British aircraft based on Crete, it was probably known that Hitler would not tolerate an Allied presence there.

The situation in Iraq was now deteriorating markedly. Furthermore, the Free French movement and the stability of the Levant States, Syria and Lebanon, French mandates under Vichy hegemony and bordering Palestine to the north, were becoming matters of increased concern. German Generalleutnant Friedrich von Paulus, a representative of Halder and the OKH, arrived at Rommel's Headquarters on 27 April 1941. His mission was 'to send back a clear picture of the situation, assess the chances of a successful defensive should Sollum be lost, try to discover Rommel's intentions, and make him understand that OKH had very few resources from which to send him any further help'.[63] This visit not only foreshadowed another determined assault on Tobruk, but Paulus's intercepted after-action report (as we shall see) was to be misunderstood by the British with serious ramifications for Wavell. In addition, British forces still had not completed the liquidation of Italian East Africa.

The barrage of signals from London continued unabated. On 24 April 1941, Churchill asked Wavell for a full report on the recent 'severe defeat' in the Western Desert. As has been demonstrated, however, the Prime Minister had been apprised fully and regularly by Wavell of the units in the Western Desert and their operational readiness, as well as which units were being despatched to Greece. In addition, London and Cairo had shared the same misperceptions about Rommel's ability to launch an offensive. The General, however, replied the next day, chronicling frankly and lucidly his understanding of the reasons for the British rout. He noted that the German attack had occurred at least a fortnight before it was expected, and that the enemy's advance had been 'hastily improvised'. The British 3rd Armoured Brigade was also an improvised unit: 'In view of state of armoured fighting vehicles at end of Cyrenaican campaign, it was best I could produce if any armoured force was to accompany troops to Greece.'[64] In commenting upon his initial instructions to Neame, for the 2nd Armoured Division to withdraw gradually if attacked by a larger enemy force, and then to counterattack after the enemy had extended himself too far, Wavell stated 'As matters turned out this was mistaken policy,'[65] and that the best course of action would have been for the British tanks to counterattack the Germans immediately. After outlining the remaining events of the British withdrawal, Wavell declared unequivocally that the 'main responsibility is mine'.[66]

In the aftermath of the German onslaughts in the Western Desert and in the Balkans, there was great concern at the potential British inability to stop Rommel at the Egyptian frontier. Indeed, on 13 April 1941, Wavell's Chief of Staff admitted to the British Ambassador that he thought the Germans would be at the Pyramids, only eight miles west of Cairo, at any moment.[67] Accordingly, on 15 April, Wavell had directed the updating of the 'Worst Possible Case' scheme which he had written originally on 25 May 1940 (see page 61). On 24 April he sent to the War Office, by the hand of a liaison officer, a copy of his revised 'Worst Possible Case' paper.

Churchill was blissfully unaware of the existence of the 'Worst Possible Case' contingency plan until 27 April 1941. That evening Kennedy, along with General Sir Alan Brooke (Commander-in-Chief, Home Forces), Captain (later Lord) David Margesson (Secretary of State for War), Professor Frederick Lindemann (later Viscount Cherwell), Ismay, and two secretaries, attended a dinner party hosted by Churchill at Chequers. After the Prime Minister had delivered a radio broadcast, he returned to his guests and dinner began. After a discussion with Brooke about the defence of the United Kingdom, the Prime Minister then turned to Kennedy and asked him what he thought of the situation in Egypt. The Director of

Military Operations responded candidly that if the German supply routes were not 'interrupted', the enemy might be able to envelop Egypt from both East and West, and that 'we could be unable to provide adequate forces for its defence'.[68] Kennedy has described Churchill's virulent reaction and the ensuing conversation:

> Churchill flushed at this, and lost his temper. His eyes flashed and he shouted, 'Wavell has 400,000 men. If they lose Egypt, blood will flow. I will have firing parties to shoot the generals.'
>
> 'You need not be afraid they will not fight', I replied. 'Of course they will fight. I am only arguing that we should decide the price we are prepared to pay, and can afford to pay, for the defence of the Middle East.'
>
> But his wrath was not appeased. He accused me of defeatism in thinking it possible that Egypt might be lost; he said that I must get such ideas out of my head – determination was what was needed.[69]

After the Prime Minister finally paused, Kennedy explained that Churchill had misinterpreted what he had said, as it did not mean defeatism to consider the worst scenario as well as all other contingencies, and in fact 'that was a normal function of any commander or of any staff'.[70] Kennedy then stated that he knew Wavell had prepared such a plan for the withdrawal from Egypt if it became necessary, but that such a drastic course of action did not indicate defeatism, since the fight could be continued from other areas. Churchill was implacable: 'At this he fairly exploded. "This comes as a flash of lightning to me", he exclaimed, "I never heard such ideas. War is a contest of wills. It is pure defeatism to speak as you have done".'[71] Wolf Heckmann called Churchill's treatment of Wavell in this incident 'disgraceful', but it was only one of a series of recent episodes in which their relationship was deteriorating rapidly.[72]

Churchill's fury did not diminish overnight, and the following morning he minuted urgently to the CIGS: 'The DMO yesterday spoke of plans which had been prepared in certain eventualities for the evacuation of Egypt. Let me see these plans, and any material bearing upon them.'[73] Dill sent him Wavell's 'Mongoose' plan, and without the knowledge or advice of the Chiefs of Staff, Churchill prepared a new directive for the conduct of the war. This directive reflected clearly Churchill's anguish at having borne upon his shoulders the enormous vicissitudes of the war effort, especially after the shattering of the British defences in the Western Desert and the evacuation from Greece, and his great concern for the ability of Great Britain to sustain the war effort. This dictate had in many respects been provoked by Churchill's knowledge of Wavell's 'Mongoose' plan, which he condemned: 'All plans for evacuation of Egypt or for closing or destroying the Suez Canal are to be called in and kept under strict personal control of Headquarters. No whisper of such plans is to be allowed.'[74] In another sense, this directive was a 'backs to the wall' order, reminiscent of that issued by Haig on 11 April 1918, since Churchill exhorted that 'The Army of the Nile is to fight with no thought of retreat or withdrawal.'[75] In addition, this directive was significant in settling the debate over the relative priorities of Malaya and the Middle East. Whereas Dill and Kennedy believed Singapore to be of the greater importance, Churchill pronounced unequivocally that 'The loss of Egypt and the Middle East would be a disaster of the first magnitude to Great Britain, second only to a successful invasion and final conquest [of the United Kingdom].'[76] Churchill, with his ability to read intercepts of German signals – Ultra – thought Rommel's forces were near exhaustion and at the end of their supply lines, and if the British would be able to inflict a defeat on the Axis anywhere, the Middle East would be the place.

The Chiefs of Staff responded to Churchill's directive on 7 May 1941. While agreeing with a number of the Prime Minister's arguments, Pound, Dill and Portal suggested that there were 'certain points which in our opinion call for amplification or amendment'.[77] Concerned with Churchill's inability to assess realistically the warning Britain would receive of a Japanese attack, for reinforcement purposes, the Chiefs of Staff were also convinced that the loss of the Battle of the Atlantic would be more decisive than the German defeat of the British in Egypt. In addition, the Chiefs of Staff endorsed heartily Wavell's preparation to meet the 'worst possible case:'

> ..., we think it necessary that these plans should be continually revised and kept up to date. However confident we may be of victory, it would be tempting providence to disregard the possibility of a reverse. In particular, should we be forced to abandon the [Suez] Canal, it is essential that it should be blocked.[78]

This did not end the controversy, as a flurry of minutes continued to pass between Churchill and Dill.

Conclusion

There were many reasons for the Germans being able to shatter the British position on the western flank of Libya in April 1941, the foremost being that the majority of troops and their equipment in Cyrenaica had been withdrawn, upon the Government's orders, and despatched to Greece. Other reasons included the return to the Delta of units depleted by 'Compass', Wavell's failure to select competent subordinate commanders, his inability to reconnoitre the potential area of operations properly, a serious overestimation of the capabilities of the British units in Cyrenaica Command, and a gross underestimation of German potential to launch an offensive operation. Wavell freely admitted his errors and responsibility in this episode, but the blame as shown, must also be placed on the shoulders of the Chief of the Imperial General Staff, who visited the Cyrenaican front with Wavell in

March 1941, the Secretary of State for Foreign Affairs, and especially with the Prime Minister. Churchill had been frequently informed of the order of battle of the force on the western flank, and the status and identification of units withdrawn from that area and sent to Greece. In addition, Churchill regularly received detailed intelligence estimates, through Ultra and from MI 14, among other sources, and similarly failed to appreciate accurately Rommel's capabilities, audacity, and potential.

In 1949, Wavell was permitted to read and comment upon the draft chapter, in Volume III of Churchill's Second World War autobiography pertaining to Rommel's initial offensive. After pointing out Churchill's misleading habit of reproducing only parts of important telegrams or documents and implying that they had been given in full, Wavell enumerated the actual composition, strength, and operational readiness of the 7th and 2nd Armoured Divisions. He emphasised that '*at no time did I have two complete armoured divisions*',[79] an impression Churchill had conveyed repeatedly in that draft chapter. Wavell admitted candidly:

> Looking back on it all, I took too big a risk in the Western Desert; but *if* the cruiser regiment [of the 2nd Armoured Division] had had 52 good tanks [instead of 26 or 27],*if* we had been able to use Bengazi as a port and thereby had the transport to push on a little further to better positions to Agheila, and *if* Rommel had not been so bold and enterprising, we might have held all right. I had reckoned on Bengazi, I had hoped the 3rd Armoured Brigade tanks would be all right in time, and I had certainly not budgeted for Rommel after my experience of the Italians.[80]

'I should have been more prudent', Wavell acknowledged, 'but no one knows better than Mr. Churchill that a little prudence is often a dangerous thing.'[81]

10

Western Desert, Iraq, Syria, and Crete, May-July 1941

'. . . threatened on no fewer than four fronts.'
Wavell, 1 August 1941[1]

As the war of words continued to be fought on the banks of the Thames, and the Prime Minister's confidence in the abilities of Dill and Wavell waned, the Germans did not remain idle in the Middle East. On 27 April 1941, a strong German force captured the strategically significant Halfaya Pass. Rommel's forces vigorously attacked the Tobruk defences three days later, and it was not until 4 May, after determined fighting in thick sandstorms, that the Germans failed in their object. On 2 May, as the battle was in progress, Paulus issued new instructions to Rommel stating he was to retain Cyrenaica and not endanger that task by continuing the fight at Tobruk. Paulus's orders, which emphasised that the German troops were 'much exhausted', were in a precarious logistical situation, and were not to advance beyond Bardia-Sollum until after the arrival of the 15th Panzer Division, were transmitted to Berlin via the German Air Force Enigma code. This message was intercepted and deciphered by the British, and Churchill was ebullient upon receipt of this singularly important report.

After receiving this information independently, Wavell, according to Gilbert, 'made no forward move'.[2] Churchill then impatiently fired off a telegram to Wavell which stated:

> Have you read OL 211 of 4th instant? Presume you realise the highly secret and authoritative character of this information? Actual text more impressive than paraphrase showing enemy 'thoroughly exhausted' unable pending arrival 15th Panzer Division and of reinforcements to do more than hold ground gained at Tobruk and assigning as main task of Africa Corps retention of Cyrenaica with or without Tobruk, Sollum, Bardia. Also definitely forbidding any advance beyond Sollum except for reconnaissance without permission.
> 2. This condition of enemy only bears out what you believed would be brought upon him by supply difficulty and his premature audacious advance. Severe

206

fighting which has attended his attacks on Tobruk imposes utmost strain on troops in this plight. It would seem to me judging from here important not to allow fighting round Tobruk to die down, but to compel enemy to fire his ammunition and to use up his strength by counter-attack. For this purpose trust you will consider reinforcing Tobruk as well as harrying enemy about Sollum. It seems to me that if you leave him quiet he will gather supplies and strength for a forward move. But if continuously engaged now, his recovery will be delayed and perhaps prevented.[3]

Ronald Lewin asserts that even though the interception and decipherment of the Paulus report was 'a considerable intelligence coup, yet it was profitless'.[4] This was due not only to the Prime Minister's preconceived – and erroneous – notions of Wavell's lack of audacity and the offensive spirit, but also with Churchill's obsession with the belief of the infallibility of his precious 'Tiger Cubs', the tanks then en route to Egypt in Operation 'Tiger'.

Wavell, unruffled, responded on 5 May 1941 that he had seen the referenced Ultra message the preceding day, and 'at once ordered Creagh [7th Armoured Division commander] to visit Beresford-Peirse [Western Desert Force commander] and discuss possibility using all available tanks for offensive operation'. He also reassured the Prime Minister that he had 'already issued orders for offensive in Western Desert at earliest possible date to be prepared on assumption "Tiger" successful'.[5] This plan, for Operation 'Brevity', was in essence a premature offspring of 'Battleaxe'. Wavell was eager to recapture the frontier positions near Sollum before Rommel could reinforce them, to use this key terrain as a 'springboard' for the subsequent British Operation 'Battleaxe'. The Halfaya and Sollum Passes were key terrain features, as they were the only places for some fifty miles where it was possible to cross the Escarpment, and whoever held the Halfaya Pass could control the lines of communication of any force from Egypt. Accordingly, on the thirteenth Wavell advised Churchill that 'without waiting "Tiger" I ordered available tanks to join Gott's force to attack enemy Sollum area. Action should take place in next day or two, and think Gott should be able to deal with forward enemy troops.'[6] If this attack was successful, Wavell planned to drive the enemy west of Tobruk.

Wavell chose the experienced Brigadier Gott to command 'Brevity' Force, which was divided into three main columns:

Desert Column: 7th Armoured Brigade Group (consisting of the two-squadron strong (29 cruiser tanks) 2nd Royal Tank Regiment and three columns of the Support Group)

Centre Column: 22nd Guards Brigade Group with 4th Royal Tank Regiment (two squadrons with a total of 24 'I' tanks)

Coast Column: 2nd Rifle Brigade and 8th Field Regiment, R A

The concept of the operation was for the Desert Column to advance from

Bir el Khireigat to Sidi Azeiz, destroying any enemy encountered along the way. The Centre Column was tasked to clear the top of the Halfaya Pass, seize Fort Capuzzo, and continue the advance northwards, while the Coast Column was designated to prevent the enemy from departing from Sollum, then to capture that town and the lower Halfaya Pass.

Early on the morning of 15 May 1941, 'Brevity' Force began its advance and initially achieved complete surprise over the Germans. During the first day, the British attack made excellent progress, capturing the positions above and below Halfaya Pass, Sollum, and Fort Capuzzo, although the last fort was recaptured by a fierce German counterattack. Concerned that the British were attempting to relieve Tobruk, Rommel hastily strengthened the force investing that garrison and sent a tank battalion to reinforce the German element at Sidi Azeiz. While the German reinforcements were moving forward Gott, concerned that the Guards Armoured Brigade located above the Escarpment could be cut off if attacked by enemy tanks, ordered its withdrawal to the Halfaya Pass while the 7th Armoured Brigade at Sidi Azeiz covered its movement. This signalled a general British withdrawal, and by the seventeenth, only Halfaya Pass remained in British possession.

Wavell, on 17 May 1941, informed the CIGS that the 'attack failed in object clearing enemy from Sollum-Bardia areas',[7] and later, after seeing Beresford-Peirse, noted that the operation came near success: 'Have instructed Beresford-Pierse [sic] to mobilise Tiger Cubs as soon as possible and try again. This will not be for fortnight anyhow and am feeling naked meanwhile. That is quite normal.'[8] The Prime Minister responded approvingly that 'Results of action seem to us satisfactory', and added proddingly, 'What are your dates for bringing Tigercubs into action?'[9] The 'Tiger' convoy, to which Churchill alluded, had reached Alexandria on 12 May with its valuable cargo of 135 'I,' 82 cruiser, and 21 light tanks. Wavell knew he would be expected to bring these armoured vehicles into action against Rommel at the earliest opportunity, but before he was able to, other campaigns had to be fought.

* * *

The main evacuation from Greece, it will be recalled, was conducted from 23/24 to 28/29 April 1941. Wilson, commander of 'W' Force in Greece, arrived on Crete on 27 April and immediately enquired about the defence of the island. Wavell, who had received indications via Ultra the day before that Crete would be the object of a German airborne assault, possibly as an intermediate objective for an Axis seizure of Cyprus, Syria, or Iraq, directed that Crete be denied to the enemy. Concerned about the relative lack of air support and the vast expanse of beaches and other possible enemy sea and

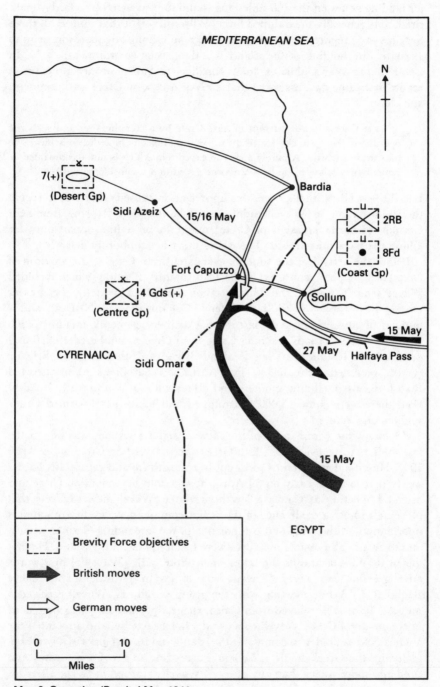

MEDITERRANEAN SEA

N

Bardia

7(+)
(Desert Gp)

Sidi Azeiz

15/16 May

2RB

8Fd

(Coast Gp)

Fort Capuzzo

4 Gds (+)
(Centre Gp)

Sollum

15 May

CYRENAICA

Sidi Omar

27 May

Halfaya Pass

15 May

EGYPT

Brevity Force objectives

British moves

German moves

0   10

Miles

Map 9. Operation 'Brevity' May 1941

air landing zones on the 160-mile-long island to be covered by a fairly small, tired, and generally unequipped force, Wilson thought that 'unless all three Services are prepared to face the strain of maintaining adequate forces up to strength, the holding of the island is a dangerous commitment, . . .'[10] In London, the War Cabinet's Joint Intelligence Subcommittee prepared a report that same day, assessing that an Axis attack on Crete was imminent, and that:

> . . . the Germans will attempt to seize Crete by a combined air and seaborne operation; these attacks are likely to be simultaneous in order to achieve the maximum surprise. A purely airborne expedition which is not accompanied or immediately followed up by a seaborne expedition is considered unlikely.[11]

Based upon Ultra intelligence, this appreciation caused Churchill to repeat this information to Wavell, adding trenchantly that 'It [the imminent German airborne invasion of Crete] ought to be a fine opportunity for killing the parachute troops. The island must be stubbornly defended.'[12]

Before the arrival of the soldiers evacuated from Greece, the garrison of Crete, or 'Creforce', consisted of the 14th Infantry Brigade (which included Wavell's old battalion, the 2nd Battalion The Black Watch), the greater part of the Mobile Naval Base Defence Organization (MNBDO), and a number of anti-aircraft and coast defence artillery elements, totalling 5,200 British soldiers. Troops reaching Crete from Greece numbered 19,950 and included the 4th and 5th New Zealand Brigades, 19th Australian Brigade (which included remnants of five Australian battalions), and assorted British troops (including gunners and others without equipment). In addition, there were some 15,000 ill-equipped and inadequately-armed Greek soldiers on Crete.

Freyberg, the commander of the New Zealand Division, was one of the last soldiers to be evacuated from Greece and arrived on Crete on 29 April 1941. He intended to return to Egypt to reconstitute and retrain his battle-weary division, but early on 30 April, he was told to remain on Crete and attend a meeting at Canea a few hours later. Wavell flew to Crete that morning to hold a conference of the senior commanders, to disseminate his information on the scale and composition of the impending German attack, and to ensure all possible measures were taken to defend the island. He first met with Wilson, and as the latter later wrote, 'His [Wavell's] first words after greeting me were, "I want you to go to Jerusalem and relieve Baghdad".'[13] While meeting with the group of officers, Wavell received a message from Dill, relayed from Cairo, suggesting that Freyberg be placed in command of Crete. Wavell concurred wholeheartedly, and appointed the Victoria Cross holder to command the island and its extemporised garrison, including the Greek soldiers. Looking, according to Freyberg, 'drawn and tired and more weary than any of us',[14] Wavell returned to Egypt after this conference and spent the night at Alexandria with Cunningham.

* * *

While Wavell was on Crete, the situation in Iraq was deteriorating significantly and bringing the British and local forces to the brink of an inevitable confrontation. After the second brigade of the 10th Indian Division had disembarked at Basra on 30 April 1941, Rashid Ali, greatly concerned about the dramatic increase in British strength in Iraq, refused permission for any additional troops to land. The Iraqi usurper determined to strike before the British could gain more strength, and his troops surrounded the Royal Air Force station at Habbaniya, some fifty miles west of Baghdad, that same day. Early on 2 May, British Wellington aircraft bombed the Iraqis, who in turn commenced shelling the British garrison with artillery.

On 2 May, Wavell candidly advised the War Office that due primarily to the expected enemy air superiority, the 'Defence of Crete will present difficult problems for all three services.'[15] Incredibly, the Defence Committee on that day also transferred 'temporarily' the responsibility for operations in Iraq to Wavell and the Middle East Command. After returning from a visit to the Western Desert, Wavell responded adamantly on the third that 'I have consistently warned you that no assistance could be given to Iraq from Palestine in present circumstances, and have always advised that commitment in Iraq should be avoided.' After suggesting that nothing short of immediate action by an artillery- and armoured vehicle-supported brigade group could restore the situation, Wavell caveated realistically: 'My forces are stretched to limit everywhere, and I simply cannot afford to risk part of forces on what cannot produce any effect.'[16] Apparently out of exasperation, Wavell recommended negotiating with the Iraqis. With Rommel then attacking Tobruk, an imminent airborne assault on Crete, rebellion in Iraq, intimations of further German infiltration in Syria, the main attack on Amba Alagi in Italian East Africa scheduled to commence the next morning, and Malta under incessant bombardment, it is no wonder that Wavell, after defeating the Countess of Ranfurly in a game of backgammon that evening after dinner, remarked dolefully: 'You seem to be the only person I can defeat these days.'[17]

The Defence Committee in London directed the Chiefs of Staff to respond urgently to Wavell. They emphasised the importance of Iraqi oil, adding that 'We much deplore the extra burden thrown upon you at this critical time by events in Iraq. A commitment in Iraq was, however, inevitable.'[18] This message further directed Wavell to send a relief force to Habbaniya as soon as possible. Upon receipt of this cable, Wavell very uncharacteristically exploded, shouting, 'He [Churchill] must face facts',[19] and his cable in reply began: 'Your 88 [Cablegram No. 65023] takes little account of reality. You must face facts.'[20] Wavell was highly sceptical of his ability to relieve Habbaniya, but understood that the earlier telegram from the Chiefs of Staff was directive in nature, and that he had no option but to do everything possible to comply; accordingly, he advised that he was assembling a relief force near the Transjordan-Iraq border. The General also stated his conviction that,

> I feel that it is my duty to warn you in the gravest possible terms that I consider prolongation of fighting in Iraq will seriously endanger defence of Palestine and Egypt. Apart from the weakening of strength by detachments such as above [incomplete mechanised cavalry brigade to be sent to Iraq], political repercussion will be incalculable and may result in what I have spent nearly two years trying to avoid: serious internal trouble in our bases.[21]

Churchill later wrote, pertaining to Iraq, that 'From the outset of this new danger General Wavell showed himself most reluctant to assume more burdens.'[22] Churchill was scathingly critical of Wavell and his reluctance to assume the responsibility for Iraq, and minuted to the Chiefs of Staff on the sixth: 'Fancy having kept the Cavalry Division in Palestine all this time without having the rudiments of a mobile column organized!'[23] Then apparently having forgotten that the responsibility for operations in Iraq had been transferred 'temporarily' from India to the Middle East only four days earlier, Churchill added harshly: 'He [Wavell] seems to have been taken as much by surprise on his eastern as he was on his western flank. . . . He gives me the impression of being tired out.'[24]

'The Prime Minister', Dill told Kennedy on 6 May 1941, 'wants to sack Wavell and put Auchinleck into the Middle East.'[25] Churchill had obviously lost confidence in Wavell, and the sentiment was further incited by his receipt of a letter from Amery, in which the Secretary of State for India wrote that he thought Wavell had lost his nerve. The Chiefs of Staff also advised Wavell that they had 'advised Defence Committee that they are prepared to accept responsibility for the force specified . . . at the earliest moment'.[26] This telegram, in essence, could have provoked Wavell's resignation, but it nonetheless achieved its desired result. Wavell's cablegrams later that day became more positive, cooperative, and less defensive, and coupled with the British actions which broke the Iraqi investment of Habbaniya, Churchill decided, at least for the time being, not to relieve Wavell. A more viable reason for Churchill's hesitation in sacking Wavell was that the Prime Minister was under a great deal of public scrutiny and criticism for his conduct of the war, especially after the evacuation from Greece, and a two-day Vote of Confidence debate had started that day in the House of Commons. Recognising the fragility of his own political position, Churchill undoubtedly knew that his relief of Wavell at this time would have given the appearance of Wavell being made a scapegoat, which, after the spectacular successes in the Western Desert only a few months earlier, would have had a negative impact on public opinion. Wavell was given, as a result, a temporary reprieve.

Wavell assumed operational control of northern Iraq officially on 5 May 1941, and of southern Iraq four days later. When informed of the latter development, Wavell responded to Dill: 'Nice baby you have handed me on my fifty-eighth birthday. Have always hated babies and Iraqis but will do my best for the little blighter.'[27] Dill reacted jovially the following day to his friend's birthday message with 'What a birthday present. Sincerely hope that you will be able to kill the little brute. Many happy returns of birthday but not of baby.'[28] Even though the Iraqi encirclement of Habbaniya had been broken on the sixth, it was still essential to send a relief force to Iraq to preempt Rashid Ali's plans for active *Luftwaffe* assistance, via Syria, to eliminate the British presence in the country.

Wavell realised that only a relatively small, mobile force could accomplish the 470-mile desert march from Palestine to Habbaniya swiftly, and he flew to Palestine on 11 May 1941, the day of Rudolf Hess's astounding yet bizarre flight to Britain, to issue guidance to Wilson and coordinate the despatch of a relief force. Major General JGW Clarke, commanding the 1st Cavalry Division in Palestine, was given this mission and organized 'Kingcol', a column under the command of Brigadier JJ Kingstone, which was to serve as the vanguard of his 'Habforce'. Kingstone's force began its movement on 11 May 1941, and three days later was augmented by elements of the Arab Legion under the command of Major (later Lieutenant General Sir) John Bagot Glubb (Pasha), who later called this incursion into Iraq 'one of the most remarkable examples of military daring in history'.[29] After being strafed for three days by German aircraft and travelling over the desert in temperatures exceeding 120 degrees Fahrenheit, 'Kingcol' reached Habbaniya on 18 May, almost coinciding with an attack by the Habbaniya garrison on the nearby town of Falluja on the route to Baghdad.

While 'Habforce' was moving to Habbaniya and then to Baghdad, elements of the 10th Indian Division (commanded after 16 May 1941 by Brigadier Slim) continued to pacify the area around Basra, being obstructed in their northward movement by seasonal floods. A significant divergence of opinion between the Middle East and India Commands had been developing as to the exact objectives and policy to follow in this operation. Concerned with his limited resources and other, more pressing, campaigns, Wavell was extremely reluctant to assume the additional burdens of occupying Mosul and Kirkuk, sites of large oil fields, as recommended by Auchinleck. Wavell believed that vital British military interests in Iraq were: '(A) Avoidance of major conflict with Arabs, (B) Security of oil supplies from Abadan, (C) Security of oil supplies from Kirkuk, (D) Maintenance of air route to India. All these', Wavell was convinced, 'are of minor importance compared with the security of Egypt and Palestine.'[30] His views were based on military as well as political factors, as he was uneasy with the possibilities of inflaming Pan-Arab sentiments and the German ability to gain a foothold in the Arab world, the former opinion also being held by the British Ambassador then besieged in Baghdad.

The War Cabinet failed to issue specific guidance or policy regarding the

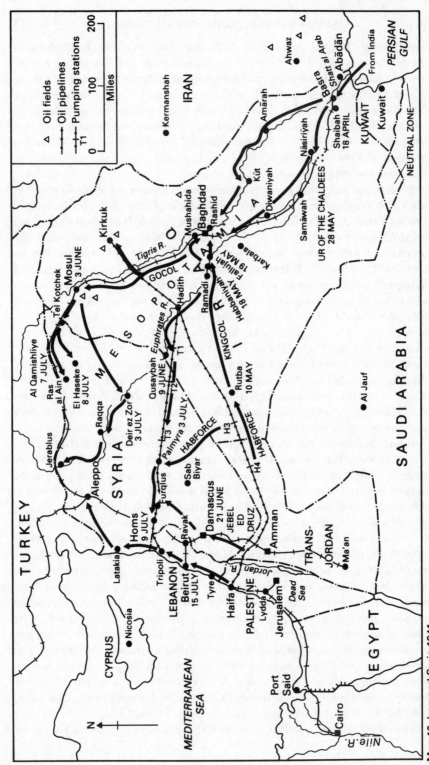

Map 10. Iraq and Syria 1941

Iraq situation; 'the argument was allowed to drift on inconclusively', Connell has suggested, 'with the War Cabinet in general approving the ends which Auchinleck desired, but hoping that they could be procured by Wavell's methods and under Wavell's authority'.[31] Wavell and Auchinleck met at Basra on 24 May 1941 to attempt to reconcile their differing attitudes towards Iraq. This was their first meeting, and was congenial and of short duration; Wavell was fully preoccupied with the battle for Crete raging at the same time in the Mediterranean. The ensuing fruitful exchange of information permitted each general to gain an appreciation of the role Iraq played in the overall defence of his counterpart's Command. It was decided that the Indian contingent would march on Baghdad at the earliest opportunity, and once that objective was reached, India Command would resume control of operations in Iraq. The interminable strain, not only as a result of Axis activities and intentions, but also from the Prime Minister's incessant bombardment of often-contradictory messages, coupled with the gnawing feeling that he had lost Churchill's confidence, continued to take its toll on Wavell. During the return flight from Basra, Wavell's fatigue was observed by his aide-de-camp, who recorded:

> We just made Lydda [Palestine], and, as we thankfully clambered out of the plane, the Chief [Wavell] had a bad giddy spell; staggered and fell against me. He recovered in a minute, but he is exhausted, I fear, mentally as well as physically.[32]

'Habforce' recommenced its advance on Baghdad, reaching the outskirts of the capital city and enemy opposition on 28 May 1941. The British found an operable telephone connected to Baghdad and an interpreter ingeniously 'seized the opportunity to spread alarm and despondency at the far end by exaggerated tales of the British strength'.[33] This deception and the Iraqi defeat in a skirmish on 30 May, during which the British were strafed by Italian aircraft, caused a frightened Rashid Ali to flee to Iran with a number of his followers. An armistice was signed the following day, followed by rioting and looting in Baghdad. British mopping up activities were now conducted to gain control of the situation, open up communications between Basra and Habbaniya, and eliminate all vestiges of pro-Axis influence, with the control of all operations in Iraq reverting to India on 18 June 1941.

The campaign in Iraq, despite Wavell's initial reluctance and consternation at having to dissipate his meagre forces even further, was clearly a British victory. Even though Ismay believed that 'Wavell's reluctance to go to the relief of Habbaniya is more understandable than he was given credit for by the Chiefs of Staff in London',[34] Churchill, Ismay's immediate superior, again failing to appreciate realistically the complexity of Wavell's commitments in the Middle East or the paucity of his resources, wrote retrospectively of the Iraqi campaign that,

The result was crowned with swift and complete success. Although no one was more pleased and relieved than Wavell himself, the episode could not pass without leaving impressions in his mind and in ours. At the same time General Auchinleck's forthcoming attitude in sending, . . ., the [10th] Indian Division to Basra so promptly, and the readiness with which Indian reinforcements were supplied, gave us the feeling of a fresh mind and a hitherto untaxed personal energy. The consequences of these impressions will be seen as the story unfolds.[35]

With the mission of 'Habforce' completed in Iraq, this element was needed desperately in Syria. British involvement in Syria was the result of many factors, and was given further impetus by the Free French General Charles de Gaulle's arrival in Cairo on 1 April 1941. He was anxious to extend Free French authority over Vichy-occupied Syria, and although he recognised that the Middle East Command was overcommitted, de Gaulle tried to press Wavell at a conference on 15 April to agree to a Free French plan to enter Syria from northern Palestine, supported by British tanks and airplanes. The French leader was given a curt refusal. Near the end of April, before it was ascertained that the objective of the German airborne assault (known to be in a state of preparation) would be Crete, there was speculation that Syria would be the German target. Dill understood that Wavell could not spare the forces to assist the Free French in a Syrian offensive but, 'On the other hand, if Germans land in Syria and [Vichy] French can be induced to resist, it would be greatly to our advantage to stiffen them to prevent [German] advance on Palestine or Iraq.'[36]

In short, it was confirmed on 14 May 1941 that the *Luftwaffe* was landing at Syrian airfields en route to Iraq, to deliver weapons to help sustain the Rashid Ali régime. On the 15th, the first day of Operation 'Brevity' in the Western Desert, Wavell advised the Chief of the Imperial General Staff that he thought the enemy intended an early attack on Crete as a preliminary to an attack on Egypt, from the West through Libya and from the North through Syria. Wavell further divulged his plans for building up a substantive force in Palestine, but assessed that it would take a 'long time' to do so. Events continued to move quickly. On 17 May, Wavell, expecting an attack on Crete hourly, indicated that the only British force he had available had been despatched to Iraq, and observed incisively: 'I am having plans examined for force to Syria but I hope I shall not be landed with Syrian commitment unless absolutely essential. Any force I could send now would be painfully reminiscent of Jameson raid and might suffer similar fate.'[37] Wavell also felt strongly that unilateral action by the Free French would be ineffective and likely to aggravate the tense situation.

French General Georges Catroux, de Gaulle's deputy in the Levant, who was keen to march into Syria, came to Wavell on 18 May 1941 and reported that the Vichy French intended to withdraw their forces into Lebanon preparatory to handing Syria over to the Germans. If this was so, Catroux contended, the road to Damascus would be open and he wanted permission from Wavell to march immediately to occupy that city. Wavell, who was sceptical of Catroux's information, stated that the immediate advance – which would depend upon British transportation – was entirely beyond his present resources, and deferred the decision to the War Office.

Wavell's reluctance to send a force into Syria at the urging of the Government, coupled with his similar reaction to the Iraqi revolt, caused the Prime Minister to decide unequivocally upon Wavell's relief. Churchill had broached the sensitive subject of Wavell and Auchinleck exchanging positions as early as 6 May 1941, and again mooted the question, as Eden recorded, after a Defence Committee meeting on 10 May:

> He [Churchill] was in favour of changing Auchinleck and Wavell about. Max [Lord Beaverbrook, Minister of State] agreed as Amery had already done. The other three of us [Clement R. Attlee, Lord Privy Seal; Margesson, Secretary of State for War; and Eden] were more doubtful. As I knew the men best, I found the advice not easy to give. I have no doubt that Archie has the better mind, but one does not know how he is bearing the strain and one cannot tell, though some of his recent reactions seem to indicate that he is flagging. In the end I weakly counselled delay and asked to wait for Crete result. Winston agreed [;] there was not unanimity.[38]

On the nineteenth, Churchill summoned Dill to Downing Street, where the Prime Minister stated that he 'had finally decided to get rid of Wavell, and to put Auchinleck in his place'. Churchill, as Dill related to Kennedy,

> . . . intended to send Wavell to India where, he thought, he [Wavell] would enjoy 'sitting under the pagoda tree.' Churchill had said he could not have Wavell hanging around in London, living in a room in his club. Dill had repeated his former advice: 'Back him or sack him.' Churchill had replied: 'It is not so simple as that. Lloyd George did not trust Haig in the last war – yet he could not sack him.' Dill had told him that Auchinleck, for all his great qualities and his outstanding record on the [North-West] Frontier, was not the coming man of the war, as the Prime Minister thought.[39]

Dill thought that Wavell was the most prominent commander of the war to date, with the full support and confidence of the public as well as the soldiers. Churchill could ill afford 'political trouble' at this time.

On 19 May 1941, Churchill discussed this proposal with Amery, who observed in his diary that,

> From the point of view of India that would be a real misfortune both from the military and even more from the political point of view, for Auchinleck is the one person in the whole government there [in India] who really inspires confidence and enthusiasm among Indians of every class.[40]

The Secretary of State for India also expressed his second thoughts in a letter to Churchill: 'I have been thinking a good deal over the Wavell-

Auchinleck problem. May I put to you some of the difficulties I see in the proposed exchange?'[41] After lauding Auchinleck's accomplishments in India, Amery stressed the future importance and involvement of India in the war effort:

> . . . India may be much more directly threatened in the almost immediate future than anything we have allowed for hitherto. There is, for one thing, the possibility of invasion of Burma from Japan. More serious is the possibility – perhaps more than a possibility – that Stalin, sooner than fight Germany, will join hands and walk into Iran and Afghanistan. In that case a tremendous strain is going to be put upon India.[42]

Amery also alluded to Churchill's apparently widespread earlier expressions of uncertainty about Wavell's aggressiveness and capabilities as a commander: 'If you have serious doubts about Wavell as a man of willpower and drive, will you feel any happier about him if he has to face the tremendous kind of crisis I have hinted at?'[43]

After Amery's earlier panegyric, his letter struck at the crux of the issue: he was now disinclined to lose Auchinleck as Commander-in-Chief, India, and even more averse to Wavell assuming that position. As a compromise solution, Amery recommended that Auchinleck assume control of operations in Iraq as well as in Palestine and Syria, and that the demarcation between the Middle East and India Commands should be extended westwards to the Suez Canal. 'Wavell's whole mind', Amery contended, 'is centred on his North African campaign and on retrieving lost ground and getting to Tripoli',[44] which would supposedly make it easier for Auchinleck to assume command of the region east of Suez. Dill met with Amery on 20 May 1941 to discuss the Wavell-Auchinleck issue, and while admitting to a number of the objections Amery raised about this exchange of positions, Dill 'thought there was no other way that would avoid political trouble'.[45]

Wavell clearly was quite unaware that his fate as Commander-in-Chief, Middle East, had already been decided in London. On 20 May 1941, the day the Germans began their assault on Crete and amidst reports of the reinforcement of the *Afrika Korps*, Wavell was astounded to learn that his recommendation to deny Catroux permission to advance into Syria had been completely overruled by the Defence Committee, which,

> . . . considered that opportunity is too good to miss and the advance must be regarded as a political *coup*, in which time is all important, rather than as a military operation. You [Wavell] should do everything you can to give Catroux not only the lorries and drivers which he requires, but also as much military and air support as possible.[46]

Wavell attributed this reversal of his recommendation to the behind-the-scenes political intrigue and influence of de Gaulle and Major General Edward Spears, Churchill's longtime Parliamentary colleague and Head of the British Mission to the Free French, who were able to circumvent Wavell and communicate directly with the Prime Minister. Wavell, provoked to the limit of his patience, responded curtly on the twenty-first:

> . . . All reports from trustworthy sources including Arab and Syrian agree that effect of action by Free French alone likely to be failure. . . . You must trust my judgment in this matter or relieve me of my command. I am not willing to accept that Catroux, de Gaulle or Spears should dictate action that is bound seriously to affect military situation in Middle East.[47]

Wavell had unwittingly played himself into his detractors' hands. Upon receipt of this message, Dill sent a note to the Prime Minister in which he stated it was his opinion that 'we have now come to the point where we must either allow Wavell to carry out the policy which he believes to be sound or relieve him of his command. My own feeling is that, at this juncture, we should trust Wavell. It is no time to make a change.'[48]

Churchill retrospectively called this situation a 'misunderstanding'.[49] Perhaps the cause of Wavell's initial irritation was unintentional and the result of a misunderstanding, but the Prime Minister's response to Wavell's protest was clearly calculated to force Wavell to stand on his principles and resign immediately or comply unquestioningly with all Government directives. After lunch on 21 May 1941, Churchill met with Dill to discuss Wavell's telegram, and also asked Eden to join them. Eden recorded his impressions of this conference in his diary:

> Wavell has misunderstood our attitude over Syria. We realise he cannot spare troops from Crete or Western desert, nor do we want him to from former in particular, but if the Free French are prepared to chance their arm in something like a Jameson raid, we are in favour of letting them have a shot, *faute de mieux*. A political more than a military venture. This Winston fully explained, but he added a last paragraph telling Wavell that if he still did not like it (tho' we took full responsibility) arrangements would be made to meet his request to relieve him. I did not like this, for I believe Wavell is the best man we have. Winston has never had much opinion of him, & I much fear that this telegram may bring about Wavell's resignation. Tho' Amery & I and David [Margesson] made it pretty plain we would have preferred to leave out last sentence, W [Winston] did not agree & was of course backed by [Albert] Alexander [First Lord of the Admiralty] with a dig at the Army and Attlee.[50]

The message drafted at this informal meeting was approved at a War Cabinet meeting that afternoon, and cabled immediately to Wavell:

> Nothing in Syria must detract at this moment from winning the battle of Crete, or in the Western Desert. . . .
>
> We do not object to your mixing British troops with the Free French who are to enter Syria; but as you have clearly shown, you have not the means to mount a regular military operation, and, as you were instructed yesterday, all that can

be done at present is to give the best possible chance to the kind of armed political inroad described in our telegram of 20th May.

You are wrong in supposing that the policy described in our previous telegram of 20th arose out of any representations made by the Free French leaders or by Spears. It arises entirely from the view taken here by those who have the supreme direction of war and policy in all theatres. Our view is that if the Germans can get Syria and Iraq with a few aircraft, tourists and local revolts, we must not shrink from running equal small-scale military risks, nor from facing the possible aggravation of political dangers from failure. We of course take full responsibility for this decision and should you find yourself unwilling to give effect to it, arrangements will be made to meet any wish you may express to be relieved of your command.[51]

That night an unhappy Dill wrote two letters, one to Wavell and one to Auchinleck, apprising them both of the seriousness of the situation, and warning the latter to be prepared to succeed Wavell as Commander-in-Chief, Middle East, not if, but when he was relieved by the Prime Minister. Dill's heartfelt letter to Wavell included:

What a time you are having. How I wish that I could be of more help to you. I do not know whether or not you will pack up on receiving the telegram from the Defence Committee – or rather the PM – which has just been drafted about Syria. . . .

From your own personal point of view you will be sorely tempted to hand in your portfolio – you could hardly go on a better wicket – but from a national point of view it would I feel be a disaster. And yet I feel that the PM has only two alternatives – to trust or to replace. But even if he does not trust it would, I feel, be disastrous for you to go *at this moment* when you are handling so many difficult, if not critical situations. . . .[52]

Despite the Prime Minister's deliberate challenge and incitement to resign, Wavell did not, to the surprise of some, including the Director of Military Operations, pick up Churchill's gauntlet. Wavell's profound sense of duty to the King, the British cause, and the profession of arms transcended any personal sentiments of self-abasement or inflated opinion of himself. Astutely understanding the implications and intent of Churchill's message, Wavell made plans to send the 7th Australian Division (less one brigade in Tobruk) to Palestine to prepare for action in Syria. In addition, late on 21 May 1941, Wavell learned that his earlier scepticism about Catroux's assessment of Vichy French intentions to withdraw to Lebanon was justified, as Catroux, who had gone to Palestine to meet a French officer from Syria, discovered that 'far from withdrawing into the Lebanon the French were moving troops south of Damascus and taking up positions to defend the routes to that city'.[53]

On 25 May 1941, while embroiled in the Battle for Crete, Wavell informed Dill of his preliminary plans for an offensive into Syria, codenamed 'Exporter'. Wavell intended to employ the 7th Australian Division (less one brigade), Free French forces, elements of the 1st Cavalry Division, and other units – a much smaller force than he estimated necessary for the occupation of Syria, but the largest force which could be improvised in view of Wavell's other concomitant campaigns. It would be commanded by 'Jumbo' Wilson.

Wavell's military and political difficulties were understood by some officers working in the War Office. Lieutenant General (later Sir) Henry Pownall, who had recently been appointed as Vice Chief of the Imperial General Staff, noted accurately that:

> Wavell is not in good odour. Indeed, if it were not for the very active operations now going on, Winston [would] certainly have him out on the grounds that he is 'losing his grip', and replace him by Auchinleck, for whom Winston has considerable admiration.[54]

As Wavell continued to assemble the transport and other assets required for 'Exporter', the Defence Committee unrealistically exhorted Wavell to advance into Syria while attacking at the same time in Cyrenaica. Lampson, the British Ambassador to Egypt, similarly failed to appreciate the logistical requirements of modern warfare: 'I warned Wavell this morning', Lampson advised Eden on 28 May 1941, 'that if, as I hoped, he [Wavell] now contemplated action against Syria, he would risk missing the bus unless he acted quickly.'[55] One week later Lampson reiterated his concern about the delay of 'Exporter' to Wavell, whose response, according to the Ambassador, was 'probably not a bad one, namely that if he is given sufficient troops he will get on with it, but that he is not prepared to risk things with insufficient forces'.[56]

'Exporter' began on 8 June 1941, with the British/Free French force numbering about fifteen battalions but with no tanks (the whole force numbering about 34,000 men) opposed to some thirty Vichy French battalions (about 37,000 soldiers), augmented by about ninety tanks. No one was sure what degree of opposition the Vichy French would offer. Wavell's general plan was to advance into Syria on a broad front, with the 5th Indian Brigade on the right given the mission to occupy Deraa and the line of the Yarmuk railway, and the 7th Australian Division on the left to advance in two columns, one by Merjayun and the other by the coast road to Beirut. The Free French were to pass through the 5th Indian Brigade and advance on Damascus.

The campaign in Syria, according to the British Official History, can be divided into three readily-identifiable phases. The first, from the first advance on 8 June 1941, witnessed initial successes but turned into a stalemate by the 13th. The Vichy French counter attacked doggedly during the second phase, 14–22 June, and the British were able to make significant progress only at Damascus. During the third phase, 23 June-12 July, the

British were able to regain the initiative by augmenting their forces with 'Habforce' and the 10th Indian Division, fresh from the fighting in Iraq.

The British/Free French advance, as noted, initially made good progress, but it soon became apparent, contrary to the predictions of de Gaulle, Catroux, and Spears, that the campaign would not succeed as easily as anticipated. There was severe fighting when the Vichy French counter-attacked, defiantly and ferociously, using their tanks with great efficacy. On 12 and 13 June 1941, Wavell was in Palestine to observe the advance on Damascus and assess the progress of the campaign. With Vichy French resistance stiffening after the discovery of the unexpected weakness of the British force, Wavell decided, in order to give additional momentum to his offensive, to reinforce Wilson's force with two brigades of the British 6th Division. By the end of the second phase, the British had captured Damascus and Sidon, had retaken Kuneitra and Ezraa, and had held Vichy counterattacks.

During the third phase of the Syrian campaign the British forces, in addition to being reinforced by 'Habforce' and the 10th Indian Division, were supported by increased naval and air contingents. Palmyra surrendered to 'Habforce' on 3 July 1941; the fortified Vichy positions at Damour, twelve miles south of Beirut, were captured on the ninth by the 7th Australian Division; and with the remainder of the Vichy defences crumbling, the end of the campaign was in sight. On 11 July, Vichy officials requested a cessation of hostilities. The Acre Convention was signed on the 14th – Bastille Day – and officially ended this bitter, fratricidal campaign.

The Syrian campaign, although successful, was extremely expensive. In terms of soldiers, the total Allied losses were about 4,700 killed, wounded, and captured, out of a total force of about 34,000, compared with 3,348 Vichy casualties out of a force of some 37,000. But of even greater significance, this 'political gesture' of sending troops into Syria had required the reluctant Wavell to withdraw forces from the Western Desert yet again. The inevitable outcome of this dispersal of assets was that both the Syrian campaign and Operation 'Battleaxe', as will be seen, were undertaken simultaneously with inadequate resources. In consequence, the Syrian campaign was prolonged unnecessarily, and Wavell's last Western Desert offensive was a failure.

* * *

Crete, it will be recalled, served as the 'receptacle' for some 20,000 British soldiers evacuated from Greece. Due to Ultra disclosures of an imminent German airborne assault (and Freyberg was an Ultra recipient), defensive preparations were accelerated. Freyberg's earlier pessimism seems to have evaporated, as he cabled Churchill: 'Cannot understand nervousness, am not in the least anxious about airborne attack, have made my dispositions and feel can cope adequately with the troops at my disposal.'[57]

While it is outside the purview of this study to detail Freyberg's preparations for the defence of the island, suffice it to note that the time and resources available were insufficient to correct the existing deficiencies in Crete's defences. The geography of Crete made the island's defence all the more difficult, and was a significant factor in the plan developed for its defence. A steep range of barren mountains, rising to some 8,000 feet, runs the entire length of the 160-mile-long lozenge-shaped island, sloping gradually to the North but steeply to the South. This resulted in the relatively large, but limited-capacity ports, Suda, Heraklion, Canea, and Retimo, being located on the northern shore of the island, facing Greece. This greatly increased their exposure and vulnerability to the expected German attack from the North, while exacerbating the difficulty of the British to conduct logistical resupply operations from Egypt. The three strategically-significant airfields at Heraklion, Retimo, and Maleme were similarly situated, and were connected by Crete's only motorable road, which ran along its northern coast. Five secondary roads, at least one of which degenerated into a goat track, traversed the island from north to south. Perhaps of greater importance, the Greek Peloponnesus lies only about eighty miles northwest of Crete, with the island of Rhodes less than one hundred miles north-east of Crete. German air support could be provided readily from these areas, whereas Crete, over 400 miles from Alexandria, was out of supporting distance of British aircraft based in North Africa.

The problem of defence was made worse by the pitiful state of readiness, equipment, and organisation of the thousands of troops evacuated from Greece. Brigadier GS Brunskill, senior administrative officer on Crete, wrote later that even though most of these soldiers had retained individual weapons and a few had crew-served weapons,

> . . . the best equipped of these men had a greatcoat and their personal equipment, but many had not even got that. Above all, there was no unit equipment or heavier weapons whatsoever, much less any transport. This meant that even in the best 'W' Force units, for example, many men, having no mess tin, had to cook their food in some kind of ration tin and eat it with their fingers until they improvised or borrowed a spoon or fork. The worst equipped 'W' Force men, of course, had nothing at all except some form of clothing.[58]

This situation made prospects for a successful defence even more remote.

Freyberg formulated his defence plan, to meet the expected German combined airborne-seaborne assault, on 3 May 1941. The essence of this plan was denial of key and vulnerable points – the aerodromes at Heraklion, Retimo, and Maleme, and the main port of Suda Bay – by establishing defences in depth. In addition, to prevent any enemy lodgement, a centrally positioned mobile reserve force was organised to reinforce defended areas if threatened. It was obvious that due to shortages of communications equipment and an underdeveloped road network, the forces responsible for the defence of the three airfields would have to fight as independent units. Each of those three forces were allocated two 'I' tanks, and additional 'I' tanks were later sent to the island.

On 5 May 1941, Ultra established that Crete was the German objective of Operation '*Merkur*' (Mercury), and revealed the following day that the attack would probably start on 17 May.[59] During this slight respite between combat operations, the British began their intervention in Iraq. Wavell continued to reinforce Crete to the best of his ability, and Freyberg hastened to position his troops and ensure the continued preparation of defensive positions. On 15 May, Wavell advised Churchill that he had 'done best to equip Colorado [codename for Crete after 14 May] against beetle pest. Recent reinforcements include 6 I tanks, 16 light tanks, 18 A.A. guns, 17 field guns, one battalion'. Wavell also added that he was preparing a small force possibly to reinforce Crete from the south, and concluded optimistically that 'Colorado is not easy commitment, and German blitzes usually take some stopping. But we have stout-hearted troops, keen and ready for fight under stout-hearted commander, and I hope enemy will find Scorcher [impending German attack on Crete] red-hot proposition.'[60] On the fifteenth, incredibly, as Operation 'Brevity' started in the Western Desert and a British relief force was advancing on Habbaniya, the Defence Committee in London made the belated decision that 'the defence of Crete should have priority over British projects in Iraq and Syria, and the interruption of enemy supplies to North Africa, . . .'[61]

On 16 May 1941 Ultra revealed a forty-eight hour postponement of the German attack, which was followed by a twenty-four hour postponement on the 19th. After six days of intense aerial strafing and bombardment, the long-awaited German assault began early on the 20th. The airborne attack was carried out primarily by elements of the XI *Fliegerkorps* (Air Corps) under the command of General Kurt Student, divided into three groups, comprising some 22,750 soldiers, with the following missions:

(a) Western Group, under Major General Meindl, was to seize possession of Maleme swiftly and suddenly in the first attack, and hold the airfield for subsequent airborne landings;

(b) Centre Group, under Lieutenant General Sussmann, was also part of the first wave, and its task was to seize Canea and the village of Suda in order to dislocate the defence and put the main harbour of the island out of action. By 15.15 the second wave was to have taken the town and airfield of Retimo.

(c) Eastern Group, under Lieutenant General Ringel, also part of the second wave, was to seize the town and airfield of Heraklion by parachute drops, and then hold the airfield open for the subsequent airborne landing of mountain troops.[62]

The parachute and glider landings were designed to secure a foothold on the island, which would then be followed up and exploited by seaborne troops.

German glider troops led the assault on Maleme and both sides of Canea, and were followed by paratroopers, landing primarily in the midst of

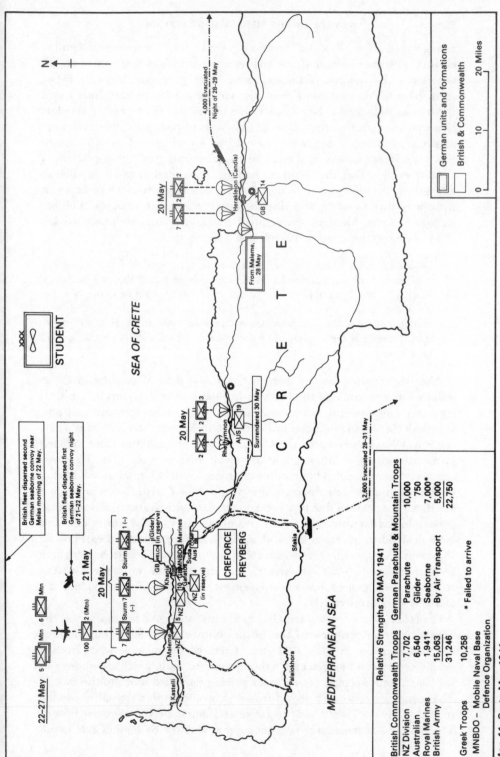

Map 11. Crete May 1941

British fleet dispersed second German seaborne convoy near Melas morning of 22 May.

British fleet dispersed first German seaborne convoy night of 21–22 May.

STUDENT

SEA OF CRETE

N

From Maleme, 28 May

Herakleion (Candia)

GB 14

20 May
7 2   2

4,000 Evacuated Night of 28–29 May

C R E T E

20 May
2   3
1   2
AUS 19
Rhethymnon

Surrendered 30 May

CREFORCE FREYBERG

2,600 Evacuated 28–31 May

22–27 May
5 Mtn   6 Mtn

20 May
100   2 (Mtn)

21 May
7   Sturm 7 (–)   3 Sturm 7 (–)

20 May
1 (–) (Glider) (in reserve)

Kastelli
Maleme
5 NZ
Khaju   GB WELCH (Glider) (in reserve)
10 NZ   MNBDO Marines
NZ Galatos   Aus Comp
4 (in reserve)   Suda Canea
Palaiokhora
Sfakia

MEDITERRANEAN SEA

Relative Strengths 20 MAY 1941

British Commonwealth Troops		German Parachute & Mountain Troops	
NZ Division	7,702	Parachute	10,000
Australian	6,540	Glider	750
Royal Marines	1,941*	Seaborne	7,000*
British Army	15,063	By Air Transport	5,000
	31,246		22,750
Greek Troops	10,258		
MNBDO – Mobile Naval Base Defence Organization		* Failed to arrive	

German units and formations

British & Commonwealth

0   10   20 Miles

camouflaged New Zealand positions. Fierce and determined fighting ensued, with the German attack greatly assisted by their overwhelming air superiority. By the end of the day, some 5,000 Germans had established themselves at Maleme and Canea. Six German airborne battalions joined the fray at Retimo and Heraklion in the afternoon. By the end of the day, however, the Germans had achieved only a small portion of their objectives and had suffered tremendous casualties, knowledge of which caused Student's Headquarters in Athens to consider calling off the operation. It became evident that the Germans had grossly underestimated the British strength, believing there were only some 5,000 defenders instead of about five times that number, and due to the excellent camouflage techniques employed, many Germans parachuted unwittingly into well-planned kill zones. Freyberg reported to Wavell that evening that,

> To-day has been a hard one. We have been hard pressed. So far, I believe, we hold aerodrome at Maleme-Heraklion and Maleme and the two harbours. Margin by which we hold them is a bare one, and it would be wrong of me to paint optimistic picture. Fighting has been heavy and we have killed large numbers of Germans. Communications are most difficult. Scale of air attacks upon Canea has been severe. Everybody here realises vital issue and we will fight it out.[63]

After the fighting began, there was actually little Wavell could do to influence the outcome of the battle, other than make decisions at the strategic level, allocate any resources available, offer encouragement, and provide periodic situation reports to London. On the night of 20/21 May 1941, the Royal Navy intercepted the German seaborne expedition and inflicted great damage to it, although at no small cost to itself. The Germans captured Maleme airfield late in the afternoon of the 21st, their task having been facilitated by the earlier withdrawal of a New Zealand battalion from a key defensive position due to a breakdown of communications and a misunderstanding. Determined but unsuccessful attempts by the Australians and New Zealanders to regain the Maleme airfield were conducted early on 22 May, but even though there was a great deal of fighting still to be done, the German capture of that area was the turning point in the battle. German reinforcements poured into the lodgement, and measures to expand the foothold were accelerated.

Churchill wrote encouragingly, but with little understanding of the enemy's air superiority over Crete or the ability of the defenders to continue their mission, on 23 May 1941 that 'Crete battle must be won. Even if enemy secure good lodgements fighting must be maintained indefinitely in the island, thus keeping enemy main striking force tied down to the task.'[64] That course of action, Churchill reasoned, would permit Wavell to use the recently-arrived 'Tiger Cubs' to strike and dominate the Western Desert. The Prime Minister should have known that with the Battle for Crete in full fury, with Wavell's limited resources being further dispersed in Iraq, and while prodding the General to send a sizeable force to Syria, an offensive in the Western Desert was not possible. In London, only two days later, the Prime Minister, according to John Colville, his Assistant Private Secretary,

> . . . criticised Wavell very heavily about tanks for Crete and expressed amazement that W should have thought he could get reinforcements ashore after the fight had begun. He [Churchill] considered the Middle East had been very badly managed. If he could be put in command there he would gladly lay down his present office – yes, and even renounce cigars and alcohol![65]

Churchill's acerbic comments reflect not only his lack of confidence in Wavell, but also his overweening desire to be in command, as a general, of soldiers in combat.

On 25 May, a large German force broke through a defensive line in Crete and captured Galatas. The situation was restored partially by a bold New Zealand counterattack, but it was becoming obvious that the tenuous position of the defenders was deteriorating rapidly. Accordingly, Freyberg informed Wavell that 'I regret to have to report that in my opinion limit of endurance has been reached by troops under my command here at Suda Bay. No matter what decision is taken by C-in-C from military point of view our situation here is hopeless.'[66] Wavell immediately relayed this information to London, but before Churchill received it, he admonished Wavell that 'Victory in Crete essential at this turning point in the war. Keep hurling in all aid you can.'[67]

Early on 27 May, Wavell reiterated to London the seriousness of the British position on Crete, and added that 'Fear we must recognise that Crete is no longer tenable and that troops must be withdrawn as far as possible.'[68] Even before the Defence Committee was able to meet to discuss the topic, Wavell advised that he had already ordered the evacuation from Crete to proceed – gloomy news which was but little offset by the sinking of the German battleship *Bismarck* that day. Driven to accept the loss of Crete, Churchill now focused his attention on other means of British force projection in the Middle East, apparently oblivious that Wavell's forces were strained to the utmost, weak in numbers and, in many cases, devoid of all except individual equipment: 'The first essential was to defeat the German army in Libya. Our second task would be to try to peg claims in Syria with the small forces which could be made available without disrupting our effort in Libya.'[69] If Churchill would have been patient enough to permit these campaigns to be conducted sequentially, rather than simultaneously, it would have been the German forces which would have been disrupted, not Wavell's.

It would have been impossible to evacuate the British troops from the northern shore of Crete, so they were required to attempt to disengage from the enemy, withdraw, and traverse the rugged mountains to ports, primarily

Sphakia, on the southern face of the island. The perilous evacuation began on the night of 28/29 May 1941 and continued until 31 May/1 June, during which time, according to Wavell, 14,580 soldiers out of 27,550 Imperial troops on the island at the beginning of the attack were evacuated (7,130 out of 14,000 British; 2,890 out of 6,450 Australians; and 4,560 out of 7,100 New Zealanders). British ground forces on Crete suffered 1,742 killed, 1,737 wounded, and 11,835 taken prisoner; the Royal Navy had 1,828 sailors killed and 183 wounded. German casualties were also very high, making their capture of Crete a Pyrrhic victory. Official German casualty figures, which were far below the original British estimates, included 1,971 killed, 2,549 wounded, and 1,888 missing (most of whom were killed), totalling 6,453. These heavy German casualties, higher than the entire German losses during the Balkan campaign in Greece and Yugoslavia the month before, persuaded Hitler not to employ his airborne forces again. Crete was, in Student's own words, 'the grave of Germany's parachutists'.[70]

During the evacuation from Crete, Wavell's morale and self-confidence were temporarily at a nadir. On 29 May Wavell visited Lampson, who described the General as 'looking the picture of gloom'. Wavell's melancholy was, however, short-lived. 'He [Wavell] said with a twinkle of his old humour', Lampson recorded, 'that it was all very well for the Prime Minister at home to send snappy, caustic telegrams saying that such and such was on the way, but telegrams, even from the British Prime Minister, didn't help him to beat the Germans.'[71] This vignette indicates not only the depth of the physical strain Wavell was under at this time as Commander-in-Chief, Middle East, but also the negative impact that Churchill's hectoring messages were having on Wavell's characteristic aplomb.

The War Office announced the evacuation from Crete on 1 June 1941. In an effort to reduce the anticipated sharp public criticism and to dissociate himself from the failure to hold Crete, Churchill immediately began the search for scapegoats. He acted swiftly, and in the midst of reports that Crete had fallen due to a lack of air support, Longmore (Air Officer Commanding-in-Chief, Middle East), who had been summoned to London on 30 April 1941 ostensibly 'for discussion on all aspects of future air operations', was relieved summarily. Indeed, Hugh Dalton, Minister of Economic Warfare, noted in his diary on 2 June that 'A search for a scapegoat is going on and already Longmore has been relieved of his command. Wavell may follow.'[72] This was, according to RW Thompson, a 'miserable injustice',[73] but the Prime Minister, convinced that it was his destiny to lead the British people to victory, was intent to use any Machiavellian method to retain his position. Gilbert also implies that the Crete defeat was Longmore's fault: 'In the aftermath of Crete, Churchill made a single change in command in the Middle East, replacing Air Chief Marshal Longmore, . . .'[74] The sacrifice of Longmore, however, would only temporarily allay further misgivings about the Government's central direction of the war.

Two days later, Dill, anticipating an adverse public reaction, sent Wavell a list of questions to answer and requested 'some preliminary account of Crete battle that would form basis of statement in the House of Commons'.[75] Undoubtedly foreseeing the requirement to respond in writing about the conduct of the Battle of Crete, Wavell quickly complied with this directive, and sent a second wire to Dill later that day noting he had formed a committee to study the battle thoroughly. 'There is a storm of criticism about Crete', the Prime Minister advised shortly thereafter,

> . . . and I am being pressed for explanations on many points. Do not worry about this at all now. Simply keep your eye on 'Exporter' and, above all, 'Bruiser' [later named 'Battleaxe']. These alone can supply the answers to criticisms, just or unjust.[76]

Churchill thus intimated that Wavell's generalship and performance as Commander-in-Chief, Middle East, were being questioned, and that his continued survival in that position was dependent upon another Western Desert offensive, to be launched at the earliest opportunity. 'There was a good deal of criticism, naturally, about Crete', recorded Pownall forebodingly after attending a Cabinet meeting, 'distinctly "catty" at times. I've no doubt Wavell's number is up as soon as there comes an interlude during which he can be got rid of.'[77]

Attlee, the Lord Privy Seal, was also acutely aware of the heavy criticism of the coalition Government as a result of Crete. On 4 June 1941, he noted to the Prime Minister that, while conceding Wavell had 'cleared up Iraq', he [Attlee] believed that Wavell had missed opportunities in both Syria and Libya, and that he should have attacked in both areas while the German Air Force was fully engaged over Crete. 'The real trouble', Attlee suggested harshly, 'has been that the Middle East forces have never been coiled to spring except in the case of the Benghazi campaign ["Compass"].'[78] The Lord Privy Seal continued to denigrate Wavell, opining that the General had never 'really freed his mind from the Maginot Line complex', and that the 'instinct to "hold a line" derived from the last war is still very strong'.[79] While Attlee's assessment of Wavell was clearly erroneous, it gave further credence to Churchill's conviction that Wavell had failed to accomplish aggressively the myriad of missions given to him.

Many people considered the German airborne assault on Crete as a dress rehearsal for an invasion of England, and continued criticism resulted in a 'noticeable slump in [Churchill's] popularity'.[80] Churchill defended British actions in Crete vociferously during a lengthy speech in the House of Commons on 10 June 1941, but that did not end the controversy. New Zealand Brigadier LM Inglis, who had commanded the Force Reserve on Crete, arrived in London as Freyberg's emissary to report to the Prime

Minister on the Crete operation. Inglis, it seems, had conspired with at least one other New Zealand brigadier (who was also a Member of Parliament in New Zealand) to undermine Freyberg's credibility and position. In his briefing to the Prime Minister on 13 June, Inglis presented many items at variance with the earlier views and statements of both Wavell and Freyberg pertaining to Crete.

On 14 June Churchill minuted his consternation at Inglis's 'shocking account of the state of troops in Crete before the battle'[81] as well as the apparent ineptitude demonstrated in the defence of the island. Churchill had been fully aware of German intentions via Ultra, as had Wavell and Freyberg, and felt 'that there was [not] any real grip shown by Middle East HQ upon this operation of the defence of Crete', who apparently 'regarded it as a tiresome commitment, while at the same time acquiescing in its strategic importance'.[82] Inglis was not only successful in tainting Freyberg's reputation, but gave further excuses to Churchill to relieve Wavell even though, as Laurie Barber and John Tonkin-Covell have suggested, 'The substance of the criticism as minuted by Churchill was partly true, partly false, and wholly misleading.'[83]

In the Western Desert, meanwhile, Wavell made every effort after the failure of Operation 'Brevity' to prepare the 'Tiger Cubs' for another offensive operation. Wasting no time, on 17 May 1941, the last day of 'Brevity', Wavell issued revised instructions to Beresford-Peirse that British policy in the Western Desert 'must be to drive the enemy to the west of Tobruk as soon as possible and to keep him west of Tobruk by means of forces in the Tobruk – El Adem area'.[84] Even though Wavell's attention was fully enmeshed with 'Habforce' in Iraq, the spectre of German intervention in Syria, the imminent German assault on Crete, and the aftermath of 'Brevity', Churchill impatiently prodded Wavell to employ the 'Tiger Cubs' in action against the Germans at the earliest opportunity. On the 19th the Prime Minister admonished Wavell: 'Tremendous risks were run to give you this aid [the 'Tiger Cubs'] and I wish to be assured that not an hour will be lost in its becoming effective', and added inquisitively, 'Are they ['Tiger Cubs'] yet in hands of troops? Why does it take a fortnight to bring them into action? What work has to be done upon them? How are they to be moved to the front?'[85] Wavell responded immediately that 'Certain unforeseen causes have delayed preparations', to include the requirement to redesign and remake the air cleaners for all the cruiser tanks, and that the estimate of employing these tanks before the end of May 'will prove optimistic'.[86]

The process of preparing the newly-arrived tanks was far more difficult than originally envisioned, especially in London. 'Weaning of tiger cubs proceeding satisfactorily', Wavell advised Churchill, 'but even tigers have teething troubles.'[87] Problems were encountered while unloading the 'Tiger' convoy transport ships: the cranes at Alexandria were unable to lift the tanks out of the hold of one ship, which then had to be sent to Port Said to unload. Radio sets had been packed haphazardly in unmarked containers, which required a vast expenditure of time and effort to sort out and assemble, and there were no tools or maintenance manuals for the tanks. The tanks required desert camouflage, the paint for which did not exist, to cover the original forest-green paint. Ten thousand gallons of desert camouflage paint was ingeniously improvised from a concoction of cement and spoiled flour (as an adhesive), rancid Worcestershire sauce (solvent), and camel dung (pigment). To deceive the enemy further, 'sunshields', a ruse based on Wavell's own ideas and sketch, were constructed. Each sunshield was an apparatus consisting of painted canvas stretched over two collapsible wooden frames, which could be erected on a tank to give it the appearance of a harmless truck. Perhaps the most significant item was the fact that the veteran ranks of the 7th Armoured Division had been thinned severely since 'Compass', with a corresponding influx of new soldiers, and the Division had been without tanks since February 1941. The cruiser Mark VI (Crusader) tanks, which had arrived on the 'Tiger' convoy, were newly-introduced to the Middle East, and the inexperienced crews would need extensive training on them. But, unconcerned with and oblivious to the logistical aspects of modern warfare, Churchill continued to pressure Wavell into taking action, even though the General advised that the 'Tiger Cubs' could not be deployed to the forward area until 14 June 1941.[88]

Wavell issued further planning guidance to Beresford-Peirse on 20 May. Seven days later, the Germans advanced, drove back the light British covering force from Halfaya Pass, and 'began to prepare intensively for defence'.[89] In the wake of this increased tension, the Western Desert Force Headquarters issued an operation order for 'Battleaxe' to Creagh, commanding 7th Armoured Division, on 29 May. This offensive was planned initially to commence on 10 June 1941, but Creagh sagely:

> . . . raised grave doubts as to his ability to equip the formation by that date. There was a serious deficiency of mechanical transport within the [7th Armoured] Division and units were very weak in AFVs. The shortage of trained personnel in some of the units necessitated a short period of time being allotted for training.[90]

Wavell, too, had trepidations about being forced to conduct a battle before he was adequately prepared. On 28 May he advised Dill that:

> I think it is right to inform you that the measure of success which will attend this operation is in my opinion doubtful. I hope that it will succeed in driving enemy west of Tobruk and re-establishing land communications with Tobruk. If possible, we will exploit success further. But recent operations have disclosed some disquieting features.[91]

These 'disquieting features' included the light armour of the British

armoured cars, which made them vulnerable to German fighter aircraft and
the more powerful German armoured cars; the slowness of the British 'I'
tanks; and the fact that 'our cruisers [tanks] have little advantage in power
or speed over German medium tanks'.[92] Three days later, Wavell gave an
updated situation report on tanks in the Middle East to the C I G S.
Including Tobruk, the British had 230 cruiser and 217 'I' tanks, although
about 90 cruisers and 50 'I' tanks were still undergoing repair. That number
of tanks was sufficient only to equip the 7th Armoured Division with one
brigade of three cruiser regiments and one brigade of three infantry tank
regiments. In spite of these obvious warnings, the Prime Minister could not
be dissuaded from continuing to exhort Wavell to attack in the Western
Desert.

Wavell flew to the Western Desert on 2 June 1941 to receive briefings
from Beresford-Peirse and Creagh on the detailed plans for 'Battleaxe'.
Wavell was not satisfied, believing the plan proposed did not make full use
of all the available British resources, especially artillery, and was not audacious enough in forcing the Germans to give battle. Accordingly, he gave
verbal instructions that another plan 'was to be prepared to include the
employment of the maximum strength in arty [artillery] and inf [infantry]
that could be made available and be maintained in the fwd [forward]
area'.[93]

As Beresford-Peirse prepared a revised plan for 'Battleaxe', Wavell had to
respond to the Prime Minister's recriminations over the British expulsion
from Crete, and finalised the preparations for Operation 'Exporter', the
British advance into Syria. Wavell again visited the Western Desert on 9
and 10 June 1941, personally seeing all commanders down to brigadier who
were going to take part in 'Battleaxe', and he 'impressed on them importance of operation and first real opportunity of inflicting heavy defeat on
Germans', adding that 'All seemed confident and in good spirits.'[94] Wavell
returned to Cairo on the tenth, and flew to Palestine two days later to check
personally on the progress of the Syrian campaign. He returned to Egypt on
13 June.

The Western Desert Force was initially organised in the following manner
for 'Battleaxe', to accomplish the various parts of the overall mission:

▷ *Escarpment Force:*
   4th Indian Division Headquarters, commanded by Major General
   FW Messervy, located in the Sidi Barrani area:
   • 4th Armoured Brigade (infantry tanks)
   • Halfaya Group
   • Artillery Group
   • Guards Brigade Group
▷ *Coast Force*, commanded by Brigadier (later Lieutenant General Sir)
   RA Savory, positioned on the line Buq Buq-Alam Samalus:

- 11th Indian Infantry Brigade
- Additional attachments

▷ *7th Armoured Division* (minus 4th Armoured Brigade), commanded by Creagh, in El Alam-Wael Qabr area:
- 7th Armoured Brigade (cruiser tanks)
- Support Group

Wavell estimated that the Western Desert Force would encounter about 5,700 Germans with about 100 medium tanks, 50 armoured cars, 20 field guns, and 70 anti-tank guns in the forward area Bardia-Capuzzo-Sollum, with an estimated 7,500 Italians with 50 guns and 20 anti-tank guns. The Germans, the British believed, had an additional 11,000 troops with 120 medium, and 70 light tanks, and the Italians about 16,000 soldiers and a few tanks, in the Tobruk-El Adem area. Counting on these figures, although the British assessment of German tank strength later proved to be high, Wavell hoped to have an initial tank superiority over the Germans in the forward area before Rommel could shift forces from the area of Tobruk.

The British plan, in brief, was to attack in three columns. Advancing along the sea coast, the 'Coast Force' was to attack and secure Halfaya and Sollum. 'Escarpment Force' was to advance along the top of the Escarpment and to secure, in turn, Halfaya, Bir Wair-Musaid, and Capuzzo, destroying the enemy forces defending these locales. Creagh's division was to advance roughly parallel and in line with the 'Escarpment Force' to screen and guard the left flank of the 4th Indian Division, and to assist in the destruction of all enemy forces in the area Bardia-Sollum-Halfaya-Sidi Omar-Sidi Azeiz. If this initial phase of the operation was successful in achieving all of its objectives, the 7th Armoured Division would continue the advance to the west of Tobruk, whose garrison would launch a 'sortie in force' as soon as the 7th Armoured Division arrived within supporting distance. This success, if achieved, would be exploited westwards to Gazala.

The Western Desert Force's two-phased approach march began early on 14 June 1941, the first stage of twenty-four miles (from Sofafi to Buq Buq) being completed by mid-morning, and the last eight miles were traversed in by moonlight early on the 15th. The British attack began at dawn with the 'Coast Force' attempting to capture the lower Halfaya Pass. This attack failed, due to the effectiveness of the enemy minefields and anti-tank fire, and a counterattack launched by the enemy. 'Escarpment Force' was more successful, having captured Capuzzo and Bir Wair, but the 7th Armoured Division had been unable to secure the Hafid position. By the end of the first day of operations, the main enemy armoured forces had not been engaged, and it was obvious that enemy reinforcements were being shifted forward from the Tobruk area. In London, Eden noted in his diary:

The opening phases of Libya appear to have gone quite well. I wish I could rid

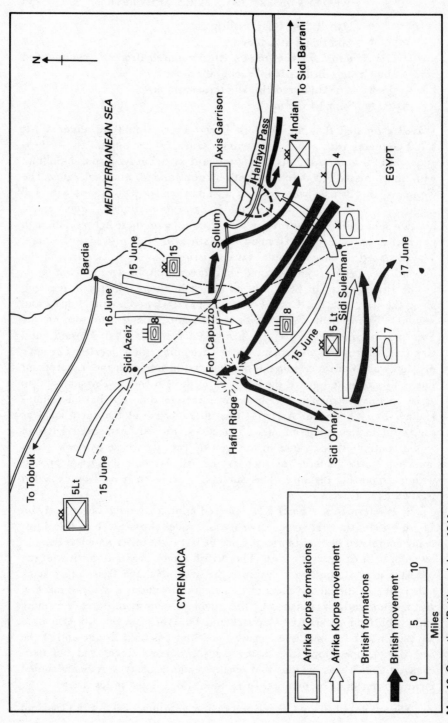

Map 12. Operation 'Battleaxe' June 1941

Afrika Korps formations

Afrika Korps movement

British formations

British movement

Miles

0   5   10

MEDITERRANEAN SEA

CYRENAICA

EGYPT

Bardia

Sollum

To Sidi Barrani

Axis Garrison

Halfaya Pass

4 Indian

4

7

Sidi Suleiman

17 June

5 Lt

7

8

15 June

Sidi Omar

Hafid Ridge

Fort Capuzzo

Sidi Azeiz

8

15

16 June

15 June

To Tobruk

5Lt

15 June

N

myself of this sinking feeling that we should have concentrated on Syria first, &, that task accomplished, switch to Libya. I fear that we may not be strong enough for decisive results in either theatre, but hope this is too gloomy a view.[95]

Eden's prediction would prove to be more accurate than he had hoped, and it is distressing that he did not relay his convictions to the Prime Minister more vocally.

The British plan for 16 June 1941 was for the 4th Indian Division to try again to seize Halfaya Pass, consolidate its positions in the Capuzzo area, and attempt to exploit towards Bardia. The 7th Armoured Division, with its 4th Armoured Brigade back under command, would 'attack and smash the enemy outflanking movement which was closing in' from the northwest.[96] Beresford-Peirse visited both division commanders early that afternoon, and Wavell, 'with his flair for knowing when he was likely to be wanted',[97] flew to the Western Desert Force Headquarters later that same afternoon. The fighting during the second day focused on repelling determined German armoured counterattacks, which succeeded in greatly reducing British tank strength. With the British Guards Brigade firmly ensconced at Capuzzo, Creagh and Messervy decided that on the 17th, the 7th Armoured Division, with its 4th Armoured Brigade still under command, would make a concerted effort to destroy the German tanks.

Anticipating the British intentions, Rommel's 5th Light Division and 15th Panzer Division launched a preemptive attack at dawn on 17 June, which struck the left flank of 4th Armoured Brigade. The British were in a precarious situation: Creagh could not attack without 4th Armoured Brigade, and Messervy could not release that formation without exposing his own flank. In addition, the Guards Brigade was in imminent danger of being surrounded by the Germans. Recognising the potential crisis, and determined to make personally the critical decision he thought would be necessary, Wavell flew to Creagh's Headquarters, only to find that Messervy, less than an hour before, had made the decision to withdraw,

> . . . as it appeared to him [Messervy] that unless he withdrew without delay, the enemy column from Sidi Omar, combined with the enemy column from the westward, would completely surround him and close his line of retreat.[98]

Wavell had little choice but to sanction Messervy's decision, adding gloomily, 'I think you were right to withdraw in the circumstances, but orders should have come from Western Desert Force.'[99] Wavell terminated the entire operation and ordered the withdrawal of Western Desert Force, then returned to Cairo to oversee the execution of the Syrian campaign.

The British sustained relatively heavy casualties during the three days of 'Battleaxe': 122 officers and men killed, 588 wounded, and 259 missing; in addition to the loss of 4 guns, 27 out of 90 cruiser, and 60 out of about 100 'I' tanks were lost due to enemy action or mechanical breakdown. German casualties included 93 officers and men killed, 350 wounded, and 235 missing; tank losses were negligible.

There were many reasons for the failure of 'Battleaxe', although most of the contributory factors were neither realised nor understood at the time. In his relevant Despatch, Wavell observed:

> The main cause of our failure was undoubtedly the difficulty in combining the action of cruiser and 'I' tanks, the cramping effect on manoeuvre of having only two regiments in each armoured brigade and the lack of training in the 7th Armoured Division.[100]

Wavell's statement is worth examining. Since the operational control of the 4th Armoured Brigade ('I' tanks) was retained by Messervy, that formation was never actually employed in conjunction with the 7th Armoured Brigade (cruiser tanks). Perhaps Wavell's intention was to imply that there were potential disadvantages in the manoeuvring and mutual support of units with infantry and cruiser tanks, due to speed differentials of the different tanks, which was about ten miles per hour for the 'I' tanks versus about twenty-five miles per hour for the Crusaders. The lack of training of the 7th Armoured Division was obvious to all who took part in 'Battleaxe': Harding, Beresford-Peirse's BGS, recalled that there was inadequate time for the tank crews to train, especially on the new Crusader tanks, some of which were still calibrating their main guns on the way to their assault positions;[101] another officer bemoaned the shortage of wireless sets, there being only one set per troop;[102] the British tanks, noted Benson succinctly, 'were chucked into battle before they were ready'.[103]

The British defeat, however, can be more directly attributed to an underestimation of German capabilities and a failure of British intelligence to ascertain German dispositions and intentions. Whereas Operation 'Compass' had been a complete surprise to the enemy, 'Battleaxe' was anything but. German wireless interception units had revealed the proposed start-time of 'Battleaxe' to be early on 15 June 1941; accordingly, the *Afrika Korps* began preparing for the British attack during the previous evening. Throughout the fighting, the Germans received and relayed to Rommel information on the British plans and objectives, perceptions of the battle, and logistical concerns. These intercepts gave Rommel confidence in the manner in which he shifted his forces and conducted the battle. Perhaps of greater significance, the British thought that their tank casualties were due primarily to an inferiority to German armour. This was only partially the case; German success was in large measure due to their adroit emplacement and employment of .88 millimeter anti-aircraft guns in a ground defence role. It would take months before the British determined the actual reasons for their defeat in 'Battleaxe' and took steps to rectify their shortcomings.

The British failure in 'Battleaxe' did not diminish the soldiers' confidence in Wavell. Lieutenant Colonel (later Major General) Donald Bateman, who served as GSO 1 of the 4th Indian Division during 'Battleaxe', summed up the sentiments of many soldiers at the time:

> From recollection, I do not think that at the time we laid blame on either the [Western Desert] Force Commander (BP) [Beresford-Peirse] or the C-in-C [Wavell] – generally the best test of battle nonsense. Rather, there was general realisation that, for unknown reasons, the C-in-C and everyone else had been bounced into a very stupid, ill-conceived, ill-prepared, and impromptu operation.[104]

When Wavell advised Dill on 17 June 1941 'Regret to report failure of Battleaxe',[105] he was certainly aware that such news signalled, as Churchill had earlier intimated, his final campaign as Commander-in-Chief, Middle East. It would be only a matter of time until he would receive official notification of his relief. A few days after the end of 'Battleaxe', Wavell's aide-de-camp, Captain (later Major) Peter Coats, walked into his Chief's office and found the General playing with a stack of coloured pencils. 'He [Wavell] seemed unusually depressed', recalled Coats;

> He [Wavell] looked up at me with his one sad eye and said, 'Is this how it goes, Peter?' and quoted some lines of a speech in Hamlet:
> If it be now, 'tis not to come;
> If it is not to come it will be now;
> If it be not now, still it will come;
> The readiness is all.[106]

* * *

Wavell, emotionally and psychologically prepared, waited fatalistically for the message he knew would soon arrive. He continued, however, to do his duty as Commander-in-Chief, Middle East, to the best of his ability.

In London, Churchill acted quickly and decisively. He had earlier warned Wavell that only the success of 'Battleaxe' could vindicate the earlier setbacks of Greece and Crete, and permit him to regain a measure of the Prime Minister's trust and confidence. The failure of 'Battleaxe' provided Churchill with the opportunity he needed to relieve Wavell, and the Prime Minister acted promptly to ensure that public opinion understood the relationship between this unsuccessful operation and Wavell's supersession to avoid any suggestions of capriciousness on his part.

On 20 June 1941, Churchill, purportedly convinced that 'Wavell was a tired man' and that the Government 'had ridden the willing horse [Wavell] to a standstill',[107] informed the Marquess of Linlithgow, Viceroy of India, that he had 'come to the conclusion that change is needed in the command in the Middle East' and proposed that Wavell and Auchinleck exchange positions.[108] Linlithgow cabled his concurrence the following day, and Dill, while believing Wavell had been under great strain and needed a rest, was not convinced that Wavell should be relieved. Dill proposed:

> [Either] (a) To let Wilson hold the Middle East Command during Wavell's temporary absence at home – say, a month or six weeks;
>
> [Or]   (b) To relieve him [Wavell] permanently by Auchinleck. (I entirely agree with you that, if Wavell is to be relieved, Auchinleck is the right man to succeed him).'[109]

'The temporary relief of Wavell', Dill continued,

> . . . has much to commend it. Wavell is undoubtedly able and has the confidence of his troops, unless Scorcher [Crete], and Battleaxe, not to mention Exporter, have shaken that confidence. Moreover, Wavell is a considerable personage in the eyes of the Public and if he were permanently superseded not a few might say that he had been made a scape-goat. On the other hand, Wavell has lost your confidence – in fact, he never had it – and that of other members of the War Cabinet. That, to my mind, is the strongest possible reason why he should be superseded.[110]

Churchill had made up his mind, and could not be persuaded to do otherwise. The inevitable cable announcing Wavell's relief arrived in Cairo early on 22 June 1941 and was given to Smith, Wavell's Chief of Staff,

> . . . who had at once dressed and gone round to Wavell's house on Gezira. He [Smith] found him [Wavell] shaving, with his face covered with lather and his razor poised. He [Smith] read out the signal. Wavell showed no emotion. He merely said: 'The Prime Minister's quite right. This job wants a new eye and a new hand'; and went on shaving.[111]

This message reached Wavell only hours before the announcement of the German attack on the Soviet Union. Wavell responded magnanimously that 'I think you are wise to make change and get new ideas and action on many problems in the Middle East and am sure Auchinleck will be successful choice.'[112] After thanking the Prime Minister for his 'generous references' to his work in the Middle East and selection to serve as Commander-in-Chief, India, Wavell asked for a short rest at home to see his son and settle some business. Rommel's forces had also been severely mauled in 'Battleaxe', and during the resultant hiatus in the fighting in the Western Desert, such a visit to England could have provided the resilient Wavell the opportunity to report on his operations and rest and relax, and return to the Middle East reinvigorated and anxious to launch a new offensive. But Churchill, perhaps thinking of what he would do if he was in Wavell's position, was fearful, as we know, of Wavell 'hanging around in London, living in a room in his club'.[113] Indeed, the Prime Minister was greatly concerned with Wavell's future employment and proximity to the press and 'opposition' in England, as he had said he had been afraid of just putting Wavell 'on the shelf', or forcing him into retirement, 'as that would excite much comment and attention'.[114] It was much easier for Churchill to 'banish' Wavell to India, to 'sit under the pagoda tree'.

Wavell continued faithfully to execute his duties as Commander-in-Chief, Middle East. He accompanied United States observer W Averell Harriman, who considered Wavell 'one of the finest characters the British Army was capable of producing, a man of real integrity and a true leader',[115] to Asmara and Addis Ababa during 25–26 June 1941. On the latter day, Wavell received, from Emperor Haile Selassie, the coveted Order of the Seal of Solomon, thus becoming only the third person, after King George VI and Haile Selassie himself, to receive this rare decoration.

Auchinleck arrived in Cairo on 1 July 1941 to take up his new appointment, which was announced officially the following day. Relinquishing command to Auchinleck at 3:00 am on 5 July 1941, Wavell departed for India two days later. Even though the departure was to be a confidential event, a number of Wavell's colleagues and loyal friends met at the Heliopolis airfield to see him off. Freya Stark, who was working in the Ministry of Information in Cairo at the time, later described the scene:

> He [Wavell] looked tired, sad, and kind, and the huge and empty airfield, the sandy edges of the hills, the pale colourwash – ochre and blue – of the early day, seemed all to lie attendant as a frame to a picture round the group of uniforms and the weather-beaten faces, and the solitary figure who was handing over the defence of all this world and what it meant. . . . The little group, . . ., made me think strangely of a Highland farewell in the Stuart wars; the image was not inspired by any thought of lost causes, but by an atmosphere of loyalty and personal devotion that hung about the scene, and with it an acceptance of all that comes.[116]

Clearly exemplifying that unrivalled sense of loyalty to Wavell was the French Major des Essarts, who had served as Weygand's liaison officer to Wavell before the fall of France: 'for daring to come and make his farewells to Wavell', des Essarts was later put under arrest by de Gaulle.[117] When Dorman-Smith, Wavell's former Brigade Major then serving as Commandant of the Staff College at Haifa, first heard of Wavell's relief, he noted sombrely and tersely in his diary: '*Sic transit gloria mundi*.'[118]

Conclusion

'It would be difficult indeed', as William L Langer and S Everett Gleason have suggested, 'to exaggerate the complexity of the situation which confronted General Wavell in April and May 1941.'[119] The pressure and strain, both mental and physical, imposed upon him throughout that period, was truly imponderable. Wavell's burden of command was never greater than in May 1941, when he was accountable for the conduct of five campaigns – the defence of Tobruk and 'Brevity' in the Western Desert, the defence of Crete,

the conclusion of the Abyssinian campaign, and the incursion into Iraq –
while simultaneously preparing the 'Tiger Cubs' for action in the Desert
and the intervention in Syria. In the light of British Government intransigence, vacillating guidance from the Chiefs of Staff, and the interminable
bombardment of unrealistic, minutely-detailed, frequently-contradictory
'advice' from the Prime Minister, and the perennial personnel and equipment shortages, let alone enemy action, it is remarkable that Wavell accomplished as much as he did.

Wavell only reluctantly improvised a task force and despatched it to Iraq.
From his standpoint, a small-scale British incursion into Iraq had the
potential to incite an Arab uprising which could have had a markedly
deleterious impact upon the fragile British position in the Middle East.
However, British attempts at negotiation or, worse still, acceptance of the
Iraqi coup could have further strengthened the impression that British
power and influence in the Middle East was waning. Although Wavell was
clearly and justifiably concerned with a large-scale pincer movement by the
Germans towards Egypt and the Suez Canal from the Balkans through
Turkey and the Levant, and from the west by Rommel's forces, the most
significant imminent threat to the Middle East (in addition to the activities
of the Germans in the Western Desert) was the forecast German airborne
assault on Crete. With Crete pinpointed as the German objective on 5 May
1941, and Ultra revealing on the 6th that the attack would probably take
place on the 17th, the British intervention in Iraq began during the interval
between the British evacuation from Greece and the known enemy invasion
of Crete. Fortunately, the gamble was a success.

The Syrian campaign, however, cannot be given the same accolades. It
was obviously important to prevent the Axis encirclement of Turkey and to
thwart German intervention in Syria, but the Iraqi armistice of 31 May
1941 indicated German reluctance to make a large commitment to foster a
nationalistic Arab uprising. In addition, on 2 June, Ultra disclosed that
German fighter aircraft had been instructed to cease attacks in Iraq and to
defend Syrian bases. But on the following day, German aircraft, again
according to Ultra, were ordered to return to their units and their base in
Athens was being disbanded.[120] But, as Hinsley has noted accurately,
'These clues were disregarded by the planners in Cairo and Whitehall',
probably due to the anxiety which existed during the days following the
German airborne invasion of Crete.[121]

An even greater indictment of the futility of the Syrian campaign is to be
found in the information, derived from Ultra, which was sent to Wavell on
31 May 1941:

1. We have firm indications that Germans are now concentrating large army
    and air forces against Russia.
2. Under this threat they will probably demand concessions most injurious to
    us. If the Russians refuse, the Germans will march.[122]

Hitler's eyes, as Churchill knew, had been focused for months, not on the peripheral areas of Iraq and the Levant, but on the Soviet Union. The intercepted German plans for Operation 'Barbarossa', juxtaposed with the intelligence on the intended *Luftwaffe* withdrawal from Syria, indicate clearly that Wavell was correct in his reluctance to advance into that country which, bereft of Axis support, could have been ignored, and would have eventually succumbed because of its relative isolation and impotence. Wavell's assessment that Free French political intrigue, combined with the Prime Minister's insatiable desire for offensive action, had served as the impetus for the Syrian campaign, was probably correct.

The Battle for Crete was the natural and inevitable denouement to the campaign in Greece. Wavell was criticised heavily for the British expulsion from Crete by many sources, including the Prime Minister who, on 29 May 1941, again believed Wavell was showing signs of defeatism, and stated, 'He [Wavell] sounds a tired and disheartened man.'[123] IMcDG Stewart, who served as a regimental medical officer during the Battle of Crete, blamed Wavell for failing to prepare the defences of the island adequately: 'a few simple measures', to include road, landing strip, and defensive position construction, 'taken during the six months of occupation before the battle, could have deprived the enemy of any hope of success'.[124] The harshest criticism came from perhaps an unexpected quarter: the 'Inter-Services Committee on Crete', which had been appointed by Wavell. Composed of three relatively junior officers (an Army Brigadier, a Royal Navy Commander and a Royal Air Force Wing Commander), this Committee was severely critical, noting the rapid turnover of commanders and, in a manner similar to that of Stewart, the Committee highlighted: 'With notable exceptions, six months of comparative peace were marked by inertia for which ambiguity as to the role of the garrison was in large measure responsible.'[125]

The report of the Inter-Services Committee on Crete was finished only a few days before Wavell's departure from the Middle East, and believing that the War Office urgently required this narrative, Wavell, to take advantage of an 'opportunity of [its] rapid despatch', forwarded the report without reading it. After learning that this report was being circulated widely, Wavell, from India, expressed his concern to the War Office. The essence of Wavell's argument was:

> In particular, circumstances in the Middle East made it quite impossible to undertake a large programme of defence works on the island of Crete. During the period from the occupation of the island until the German attack, RE [Royal Engineer] personnel, stores and material, transport, and labour were utterly insufficient for our needs. GHQ had to decide how resources available should be distributed, and had far more pressing and important commitments to meet, both for personnel and material, in the Western Desert, in Greece and on the northern frontiers of Palestine.[126]

He also gave the example of the extreme shortage of steel for reinforced concrete, and what was available was insufficient even for the needs of the defence of the western flank of Egypt, 'where the most serious threat to our whole position was at the time. Even had material been available', Wavell continued, 'there was always a lack of sufficient shipping for Crete, especially after we had undertaken to send an expedition to the assistance of Greece.'[127]

The criticisms of Stewart, the Inter-Services Committee on Crete, and others, generally failed to consider the Crete episode within the overall military and political context of the Middle East at the time, and considered the defence of Crete as an isolated incident. Authors of the official histories, with unlimited access to primary source material and documents, were able to view the Battle for Crete in a much more balanced manner. Hinsley realistically assessed the 'acute shortage of shipping, equipment and troops throughout the Middle East theatre', and believed this 'had prevented the British from giving much attention to Crete's defences since their arrival there'.[128] Nothing would have been more convenient', declared Playfair, 'than to be able to provide a strong force for Greece and at the same time fortify Crete. In reality it was necessary to scrape together units and equipment from all over the Middle East to fit out the expedition to Greece.'[129] In stronger and all-inclusive terms, Playfair addressed Stewart's and the Inter-Services Committee's criticisms by stating adamantly:

> Nothing is easier to say than that in the six months from November 1940 to April 1941 Crete should have been turned into a fortress. In fact, all this time the preparation of the island for defence was very low on the list of things to be done; not even the resources for the local protection of Suda Bay could be provided in full.[130]

Thus, in the light of Wavell's numerous divergent commitments and inadequate resources, it would be neither fair nor accurate to place on Wavell's shoulders the fault for the lack of defensive preparations on Crete.

Wavell had been under incessant pressure from Churchill to use the mobility, firepower, and shock effect of the precious 'Tiger Cubs' to launch the decisive battle of the Western Desert to relieve Tobruk and soundly defeat Rommel once and for all. Churchill's insistence upon the execution of the unnecessary Syrian campaign forced Wavell to dissipate his resources, as he had had to do earlier to send troops to Greece, and condemned Operation 'Battleaxe' to failure. Even though 'Battleleaxe' was not successful, Rommel observed of Wavell:

> Wavell's strategic planning of this offensive had been excellent. What distinguished him from other British army commanders was his great and well-balanced strategic courage, which permitted him to concentrate his forces regardless of his opponent's possible moves. He knew very well the necessity of avoiding any operation which would enable his opponent to fight on interior

lines and destroy his formations one by one with locally superior concentrations. But he was put at a great disadvantage by the slow speed of his heavy infantry tanks, which prevented him from reacting quickly enough to the moves of our faster vehicles. Hence the slow speed of the bulk of his armour was his soft spot, which we could seek to exploit tactically.[131]

Wavell, however, against his better judgement and after providing numerous admonitions to the Government doubting the success of the proposed operation, gave way to Churchill's pressure. If Wavell would have demurred, he would surely have suffered the same fate as Longmore, even earlier than he eventually did.

11

The Generalship of Wavell:
An Assessment

> *'We have won some great successes, . . .*
> *We have had some failures and setbacks, . . .'*
> Wavell, July 1941[1]

Wavell's primary responsibility as Commander-in-Chief, Middle East, was to command all of the British, Dominion, and Allied ground forces in that vast theatre of operations. Inherent in that position was the colossal requirement to serve as the British Government's *ex officio* chief diplomat for the Middle East, attempting to establish and implement, with Sir Miles Lampson's assistance, a coherent and consistent British policy for the region in the midst of latent Pan-Arabism and potential pro-Axis infiltration. In addition, Wavell served as the chief logistician for his embryonic command, to ensure that not only did his command receive the administrative and logistical support it required, but also, with foresight, to endeavour to establish a logistical base for future large-scale operations. He also emerged as the unofficial but *de facto* representative, spokesman, and leader of the three Middle East Commanders-in-Chief. In this multi-faceted position, Wavell, to quote Air Chief Marshal (later Marshal of the Royal Air Force, Lord) Arthur Tedder, Longmore's successor as Air Officer Commanding-in-Chief, Middle East, 'had to put up with, and even worse, act upon, the imperious directives from the Prime Minister',[2] prodding messages which Admiral Cunningham characterised as 'singularly unhelpful and irritating in times of stress'.[3] Wavell's tenure as Commander-in-Chief, Middle East, was clearly his greatest challenge and, up until that time, the most demanding test of his generalship.

Wavell's Relief – Justification and Perceptions

Prior to an assessment of Wavell's generalship, it is necessary to scrutinise the vexed question of Wavell's alleged 'excessive fatigue', since this formed, at least according to Churchill, the basis for Wavell's relief. This was a controversial topic at the time, and remains so in some circles, especially among Wavell's supporters who believed his relief for this cause to be unjustified. War correspondent Cecil Brown broadcast from Cairo on 2 July 1941 that,

> The explanation that General Wavell needed a rest caused many a British and Egyptian eyebrow out here to be raised considerably. Wavell is an energetic, dynamic commander, strong-minded for one thing and able for another. He is a military man in the true sense.[4]

Fergusson (then Brigadier The Lord Ballantrae), who travelled with Wavell as his Private Secretary from Egypt to India, wrote forcefully:

> Lord Wavell's 'exhaustion' has often been alleged, but I dispute it. If he had been 'exhausted' he would surely have slept most of the way to India. I accompanied him on that journey . . ., and I do not remember him closing an eye in flight at all. He had only one, anyway; and for the first leg of the flight, to Lydda, he was peering with it out of the window at Sinai and southern Palestine, the scene of his experiences with Allenby during World War I. On the second leg, to Habbaniya, as soon as we had overflown Amman, he asked me if I had anything to read; and I lent him the copy of Flecker's *Hassan*, which I was reading myself. Before opening it, he quoted the whole of *Ishak's Song*, by heart, and then read it happily until we touched down.
> At Habbaniya, where it was devilish hot, he insisted on being driven all around the scene of the recent fighting. At Baghdad, he was dissuaded only with difficulty from flying up to Deir-ez-Zor, which had just fallen, on the grounds that it no longer came under his command: he took me and his ADC for a swim at the Al Wiya Club instead. At Basra, which in July was even hotter than Habbaniya, he was tireless in looking around the docks and inspecting the unloading of ships where men were actually dying of heat stroke on the job. At Sharja, . . .
> Next morning, with me on his heels, he took formal possession of GHQ, India. His full vigour was at once apparent; and within forty-eight hours he had despatched proposals, which were implemented within six weeks, to the Chiefs of Staff for the invasion of Iran. . . .
> Fighting on many fronts, as he was, with meagre resources, and bombarded with daily thunderbolts from the Prime Minister, I will concede that he was harassed; but that he was 'exhausted', I strenuously deny.[5]

Ronald Lewin believed that Fergusson's testimony provided 'clinching evidence' that 'for the time being, translation from Cairo to Delhi gave Wavell a second wind'.[6] It is undoubtedly true that the robust Wavell was indeed mentally and physically resilient. However, the mere fact of the removal of the tremendous responsibility of serving as Commander-in-Chief, Middle East, gave him a 'second wind' before assuming command in India. Both Fergusson and Lewin, however, clearly imply that Wavell was not over-tired, and should not have been relieved for that reason.

Such a view is not consistent with the historical record, as Fergusson later conceded privately when referring to mistakes Wavell made in the Western Desert:

> I think it [Wavell sending O'Connor to 'assist' Neame in Cyrenaica in April 1941] must have been a symptom of his weariness. Oddly enough, people at the time were saying that he [Wavell] was tired; and yet I, at close quarters, could not see it – not even in the aircraft in which I finally travelled with him to India.[7]

Fergusson's oblique admission of Wavell's weariness coincides with the observations and impressions of Freyberg, Coats, Lampson, and Stark made during the period from 30 April 1941 until Wavell's 7 July 1941 departure from the Middle East, which were recounted in the previous chapter. Dorman-Smith, who worked closely with Wavell on a daily basis from April to June 1941, wrote of him after conducting a briefing in early June: 'Looking very tired, he [Wavell] was. I wish he'd take some leave. This unending responsibility is so utterly wearing.'[8] Julian Amery, who visited Wavell in Cairo later in June, observed that Wavell 'seemed physically tired and fatalistic in his approach to his problems';[9] shortly after Wavell's departure from Egypt, Air Vice Marshal Thomas Elmhirst, back from Turkey and then commanding 202 Group, Royal Air Force, Egypt, wrote that Wavell 'certainly needed one [a rest]'.[10] Coats, who, as Wavell's aide-de-camp, probably knew him better than anyone else except the General's family, recently reflected:

> He [Wavell] had had an exhausting time, certainly – & I did think he was tired. His unfortunate habit of not talking did not help. Some people (generals, etc.) did think him tired, but it was never discussed. He had a lot to depress him.[11]

'One week', concluded Coats thoughtfully, '[Wavell was] the Empire's Hero – and the next . . .?'[12]

The most convincing evidence of Wavell's weariness comes from the General himself. In response to the request of his former divisional commander, General Sir Henry Jackson, to autograph a copy of his pamphlet *Generals and Generalship*, Wavell wrote candidly and dejectedly on 5 June 1941:

> So many thanks for your charming letter which I only received yesterday at a time when I am feeling very far from being a successful commander, after Cyrenaica, Greece and Crete. I think I only made one bad mistake, but that was the beginning of all our troubles. I've had a very difficult time for some months with Cyrenaica, Greece, Crete, Iraq, Syria and we still have troubles in plenty.
>
> It's all a matter of equipment and that is still desperately slow to come out. It also makes things difficult when one's supposed allies fail. I am afraid Victory has definitely joined the enemy, there is still plenty of trouble likely in Iraq, and Turkey will certainly not come down on our side of the fence at present.

America is terribly slow in getting started and altogether it will be a long and unpleasant business.

Good luck to you, I've signed the lectures, wish I could have lived up to them in some precepts.[13]

Even though his oak-like body did not reveal it, Wavell knew he was tired, and informed Dill the next day: 'If Syria and Battleaxe go well there may be a partial lull in Middle East till the autumn. If so I should like some weeks rest and possibly you might like me home part of the time to report.'[14] He was also concerned that his judgement might have become affected by his fatigue, and appears to have considered this a valid cause for relief, as he added 'that, if he were told to go, he would go without making any trouble'.[15] The preponderance of the evidence, from others and from Wavell himself, indicates that he had been fatigued greatly throughout the last few months of his command. Considering the multiplicity of military and political responsibilities he had borne from April to June 1941, including the conduct, with grossly inadequate resources, of simultaneous campaigns on the periphery of his enormous command, it would have been difficult to conclude otherwise.

It has also been suggested that neither Wavell's fatigue, nor any other reason, justified his dismissal from Command in the Middle East. Writing shortly after Wavell's relief, Major General H Rowan-Robinson wrote that:

The reasons for relieving Wavell from his former command are obscure. . . . He has the confidence of his troops and of the nation. His known toughness of fibre and his transfer to another high command altogether preclude any doubt as to his health, though the appointment of a triumvirate to replace him is an indication that he must have been subjected to a colossal strain.[16]

Correlli Barnett, in 1960 in *The Desert Generals*, argued compellingly that 'There was no valid case for relieving Wavell.'[17] After more than two decades of additional research and introspection, during which Ultra and other information was declassified, it became clear that it was 'a crude and superficial reading of *Ultra* information on Churchill's part [which] provided the key factor in his insistence that Wavell should launch . . . "hopelessly premature" offensives' which, Barnett remained convinced, 'lends extra weight to the charge that Churchill's decision finally to sack Wavell because of the failure of *Battleaxe* was "an amazing injustice".'[18]

Rowan-Robinson's statement and Barnett's conviction that 'there was no valid case for relieving Wavell' fail to take into consideration the legacies and realities of civil-military relations in a democratic nation. 'We see, therefore', observed Clausewitz, 'that war is not merely an act of policy but a true political instrument, a continuation of political intercourse, carried on with other means.'[19] Even though the military and civilian aspects of society became less distinct in the totality of the Second World War, it remained the function of the military to implement the will of the State. Whereas the military leader, a general, is a specialist, it is the responsibility of a single civilian authority to understand and coordinate overall policy, and maintain primacy over the military. 'In other words', as Harry L Coles has stated, 'in a democracy all basic policy, including military policy, is made by officials responsible to the people with whom sovereignty ultimately rests.'[20] Churchill, therefore, despite Barnett's *post-facto* condemnation, possessed the authority to relieve Wavell of command if he lacked confidence in the General or believed him to be tired – or for any other reason, real or perceived. The prerogative of the civil authority and the subordination of the military to that authority, rather than fairness or some emotional conception of 'justice', is the dominant issue in the debate over Wavell's supersession.

'In time of war, there must be complete confidence between any Commander and his subordinates', wrote Fergusson in 1965,

> . . . and many subordinates were unlucky in that they forfeited that confidence and had to go. In the light of the clash of character between Churchill and Wavell, it seems to me that Wavell's dismissal was justified, and that he himself would be the first to agree.[21]

After having spent only a fortnight in his new position as Commander-in-Chief, India, Wavell, without rancour, wrote to Dill:

> I was sorry, very sorry, to leave [the] Middle East and should have loved to see it through there, but as the PM had obviously lost confidence in me, and he bears the supreme responsibility, he was right to make a change of bowling and I had had several sixes hit off me, some perhaps through bowling to orders. Anyway I had a long spell, got some wickets, and have no grouse at being taken off.[22]

Fergusson's assessment of his former Chief's reaction to his own relief was entirely correct: Wavell clearly understood the respective roles of the soldier and the statesman.

Even though Wavell had lost the confidence of the Prime Minister, he definitely did not lose the trust and respect of his subordinate officers and troops. A few days after being notified of his relief, Wavell personally announced to his senior staff officers the confidential news of his imminent departure. 'The silence – a hush of gloom – which fell on the room', wrote Collins, 'was perhaps more eloquent of the news than any words.'[23]

Many of the soldiers of the Middle East Command felt consternation, a sense of personal loss, and even anger, at the dismissal of their leader, who had led them, against numerically-overwhelming forces, to unmitigated victory in the Western Desert and Italian East Africa. As Dill had intimated to the Prime Minister earlier, many soldiers viewed Wavell's relief as little more than a feeble attempt by Churchill to shift the blame for the recent setbacks in the Middle East onto its commander. 'The feeling of the troops', recently observed HJ Fischer, who served in the 1st South African Brigade Group, 'was that Wavell was made a scapegoat due to poor organisation and Intelligence of the British Government.'[24] WJ Kennedy, who served in the 2nd New Zealand Division, believed Wavell's relief to be 'quite unjustified';[25] 'I was aware that Sir Archie Wavell, as we called him', retrospectively wrote Ernest Mason, a 'Desert Rat' of the 7th Armoured Division, 'had been posted to India, and most of the lads were very sorry[;] we [had] a lot of confidence in him. Wavell was a scapegoat for Churchill.'[26] George Rose, who was a Royal Horse Artilleryman also serving in the 7th Armoured Division, was clearly perplexed and dismayed by Wavell's replacement: 'he [Wavell] was a very likeable man and for the life of me, I don't know why they pulled him out, and sent him to India';[27] expressing similar sentiments was John Whyatt, 2nd Battalion The York and Lancaster Regiment:

> To this day I do not know why the troops' most liked general was sacked. If it was because of the failures in Greece and Crete it is a disgusting affair. Having to withdraw [from the Western Desert] a high percentage of a successful force and throw them into a completely different kind of warfare, and sadly lacking a comparable air force[,] was a foregone prelude to disaster. My humble opinion is that Wavell was a scapegoat.[28]

Other soldiers expressed disgust, being angered and feeling betrayed by Wavell's removal from command. 'He [Wavell] got a rum deal', Jack Fuller, who had participated in Operation 'Compass', complained bitterly, 'First they take all his men and equipment and ship it to Greece, then they expect him to fight the whole bloody German Army with tanks that don't work and fuzzy-cheeked platoons.'[29]

The public reaction to Wavell's dismissal was much more subdued than expected, being greatly overshadowed by the news of the German attack on the Soviet Union. The private opinions of British soldiers have been previously described and coincide greatly with the personal impression of a knowledgeable United States Army officer. When asked if he had been shocked by the news of Wavell's relief, Brigadier General Raymond E Lee, US Military Attaché in London, admitted in his journal,

> . . . that I was, for Wavell is the only British general who has had anything approaching success, in spite of the fact that he has had to make all his 'bricks without straw.' I don't know that this is a political blunder of the first magnitude, but certainly it is not going to do anything to relieve the gradual tide of uneasiness which people are feeling over the one-man conduct of this war.[30]

The official United States Army interpretation of Wavell's transfer appears to have been very imaginative, although it was a version later accepted by many people. 'General Wavell was selected to appear as a scapegoat', wrote Lieutenant Colonel Frederick D Sharp, of the US Army Military

Intelligence Division's New York Office, 'his transfer to India giving the appearance of a demotion but in reality being a promotion in view of the opinion held that a Nazi attack on India or intervening points is part of the Hitler program to follow the Russian campaign.'[31]

Eliciting little public attention, Wavell's dismissal was seen by many as a routine administrative action in which a successful general was transferred to another, similar position. With the rapidity of the German advance into the Soviet Union, there was widespread apprehension about the Soviet ability to survive the onslaught. It appeared that the German juggernaut might sweep through the Caucasus, threatening Turkey, Iraq, and Iran, and ultimately, India, in addition to the British position in the Middle East. The loss of the oil fields of Northern Iraq and South-Western Iran could have been a decisive blow to the British war effort, and their protection became a matter of paramount importance. Accordingly, to expel the Germans and other pro-German elements established there, the British, under the strategic direction of Wavell (now in India) and in conjunction with Soviet units, advanced into Iran on 25 August 1941.

This brief and successful campaign was followed with a 15 October 1941 meeting at Tiflis where Wavell discussed with General Koslov, the Soviet commander in the Caucasus, the coordination of joint contingency plans for the defence of that important region. Since Wavell's service during the Great War as a liaison officer to the Grand Duke Nicholas (Commander-in-Chief of the Russian Army of the Caucasus), his observation of the 1936 Soviet Army manoeuvres, and his fluency in the Russian language were all well-known facts, they combined at this time, as Robert Woollcombe has suggested, to create 'a feeling among the uninformed public that the War Cabinet had probably shown Olympian foresight all along in sending him [Wavell] to India in good time to make fast'.[32] Thus, the German attack on the Soviet Union served to deflect negative public opinion over Wavell's relief, and the requirement for British-Soviet cooperation gave credence to the impression that Wavell had been transferred to India expressly for that purpose.

* * *

The Generalship of Wavell – An Assessment

The primary purpose of this study, as stated in the Introduction, has been 'to make a full and fair assessment of what Wavell achieved as a fighting commander during the first two years of the Second World War' as Commander-in-Chief, Middle East. This has been done, initially, by chronicling Wavell's formative experiences in his professional development, and by elucidating and evaluating his philosophies of command, leadership, and training. The high point of Wavell's almost four decades of military service was his tenure as Commander-in-Chief, Middle East, when he was able to distill the intrinsic qualities of high command and put them into practice under the most demanding conditions.

No one man can win a battle by himself, but throughout history battles have been won and lost because of the strengths or weaknesses of one individual – the commander. Indeed, it was Napoleon who observed astutely that 'An army is nothing without a head.'[33] Since Wavell served as the 'head' of the Middle East Command, it is essential to assess his performance and strengths and weaknesses in that position.

Generalship is undoubtedly one of the most difficult and complex arts to master, dealing 'not with dead matter but with living things, who are subjected to every impression of the moment, such as fear, precipitation, exhaustion – in short, to every human passion and excitement.'[34] Wavell astutely and realistically recognised the paramount importance of the fragile and volatile human element of leadership and warfare, as he wrote to Liddell Hart shortly after assuming command of the 2nd Division in 1935:

> How are your studies in war progressing? If I had time, and anything like your ability and industry to study war, I think I should concentrate almost entirely on the 'actualities' of war – the effects of tiredness, hunger, fear, lack of sleep, weather, inaccurate information, the time factor, and so forth. The principles of strategy and tactics, and the logistics of war are really absurdly simple, it is the 'actualities' that make war so complicated and so difficult, and are usually so neglected by historians.[35]

A general must control a multitude of intangible factors simultaneously, including time and weather, while at the same time being confronted by an armed and hostile adversary intent on his total destruction. The mantle of responsibility borne by a general, and especially a commander-in-chief, is enormous, and has evolved through the centuries, in conjunction with numerous technological and societal changes, into an even greater challenge more difficult to master.

Of course, there is no set equation or magic formula or textbook definition of generalship, no recipe of essential ingredients for the successful general. Perceptions of the qualifications of generalship have evolved only slightly through the centuries, the human elements of leadership remaining relatively constant. And human beings are, naturally, not perfect. Indeed,

> A perfect general, like Plato's republic, is a figment. Either would be admirable, but it is not characteristic of human nature to produce beings exempt from human weaknesses and defects. The finest medallions have a reverse side. But in spite of this awareness of our imperfections it is not less necessary to consider all the different talents that are needed by an accomplished general. These are the models that one attempts to imitate and which one would not try to emulate if they were not presented to us.[36]

Wavell's Lees Knowles Lectures, entitled 'Generals and Generalship', attracted little notice when delivered at Trinity College, Cambridge, in February 1939, only five months prior to his appointment as Commander-in-Chief, Middle East. Two years later, after the unmitigated success of Operation 'Compass' in the Western Desert, Wavell's name was veritably a household word in England and he was at the height of his popularity, considered 'Britain's Soldier of the Hour'. At this time, as noted earlier, his lectures were published in pamphlet form and were extremely popular and well-received.

Wavell's first lecture was entitled 'The Good General', and he introduced it by an exposition on generalship attributed to Socrates:

> The general must know how to get his men their rations and every other kind of stores needed for war. He must have imagination to originate plans, practical sense and energy to carry them through. He must be observant, untiring, shrewd; kindly and cruel; simple and crafty; a watchman and a robber; lavish and miserly; generous and stingy; rash and conservative. All these and many other qualities, natural and acquired, he must have. He should also, as a matter of course, know his tactics; for a disorderly mob is no more an army than a heap of building materials is a house.[37]

Wavell pointed out that Socrates's definition of generalship began with the logistical and administrative aspects of war, which, he believed, 'is the real crux of generalship'.[38] He learned this lesson while serving on the Western Front during the Great War, and during his service with Allenby in Palestine. When preparing his own offensives according to his own time-tables, most notably 'Compass' and to a lesser extent the Italian East African campaign, Wavell shepherded his meagre resources and ensured the establishment of prepositioned supply and fuel depots to sustain the respective operation. When being pressured to initiate simultaneous offensives Wavell, primarily due to his shortage of resources and competing demands, was less successful in this regard, although he ensured that all logistical preparations which could be made were completed.

'The first essential of a general', according to Wavell, is 'the quality of robustness, the ability to stand the shocks of war.'[39] A commander must be physically and mentally robust, and Wavell clearly lived up to this precept. During April, May, and June 1941, the last three months of Wavell's command in the Middle East, he bore an incredible burden of responsibility. His stamina and energy were remarkable, although on a few occasions, as we have seen, Wavell was excessively tired, but his strong powers of resilience allowed him to recover quickly. It is quite possible, however, that his fatigue resulted in a decrease in his ability to resist Churchill's omnipresent pressures to launch simultaneous and premature offensives (Iraq, 'Brevity', Syria, and 'Battleaxe'). O'Connor suggested that Churchill's incessant 'badgering' in the end affected Wavell with a sense of deficiency and of a need to show that he (Wavell), too, could be strong.[40] Wavell warned the

Government against undertaking these operations, but he eventually acquiesced and initiated them. According to Ismay, Wavell should have 'made it absolutely clear to the P M, in the simplest possible language, that he had not got the resources for the multifarious operations that the P M wanted him to undertake'.[41] The example of Longmore's relief, and Wavell's desire to act in a positive and aggressive manner, were also factors in Wavell agreeing to conduct these operations as ordered, as was his ardent desire to avoid new reproaches for being excessively cautious. Wavell believed that since the 'general is dealing with men's lives, [he must] have a certain mental robustness to stand the strain of responsibility'.[42] He stood this strain remarkably well himself.

The physical attributes of courage, health, and youth, according to Wavell, are also required of the general. His physical courage was never in doubt, manifested by his frequent flights in unreliable aircraft to decisive areas in the midst of hostilities and his willingness to observe and direct operations from the forward area of the battlefield was evident on numerous occasions. The timing of Wavell's visits was propitious, and, according to the British Official History, they were 'a tonic'.[43] Wavell's unsurpassed imperturbability and ability to maintain his calm in the most demanding situations was one of his hallmarks.

Moral courage is an essential component of command. There were many moral dilemmas which Wavell encountered while commanding in the Middle East. Always willing to challenge orthodoxy, he courted Churchill's displeasure by not informing him of Operation 'Compass' until the planning was completed. Another quandary Wavell faced, as stated earlier, was the question of conducting simultaneous and premature operations. O'Connor, who generally had an extremely high opinion of Wavell's performance in the Middle East and was a close friend, criticised him for failing to stand up to Churchill and refusing to act on military grounds when he believed, on military grounds, that it was wrong to do so[44] – as in the case of Iraq, Syria, and Wavell's last two Western Desert offensives. This lapse in moral courage can, perhaps, be attributed to Wavell's weariness, or fear of supersession if he demurred. Furthermore, failure to comply with a legal directive from his constitutionally-sanctioned political master would have been anathema to Wavell's highly-developed sense of selfless duty to his King and country. Similarly, resignation would have been out of the question. He knew full well that to have abandoned his Command voluntarily could only have exacerbated an already precarious situation.

Health and youth, according to Wavell, are also requirements of generalship. He unquestionably possessed the former, but the latter is more difficult to define and assess. 'It is impossible', Wavell observed,

> . . . really to give exact values to the fire and boldness of youth as against the judgment and experience of riper years; if the mature mind still has the capacity to conceive and to absorb new ideas, to withstand unexpected shocks, and to

put into execution bold and unorthodox designs, its superior knowledge and judgment will give the advantage over youth.[45]

It is indisputable that Wavell possessed both 'the judgment and experience of riper years' and 'the mature mind'. At what point a general becomes too old to serve effectively as a combat commander is a function of the individual's mental and physical characteristics, the nature of the war, and a host of additional factors.

Liddell Hart, who had been an active advocate for Wavell's selection to be Chief of the Imperial General Staff in 1937, later believed that Wavell had actually reached his peak of effectiveness some time before 1941, probably when he was commanding the 2nd Division from 1935 to 1937. When Wavell took over Southern Command in 1938, after having spent the previous year in Palestine, Liddell Hart visited him. 'I went down to visit him [Wavell] at Salisbury', Liddell Hart later recorded, and 'was dismayed to find that he had become only a shadow of the man he had been, having developed a hesitancy and conservatism that he never had before.'[46] Liddell Hart attributed this to the fact that the prolonged promotion stagnation immediately following the Great War forced officers to hold positions of limited scope for lengthy periods prior to reaching positions in which they could exercise their own individual ideas and initiative.[47] Although Liddell Hart is the only person known to have made this observation, and Wavell's subsequent performance in the Middle East, especially during 'Compass', would seem to belie this impression, it is one that is nevertheless worth considering.

Wavell was adamant that a general must have 'character', which simply means that he knows what he wants and has the courage and determination to get it'.[48] A more recent definition of 'character' is more inclusive:

> ... there appears to be an aggregate of qualities in an individual's make-up, particularly those concerning his integrity and ethical foundation which are absolutely essential in the potential leader, and which cannot be added through schooling or experience.[49]

Wavell certainly possessed a solid foundation of character, with unimpeachable integrity, and the determination to accomplish all his specified and implied missions in a highly professional manner. 'The fighting spirit, the will to win', was an essential item in the composition of Wavell's theoretical general, as was a genuine interest in and real knowledge of humanity, both of which were also a part of Wavell's character.

Wavell emphasised that 'the mark of the really great commander, as distinguished from the ordinary general [is that] he must have a spirit of adventure, a touch of the gambler in him.'[50] This quality of audacity in Wavell can be traced from his experiences with Allenby, through his realistic field training exercises while commanding the 2nd Division, and culminating with the remarkably audacious execution of 'Compass'. His adroit shifting of forces to meet his divergent contingencies was clearly within the realm of boldness. His normal proclivity to take risks was evident in 'Compass', the Italian East African campaign, and the expedition to Greece, but he faltered in his reluctance to exploit 'Compass' and continue the advance to Tripoli. 'A bold general may be lucky, but no general can be lucky unless he is bold': by taking advantage of all situations, and by not permitting one to be bound by the fetters of orthodoxy, the general, as did Wavell, could create his own 'luck'.

Wavell also considered 'common sense', based on 'a really sound knowledge of the "mechanism of war," i.e., topography, movement, and supply'[51], to be a requirement of the general. This is totally consistent with Wavell's conviction that:

> A real knowledge of supply and movement factors must be the basis of every leader's plan; only then can he know how and when to take risks with those factors; and battles and wars are won only by taking risks.[52]

Careful attention to the logistics of war, Wavell believed, and adequate logistical preparations, were matters of signal importance, 'the real crux of generalship'. Especially noteworthy is his foresight in initiating the establishment of a significant logistical base for the large forces he knew would eventually flow into the Middle East.

'The General and His Troops' was the title and theme of Wavell's second Lees Knowles Lecture. He began that lecture with what he considered to be two important, yet simple, rules which every general should observe: 'first, never try to do his own staff work; and secondly, never to let his staff get between him and his troops'.[53] The general should issue guidance to the staff, give them the authority and responsibility they need for their actions, and let them work out the details. The general should not let himself be overworked by minutiae, or let details of staff work stifle his imagination or strategic vision of operations. Wavell adhered to that tenet very well, and frequently visited his subordinate commanders and soldiers. The perception of his visits being a 'tonic' has been remarked upon earlier. 'Jumbo' Wilson's belief that Wavell's frequent visits 'acted as a stimulant to all ranks', and that 'the effect of his arrival on the inspiration and energy of those he came to see was remarkable',[54] is supported by the reminiscences of many former soldiers of Wavell's Middle East Command. John Whyatt, for example, one of the 'Other Ranks' of the 2nd York and Lancaster Regiment, met Wavell during one of his visits to Crete in November 1940. Wavell had a short conversation with Whyatt, and shared a mug of tea with him. The following month 'Compass' was initiated, and Whyatt recalled that:

> We had been soundly thrashed in France and Norway, and now good news was coming through about the Western Desert and Abyssinia. That the opposition was not of the same calibre as the Germans didn't matter, we were winning something at last and now everyone knew of General Wavell. I felt a little smug – I had spoken with the man, and he had shared my tea. From then on he was my man.[55]

Indeed, 'The less time a general spends in his office and the more with his troops the better.'[56]

A higher commander, Wavell submitted, must be a good judge of character. This maxim is easier to state than to put into practice, and Wavell's ability to judge character may have been one of his shortcomings. Lady Wavell observed, in 1961, that 'Archie [Wavell] was apt to tolerate people, and keep them on his personal staff too long, if they amused him. He was easily bored by people . . ., and would forgive anyone who amused him.'[57] There is no evidence of this, but the retention of less-than-proficient personal staff members – aides-de-camp, private secretaries, military assistants – would have had little impact on the conduct of operations.

Field Marshal Viscount Montgomery's declaration that Wavell 'was not sufficiently ruthless with those below him whom he reckoned were not fit for their jobs'[58] has, however, a certain amount of truth, which Wavell himself fully recognised. The most significant example is that of the commanders in the Western Desert after Operation 'Compass', as Wavell later wrote:

> Finally, though I have never said this officially, and have always accepted full responsibility, I was very poorly served in the matter of commanders. It was, I suppose, largely my own fault, since the two chief culprits were my own selections. I know that Philip Neame is a friend of yours, and I have great admiration for his character, but as a Commander and a tactician, his dispositions were simply deplorable, and his conduct of the battle equally so, I consider. . . . When I went out there in the middle of March, I found that he was proposing to place an Infantry Brigade in one long thin line. . . . It would have been completely sacrificed. . . . In the battle, he seemed to me never to have any idea whatever where his troops were, or to make any particular effort to find out, . . .
>
> The second complete failure was Gambier-Parry, who was, I think, equally inept in his handling of his Command. This was my fault; I had recommended him for the Command. . . .
>
> I don't think that either Rimington or Younghusband were fit for their jobs. I did not know Rimington well, but I very nearly removed him from his Command a week or two before the battle, as from the little I saw of him he did not inspire me with confidence. But as I did not think a battle was likely to take place for some time, I decided to give him a chance.[59]

Thus, by his own admission, Wavell knew he had selected commanders who eventually appeared unable properly to execute their assigned tasks, yet he kept them in command after detecting their shortcomings because he did not expect an attack as quickly as one occurred. While, therefore, he could have been a better judge of character, the important point is that he should have immediately replaced those senior officers he deemed incompetent.

Tradition and discipline, Wavell was convinced, were the key factors in the general's relations with his troops. 'The general who sees that the soldier is well fed and looked after', Wavell surmised sagely, 'and who puts him into a good show [battle] and wins battles, will naturally have his confidence.'[60] 'Wavell always [,] through good planning', recently wrote Lieutenant Colonel JAE Deane, 'kept his casualties as low as possible [;] he was loved by the men under him as he was meticulous in looking after them and ensuring that hardships were reduced to a minimum.'[61] Wavell always took great care to look out for the health and welfare of his soldiers, which they realised and reciprocated by placing their full confidence in him.

Although Wavell always held that a general 'must certainly never court popularity. If he has their [the soldiers'] appreciation and respect it is sufficient',[62] it is abundantly clear, as Lieutenant Colonel Deane has told us above, that he was indeed held in great affection as well as deep respect, by all who served under him. This he achieved, quite unconsciously, by his scrupulous care of the soldiers' best interests and needs, by demanding the highest standards in challenging training and by meticulous preparation before battle. Quite simply, the troops knew they could trust him implicitly – which is all they ask of any general. It was deeply regrettable that Ronald Lewin, in his biography *The Chief*, should have suggested that while Wavell's loyal supporters, in their memoirs, should have referred 'not infrequently to the impression he made upon the troops in his wartime commands there was little evidence from the troops themselves of such impressions.'[63]

The tributes which follow leave us in no doubt that Wavell gained not only the respect but also the affection and admiration of his soldiers. That an historian of Lewin's standing should have made so misleading a statement is beyond comprehension.

> . . . Wavell to us troops was really the *tops*. He was regarded by all as a good and reliable man, whom everyone loved and respected; and . . . Archie Wavell to the common soldier was the essence of good military stature. Someone who we always [knew] would give [us] a fair deal.[64]
>
> – *SG Smith, 11th Hussars, 1938–43.*

> Wavell was probably the most respected of all British army commanders; and . . . along with all other allied troops at the time, I gained a very deep respect for him [Wavell], and have always believed that he was one of our most outstanding military leaders.[65]
>
> – *WJ Kennedy. 2nd New Zealand Division, 1940–43*

> I think I am correct in saying that all who served under Wavell during his time in the Middle East had nothing but praise and admiration for the man . . . with these limited forces, he accomplished miracles.[66]
>
> – *Reuben Ashington, 1st South African Division, 1940–42*

> . . . He [Wavell] was very well liked, that kind of praise coming from the rank and file speaks volumes, he was a soldier's soldier, a compassionate man, who I personally felt had not been given credit for his organisational abilities and [the] successful culmination of what in my opinion was the first British and Commonwealth victory in WW II.[67]
>
> *John Barnard, 4th Indian Division, 1940–42*

Wavell was in my opinion a brilliant General vastly underrated by Churchill and the War Cabinet. Every one of us thought the world of him, and under the circumstances I know of no one who could have done as well, certainly not any better. . . . Wavell in my opinion accomplished the impossible dream.[68]
– R J Mathews, Royal Artillery, 1939–43.

General Wavell, in my humble opinion, was one of the best generals in the British Forces.[69]
Harold Van Santen, 1st South African Division 1939–43

Christopher Sykes observed that 'He [Wavell] was in the singular position of being loved equally by the ordinary soldiers and officers, by his senior commanders and by his staff';[70] after Wavell's relief, correspondent Alexander Clifford was surprised that 'the curious thing was that, in spite of Greece, Crete, Cyrenaica, Wavell still retained the respect and affection and confidence of the troops in the Middle East'.[71] 'Since Wavell had left us', wrote another veteran of the Western Desert, 'our C-in-Cs had been so dreary that I hadn't bothered to find out the name of our latest acquisition.'[72] Although Wavell 'certainly never courted popularity', he did in fact gain more than the appreciation and respect of his soldiers by sparing no efforts in taking care of their physical and psychological needs.

In summing up his second Lees Knowles lecture, Wavell had stated that,

> the relationship between a general and his troops is very much like that between the rider and his horse. The horse must be controlled and disciplined, and yet encouraged: he should, according to an old hunting maxim, 'be cared for in the stable as if he was worth £500 and ridden in the field as if he were not worth half-a-crown.' And the horse knows not only by his own comfort whether he is being ridden well or badly, but he knows if his rider is bold or frightened, determined or hesitating.[73]

He followed this philosophy throughout his tenure in the Middle East.

The last and shortest, of the Lees Knowles Lectures dealt with the relations of higher commanders to their political masters. It was entitled 'The Soldier and the Statesman'. Wavell alluded to the Great War experience, in which 'the politician charged the soldiers with narrowness of outlook and professional pedantry, while the soldier was inclined to ascribe many of his difficulties to "political interference."'[74] It was certainly also a portent of Wavell's experience in the Middle East. Many of his difficulties would indeed be attributable to continual 'political interference', although he would not and did not blame his political superiors for any of those difficulties.

Wavell, with only a few exceptions, was able to live up to his expostulated precepts of generalship while serving as Commander-in-Chief, Middle East. To obtain a more thorough assessment of his generalship, and to gain a better appreciation of the possible severity of his few demonstrated shortcomings, one can also evaluate Wavell's generalship within the parameters stated by Norman Dixon in his seminal work *On the Psychology of Military Incompetence*. From an examination of historical case studies, Dixon identified the following fourteen components of military incompetence:[75]

1. *A serious wastage of human resources and failure to observe one of the first principles of war – economy of force*. Wavell cannot be faulted in this regard, since he planned, or ensured that all operations were planned, using the minimum forces required to accomplish the respective mission and avoiding frontal assaults whenever possible. He had seen, and experienced, the human slaughter which resulted from inadequately planned operations during the Great War, and was committed to preventing its recurrence. In addition, primarily due to his acute manpower shortage, Wavell was forced to task-organise his respective forces and allocate them carefully to meet the many dynamic operational commitments throughout his enormous theatre of operations. The conquest of Italian East Africa, representative of many of Wavell's campaigns, was executed, as noted previously, 'on two fronts with an economy and flexibility of force that ought to rank as a feat of spontaneous exploitation unsurpassed in war'.[76] Wavell's ardent desire to conduct campaigns as expeditiously as possible also helped him conserve human resources.

2. *A fundamental conservatism and clinging to outworn tradition*. Wavell continually eschewed the shackles of conservatism and orthodoxy, and this trait can most readily be discerned during his advancement in rank and in positions of increasing command responsibility in the 1930s. He was an advocate of the mechanisation of the Army and combined arms operations, and he championed demanding, realistic infantry training, which included deception, ruses, and night training. In addition, he sponsored the formation of Wingate's Special Night Squads in Palestine, and later employed him leading indigenous forces in Ethiopia. The Long Range Desert Group and other special military formations owed their existence either to Wavell's own ideas or advocacy. Wavell was very open-minded, willing to employ new weapons and tactics, as Harvey Arthur DeWeerd has written:

> Wavell was the first British soldier in World War II to grasp the full lessons of the German campaigns in Poland and France and apply them to the conditions of desert fighting. He was the first British soldier in this war to coordinate effectively the full power of British sea, land, and air forces in a single campaign.[77]

Wavell was afraid of nothing, including the implementation of a new idea.

3. *A tendency to reject or ignore information*. Wavell was generally receptive to any new information or confirmed, accurate intelligence, regardless of how unpalatable it might have been. One exception to this maxim must be noted. After the relatively easy defeat of the Italians in

Operation 'Compass', Wavell became temporarily imbued with the notion of the marked superiority of his forces, and believed the newly-arrived German forces were of the same low quality as the Italians. As a result, as he later wrote, 'I [had] made up my mind that the enemy could not put in any effective counter-stroke before May [1941] at the earliest.'[78] In this instance, he demonstrated uncharacteristically an inflexibility of mind which prohibited him from accepting this possibility.

4. *A tendency to underestimate the enemy*. Wavell's estimate of enemy strengths and dispositions was usually accurate. His estimates of German unit identifications, strengths, dispositions, and capabilities, having been based on orthodox logistical considerations, were also realistic. However, due to the shortcomings mentioned above, Wavell also underestimated Rommel's audacity and ability to launch an offensive earlier than anticipated, while concurrently overestimating the mechanical status and operational readiness of the British 2nd Armoured Division. The juxtaposition of these two errors of judgement had disastrous repercussions for the British, and led directly to Rommel's breach of the British positions guarding the western flank of Cyrenaica. In addition, the German defensive capabilities were seriously underestimated in Operation 'Battleaxe'.

5. *Indecisiveness*. That Wavell was decisive is shown by the timing and range of his offensives. He also possessed the uncanny ability of showing up at the crucial point of a battle and, after quickly and accurately assessing the situation with the information available, would decide upon the next course of action. When he felt that a situation demanded decisions of signal importance, he made them unhesitatingly and accepted full responsibility for them. Cases in point include the evacuations from Greece and Crete, the decision to hold Tobruk, and his order to call off Operation 'Battleaxe'.

6. *An obstinate persistance in a given task*. Generally, Wavell was very open-minded and flexible and not obstinate. Two episodes are worth remarking upon, however. The first is his insistence on withdrawing the 4th Indian Division from the Western Desert during Operation 'Compass', after underestimating the potential success of that offensive, and sending the division to the Sudan. As suggested earlier, he should have been less rigid, and waited a few more days to be able to assess properly the successful outcome of 'Compass' before withdrawing one-half of the attacking force. The second example is Wavell's insistence upon favouring the despatch of a British force to Greece, despite strong evidence to suggest that the expedition could only end in defeat.

7. *A failure to exploit a situation gained*. Wavell was a bold and aggressive commander, willing to take calculated risks. However, he demonstrated flawed judgment in prematurely taking the 4th Indian Division out of Operation 'Compass', but, more importantly, in his untypical hesitation and failure to exploit 'Compass' by pushing on to and seizing Tripoli – although the feasibility of staying there is still a matter of deep controversy.

8. *A failure to make adequate reconnaissance*. 'He [the general] must as far as possible', Wavell wrote, 'see the ground for himself to confirm or correct his impressions off the map.'[79] Wavell, rightly, believed it was imperative personally to reconnoitre a future or potential area of operations. Shortly after his arrival in Cairo in August 1939, he indefatigably conducted a reconnaissance of the significant regions of the Middle East Command. He also reconnoitred vast expanses of the Western Desert, on the ground as well as from the air, but the arrival of the Eden-Dill mission in Egypt in February 1941 diverted his attention elsewhere. As a result, he was unable to reconnoitre the western flank of Cyrenaica, and his plans for the defence of the area were, by his own admission, based on entirely erroneous perceptions of the nature of the terrain, the salt marshes, and the Escarpment in the area. He belatedly recognised this deficiency: 'I think my first error [regarding the German breakthrough in Cyrenaica] was that I never went out and looked at the ground for myself till too late.'[80] Similarly, he failed to conduct a personal reconnaissance of the proposed Aliakhmon positions in Greece; had he done so, it is quite possible that he would not have favoured sending a British force to Greece to defend along that line.

9. *A predilection for frontal assaults*. Wavell was a firm believer in the 'indirect approach', and used a number of imaginative stratagems, as had Allenby at the Third Battle of Gaza, to mislead his opponent and attack at an unexpected location.

10. *A belief in brute force*. Wavell never possessed the advantage of numerically-superior forces, and although he endeavoured to mass his forces whenever possible to achieve a local superiority, he characteristically integrated clever ruses, camouflage, and deception into his battle plans and operations. He exhorted his subordinate commanders to 'Always try to devise means to deceive and outwit the enemy and throw him off his balance,'[81] advice to which he regularly adhered himself.

11. *A failure to make use of surprise*. Surprise and deception, as noted earlier, were inherent facets of all Wavell's plans and operations. Of Operation 'Compass', one contemporary military journal stated unequivocally:

> Generations hence, when the military student or the embryo military leader is looking in the pages of history for examples of leadership calling for thorough preparation, blinding surprise, whirlwind attack, and relentless pursuit he will turn to the Libyan Campaign and need look no further.[82]

In addition, Wavell's commitment to tactical and strategic deception was so significant that Professor Michael Howard wrote recently: 'No one understood better than he [Wavell] the role which deception and its child, surprise, should play in all military operations – especially operations conducted by numerically inferior forces far from home.[83]

12. *An undue readiness to find scapegoats.* Wavell unflinchingly assumed responsibility for every setback that occurred in the Middle East during his command, and never once attempted to shift the blame onto anyone else. With similar and sincere magnanimity, he ensured his subordinates received the lion's share of recognition, to include public praise, promotions, and honours, in the wake of battlefield successes. After being congratulated by Churchill upon the success of 'Compass', for example, Wavell's immediate rejoinder was:

> Very grateful for congratulations. Success was mainly due to planning of Wilson and O'Connor and careful training over long period and fine leading of Seventh Armoured Division and Fourth Indian Division, to which 16 Inf. Brigade was attached. Operation could not have been executed without the magnificent support given by RAF and RN. Some Free French troops also took part.[84]

It was anathema to Wavell to seek scapegoats for any reason or purpose.

13. *A suppression or distortion of news.* Wavell was always completely forthright in the situation reports he sent to London, and never distorted the causes and results of unsuccessful operations. Likewise, he was brutally honest in the estimates of the chances of success of prospective operations. His realistic appraisals and reluctance to assume additional burdens, such as the defence of Iraq, were interpreted by the impetuous Churchill as excessive caution and pessimism.[85] Pownall, the Vice Chief of the Imperial General Staff, commented:

> Wavell's judgment is clearly as good as ever. He didn't take a rosy view of our chances in Crete, nor of the recent attack in Libya ['Battleaxe']; and he made a good prophecy about Syria. Taking a gloomy view, tho' an accurate one, he came under suspicion of being a commander without self-confidence. In point of fact Wavell's prophecies have proved precise.[86]

Wavell was always honest in his reports and appreciations to Whitehall, even though his candour led to him being misinterpreted at times.

14. *A belief in mystical forces.* Wavell approached his military duties on many occasions in a detached and fatalistic manner, as observed by Coats and Julian Amery and noted earlier. Wavell, wrote Dorman-Smith, 'had a curious, static loyalty to over-ruling authority, as if it was "fate"',[87] Field Marshal Lord Carver recently observed perceptively that 'I think that Wavell suffered . . . from a rather fatalistic outlook, that if things went wrong, oh well, that's just another of those things, and it happened, and this is what life is like.'[88] Wavell's tendency to succumb to fate can be traced to a multitude of factors and experiences, including his classical education at Winchester, his thorough study and knowledge of Greek and Roman generals and history, and his experiences on the Western Front during the Great War, where one almost inevitably became a casualty if not a fatality.

Wavell's belief that 'war is an option of difficulties' sums up this philosophy and his outlook on life.

Placed within the context of Wavell's attitude towards fate, many of his hitherto inexplicable decisions and actions can be better understood, although it is imperative to realise that this is not an attempt to rationalise or justify those controversial issues. Wavell's failure to push on to Tripoli in the final phase of 'Compass', after receiving revised guidance that assistance to Greece would take priority over all Middle East operations once Tobruk was taken, also reveals his acceptance of fate, that assistance to Greece would in fact have priority over his resources regardless of anything he did. The same can be said for the despatch of the force to Greece: it was destined to happen, Wavell believed, whether he favoured or opposed it. O'Connor recalled that when he proposed plans to Wavell, the latter tended to say succinctly, 'If you think it's OK, fine.'[89] A similar exchange took place on 8 April 1941, when Wavell asked Harding if Tobruk could be held. After Harding responded in the affirmative, Wavell stated 'Well if you think you can hold it you had better hold it.'[90] While Wavell's actions in these episodes may have instilled confidence in his respective subordinates, they again indicate an acquiescence of fate, which appears to have become more pronounced as he became more fatigued, and in part also explains his relatively passive reaction to the execution of 'Brevity' and 'Battleaxe' and to his own relief. Correspondent Alan Moorehead also recognised Wavell's sense of fatalism, and wrote that Wavell 'simply threw out an air that suggested that everything was moving on toward its own inevitable conclusion, everything turned upon a cycle, and the best one could do was to ensure that every man moved at his own predestined pace.'[91]

Wavell, based upon his demonstrated performance and attributes of generalship, as compared with his own precepts of the requirements of the higher commander and with indicators of military incompetence, clearly performed his duties as Commander-in-Chief, Middle East, in a highly laudable and outstanding manner. His final ledger of military accomplishments in the Middle East reveals:

Credits
▷ His incisive measures on assuming command in the Middle East in 1939. These included a series of shrewd and highly professional appreciations of the strategic, political, and purely military factors which would be likely to influence his exercise of command and led to the establishment of a viable headquarters, the creation of a planning staff, and an estimate of the scale of reinforcement which might become necessary as the impending war progressed. This last item led to the establishment of a logistic base without which few, if any, of his subsequent campaigns would have been sustainable. In all these things, he demonstrated a vision and a level of military

competence which showed that he had no rival as a commander in the British Army at that time.

▷ The reconquest of Italian East Africa (Italian Somaliland, Eritrea, and Ethiopia). The capture of Eritrea and the port of Massawa removed the threat to shipping on the Red Sea. As a result President Roosevelt, on 11 April 1941, declared that the Red Sea and the Gulf of Aden were no longer a combat zone and authorised American vessels to carry war supplies to the beleaguered Middle East by this route. The results of the entire campaign included the capture of some 250,000 enemy soldiers and their equipment, and about one million square miles of colonial territory being wrested from Italy.

▷ The successful evacuation of British troops from British Somaliland.

▷ The conception, planning, and execution of 'Compass', in which a British force never exceeding two divisions advanced over 500 miles in two months and destroyed an Italian army of nine-and-a-half divisions and captured some 130,000 enemy soldiers. The success of 'Compass' incalculably raised morale on the home front (after the débâcles of Norway and Dunkirk), and facilitated the passage of Lend-Lease legislation in the United States House of Representatives on 8 February 1941.

▷ The reconquest of British Somaliland.

▷ The British expedition to Greece was a key factor in inspiring the Yugoslav *coup d'état*, and the German reaction to these two activities, arguably, delayed the German invasion of the Soviet Union by up to six weeks.

▷ The decision to hold Tobruk, which prevented Rommel from using this important port and forced him to extend his lines of communication some 1,400 miles from Tripoli. In addition, the existence of an enemy position on his flank forced Rommel to disperse his forces to attempt to capture the British position, which in turn impaired his forward advance.

▷ The successful evacuation of 50,732 British soldiers from Greece.

▷ The defence of Crete inflicted such heavy casualties on the German airborne troops that these forces were not used to capture Cyprus or Syria, as had been feared.

▷ Successful evacuation of 14,580 British soldiers from Crete.

▷ The suppression of the Rashid Ali revolt and the re-establishment of a pro-British government in Iraq.

▷ The defeat of the Vichy French and elimination of Axis influence in the Levant States.

▷ The consolidation of the British position in the Middle East, and the retention of the Suez Canal and the short sea route to India and the Far East.

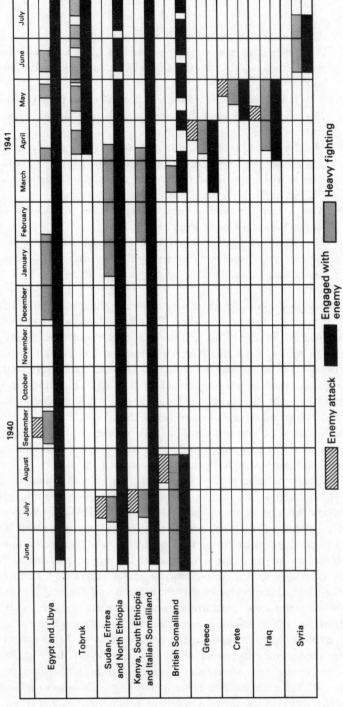

Fig. 1 Timing and Intensity of Wavell's Middle East Campaigns, 1940–41

Debits:

▷ The withdrawal from British Somaliland.

▷ An underestimation of the potential of 'Compass' and the premature withdrawal of the 4th Indian Division from the Western Desert to the Sudan.

▷ The failure to exploit 'Compass' properly and push on to Tripoli.

▷ His adamant support for the despatch of a British expeditionary force to Greece.

▷ His decision to send O'Connor to 'assist' Neame in Cyrenaica, with a resultant confusion in command and the capture of both.

▷ The British expulsion from Greece and Crete, although the British did not suffer a tactical defeat in either episode.

▷ The underestimation of German capabilities to launch an offensive in the Western Desert in February 1941.

▷ His relatively passive reaction to and acquiescence in conducting premature offensives ('Brevity' and 'Battleaxe') and simultaneous operations (Iraq/'Brevity' and Syria/'Battleaxe').

Where there were setbacks, they were generally the result of misjudgements, not incompetence, and never malice. That Wavell was able to avoid decisive defeats, and at the same time achieve two of the most resounding military victories in history – in the Western Desert and in Italian East Africa – while involved in operations in Cyrenaica, Greece, Iraq, Crete, and Syria, is an indication that he was a general of the highest calibre. It is highly doubtful if anyone else serving as Commander-in-Chief, Middle East, from 1939 to 1941, could have done any better than Wavell. In fact, considering the multiplicity of commitments in his enormous Command, and his marked paucity of manpower and material resources, it is quite probable that someone else would have done far worse.

In addition to being a superb general, Wavell was a man of immense strength, simplicity, and dignity of character. He possessed a keen strategic insight and breadth of vision beyond compare. His finely-honed intellect, sagacity, powers of analysis, and elephantine memory enabled him to reduce any problem to its simplest form, which was then acted upon decisively. He was a master of the written word, his reports and despatches being models of clarity and lucidity, and he spoke Russian and some French. Wavell possessed a superb capacity for making and keeping friends, with his strength of character permitting him to treat everyone with respect. Kindness and thoughtfulness were two of his other qualities, as was an indisputable loyalty, to subordinates and peers as well as to superiors. His unimpeachable integrity, personal dignity, and obvious honesty, in addition to his innate sincerity, were readily apparent to all with whom he came in contact. Wavell's unflinching imperturbability, calmness in adversity, and optimistic attitude, juxtaposed with his other attributes, earned him the respect and confidence, and in some cases the veneration, of those with whom he served.

Wavell seems to have been able to put different aspects of his life into different compartments to a remarkable degree. This has led many people to misunderstand him and to misinterpret his dedication to soldiering and his many accomplishments. Wavell, with his well-developed intellect, immense range of curiosity, and impeccable sense of history, had many interests outside soldiering. He was fond of poetry and books, thought to be unusual and 'unmilitary' pastimes for a fighting commander. Periodic flashes of self-revelation show Wavell's diverse interests, as he once told Pownall, his Chief of the General Staff in ABDACOM (See page 272), that 'My trouble is that I am not really interested in war.'[92] Similarly, Wavell inscribed in the journal he kept while Viceroy of India, after a meeting with Lieutenant General Sir Francis Tuker, General Officer Commanding-in-Chief, Eastern Command, India, that 'I like him, he has many more interests than soldiering, in fact his defect as a soldier is probably the same as mine, that soldiering rather bores him and books and history and art interest him more.'[93] Wavell also disclosed similar personal thoughts in some of the explanatory comments he wrote in his poetry anthology: 'War is not only a grim but mainly dull business and does not tend to inspire poetry in those who practise it',[94] and 'The gipsy in real life is usually both dirty and dull. So is war.'[95] One may infer that the diversity of Wavell's outside interests and his belief that war was monotonous indicated apathy or a lack of drive on his part. Nothing could be further from the truth. Wavell's ability to compartmentalise the various activities of his life permitted him, during times of intense strain, to withdraw periodically into more familiar, less threatening spheres, which, in turn, enhanced his inner strength, resolve, and stamina, and gave him the resilience to carry out his responsibilities of command during that and the next crisis.

His renowned and enigmatic taciturnity served, on occasion, the same purposes. The master of deception, Wavell's apparent detachment and phlegmatic behaviour conveyed the perception, when he wanted it to, of aloofness and apathy. This 'air of inattention, the secrecy, the silence', as Philip Mason has written, 'combined to make his subordinates regard him as primitive people regard a force of nature, something beyond their calculations, something liable at any moment to surprise them'.[96] Indeed, individuals underestimated Wavell in these situations, and did not expect him to be such a bold and audacious commander. In addition, his reticence helped serve as a reservoir of inner strength.

Wavell's taciturnity, however, could produce the opposite results. His disinclination to speak was perceived by Churchill to indicate a lack 'of mental vigour and resolve to overcome obstacles',[97] and it is quite probable that as a result, Churchill thought Wavell little more than 'a rather dumb

Scotsman'.[98] This trait of Wavell's damaged irreparably the Churchill-Wavell relationship from their initial meeting in August 1940. Arthur Smith, Wavell's Chief of Staff, once asked him why Churchill did not like him. Wavell replied: 'Perhaps because I don't talk enough. (SILENCE).'[99]

In large groups, Wavell's shyness and awkwardness, the product of his humility and, at times, boredom, could prove embarrassing. But when he was with friends, or others with whom he had common interests, Wavell could 'unbend', as Lieutenant Colonel John Benson, who knew him well, reflected recently:

> [Wavell was] on the whole very taciturn but could unbend at times if amused or interested – little or no small talk at any rate to those who *tried* to converse with him about things in which he was not interested. But on the other hand [he] did not mind being teased. If you had the guts to do so, or were in the position to tease him. I can think of more than one person of either sex who was able to do this and who would draw him out and amuse him. It was not much good talking in general terms – you needed to particularise.[100]

Indeed, Wavell 'talked best *à deux*', as Lieutenant Colonel David Walker, who served as Wavell's Comptroller of the Viceregal Household, recently wrote, 'or with a few people. But between him and an audience there seemed to dangle an awkward curtain of reserve.'[101] Favourite topics of discussion included his Regiment, The Black Watch, literature, poetry, and a host of other items: 'a warm and witty raconteur he [Wavell] was when in the mood'.[102] Queen Elizabeth, the Queen Mother, told Lieutenant Colonel FJ Burnaby-Atkins not long ago that she never had any difficulty talking with Wavell. 'All she had to do was immediately to introduce the subject of The Black Watch',[103] a task made easier since she was Colonel-in-Chief of the regiment.

Wavell's tenure and achievements as Commander-in-Chief, Middle East, were very similar to the career of his favourite historical general, Belisarius, of whom Wavell wrote:

> He seems to have had more imagination and originality than any great commander of whom I have read. He was always devising means to outwit his enemy and to attain his objectives by stratagem as much as by fighting. Yet he was a great fighter and a great trainer of fighting men. He served his ungrateful master Justinian with loyalty and discretion; and certainly had the power of handling allies successfully. A very great commander in every way, with a very gallant heart in adversity, . . .[104]

This, then, was Wavell the general and Wavell the man.

* * *

This study has shown conclusively that Wavell's service and accomplishments as Commander-in-Chief, Middle East, clearly deserve to be acknowledged as singularly outstanding. Inaccurate perceptions of Wavell's sub-sequent military and political service in India and South-East Asia, as well as the accomplishments of generals who, given a manpower and material superiority, were able to achieve better-publicised successes during the second half of the war, should not be permitted to overshadow Wavell's Middle East achievements. Nor should any previous lack of understanding of Wavell's somewhat enigmatic personality and his own reluctance to attempt to exonerate himself from any shortcoming or accusation. The apparently conscious efforts of others, notably the 'Churchillians', should also not be allowed to diminish the significance of Wavell's Middle East performance. Wavell and his stout-hearted soldiers in the Middle East deserve to be recognised and remembered, not only for the superb execution of 'the best-planned and most remarkable series of campaigns since those of Wellesley in the Peninsula',[105] but perhaps more importantly, as stated in the Introduction, for holding the Middle East 'against vastly superior armies for two years and [keeping] them away from the Nile when mail took months, comforts were few, and numbers were still fewer'.[106]

Authoritative opinion supports this conclusion. In 1950, the year of Wavell's death, Basil Liddell Hart, in an appraisal of his accomplishments and his standing in the eyes of the Nation at the peak of his fame, wrote:

> Lord Wavell's star rose high at an early stage of the war. Its glow was the more brilliant because of the darkness of the sky. His victories over the Italian armies in North Africa and East Africa in the winter of 1940–41, were Britain's first striking successes after the catastrophic run of defeats in the West. They came as a great tonic – not only to the British people but even more to others who had been shocked and alarmed by the apparently irresistible advance of the Nazi and Fascist dictators. Within a few months, Wavell was a world famous figure, and well on his way to becoming a living legend. At that moment, his fame almost dimmed Mr. Churchill's. No other Allied soldier perhaps attained quite such a peak, for those who rose to fame later formed part of a cluster that shared public attention.

General Sir Ian Hamilton, Commander-in-Chief of the Mediterranean Expeditionary Force during the Great War, was asked during the Second World War if the war in progress had produced a great soldier who was also a great man. 'Without hesitation', responded Hamilton unequivocally, 'I say yes, and without hesitation I say that the man is Wavell.'[107] Wavell 'was a very great man', wrote General Sir James Marshall-Cornwall, who worked closely with him for many years, 'and in my opinion the best soldier we threw up in the War'.[108] General Lord Ismay wrote interestingly that:

> [Field Marshal Viscount] Bill Slim spent the weekend with me and we chatted a lot about men and affairs. We agreed that Wavell and [US General of the Army Douglas] MacArthur were the outstanding Campaign Generals, i.e., the Generals in the Napoleonic mould, of the Second World War. History will I am

sure endorse this verdict, but how I wish Wavell had never backed the Greek venture.[109]

General Sir John Hackett, who fought under Wavell in the Middle East, suggested recently that Wavell, as Commander-in-Chief, Middle East, was 'outstandingly good in the handling of a very complicated situation, fighting with less than adequate forces on so many fronts',[110] and Field Marshal Lord Harding was convinced that Wavell 'had the heaviest burden that any general officer of any nation has had to bear, this century or before'.[111] Even Wavell's dauntless adversary, German General Erwin Rommel, conceded that the only British general 'who showed a touch of genius was Wavell'.[112] The British Official History ably summed up these sentiments: 'He [Wavell] was essentially a soldier's soldier, and takes an assured place as one of the great commanders in military history.'[113]

The preceding viewpoints are indeed enlightening, but the most stringent and accurate test of good generalship is, according to Wavell, that 'A general may succeed for some time in persuading his superiors that he is a good commander: he will never persuade his army that he is a good commander unless he has the real qualities of one.'[114] Thus the keenest and most perceptive judges of leadership and generalship are the soldiers themselves, and some of those who served under Wavell in the Middle East made their opinions on this topic unmistakably clear. One former soldier of Wavell's Middle East Command expressed sentiments shared by many of his former comrades:

> I hope that a small tribute from one who knew Lord Wavell well and served in the ranks of the Army will be permitted at this time. Many thousands of men of all ranks will feel that they have lost a true friend. The two qualities which most closely characterised him were simplicity and kindliness; he had a truly human understanding of men and their problems and was always ready to give a friendly word of cheer or advice to any who needed it. It was these things, together with his great generalship, which were the secret of the Army's love and admiration for him. Lord Wavell was not only a great general: he was something more – a great soldier.[115]

Even after the passage of a half-century, George Rose, who served under Wavell in the 7th Armoured Division, declared resolutely that 'I was very proud to serve under him and would do [so] again.'[116]

One cannot do better than that.

Epilogue

Less than ten short years were to pass before Wavell died on 24 May 1950. If ever a man deserved a period of happiness in the evening of his life, it was he. Instead, he would spend nearly six weary years in India, first as Commander-in-Chief and later as Viceroy and Governor General, until unceremoniously dismissed by Clement Attlee in February 1947. It is hard to find any other great national figure to whom the British public owed so much and yet who had been given such scurvy treatment by the politicians he had served so loyally and well – even when their views were in conflict. To the people of Britain he had become a legend in his own time; to the armies of his country and the Commonwealth, as this study has shown, he was a deeply respected and revered commander to whom they gave their unstinted loyalty and affection.

The inevitable comparisons between Wavell and Montgomery have been made time and again but they are simply not valid. Wavell was a Theatre commander, Montgomery an Army and Army Group commander, concerned with the operational level of command only. To pursue the comparison is futile.

For two years, from 1941 to 1943, Wavell wrestled with the military problems of India and even served a short spell as the first Supreme Allied Commander of the ill-fated American British Dutch Australian Command (ABDACOM), charged with responsibility for the South-West Pacific area. But the sweeping success of the Japanese in South-East Asia soon changed all that and Wavell's energies were refocused on the defence of India and the recovery of Burma, for which India supplied all the base facilities. It was during this time that he also found himself closer to the Allied central direction of the war, attending the great conferences in Cairo, Moscow, and Washington at Churchill's side. But such gatherings were not his scene and his old taciturnity was to create an impression upon both the Americans and the Chinese that once more led to Churchill losing confidence in him. In a typically Churchillian political expedient, Wavell was made Viceroy and Governor General of India with Auchinleck, himself a victim of Churchillian mistrust, as Commander-in-Chief.

271

Wavell had been promoted Field Marshal on 1 January 1943 and then, on assuming his new appointment, was elevated to the peerage as Viscount Wavell of Cyrenaica and Winchester.

It had been thought that he would serve as a stop-gap Viceroy but any such idea was completely out of keeping with a man of his energy, initiative, and strong sense of duty combined with humanity and progressive views. He worked tirelessly for what he felt to be the best interests of the great continent which was then, effectively, his realm, dealing with the ravages of famine and employing all his skills to keep India in the war. The lamentable failure of both the Churchill and Attlee governments to produce any coherent policy upon which the inevitable independence of India could be based and the intransigence of the Indian politicians made his task doubly hard and intolerably frustrating, so that when the final break with Attlee came, it was not surprising that he found life in retirement depressing, giving him, as he himself put it, a feeling of being rootless and unable to settle down.

Created an Earl on his return to England, he involved himself with the work of the House of Lords and became Constable of the Tower of London. He was also appointed Lord Lieutenant of London. He tried to interest himself in the work of the numerous literary societies of which he became President – but it was all of little avail. Ill health plagued him throughout 1949 and in May 1950 he died.

After lying in state in the Norman chapel of the Tower, his coffin was brought by river to Westminster for a service in Westminster Abbey before going on to Winchester – home of the Wavells for so many centuries – to be buried in William of Wykeham's cloister garth in the heart of his old college. A very great Englishman had gone to his rest.

Source Notes

Chapter 1

1. Brig. CN Barclay, *On Their Shoulders* (London: Faber and Faber, 1964), 65.
2. Dr HA DeWeerd (i), 'Wavell's Middle East Command', IJ 31 (September 1941): 13.
3. 'Britain's Soldier of the Hour', MR 21 (March 1941): 8.
4. Ltr, Lt.Col. David Walker to author, 13 March 1987.
5. Ltr, The Rt Hon Sir James Grigg to John Connell, 15 February 1962, File (XII), Folder 2, [Wavell II], CP, MU.
6. Eden, interview by David Elstein, 5 April 1972. Transcript on file in Dept. of Film, IWM.
7. Ltr, Maj. Arthur Irwin to author, 7 June 1989.
8. Alex Danchev has ably elucidated the role of the intensely-loyal members of Churchill's war-time 'Secret' or 'Inner Circle' in its treatment of General (later Field Marshal) Sir John Dill in 'Dilly-Dally,' or Having the Last Word: Field Marshal Sir John Dill and Prime Minister Winston Churchill', JCH 22 (January 1987): 21–44. The treatment of Wavell by the 'Churchillians' has generally been more severe than that meted out to Dill, since Wavell's reputation throughout the British Army and the overwhelming popular acclaim he received after the North African and East African campaigns, as will be seen, were so considerable that Churchill found it impossible to 'sack' Wavell as Commander-in-Chief, Middle East, in June 1941, and instead 'transferred' him to India. See also Alex Danchev, review of *Never Despair: Winston S. Churchill*, vol. VIII, *1945-1965*, by Martin Gilbert, in JRUSI 113 (Winter 1988): 91.
9. CR Attlee, *As It Happened* (NY: Viking, 1954), 166.
10. Cyril Falls, 'Aftermath of War: The Career of Field Marshal Lord Wavell', review of *Lord Wavell (1883–1941): A Military Biography*, by Maj. Gen. RJ Collins, in ILN, 31 January 1948, 122.
11. FM Viscount Alanbrooke of Brookeborough, foreword to Robert Woollcombe, *The Campaigns of Wavell, 1939–1943* (London: Cassell, 1959), x.
12. Ltr, Col. JL Waddy to author, 27 January 1987.
13. Gen. Sir Archibald Wavell (i), *Allenby: A Study in Greatness* (NY: OUP, 1941), 15.
14. Capt. Alec Walkling, 'The Desert War, 1940–42. A Letter to a Young Wife', JRA 115 (September 1988): 116.

Chapter 2

1. Quoted in RH Kiernan, *Wavell* (London: George G Harrap, 1945), 50.
2. Wavell, quoted in John Connell [John Henry Robertson] (i), *Wavell: Scholar and Soldier* (London: Collins, 1964), 34.
3. Maj. Gen. RJ Collins, *Lord Wavell (1883–1941): A Military Biography* (London: Hodder and Stoughton, 1947), 39.
4. Wavell, quoted in Connell (i), 57.
5. Brian Bond (i), *The Victorian Army and the Staff College, 1815–1914* (London: Eyre Methuen, 1972), 262.
6. Ibid., 281.
7. Collins, 50.
8. Facsimile reproductions of selected portions of this essay of Wavell's, to include this quoted extract, with transcriptions, can be found in Victor Bonham-Carter, *The Strategy of Victory, 1914–1918* (1963; rpt., NY: Holt, Rinehart and Winston, 1964), 334–337.
9. Collins, 50.
10. Robertson, quoted in Kiernan, 63.
11. Connell (i), 78.
12. Ltr, Wavell to Maj. Gen. AG Wavell (father), 29 March 1914, quoted in Connell (i), 88.
13. Ltr, Wavell to Miss Anne Wavell (sister), 12 September 1914. Typescript copy in File (XII), Folder 10, CP, MU.
14. Buchanan, quoted in Connell (i), 102.
15. Connell, 'Wavell: Aide-Memoire', 24 June 1961, File (XII), Folder 2, [Wavell II], CP, MU.
16. Brig. AP Wavell (ii), 'The Training of the Army for War', JRUSI 78 (May 1933): 255.
17. Wavell, quoted in Connell (i), 112.
18. Wavell (i); FM Viscount Wavell of Cyrenaica and Winchester (iii), *Allenby in Egypt* (1943; rpt., NY: OUP, 1944); and Col. AP Wavell (iv), *The Palestine Campaigns*, Campaigns and Their Lessons, ed. Maj. Gen. Sir Charles Callwell (1928; rpt., London: Constable, 1931).
19. Connell (i), 134.
20. Wavell, quoted in Ibid., 136.
21. Wavell, quoted in Ibid., 144.
22. Wavell (iv), 242.

Chapter 3

1. Ltr, Congreve to Wilson, 1 April 1920, quoted in Keith Jeffery, ed., *The Military Correspondence of Field Marshal Sir Henry Wilson, 1918–1922* (London: Bodley Head for the Army Records Society, 1985), 155–156.
2. Connell (i), 149.
3. Ltr, Lawrence to Wavell, 21 May 1923, quoted in David Garnett, ed., *The Letters of TE Lawrence* (NY: Doubleday, Doran, 1939), 422. Italics in original.
4. Ltr, Stimson to Connell, 12 June 1963, File (XII), Folder 7, [Wavell IX], CP,

MU. Italics in original.

5. Vesey, interview by Connell, 26 August 1961. Notes in File (XII), Folder 2, [Wavell II], CP, MU.

6. Review of Wavell (iv), in AQ 16 (July 1928): 441.

7. Wavell, quoted in 'Cross-references: Inter-war – November 1926 – March 1935', File (XII), Folder 4, [Wavell VI], CP, MU.

8. Liddell Hart, quoted in Col. H Rowan-Robinson (i), *Some Aspects of Mechanization* (London: William Clowes & Sons, 1928), 4

9. Quoted in Harold R Winton, *To Change an Army* (Lawrence, Kansas: University Press of Kansas, 1988), 91.

10. Wavell, quoted in Capt. BH Liddell Hart (i), *The Tanks*, vol. 1, *1914–1939* (NY: Frederick A Praeger, 1959), 262.

11. Collins, 131.

12. Burnett-Stuart, quoted in Connell (i), 154–155.

13. Quoted in Collins, 134.

14. Ltr, FM Sir Francis Festing to Connell, 13 May 1962, File (XII), Folder 7, [Wavell IX], CP, MU.

15. Burnett-Stuart, 'Memoirs', n.d., 2 vols., 2:51. Photostatic copy in Burnett-Stuart Papers, LHCMA.

16. Brig. AP Wavell (v), 'The Army and the Prophets', JRUSI 75 (November 1930): 667.

17. Ibid., 670–671.

18. Wavell, quoted in Connell (i), 160.

19. Collins, 139.

20. Collins, quoted in Connell (i), 167.

21. Ltr, Maj. Gen. E Dorman-Smith to Connell, 9 December 1961, File (XII), Folder 11, CP, MU.

22. FM Earl Wavell (vi), *The Good Soldier* (London: Macmillan, 1948), 129.

23. Wavell, quoted in Connell (i), 169.

24. Wavell (ii), 258.

25. Ibid., 260.

26. Ibid., 270.

27. Collins, 149.

28. James Marshall-Cornwall, *Wars and Rumours of Wars* (London: Leo Cooper, Secker & Warburg, 1984), 95.

29. Bernard Fergusson, *Wavell: Portrait of a Soldier* (London: Collins, 1961), 37.

30. Ibid., 38.

31. Connell (i), 176.

32. Gathorne-Hardy, quoted in Ibid., 177.

33. Marshall-Cornwall, 100.

34. Burnett-Stuart, quoted in Connell (i), 182.

35. 'The Argonauts Trapped', *The Times* (London), 15 August 1936, p. 12.

36. Lt. Gen. Sir Brian Horrocks, *Escape to Action* (1960; rpt., NY: St. Martin's Press, 1961), 72.

37. Brian Bond (ii), 'Leslie Hore-Belisha at the War Office', in *Politicians and Defence*, ed. Ian Beckett and John Gooch (Manchester: Manchester University Press, 1981), 111.

38. HQ, British Forces Palestine, 'Information for Commanders of Reinforcing

Troops', 7 September 1936, quoted in Charles Townshend, 'The Defence of Palestine: Insurrection and Public Security, 1936–1939', EHR 103 (October 1988): 922.

39. Ltr, Professor Wesley K Wark to author, 17 February 1988. Wark has been selected by FM Lord Ironside's son, the present Lord Ironside, to write the biography of his father, and in doing so has unlimited access to the FM's voluminous unpublished diaries. Ltr, The Rt Hon Lord Ironside to author, 23 December 1987.

40. Christopher Sykes, *Orde Wingate* (London: Collins, 1959), 143.

41. Hore-Belisha, quoted in RJ Minney, *The Private Papers of Hore-Belisha* (London: Collins, 1960), 55.

42. Ltr, Capt. BH Liddell Hart to Brig. Bernard Fergusson, 21 January 1959. Typescript extract as enclosure to ltr, Liddell Hart to Connell, 19 July 1961, File (XII), Folder 2, [Wavell II], CP, MU. Italics in original.

43. Liddell Hart diary, 1 October 1937, quoted in BH Liddell Hart (ii), *The Liddell Hart Memoirs* (NY: GP Putnam's Sons, 1965), 2:32.

44. 'Editorial', AQ 35 (January 1938): 196.

45. Ltr, Wavell to Swinton, 22 May 1938. Copy in File 1/733, Liddell Hart Papers, LHCMA.

46. Ltr. Maj. PS Huggett to author, 16 June 1988.

47. Connell (i), 203–204.

48. Keitel, quoted in Kiernan, 112.

49. Collins, 187.

50. '50 Years Ago . . . July 20, 1939: British Army Commander for Middle East', *Daily Telegraph*, 20 July 1989, page unknown. I am indebted to Lt. Col. FJ Burnaby-Atkins for sending me a photostatic copy of this article. Enclosure to ltr, Burnaby-Atkins to author, 31 July 1989.

Chapter 4

1. FM Viscount Wavell, 'Notes for Talk with Australians, February 1940', in *Speaking Generally* (London: Macmillan, 1946), 7. This book will be hereafter cited as Wavell (vii).

2. See Maj. Gen. ISO Playfair, et al., *The Mediterranean and Middle East*, vol. I, *The Early Successes against Italy (to May 1941)* (1954; rpt., London: HMSO, 1974), 1–32, 457–459.

3. Jules Menken, 'Wavell in the Mediterranean: I. The Beginnings, Somaliland, and Cyrenaica', NR 127 (November 1946): 407.

4. Memo, 'Notes for BGS, Middle East Command', 31 July 1939, p. 1, WO 201/2379, PRO.

5. Ibid.

6. Ibid., pp. 1–2. Italics in original.

7. Ibid., pp. 2–3.

8. Demi-official ltr, Wavell to Gort, 3 August 1939, WO 201/2119, PRO.

9. Demi-official ltr, Wavell to Gort, 10 August 1939, WO 201/2119, PRO.

10. Memo, 'Note on Strategical Situation in Middle East by GOC in C, Middle East', 14 August 1939, p. 1. Enclosure to demi-official ltr, Wavell to Gort, 14

NOTES pp. 44–50 277

August 1939, WO 201/2119, PRO.
11. Playfair, 1:33.
12. WGF Jackson, *The North African Campaign, 1940–43* (London: BT Batsford, 1975).
13. App. V, memo, 'Middle East Inter-Service Conference', 23 August 1939, p. 1, to 7 WD, Military HQ, ME, Vol. 1: 2–31 August 1939, WO 169/1, PRO.
14. Demi-official ltr, Wavell to Gort, 18 [19] August 1939, WO 201/2119, PRO.
15. Memo, 'Notes on Strategical Situation in the Middle East', 24 August 1939, p. 3. Enclosure to demi-official ltr, Wavell to Gort, 24 August 1939, WO 201/2119, PRO.
16. Playfair, 1:38.
17. Memo, 'Note for CIGS on Command in the Western Desert in the Event of War', 14 August 1939. Enclosure to demi-official ltr, Wavell to Gort, 14 August 1939, WO 201/2119, PRO.
18. Demi-official ltr, Wavell to Gort, 29 August 1939, WO 201/2119, PRO.
19. Memo, 'Appreciation Regarding a British Offensive into Libya based on the Assumption that the Italians do not carry out a Main Offensive against Egypt', July 1939, p. 1, WO 201/327, PRO.
20. Gen. Sir Archibald P Wavell, Despatch (i): 'Operations in the Middle East from August, 1939 to November, 1940', third supplement to TLG, 13 June 1946, p. 2297.
21. The two quotes in this paragraph are from General Maxime Weygand, *Recalled to Service*, trans. EW Dickes (1950; rpt., London: William Heinemann, 1952), 6.
22. The two quotes in this paragraph are from demi-official ltr, Gordon-Finlayson to Gort, 17 May 1939, pp. 1 and 2, WO 216/44, PRO. Italics in original.
23. Count Galeazzo Ciano diary, 24 August 1939, quoted in Hugh Gibson, ed., *The Ciano Diaries, 1939–1943*, (1945; rpt., Garden City, NY: Doubleday, 1946), 127.
24. MacGregor Knox, *Mussolini Unleashed, 1939–1941* (1982; rpt., Cambridge: CUP, 1986), 43.
25. Memo, 'Note for Long Term Policy for Middle East', 4 September 1939, WO 201/1956, PRO.
26. Ltr, Wavell to: '1. GOC, British Troops in Palestine and Trans-Jordan; 2. GOC-in-C, British Troops in Egypt; 3. GOC, British Troops in the Sudan; 4. GOC, East African Forces', 8 September 1939, WO 201/1956, PRO.
27. Collins, 203.
28. Lt. Col. John E Benson, interview by author, 24 June 1989, audio cassette recording in author's possession.
29. Lampson diary, 24 September 1939, quoted in Trefor E Evans, ed., *The Killearn Diaries, 1934–1946* (London: Sidgwick & Jackson, 1972), 112.
30. This and the following quote are from Appx. 4, ltr, 'GOC in C, Middle East to the GOC, British Troops in Egypt', 3 October 1939, to WD, Military HQ, ME, Vol. 3: 1–31 October 1939, WO 169/1, PRO.
31. This and the following quote are from Appx. 5, memo, 'Note on Operations against Italian East Africa. By GOC-in-C, ME', 3 October 1939, to Vol. 3, WO 169/1, PRO.
32. App. 6, memo, 'Statement of the Relationship between HE the British Ambassador and the GOC-in-C, ME; Between the GOC-in-C, ME, and the GOC-in-C, BTE; and the Position of the British Military Mission', [3 October 1939], to Vol. 3, WO 169/1, PRO.

33. Cable No. 3289/39, 14 October 1939, WO 201/1956, PRO.
34. Playfair, 1:49.
35. Ltr, Ironside to Wavell, 11 September 1939, quoted in Connell (i), 216–217.
36. Ironside diary, 20 September 1939, quoted in Col. R Macleod and Denis Kelly, eds., *The Ironside Diaries, 1937–1940* (London: Constable, 1962), 112.
37. Playfair, 1:60.
38. Ltr, Benson to author, 15 December 1988.
39. On 3 November 1939, Wavell's Military HQ, ME, was officially redesignated GHQ, ME.
40. WDs, GHQ, ME, Vol. 4: G & A, 1–30 November 1939, passim; and Vol. 5: G & A, 1–31 December 1939, passim, WO 169/1, PRO.
41. This and the following two quotes are from Dudley Clarke, *Seven Assignments* (London: Jonathan Cape, 1948), 29, 31, and 31 respectively.
42. Weygand, 23.
43. Playfair, 1:61.
44. Ironside diary, 7 December 1939, quoted in Macleod and Kelly, 171.
45. Bernard Fergusson, ed., *The Business of War* (London: Hutchinson, 1957), 41. This entire vignette is from Ibid., and the following three quotes are from Ibid., 41, 43–44, and 44 respectively. Italics in original.
46. Ltr, Lord Wilson of Libya to author, 11 December 1988, FM Lord Wilson's son, Patrick, the second and present Lord Wilson, served on his father's staffs in the Middle East and Mediterranean from 1940–1944. Patrick Wilson also lived, from May 1940 until January 1941, in the house shared with the Wavell family, and thus had the opportunity to observe Wavell and his family closely in a relatively relaxed, congenial atmosphere. Ltr, Lord Wilson to author, 25 March 1989.
47. Lord Wilson, interview by author, 12 June 1989, audio cassette recording in author's possession.
48. Weygand, 28.
49. This and the following quote are from Appx. 96, ltr, Wavell to War Office, 26 January 1940, to WD, GHQ, ME, Vol. 6: G & A, 1–31 January 1940, WO 169/6, PRO.
50. WD, GHQ, ME, Vol. 7: G & A, 1–29 February 1940, passim, WO 169/6, PRO. A few days after these conferences were held, on 15 February 1940, Wavell's position and title were upgraded to 'Commander-in-Chief, Middle East'.
51. The Rt Hon The Earl of Avon, *The Eden Memoirs: The Reckoning* (London: Cassell, 1965), 85–86.
52. Playfair, 1:62.
53. This and the following two quotes are from Appx. 9, ltr, 'War Against Italy', Wavell to Ironside, 2 April 1940, to WD, GHQ, ME, Vol. 9: G(O) Branch, 1–30 April 1940, WO 169/8, PRO.
54. Ironside diary, 22 April 1940, quoted in Macleod and Kelly, 278.
55. Winston S Churchill, *The Second World War*, vol. I, *The Gathering Storm* (Boston: Houghton Mifflin, 1948), 613.
56. RW Thompson (i), *Generalissimo Churchill* (NY: Charles Scribner's Sons, 1973), 61.
57. Churchill, 1:617.
58. Thompson (i), 65.

NOTES pp. 58–64   279

59. Churchill, 1:660.
60. Ibid., 1:667.
61. This and the following quote are from Winston S Churchill, *The Second World War*, vol. II, *Their Finest Hour* (Boston: Houghton Mifflin, 1949), 16.
62. AJP Taylor, *The Oxford History of England*, vol. XV, *English History, 1914–1945* (NY: OUP, 1965), 479.
63. This and the following quote are from Gen. Lord Ismay, *The Memoirs of General Lord Ismay* (NY: Viking, 1960), 160.
64. RW Thompson (ii), *The Yankee Marlborough* (London: George Allen & Unwin, 1963), 294.
65. This and the following two quotes are from Appx. 23, Cable No. 69887, 3 May 1940, to WD, GHQ, ME, Vol. 10: G(O) Branch, 1–31 May 1940, WO 169/9, PRO.
66. This and the following two quotes are from Appx. 40, Cable No. 0/10326, 6 May 1940, to Vol. 10, WO 169/9, PRO.
67. The British policy of non-provocation and the desire not to violate the neutrality of Greece was one of the most significant reasons for the island's ill-preparedness to defend against a German invasion the following year. The Middle East Commanders-in-Chief were not directly at fault in this issue; prior to receiving an 8 June 1940 message, stating that the British occupation of Crete could only be carried out if Italy first attacked Greece, all arrangements had been made by 29 May 1940 to transport British and French troops to Crete. The 8 June directive, however, countermanded all earlier orders and prohibited the despatch of British troops to Crete unless Italy attacked Greece. Admiral of the Fleet Viscount Cunningham of Hyndhope, *A Sailor's Odyssey* (London: Hutchinson, 1951), 230, 233.
68. This and the following quote are from ltr, Wavell to Wilson, 10 May 1940, WO 201/152, PRO.
69. Lynn H Curtright, 'Great Britain, the Balkans, and Turkey in the Autumn of 1939', IHR 10 (August 1988): 454–455.
70. Wavell, cover ltr to 'The Worst Possible Case', 24 May 1940. Typescript copy in File (XII), Folder 7, [Wavell IX], CP, MU.
71. Wavell, 'The Worst Possible Case', 24 May 1940. Typescript copy in File (XII), Folder 7, [Wavell IX], CP, MU.
72. Ibid.
73. App. 277, memo, 'The Position – May 1940', 27 May 1940, to Vol. 10, WO 169/9, PRO.
74. App. 272, Cable No. 72619, 30 May 1940, to Vol. 10, WO 169/9, PRO.
75. Demi-official ltr, Wavell to Dill, 7 June 1940, WO 201/2119, PRO.
76. Ibid.
77. Memo, 'Note for CIGS: Middle East, Situation – 6th June 1940'. Enclosure to Ibid.
78. Minute, PM to S of S for War [Eden], 6 June 1940, quoted in Churchill, 2: 163.
79. Martin Gilbert, *Winston S. Churchill*, vol. VI, *Finest Hour, 1939–1941* (London: Heinemann, 1983), 477.
80. Pietro Badoglio, *Italy in the Second World War*, trans. Muriel Currey (London: OUP, 1948), 14.
81. These figures are from Wavell, Despatch (i): 2998–2999, and Playfair, 1:93, fn 2.

82. Weygand, quoted in BH Liddell Hart (iii), *History of the Second World War* (NY: GP Putnam's Sons, 1970), 85.

Chapter 5

1. Wavell (vii), 'Order of the Day, June 17, 1940', 11.
2. Rommel and von Ravenstein, quoted in Ludovic Kennedy, introduction to Roger Parkinson (i), *The War in the Desert* (London: Book Club Associates, 1976), 7.
3. Hans-Otto Behrendt, *Rommel's Intelligence in the Desert Campaign, 1941–1943* (Freiburg im Breisgau: Rombach, 1980; rpt., London: William Kimber, 1985), 41.
4. Playfair, 1:116.
5. Correlli Barnett, *The Desert Generals* (1960; rpt., Bloomington, Indiana: IUP, 1982), 23.
6. Parkinson (i), 11.
7. Maj. Gen. GL Verney, *The Desert Rats* (London: Hutchinson, 1954), 19.
8. App. 47, ltr, GHQ, ME, Cairo, to HQ, BTE, 8 June 1940, to WD, GHQ, ME, Vol. 11: G(O) Branch, 1–30 June 1940, WO 169/10, PRO.
9. App. A, to WD, HQ, WDF, Vol. 10: GS, 1–30 June 1940, WO 169/53, PRO.
10. Maj. Gen. Pip Roberts, *From the Desert to the Baltic* (London: William Kimber, 1987), 15.
11. Wavell, quoted in Julian Amery, *Approach March* (London: Hutchinson, 1973), 206.
12. Wavell (vii), 'Order of the Day, June 17, 1940', 11.
13. Eleanor M Gates, *The End of the Affair* (Berkeley: University of California Press, 1981), 310.
14. Wavell, Despatch (i): 3000.
15. App. 283, Cable No. 0/12825, 28 June 1940, to Vol. 11, WO 169/10, PRO.
16. App. 2, Cable No. 75263, 1 July 1940, to WD, GHQ, ME, Vol. 12: G(O) Branch, 1–31 July 1940, WO 169/11, PRO.
17. Wavell, quoted in Connell (i), 241.
18. Alan Moorehead, *The March to Tunis* (1943; rpt., NY: Harper & Row, 1965), 18.
19. John Charteris, 'The Operations in Libya', *Nineteenth Century and After* 131 (February 1942): 73.
20. Cable No. 0/13037, 3 July 1940, PREM 3/293/3, PRO.
21. Moorehead, 23.
22. Ibid.
23. Ltr, 'Action this Day', Churchill to Ismay, 5 July 1940, PREM 3/293/3, PRO.
24. Ibid.
25. App. 52, Cable No. 75820, 8 July 1940, to Vol. 12, WO 169/11, PRO.
26. App. 64, Cable No. 0/13422, 9 July 1940, to Vol. 12, WO 169/11, PRO.
27. Connell (i), 248.
28. Maj. Gen. BC Freyberg, memo, 'The Position in Egypt', 29 July 1940, p. 1, PREM 3/295/2, PRO. The following three quotes are from Ibid., pp. 1, 2, and 10 respectively.
29. War Cabinet, Ministerial Committee on Military Policy in the Middle East,

NOTES pp. 74–82 281

'Situation in the Middle East: Report', 29 July 1940, p. 1, PREM 4/32/6, PRO.
30. Ibid., p. 2.
31. App. 296, Cable No. 0/14957, 30 July 1940, to Vol. 12, WO 169/11, PRO.
32. Avon, 129.
33. Ibid.
34. Both quotes in this sentence are from 'Editorial', AQ 46 (August 1943): 130.
35. As quoted in Wavell, Despatch (ii): 'Operations in the Somaliland Protectorate, 1939–1940', supplement to TLG, 5 June 1946, p. 2720.
36. Ibid., p. 2721.
37. Ltr, Eden to Churchill, [13 or 14] June 1940, PREM 3/293/3, PRO.
38. App., 'JPS Paper No. 13: British Somaliland', 6 July 1940, p. 1, to WD, GHQ, ME, JPS, August 1939-December 1940, WO 169/3, PRO.
39. These two quotes are from Ibid., pp. 3 and 4 respectively. Italics in original.
40. Col. Hon. EH Wyndham, 'Italy's One Victory', AQ 46 (August 1943): 209.
41. Connell (i), 253.
42. Avon, 130.
43. Churchill, 2:424.
44. Barrie Pitt, Churchill and the Generals (London: Sidgwick & Jackson, 1981), 45.
45. Shearer, quoted in Ronald Lewin (i), The Chief: Field Marshal Lord Wavell, Commander-in-Chief and Viceroy, 1939–1947 (NY: Farrar, Straus and Giroux, 1980), 23.
46. Both quotes are from Shearer, quoted in Lewin (i), 24–25.
47. Churchill, quoted in Colville diary, 9 August 1940, quoted in John Colville, The Fringes of Power (London: Hodder and Stoughton, 1985; rpt., NY: WW Norton, 1986), 214.
48. Avon, 130.
49. Eden diary, 12 August 1940, quoted in Ibid., 131.
50. Eden diary, 13 August 1940, quoted in Avon, 131.
51. Ltr, Churchill to Eden, 13 August 1940, PREM 3/296/17, PRO.
52. Quoted in Avon, 132.
53. Churchill, quoted in Ibid., 133.
54. Churchill, 2:425.
55. Wavell, quoted in Connell (i), 256.
56. Ltr, Lord Annan to author, 11 September 1987.
57. Ibid.
58. Ltr, Lt. Gen. Sir Ian Jacob to author, 18 November 1988.
59. Ltr, Lord Home of the Hirsel to author, 8 September 1987.
60. Ltr, Dorman-Smith to Connell, 29 January 1962, File (XII), Folder 7, [Wavell IX], CP, MU.
61. Ltr, Jacob to author, 18 October 1988.
62. Ibid.
63. Jacob, interview by author, 26 June 1989, audio cassette recording in author's possession.
64. Lloyd George, quoted in Lord Boothby, Recollections of a Rebel (London: Hutchinson, 1978), 147.
65. Wavell, Despatch (ii): 2724.
66. Ltr, 'Instructions to Major-General Godwin Austen', 10 August 1940, Godwin Austen 1, Godwin Austen Papers, LHCMA.

67. FM Lord Wilson of Libya, *Eight Years Overseas* (London: Hutchinson, [1948]), 42.
68. App. 157, Cable No. 0/16333, 15 August 1940, to WD, GHQ, ME, Vol. 13: G(O) Branch, August 1940, WO 169/12, PRO.
69. App. 156, Cable No. 0/16335, 15 August 1940, to Vol. 13, WO 169/12, PRO.
70. Wavell, quoted in Connell (i), 264.
71. App. 165, Cable No. 79127, 15 August 1940, to Vol. 13, WO 169/12, PRO.
72. Mitchell diary, 17 August 1940, MSS. Afr.r. 101, Mitchell Papers, RHL.
73. Wavell, Despatch (ii): 2724.
74. Dill, quoted in Lewin (i), 12.
75. Ltr, Morton to Thompson, 21/24 August 1961, quoted in RW Thompson (iii), *Churchill and Morton* (London: Hodder and Stoughton, 1976), 175.
76. Lewin (i), 12.
77. Churchill, 2:428.
78. JRM Butler, *Grand Strategy*, vol. II, *September 1939-June 1941*, History of the Second World War (London: HMSO, 1957), 310.
79. Gavin Long, *Australia in the War of 1939-1945*, series 1 (Army), vol. I, *To Benghazi* (Canberra: AWM, 1952), 111.
80. Gordon A Craig, 'The Political Leader as Strategist', in *Makers of Modern Strategy*, ed. Peter Paret (Princeton, New Jersey: Princeton University Press, 1986), 499-500.
81. Wavell, quoted in Connell (i), 267.
82. Wavell, understanding keenly the historical significance of 'Compass', wrote on 15 December 1940 a paper entitled 'Operations in Western Desert, October to December 1940 (Notes on Genesis and Working Out of "Compass" Plan)'. It is of the utmost importance that the following entry appears near Wavell's signature block on this document: 'Note: Generals Wilson and O'Connor have read the above note and agree with it.' Wavell enclosed the seminal directives leading up to this operation: App. A (memo, 'Gen. Sir Archibald P Wavell to Deputy Chief of the General Staff', 11 September 1940); App. B (memo, 'Note to Gen. Wilson', 21 September 1940); App. C (memo, 'GOC in C, British Troops in Egypt', 20 October 1940); App. D (memo, 'GOC in C, BTE', 2 November 1940); App. E (memo, 'A Method of Attack on an Entrenched Camp in the Desert', [25/26 November 1940]); App. F (memo, 'Lt. Gen. Wilson: Compass – Exploitation', 28 November 1940); and App. G ('HQ, BTE Operation instruction No. 17', 5 December 1940). All of these documents were collected by the US Army Military Attaché, Great Britain, and forwarded to Washington, DC: [US] Military Intelligence Division, War Department General Staff, Military Attaché Report Great Britain, Subject: 'British Campaign in the Western Desert', Report No. BES-134, 1 May 1941, File No. 2017-744/26, Record of the War Department General and Special Staffs, Record Group 165, NA. Wavell's 15 December 1940 memorandum was listed as Enclosure A to BES-134, and the appendices, as listed above, were included as appendices to Enclosure A, and will henceforth be cited in that manner.
83. Quoted in Knox, 164.
84. Both quotes quoted in Great Britain, Ministry of Information, War Office, *Destruction of an Army* (London: HMSO, 1941), 27.
85. Wilson, 44.

86. This and the following two quotes are from Appx. B to Inclosure A, BES-134, RG 165, NA.

87. Avon, 142.

88. Peter Coats, *Of Generals and Gardens* (London: Weidenfeld and Nicolson. 1976), 69.

89. Appx. 86, memo, 'Note on Strategy in the Middle East in the Winter 1940/41', 20 October 1940, to WD, GHQ, ME, Vol. 15: G(O) Branch, October 1940, WO 169/14, PRO.

90. Appx. C, p. 1, to Inclosure A, BES-134, RG 165, NA.

91. Ibid., p. 2.

92. Wilson, 47.

93. App. D to Inclosure A, BES-134, RG 165, NA.

94. Cable No. AE 45A, 1 November 1940, Great Britain, Cabinet Office, *Principal War Telegrams and Memoranda, 1940–1943: Middle East*, vol. I, Cabinet History Series (Nendeln, Liechtenstein: KTO Press, 1976). This source will be hereafter cited as PWT.

95. Ibid.

96. Wavell, quoted in Maj. KJ Macksey, *Beda Fomm* (1971; rpt., London: Pan/Ballantine, 1972), 50.

97. Cable No. AE 53, 3 November 1940, PWT.

98. Cable No. AE 54, 3 November 1940, PWT.

99. Cable No. AE 58/04809, 5 November 1940, PWT.

100. Churchill, 2:537.

101. Ibid., 2:543.

102. Ismay, 197.

103. Cable No. 90494, 26 November 1940, PREM 3/288/1, PRO.

104. Inclosure A, p. 3, to BES-134, RG 165, NA.

105. Gen. Sir Archibald Wavell (viii), *Generals and Generalship*, The Lees Knowles Lectures for 1939 (London: Times, 1941), 2.

106. Michael Carver (i), *Out of Step: Memoirs of a Field Marshal* (London: Hutchinson, 1989), 61.

107. [US] Military Intelligence Division, War Department General Staff, Military Attaché Report Egypt, Subject: 'Training Exercise, Western Desert, Nov. 25–26', Report No. 2, 7 December 1940, File No. 2017–744/20, p. 4, RG 165, NA.

108. Ibid., p. 5.

109. Wavell (viii), 7.

110. App. F, p. 2, to Inclosure A, BES-134, RG 165, NA.

111. Lt. Gen. Sir Richard N O'Connor (i), 'Report on Operations in Libya from September 1940 to April 1941', p. 5, Folder 6312/29, O'Connor Papers, NAM.

112. Miles Reid, *Last on the List* (London: Leo Cooper, 1974), 83.

113. Appx. G, p. 1, to Inclosure A, BES-134, RG 165, NA.

114. Ibid., p. 2.

115. Coats, 73.

Chapter 6

1. Wavell (vii), 'Special Order of the Day, GHQ, Cairo, February 14, 1941', 23.

2. Alexander Clifford, *Three Against Rommel* (London: George G Harrap, 1943), 36.

3. Moorehead, 65.
4. Wavell, quoted in Ibid.
5. Clifford, 36.
6. Benson, interview by author, 24 June 1989.
7. O'Connor (i), p. 6.
8. Wavell (vii), 'Special Order of the Day, December 1940', 18–19.
9. Quoted in Churchill, 2:611.
10. O'Connor (i), p. 8.
11. Churchill, 2:612.
12. Compton MacKenzie, *Eastern Epic*, vol. I, *September 1939-March 1943: Defence* (London: Chatto & Windus, 1951), 62.
13. JC Smuts, *Jan Christian Smuts* (London: Cassell, 1952), 409.
14. Cable, 26 November 1940, PREM 3/278/1, PRO.
15. Appx. 26A, Cable No. 0/28314, 2 December 1940, to WO 106/2340, PRO.
16. Both quotes in this sentence are from Appx. 33, Cable No. 0/29224, 8 December 1940, to WD, GHQ, ME, Vol. 17: G(O) Branch, December 1940, WO 169/16, PRO.
17. Appx. 36, Cable No. 0/29394, 9 December 1940, to Vol. 17, WO 169/16, PRO.
18. Ltr, Wavell to O'Connor, 27 June 1945. Typescript copy in RLEW 4/6, Lewin Papers, CAC. Italics added.
19. Brig. JAL Caunter, 'Some Lessons from the [1st Libyan] Campaign', p. 1, Caunter Papers, LHCMA.
20. Michael Carver (ii), *Dilemmas of the Desert War* (Bloomington, Indiana: IUP, 1986), 17.
21. O'Connor (i), p. 9.
22. Carver (i), 62.
23. Wilson, 53.
24. O'Connor, interview by Peter Batty, 17 October 1972. Transcript on file in Dept. of Film, IWM.
25. Carver (ii), 17.
26. Both quotes in this sentence are from one of O'Connor's replies to a question asked of him by Maj. JK Nairne, and contained in 'Questions & Answers (Prepared in 1970, 1971, 1972) 1909–1948. Western Desert Campaign, 1940–1941', n.p., Folder 1/15, O'Connor Papers, LHCMA.
27. Winston S Churchill, 'The Victory at Sidi Barrani', in *The War Speeches of Winston Churchill*, vol. II, *The Unrelenting Struggle*, comp. Charles Eade (London: Cassell, 1942), 15.
28. The three quotes in this and the preceding sentence are from Cable No. 92792, 13 December 1940, PWT.
29. These cablegrams are respectively Cable No. 93374, 18 December 1940, and Cable No. 0/30879, 19 December 1940, both in PWT.
30. App. 35A, Cable No. 0/30497, 17 December 1940, to WO 106/2136, PRO.
31. Cable, Wavell to CIGS, 20 December 1940, quoted in Connell (i), 300.
32. O'Connor (i), pp. 11–12.
33. Wavell (viii), 11.
34. App. 5, 'ME JPS Paper No. 35: Advance into Libya', 20 December 1940, p. 6, to WD, GHQ, ME, JPS, Vol. 15: 1–31 December 1940, WO 169/3, PRO.
35. Ibid., p. 2.

36. Mackay, quoted in Long, series 1 (Army), 1:154–155.

37. O'Connor (i), p. 15.

38. Wavell, Despatch (iii): 'Operations in the Western Desert from December 7th, 1940, to February 7th, 1941', supplement to TLG, 26 June 1946, p. 3265.

39. FH Hinsley (i) et al., *British Intelligence in the Second World War: Its Influence on Strategy and Operations*, vol. I, History of the Second World War (1979; rpt., London: HMSO, 1986), 352.

40. Both quotes in this sentence are from Cable, PM to Wavell, 6 January 1941, quoted in Connell (i), 303–304.

41. Cable No. 95942 (MO5), 7 January 1941, PWT.

42. Ian Jacob, 'Churchill and his Generals', *Listener* 102 (25 October 1979): 548.

43. Wavell, quoted in Connell (i), 256.

44. Winston S Churchill, *The Second World War*, vol. III, *The Grand Alliance* (Boston: Houghton Mifflin, 1950), 10.

45. Quoted in Roger Parkinson (ii), *Blood, Toil, Tears and Sweat* (London: Hart-Davis MacGibbon, 1973), 177.

46. Cable No. X744, 9 January 1941, PWT.

47. Cable No. 46, 10 January 1941, PREM 3/209, PRO.

48. Cable No. 0/34651, 10 January 1941, PWT.

49. Wavell received the first Ultra message, numbered OL 1, on 14 March 1941. Ultra messages OL 1 to OL 500, sent to Cairo during 14 March-29 May 1941, are found in DEFE 3/687, PRO.

50. App., 'ME JPS Paper No. 30: Immediate Assistance to Greece and Turkey', 30 October 1940, p. 1, to WD, GHQ, ME, JPS, Vol. 13: 1–31 October 1940, WO 169/3, PRO.

51. 'ME JPS Paper No. 34: Assistance to Greece and Turkey in April, 1941', 17 December 1941, extract in ELMT 2/4, Elmhirst Papers, CAC.

52. App. 1, 'ME JPS Paper No. 36: Memorandum for British Liaison Staff to Turkey', 4 January 1941, p. 1, to WD, GHQ, ME, JPS, Vol. 16: 1–31 January 1941, WO 169/914, PRO. Italics in original.

53. App. 3, memo, 'Minutes of the 123rd Meeting of the JPS held at GHQ ME at 1830 hours on Thursday, 9th January 1941', p. 1, to Vol. 16, WO 169/914, PRO.

54. Cable No. 96572 (MO5), 11 January 1941, PWT.

55. Hopkins, quoted in Robert E Sherwood, *The White House Papers of Harry L Hopkins*, vol. I, *September 1939-January 1942* (London: Eyre & Spottiswoode, 1948), 240.

56. Cable No. P26, 15 January 1941, PWT.

57. Martin van Creveld, 'Prelude to Disaster: The British Decision to Aid Greece, 1940–41', JCH 9 (1974): 78–79.

58. FM Earl Wavell (ix), 'The British Campaign in Greece in 1941', address to the US Army National War College, 30 November 1949, Washington, DC. Typescript copy in Special Collections and History, US Dept. of Defense, NDUL.

59. O'Connor (i), p. 17.

60. Ltr, O'Connor to Brig. A Galloway, 19 January 1941, CAB 106/685, PRO.

61. O'Connor (i), p. 17.

62. FM Lord Harding of Petherton, interview by author, 14 April 1988, notes in

author's possession.

63. Churchill, quoted in Ismay, 'Notes on Intervention on the Greek Mainland', 22 April 1948, p. 5, Ismay II/3/43/2e, Ismay Papers, LHCMA.
64. 'Notes taken from General Creagh on Desert War', p. 1, Creagh Papers, LHCMA.
65. Annex, War Cabinet, JPS, 'Strategy in the Balkans and Eastern Mediterranean', 28 January 1941, p. 7, to COS(41), 33rd Meeting, CAB 79/8, PRO.
66. Robin Higham (i), *Diary of a Disaster* (Lexington, Kentucky: University Press of Kentucky, 1986), 76.
67. Cable No. 0/38391, 30 January 1941, PWT.
68. PM's Personal Minute, D27/1, 31 January 1941, PREM 3/209, PRO.
69. Cable No. 99737 (MO5), 1 February 1941, PWT.
70. Verney, 37.
71. O'Connor (i), p. 25.
72. Mitchell diary, 7 February 1941, Mitchell Papers, RHL.
73. O'Connor (i), p. 26.
74. Churchill, 'Give Us the Tools and We Will Finish the Job', in *War Speeches*, 2: 57.
75. Ibid.
76. *Destruction of an Army*, 51.
77. O'Connor (i), p. 27.
78. Wavell, quoted in Connell (i), 330.
79. War Cabinet, Defence Committee (Operations), 'Minutes of Meeting held in the Cabinet War Room on Monday, 10 February, 1941, at 9: 30 pm', DO(41), 7th Meeting, p. 3, CAB 69/2, PRO.
80. Ibid.
81. Ibid., pp. 3–4.
82. Cable No. 51265, 12 February 1941, PWT.
83. Quoted in FH Hinsley (ii), *Hitler's Strategy* (Cambridge: CUP, 1951), 119–120.
84. Quoted in Butler, 2:386.
85. FM Earl Wavell (x), 'The British Expedition to Greece, 1941', AQ 60 (January 1950): 179–180.
86. Gen. Sir Richard N O'Connor (ii), 'The British Expedition to Greece', p. 3, Folder 3/d, O'Connor Papers, LHCMA.
87. Ibid., p. 4(b).
88. ACM Sir Arthur Longmore, *From Sea to Sky, 1910–1945* (London: Geoffrey Bles, 1946), 257.
89. Ltr, Longmore to Woollcombe, 11 July 1957, Folder DC 74/102/33, Longmore Papers, RAFM.
90. O'Connor (ii), p. 4(c).
91. Cunningham, 310.
92. Ltr, Cunningham to Admiral of the Fleet Sir Dudley Pound, 6 [16?] February 1941, Folder 52561, Cunningham Papers, BL.
93. Ltr, Roskill to Connell, 15 September 1961, File (XII), Folder 2, [Wavell II], CP, MU.
94. O'Connor (ii), p. 4.

95. Wilson, 62.
96. Ltr, Dorman-Smith to Connell, 12 July 1961, File (XII), Folder 11, CP, MU.
97. Ltr, Dorman-Smith to Connell, 9 September 1961, File (XII), Folder 2, [Wavell II], CP, MU.
98. Cable No. 0/40808, 10 February 1941, PWT.
99. Quoted in Connell (i), 323.
100. Ibid.
101. War Cabinet, JPS, 'Examination of a Suggestion for the Capture of Tripoli: Aide-Mémoire by the JPS', 8 February 1941, CAB 79/9, PRO.
102. Ltr, Jacob to author, 29 January 1988.
103. Ltr, Dorman-Smith to Connell, 18–22 August 1962, File (XII), Folder 11, CP, MU.
104. Robert Rhodes James, *Churchill: A Study in Failure, 1900–1939* (London: Weidenfeld and Nicolson, 1970; rpt., Harmondsworth, Middlesex: Penguin, 1973), 87.
105. David Day, *Menzies & Churchill at War* (NY: Paragon House, 1988), 65.
106. Kennedy, quoted in Fergusson, ed., 139.
107. Maj. Gen. Sir Francis de Guingand (i), *Operation Victory* (London: Hodder and Stoughton, 1947), 47.
108. Maj. Gen. David Belchem, *All in the Day's March* (London: Collins, 1978), 67–68.
109. Ltr, Belchem to Lewin, 22 July 1979, RLEW 2/13, Lewin Papers, CAC. Italics in original.
110. App. 1, 'ME JPS Paper No. 41: Advance to Tripoli', 11 February 1941, p. 5, to WD, GHQ, ME, JPS, Vol. 2: 1–28 February 1941, WO 169/914, PRO. Italics in original.
111. Ltr, Ernest A Mason to author, 6 June 1988.
112. Ltr, RJ Mathews to author, 17 November 1989.
113. Ltr, George A Rose to author, 8 August 1989.
114. Rommel, quoted in BH Liddell Hart, ed., *The Rommel Papers*, trans. Paul Findlay (1953; rpt., NY: Harcourt, Brace, n.d.), 95.
115. Ltr, Generalmajor Friedrich W von Mellenthin to author, 14 April 1989.
116. O'Connor (i), p. 29.
117. FM Lord Harding, interview by author, 14 April 1988.
118. FM Lord Carver, interview by author, 11 April 1990, audio cassette recording in author's possession.
119. Carver (ii), 17.
120. Benson, interview by author, 24 June 1989.
121. O'Connor (ii), p. 4.
122. Wavell (viii), 7.
123. Lieut. Richard J Riddell and Lieut. Harvey S Ford, 'The War in North Africa', FAJ 31 (November 1941): 838.
124. Col. Frederick M Barrows, 'The War in Africa', MR 21 (March 1941): 23.

Chapter 7

1. Wavell (vii), 'Notes for Address to Defence Consultative Committee of the [Indian] Legislature, August 1, 1941', 35.

2. 'A Master of War', ILN, 15 February 1941, p. 197.
3. Both quotes in this sentence are from 'The Leader in War', *The Times* (London), 17 February 1941, p. 5.
4. WR Titterton, Letter to the Editor, *The Times* (London), 21 February 1941, p. 5.
5. 'Britain's Soldier of the Hour', MR 21 (March 1941): 8.
6. Sir Henry 'Chips' Channon diary, 9 February 1941, quoted in Robert Rhodes James, ed., *Chips: The Diaries of Sir Henry Channon* (London: Weidenfeld and Nicolson, 1967), 291.
7. Long, series 1 (Army), 1: 282.
8. O'Connor (i), p. 6.
9. Sherwood, 1: 240.
10. Cable No. 98778, 26 January 1941, PWT.
11. Hugh Dalton diary, 3 February 1941, quoted in Day, 56.
12. Ltr, Wavell to The Rt Hon Viscount Cranborne, 31 October 1942. Typescript extract in PREM 3/288/7, PRO.
13. Ltr, Jacob to Ismay, 24 January 1959, Ismay I/14/69b, Ismay Papers, LHCMA. Italics in original.
14. Alanbrooke, quoted in Arthur Bryant, *The Turn of the Tide, 1939–1943* (London: Collins, 1957), 248.
15. Mark Arnold-Forster, *The World at War* (NY: Stein and Day, 1973), 100.
16. Jackson, 82.
17. Connell (i), 336.
18. Robin Higham (ii), 'British Intervention in Greece, 1940–1941: The Anatomy of a Grand Deception', *Balkan Studies* 23 (1982): 111.
19. Higham (i), 236.
20. Memo, 'Notes for BGS, Middle East Command', 31 July 1939, HQ, ME, p. 1, WO 201/2379, PRO.
21. Ibid., p. 2. Italics in original.
22. Fergusson, ed., 44.
23. App. 53A, 'Balkan Situation', 8 June 1940, to Vol. 11, WO 169/10, PRO.
24. App. 104, memo, 'Notes on a Meeting held at Alexandria on Morning of 28/10/40 in Connection with Outbreak of War between Italy and Greece', to Vol. 15, WO 169/14, PRO.
25. Cable No. AE 45A, 1 November 1940, PWT.
26. App. 33, Cable No. 0/25034, 7 November 1940, to WD, GHQ, ME, Vol. 16: G(O) Branch, November 1940, WO 169/15, PRO.
27. Appx. 152, memo, 'Notes on Future Plans in Middle East', 27 November 1940, p. 3, to Vol. 16, WO 169/15, PRO.
28. Cable No. 46, 10 January 1941, PWT.
29. Cable No. 51265, 12 February 1941, PWT.
30. Ibid.
31. Dill, quoted in Fergusson, ed., 75.
32. Dill, quoted in Ibid.
33. The two quotes in this sentence are from Ibid., 75 and 76 respectively.
34. Ltr, Lady NIC Dill (Dill's second wife) to author, 21 August 1989.
35. Cable No. 0/36206, 18 January 1941, PWT.
36. Maj. Gen. Sir Francis de Guingand (ii), *Generals at War* (London: Hodder and Stoughton, 1964), 24.

37. Ltr, Fergusson to Nairne, 7 March 1971. Typescript copy in 'Questions and Answers', Folder 1/15, O'Connor Papers, LHCMA.
38. Ltr, Benson to author, 2 March 1989.
39. de Guingand (i), 77.
40. Kennedy, quoted in Fergusson, ed., 85.
41. Ltr, Jacob to author, 29 December 1988.
42. Carl von Clausewitz, *On War*, ed. and trans. Michael Howard and Peter Paret (1976; rpt., Princeton, New Jersey: Princeton University Press, 1984), 607.
43. Wavell (x), 181.
44. Bond (i), 272.
45. Robertson, quoted in Bonham-Carter, 337.
46. Anthony Eden, 'Story of Greece', n.p., AP 16/1/82A, Avon Papers, UB.
47. Avon, 190.
48. Col. Vivian Dykes diary, 8, 12, 15, 16, and 17 January 1941, respectively pp. 11–13, 18, 20, and 21 (twice), Document 940, Box 75B, Donovan Papers, USAMHI.
49. Ibid., 8 February 1941, p. 41.
50. Ibid., 10 February 1941, p. 44.
51. Ltr, Lord Wilson to author, 22 February 1989.
52. Wavell, (x), 179.
53. App. X37, 'Weekly Review of the Military Situation Up to 1800 hours 24 February 1941', p. 1, to WD, GHQ, ME, Vol. 2 (Part 10): GS Intelligence, 1–28 February 1941, WO 169/924, PRO.
54. Wavell, Despatch (iii): 3425.
55. Ibid.
56. Cable No. 0/41285, 12 February 1941, WO 106/2144, PRO.
57. Long, series 1 (Army), 1:101.
58. Christopher Buckley (i), *Greece and Crete. 1941*, vol. in The Second World War, 1939–1945 (London: HMSO, 1952), 29.
59. App., memo, 'The New Zealand Division in Greece – Report by General Freyberg (Notes Only)', to WD, HQ, New Zealand Division, 6 March-28 April 1941, WO 179/712, PRO.
60. Freyberg, quoted in WG McClymont, *To Greece*, Official History of New Zealand in the Second World War, 1939–45 (Wellington: Dept. of Internal Affairs, War History Branch, 1959), 99.
61. App. 63, 'Despatch of British Forces to Balkans', 17 February 1941, p. 1, to WO 169/918, PRO.
62. Ibid.
63. Ibid., p. 4.
64. de Guingand (i), 55.
65. Appx. X25, 'German Intentions in South-East-Europe and in North Africa', 17 February 1941, p. 3, to Vol. 2 (Part 10), WO 169/924, PRO.
66. Ibid., p. 4.
67. Blamey, quoted in DM Horner, *High Command* (Canberra: AWM, 1982), 67.
68. SF Rowell, *Full Circle* (Carlton, Victoria: Melbourne University Press, 1974), 61.
69. Blamey, quoted in John Hetherington, *Blamey* (Melbourne: FW Cheshire, 1954), 92.

290   WAVELL IN THE MIDDLE EAST 1939–1941

71. Pierson Dixon diary, 13 February 1941, quoted in Pierson Dixon, *Double Diploma* (London: Hutchinson, 1968), 57.
72. The quotes in this and the preceding sentence are from memo, 'Note for the Foreign Secretary', 12 February 1941, p. 1, PREM 3/294/2, PRO. The following three quotes are from Ibid., pp. 2, 3, and 7 respectively.
73. Memo, 'Memorandum by FM Sir John Dill on the Decision to Send British Forces to Greece', 21 April 1941, p. 2, FO 371/33145, PRO. Hereafter cited as 'Dill Report'.
74. Cable No. 4617, 18 February 1941, FO 371/29813, PRO.
75. 'Appx. 4A, memo, '"War is an Option of Difficulties" (Wolfe)', 19 February 1941, to Military HQ Papers, ME Forces, January-May 1941: Appreciations of Possible German Intentions, WO 201/2574, PRO.
76. Ibid., p. 1.
77. Ibid., p. 2.
78. Marshall-Cornwall, 185.
79. Dykes diary, 19 February 1941, p. 51.
80. Wavell, Despatch (iv): 'Operations in the Middle East from 7th February, 1941 to 15th July, 1941', supplement to TLG, 3 July 1946, p. 3424.
81. Wavell, quoted in Avon, 195.
82. Avon, 195.
83. Memo, 'Col. Donovan's Report on the Situation in the Mediterranean Area', 20 February 1941, n.p., FO 371/29782, PRO.
84. Ibid.
85. Eden diary, 20 February 1941, quoted in Avon, 195.
86. App. III, 'Assistance for Greece: Record of Meeting held at His Majesty's Embassy, Cairo, at 6 pm, 20th February 1941', p. 3, to Brig. AWS Mallaby, 'Diary of CIGS Tour to Mediterranean, February-April 1941', 11 April 1940 [1941], WO 106/2145, PRO.
87. Dykes diary, 20 February 1941, p. 52.
88. Cable No. 0/43125, 21 February 1941, PREM 3/206/3, PRO.
89. Dill Report, p. 2.
90. Ibid., p. 6.
91. Dixon diary, 20/21 February 1941, quoted in Dixon, 63.
92. This and the preceding quote are from Cable No. 355, 21 February 1941, PWT.
93. Churchill, quoted in Gilbert, 6:1012.
94. This and the following quote are from Cable No. 467, 21 February 1941, PREM 3/206/3, PRO.
95. Cable No. 358, 21 February 1941, PWT. Italics added.
96. Lord Caccia, interview by author, 5 April 1990, audio cassette recording in author's possession.
97. Ibid.
98. de Guingand (ii), 22.
99. Ltr, Belchem to Lewin, 22 July 1979, RLEW 2/13, Lewin Papers, CAC.
100. Annex 3, 'Record No. 2: Record of Meeting of the British and Greek Military Representatives held at Royal Palace at Tatoi, February 22, 1941', to Pierson Dixon, 'Report on the Mission of the Secretary of State for Foreign Affairs to

the Eastern Mediterranean, February-April, 1941', 21 April 1941, p. 24, FO 371/39777, PRO. The latter document will be hereafter cited as the 'Pierson Dixon Report'.
101. Wavell, quoted in Connell (i), 339.
102. de Guingand (i), 59.
103. Cable No. 260, 23 February 1941, PWT.
104. Churchill, quoted in Gilbert, 6:1013.
105. War Cabinet, COS Committee, 'Policy in the Middle East and Eastern Mediterranean', 24 February 1941, p. 1, to WP (41) 39 (Revise), CAB 66/15, PRO.
106. Ibid., p. 3.
107. Menzies diary, 24 February 1941, quoted in Day, 63–64. First set of italics added.
108. Day, 65.
109. Cable No. 516, 24 February 1941, PWT.
110. Quoted in Hinsley (i), 1:361.
111. Wavell, Despatch (iv): 3426.
112. Cable No. 0/45279, 2 March 1941, PWT.
113. Cable No. 313, 5 March 1941, PWT.
114. 'Record of a Meeting held at the British Legation, Athens, at 1830 hours on March 3, 1941', Pierson Dixon Report, p. 59.
115. Dill Report, pp. 10–11.
116. Day, 72.
117. Churchill, quoted in Parkinson (ii), 202.
118. This and the preceding quote are from Cable No. 607, 6 March 1941, PWT.
119. Annex 12, 'Assistance to Greece: Record of Meeting held at GHQ, ME, on March 6, 1941, at 5 pm', to Pierson Dixon Report, p. 75.
120. Ibid., p. 76.
121. Cable No. 455, 6 March 1941, PWT.
122. Connell (i), 354–356.
123. This vignette is from Eden, 'Story of Greece', p. 1.
124. The three quotes in this sentence are from Annex 13, 'Assistance to Greece: Record of Meeting held at His Majesty's Embassy, Cairo, at 10.15 pm on March 6, 1941', to Pierson Dixon Report, pp. 79, 80, and 81 respectively.
125. Cable No. 461, 7 March 1941, PREM 3/206/3, PRO.
126. Cable No. 632, 7 March 1941, PWT.
127. Cable No. 1295, 10 March 1941, PREM 3/206/3, PRO.
128. Churchill, 3:168.
129. Hinsley (i), 1:405.
130. Wavell, Despatch (iv): 3427.
131. Wilson, 84.
132. Cable No. 855, 6 April 1941, PREM 3/288/8, PRO.
133. OL 34, 0434/5/4/41 [Time/day/month/year], DEFE 3/687, PRO.
134. Hinsley (i), 1:409.
135. de Guingand (ii), 76–77.
136. Cunningham, 352.
137. Cable No. 61936, 17 April 1941, PWT.
138. Appx. G, 'Record of a Meeting held at Gen Wilson's House on 18th [19] April,

1941, to Consider the Question of Evacuation', p. 3, to Lt. Gen. Sir HM Wilson, 'Report on Military Operations in Greece', 5 May 1941, WO 201/72, PRO.
139. Hetherington, 105.
140. Anthony Heckstall-Smith and Vice Admiral HT Baillie-Grohman, *Greek Tragedy* (London: Anthony Blond, 1961), 61.
141. Cable No. 0/58960, 22 April 1941, PWT.
142. Cable No. 64484, 1 May 1941, PWT.
143. Draft, CIGS amendment to proposed telegram (never sent) to send to the Australian Government in response to their Cable No. 749, 22 November 1941, about the campaign in Greece, 17 December 1941, PREM 3/206/2, PRO.
144. Fraser, quoted in Official Archivist, 2 NZEF, Middle East, *Campaign in Greece* (Wellington: Army Board, 1943), 55.
145. Capt. KM Oliphant, Private Diary (Unofficial) of Operations in Greece, preface to diary, p. 1, WO 217/33, PRO.
146. Ltr, Wavell to O'Connor, 27 June 1945. Typescript copy in RLEW 4/6, Lewin Papers, CAC.
147. Ltr, Dorman-Smith to Connell, 1 July 1961, File (XII), Folder 11, CP, MU.
148. Ltr, Correlli Barnett to O'Connor, 16 August 1965, Folder 1/5, O'Connor Papers, LHCMA.
149. Wavell, Despatch (iv): 3432.
150. Ltr, FM Lord Harding to author, 21 September 1987.
151. Jacob, interview by author, 26 June 1989.

Chapter 8

1. Wavell (vii), 'Notes for Address to Defence Consultative Committee of the [Indian] Legislature, August 1, 1941', 34.
2. Memo, 'Note on Strategical Situation in the Middle East by GOC in C, Middle East', 14 August 1939, p. 2. Enclosure to demi-official ltr, Wavell to Gort, 14 August 1939, WO 201/2119, PRO.
3. Memo, 'Notes on Strategical Situation in the Middle East', 24 August 1939, p. 2. Enclosure to demi-official ltr, Wavell to Gort, 24 August 1939, WO 201/2119, PRO.
4. Appx. 5, memo, 'Note on Operations against Italian East Africa. By GOC in C, ME', 3 October 1939, to Vol. 3, WO 169/1, PRO.
5. Wavell, Despatch (ii): 2721.
6. App. 23, memo, 'Operations Against Italian East Africa', 3 August 1940, p. 3, to Vol. 13, WO 169/12, PRO.
7. Playfair, 1:184.
8. Sykes, 230.
9. Appx. 86, memo, 'Note on Strategy in the Middle East in the Winter 1940/41', p. 2, to Vol. 15, WO 169/14, PRO.
10. Memo, 'Notes of Conference Held at the Palace, Khartoum, at 2000 hours, 28th October 1940', p. 4, WO 106/2340, PRO.
11. Messervy, quoted in Henry Maule, *Spearhead General* (London: Odhams, 1961), 31.

12. Ibid., 43.
13. Wavell, Despatch (i): 3002.
14. Playfair, 1:393.
15. Ltr, Viscount Slim to author, 7 December 1988.
16. Annex, 'Report by Lt. Gen. Sir William Platt on the Operations in Eritrea and Abyssinia', to Wavell, Despatch (v): 'Operations in East Africa, November, 1940-July, 1941', supplement to TLG, 10 July 1946, p. 3531.
17. Quoted in Michael Glover, *An Improvised War* (London: Leo Cooper, 1987), 63.
18. Cable No. 0/27133, 23 November 1940, PREM 3/278/1, PRO.
19. Parkinson (ii), 161.
20. Churchill, 3:83.
21. Wavell, Despatch (v):3527.
22. Gen. Sir William Platt, *The Campaign Against Italian East Africa, 1940/41*, The Lees Knowles Lectures for 1951 (N.p., Privately printed, 1962), II-11.
23. Cable No. 93181, 17 December 1940, PWT.
24. Cable, Smuts to Churchill, 8 January 1941, quoted in Churchill, 3:16–17.
25. Ltr, Cunningham to Wavell, 26 January 1941, quoted in Connell (i), 367–368.
26. Both quotes in this sentence are from Churchill, 3:84.
27. Neil Orpen, *South African Forces, World War II*, vol. I, *East African and Abyssinian Campaigns* (Cape Town: Purnell, 1968), 113.
28. Cable No. 0/38950, 2 February 1941, PREM 3/278/1, PRO.
29. Ltr, Reuben Ashington to author, 28 October 1989.
30. Quoted in Great Britain, Ministry of Information, War Office, *The Abyssinian Campaigns* (London: HMSO, 1942), 39.
31. Cable No. 51265, 12 February 1941, PWT.
32. Cable No. 54339 (MO5), 2 March 1941, PWT.
33. Ltr, Capt. SHJ Harrison to author, 9 April 1988.
34. Wavell, Despatch (v): 3529.
35. Platt, quoted in Playfair, 1: 439.
36. The two quotes in this sentence are from respectively Cable No. 0/5033, 20 March 1941, and Cable No. 828, 22 March 1941, both in PWT.
37. Cable No. 0/50992, 23 March 1941, PWT.
38. Wavell, quoted in Connell (i), 375.
39. WE Crosskill, *The Two Thousand Mile War* (London: Robert Hale, 1980), 135.
40. Annex, 'Report by Platt', to Wavell, Despatch (v): 3545.
41. Glover, 180.
42. Bisheshwar Prasad, ed., *Official History of the Indian Armed Forces in the Second World War, 1939–45*, Campaigns in the Western Theatre, *East African Campaign, 1940–41* (Combined Inter-Services Historical Section (India & Pakistan), 1963), 155.
43. Wavell, Despatch (v):3530.
44. Woollcombe, 42.

Chapter 9

1. Wavell (vii), 'Notes for Address to Defence Consultative Committee of the [Indian] Legislature', 34.

2. Falls, 122.
3. Lt. Gen. Philip Neame, 'Operations in Cyrenaica from 27th February, 1941, when Lt. Gen. P Neame assumed command, until his capture on 7th April, 1941', par. 2, RLEW 4/6, Lewin Papers, CAC.
4. Ibid., par. 3.
5. Ltr, Wavell to O'Connor, 27 June 1945.
6. Walkling, 117.
7. Wavell, quoted in Connell (i), 386.
8. Ltr, Wavell to O'Connor, 27 June 1945.
9. This and the preceding quote are from App. 19, memo, 'Defence of Cyrenaica', 19 March 1941, p. 1, to WO 216/14, PRO.
10. Cable No. 0/50330, 20 March 1941, PWT.
11. Hinsley (i), 1:390.
12. This and the preceding quote are from Appreciation, 'German Forces in Tripolitania', 20 March 1941, MI 14, FO 371/27549, PRO.
13. Ibid.
14. Quoted in David Irving, *The Trail of the Fox* (NY: EP Dutton, 1977), 70.
15. Larry H Addington, 'Operation Sunflower: Rommel Versus the General Staff', MA 31 (Fall 1967): 122.
16. Behrendt, 68–69.
17. App. XI38, memo, 'Counter Offensive from Tripolitania', 24 March 1941, p. 6, to WD, GHQ, ME, Vol. 2 (Part 11): GS Intelligence, 1–31 March 1941, WO 169/924, PRO.
18. App. 1, 'ME JPS Paper No. 44: Immediate Policy in Cyrenaica', 25 March 1941, p. 4, to WD, GHQ, ME, JPS, Vol. 18: 1–31 March 1941, WO 169/914, PRO.
19. Ibid., p. 6.
20. Cable No. 58386, 26 March 1941, PWT.
21. Cable No. 0/52146, 27 March 1941, PREM 3/288/8, PRO.
22. Quoted in Connell (i), 390.
23. Ibid.
24. Neame, par. 4.
25. Gambier-Parry, quoted in Barton Maughan, *Australia in the War of 1939–1945*, series 1 (Army), vol. III, *Tobruk and El Alamein* (Canberra: AWM, 1966), 50.
26. Wavell, quoted in Connell (i), 391.
27. Liddell Hart, ed., 109.
28. This and the preceding quote are from Cable No. 0/53520, 1 April 1941, PWT.
29. This and the preceding quote are from Cable No. 002, 2 April 1941, PWT.
30. 'Defence of Cyrenaica', p. 1.
31. Maughan, 55.
32. Maj. Gen. ISO Playfair et al., *The Mediterranean and Middle East*, vol. II, '*The Germans come to the Help of their Ally*' *(1941)* (1956; rpt., London: HMSO, 1974), 20–21.
33. Maughan, 57–58.
34. Michael Carver (iii), *Harding of Petherton* (London: Weidenfeld and Nicolson, 1978), 67.
35. Ltr, Wavell to O'Connor, 27 June 1945.
36. O'Connor (i), p. 36.

37. Wavell, Despatch (iv): 3428.
38. This and the preceding quote are from O'Connor (i), p. 37.
39. Gen. Sir Richard N O'Connor, interview by Ronald Lewin, 9 November 1977. Notes on file in RLEW 4/1, Lewin Papers, CAC.
40. Churchill, 3:344.
41. O'Connor (i), p. 37.
42. Ltr, FM Lord Harding to author, 21 September 1987.
43. Benson, interview by author, 24 June 1989.
44. de Guingand (i), 75.
45. Cunningham, 338–339.
46. de Guingand (i), 73.
47. Ltr, FM Lord Harding to author, 21 September 1987.
48. Ibid.
49. Cable No. 61791 (MO5), 16 April 1941, PWT.
50. Fergusson, ed., 94.
51. Cable No. 62176 (MO5), 18 April 1941, PWT.
52. Parkinson (ii), 227.
53. MacKenzie, 90.
54. Memo, CIGS to PM, 19 April 1941, p. 2, PREM 3/52/1, PRO.
55. Ibid.
56. Ibid.
57. App. 23, Cable No. 69887, 3 May 1941, to Vol 10, WO 169/9, PRO.
58. Cable No. 0/57713, 18 April 1941, PWT.
59. Hinsley (i), 1: 395–396.
60. Butler, 2: 453.
61. Quoted in Churchill, 3: 248.
62. Quoted in Ibid., 3: 249.
63. Playfair, 2: 153.
64. Cable No. 0/59719, 25 April 1941, PWT.
65. Ibid.
66. Ibid.
67. Artemis Cooper, *Cairo in the War, 1939–1945* (London: Hamish Hamilton, 1989), 67.
68. Fergusson, ed., 105.
69. Quoted in Ibid., 106.
70. Ibid.
71. Ibid.
72. Wolf Heckmann, *Rommel's War in Africa*, trans. Stephen Seago (1976; rpt., Garden City, NY: Doubleday, 1981), 119.
73. PM's Personal Minute, M479/1, 28 April 1941, PREM 3/295/4, PRO.
74. Memo, 'Directive by the PM and Minister of Defence', War Cabinet, 28 April 1941, p. 2, PREM 3/296/2, PRO.
75. Ibid.
76. Ibid., p. 1.
77. Memo, COS to PM, 7 May 1941, p. 1, PREM 3/296/2, PRO.
78. Ibid., p. 2.
79. FM Earl Wavell, memo, 'Written in 1949, after having seen in proof Ch XI of Volume III of WS Churchill's *The Second World War* "Germany Drives East"',

n.d., p. 1. Typescript copy in File (XII), Folder 7, [Wavell IX], CP, MU. Italics in original.
80. Ibid., pp. 3–4. Italics in original.
81. Ibid., p. 4.

Chapter 10

1. Wavell (vii), 'Notes for Address to Defence Consultative Committee of the [Indian] Legislature, August 1, 1941', 35.
2. Gilbert, 6: 1081.
3. Cable No. 012, 4 May 1941, PWT.
4. Ronald Lewin (ii), *Ultra Goes to War* (London: Hutchinson, 1978), 163.
5. This and the preceding quote are from Cable No. 0/61916, 5 May 1941, PWT.
6. Cable No. 0/64081, 13 May 1941, PWT.
7. Cable No. 0/64952, 17 May 1941, PWT.
8. Cable No. 0/65155, 17 May 1941, PWT.
9. This and the preceding quote are from Cable No. 023, 17 May 1941, PREM 3/288/8, PRO.
10. Wilson, quoted in Playfair, 2: 125.
11. War Cabinet, Joint Intelligence Sub-Committee, 'Scale of Attack on Crete. Report by the Joint Intelligence Sub-Committee', 27 April 1941, p. 1, PREM 3/109, PRO.
12. PM's Personal Telegram, T117, 28 April 1941, PREM 3/109, PRO.
13. Wavell, quoted in Wilson, 102.
14. Freyberg, quoted in Gavin Long, *Australia in the War of 1939–1945*, series 1 (Army), vol. II, *Greece, Crete and Syria* (1953; rpt., Canberra: AWM, 1962), 208.
15. Cable No. 0/61232, 2 May 1941, PWT.
16. This and the preceding quote are from Cable No. 0/61267, 3 May 1941, PWT.
17. Countess of Ranfurly diary, 3 May 1941, quoted by the Countess of Ranfurly, interview by author, 12 April 1990, audio cassette recording in author's possession.
18. Cable No. 65023 (MO5), 4 May 1941, PWT.
19. Wavell, quoted in Lavinia Greacen, *Chink* (London: Macmillan, 1989), 178.
20. Cable No. 0/61872, 5 May 1941, PWT.
21. Ibid.
22. Churchill, 3: 256.
23. Quoted in Parkinson (ii), 237.
24. Ibid.
25. Dill, quoted in Fergusson, ed., 116.
26. Quoted in Connell (i), 439.
27. Quoted in Ibid., 438.
28. Quoted in Ibid., 440.
29. Lt. Gen. Sir John Bagot Glubb, *A Soldier with the Arabs* (NY: Harper & Brothers, 1957), 42.
30. Cable No. 0/63234, 10 May 1941, PWT.
31. John Connell [John Henry Robertson] (ii), *Auchinleck* (London: Cassell, 1959), 227.

32. Quoted in Coats, 108.
33. Playfair, 2: 192.
34. Ltr, Ismay to Connell, 21 August 1961, File (XII), Folder 2, [Wavell II], CP, MU.
35. Churchill, 3: 266–267.
36. Cable No. 63761 (MO5), 27 April 1941, PWT.
37. Cable No. 0/65182, 17 May 1941, PWT.
38. Eden diary, 10 May 1941, quoted in Avon, 250–251.
39. This and the preceding quote are from Fergusson, ed., 119.
40. Amery diary, 19 May 1941, quoted in John Barnes and David Nicholson, eds., *The Empire at Bay: The Leo Amery Diaries, 1929–1945* (London: Hutchinson, 1988), 688–689.
41. Ltr, Amery to Churchill, 21 May 1941, p. 1, PREM 3/52/1, PRO.
42. Ibid.
43. Ibid., pp. 1–2.
44. Ibid., p. 2.
45. Amery diary, 20 May 1941, quoted in Barnes and Nicholson, 689.
46. Cable No. 027 (MO5), 20 May 1941, PWT. Italics in original.
47. Quoted in Connell (i), 462.
48. Quoted in Fergusson, ed., 120.
49. Churchill, 3: 324.
50. Eden diary, 21 May 1941, AP 20/1/21, Avon Papers, UB.
51. Quoted in Fergusson, ed., 121.
52. Quoted in Connell (i), 462–463.
53. Wavell, Despatch (iv): 3440.
54. Pownall diary, 25 May 1941, Pownall Papers, LHCMA.
55. Cable No. 1572, 28 May 1941, FO 954/15, PRO.
56. Cable No. 1679, 4 June 1941, FO 954/15, PRO.
57. Cable No. 4231, 5 May 1941, PWT.
58. Brig. GS Brunskill, 'The Administrative Aspect of the Campaign in Crete', AQ 54 (July 1947): 210–211.
59. Hinsley (i), 1: 412, 418.
60. This and the preceding quote are from Cable No. 0/64501, 15 May 1941, PWT.
61. Hinsley (i), 1: 418–419.
62. Karl Gundelach, 'The Battle for Crete 1941', in *Decisive Battles of World War II: The German View*, ed. HA Jacobsen and J Rohwer, trans. Edward Fitzgerald (1960; rpt., NY: GP Putnam's Sons, 1965), 120.
63. Cable No. 0/66006, 21 May 1941, PWT.
64. Cable No. 030, 23 May 1941, PWT.
65. Colville diary, 25 May 1941, quoted in Colville, 391.
66. Freyberg, quoted in Cable No. 0/67710, 26 May 1941, PWT.
67. Cable No. 68836 (MO5), 26 May 1941, PWT.
68. Cable No. 0/67808, 27 May 1941, PREM 3/109, PRO.
69. Churchill, quoted in Parkinson (ii), 250.
70. Student, quoted in Gundelach, 131.
71. Lampson diary, 29 May 1941, quoted in Evans, 179.
72. Dalton diary, 2 June 1941, quoted in Ben Pimlott, ed., *The Second World War*

Diary of Hugh Dalton, 1940-45 (London: Jonathan Cape in association with the London School of Economics and Political Science, 1986), 218.
73. Thompson (i), 121.
74. Gilbert, 6: 1101.
75. Cable No. 70091 (MO5), 3 June 1941, PWT.
76. Cable No. 040, 3 June 1941, PWT.
77. Pownall diary, 4 June 1941, Pownall Papers, LHCMA.
78. Ltr, Lord Privy Seal to PM, 4 June 1941, pp. 3-4, PREM 3/109, PRO.
79. This and the preceding quote are from Ibid., p. 4.
80. Channon diary, 6 June 1941, quoted in Rhodes James, 307.
81. PM's Personal Minute, D186/1, 14 June 1941, p. 1, PREM 3/109, PRO.
82. This and the preceding quote are from Ibid., p. 2.
83. Laurie Barber and John Tonkin-Covell, *Freyberg* (1989; rpt., London: Hutchinson, 1990), 114.
84. Memo, 'Report on the Battle of Capuzzo, 15-17 June 1941', 6 August 1941, WDF, par. 1, WO 201/357, PRO.
85. This and the preceding quote are from Cable No. 025 (MO5), 19 May 1941, PREM 3/284/15, PRO.
86. This and the preceding quote are from Cable No. 0/65675, 19 May 1941, PREM 3/284/15, PRO.
87. Cable No. 0/67417, 25 May 1941, PWT.
88. Cable No. 0/66046, 21 May 1941, PREM 3/287/1, PRO.
89. Wavell, Despatch (iv): 3441.
90. Maj. Gen. Sir Michael O'Moore Creagh, memo, 'Notes on Action 7 Armd Div, 14-17th June, 1941', n.d. [c. 23 June 1941], Creagh Papers, LHCMA.
91. Cable No. 0/68331, 28 May 1941, PWT.
92. Ibid.
93. 'Report on the Battle of Capuzzo', par. 5.
94. The two quotes in this sentence are from Cable No. 1507, 10 June 1941, PREM 3/287/1, PRO.
95. Eden diary, 15 June 1941, AP 20/1/21, Avon Papers, UB.
96. 'Report on the Battle of Capuzzo', par. 14.
97. Playfair, 2: 169.
98. Wavell, Despatch (iv): 3442.
99. Wavell, quoted in Maule, 123.
100. Wavell, Despatch (iv): 3443.
101. FM Lord Harding. interview by author, 14 April 1988.
102. Roberts, 46.
103. Benson, interview by author, 24 June 1989.
104. Ltr, Bateman to Connell, 3 July 1961, File (XII), Folder 1, [Wavell I], CP, MU.
105. Cable No. 0/74021, 17 June 1941, PWT.
106. Wavell, quoted in Coats, 113.
107. This and the preceding quote are from Churchill, 3: 344.
108. PM's Personal Telegram, T309, 20 June 1941, PREM 3/52/1, PRO.
109. Memo, CIGS to PM, 21 June 1941, p. 1, Dill Papers. Original lent to author by Lady Dill.
110. Ibid., pp. 1-2.

111. Fergusson, 59.
112. PM's Personal Telegram, T325, 22 June 1941, PREM 3/52/1, PRO.
113. Fergusson, ed., 119.
114. Colville diary, 21 June 1941, quoted in Colville, 404.
115. Harriman, quoted in W Averell Harriman and Elie Abel, *Special Envoy to Churchill and Stalin* (NY: Random House, 1976), 65.
116. Freya Stark, *The Arab Island* (NY: Alfred A Knopf, 1945), 144.
117. Fergusson, 59.
118. Dorman-Smith diary, 22 June 1941, quoted in Greacen, 181.
119. William L Langer and S Everett Gleason, *The Undeclared War, 1940–1941* (1953; rpt., Gloucester, Massachusetts: Peter Smith, 1968), 497.
120. Hinsley (i), 1: 424.
121. Ibid.
122. Cable No. 69821 (MO5), 31 May 1941, PWT.
123. Churchill, quoted in Colville diary, 29 May 1941, quoted in Colville, 392.
124. IMcDG Stewart, *The Struggle for Crete, 20 May–1 June 1941* (London: OUP, 1966), 479.
125. Memo, 'Report by the Inter-Services Committee on Crete on Operations in Crete', 2 July 1941, GHQ, ME, p. 33, WO 201/99, PRO.
126. Ltr, Wavell to Under-S of S, War Office, 19 August 1941, p. 1. Typescript copy in WO 106/3126, PRO.
127. Ibid.
128. The two quotes in this sentence are from Hinsley (i), 1: 418.
129. Playfair, 2: 122.
130. Ibid., 2: 124.
131. Rommel, quoted in Liddell Hart, ed., 146.

Chapter 11

1. Wavell (vii), 'Farewell Order, July 1941', 25.
2. MRAF Lord Tedder, *With Prejudice* (London: Cassell, 1966; rpt., Boston, Massachusetts: Little, Brown, 1966), 34.
3. Cunningham, 402.
4. Quoted in Cecil Brown, *Suez to Singapore* (NY: Random House, 1942), 76.
5. Brig. Lord Ballantrae, Letter to the Editor, 'Correspondence', JRUSI 124 (December 1979): 83–84.
6. Lewin (i), 128, 129.
7. Ltr, Fergusson to Connell, 15 December 1964, ACC 9259/316, Ballantrae Papers, NLS.
8. Dorman-Smith, quoted in Greacen, 180.
9. Amery, 276.
10. Ltr, Elmhirst to Katherine Elmhirst, 15 July 1941, ELMT 2/4, Elmhirst Papers, CAC.
11. Ltr, Peter Coats to author, 19 December 1988.
12. Ibid.
13. Ltr, Wavell to Jackson, 5 June 1941. Typescript copy in File (XII), Folder 2, [Wavell II], CP, MU.

14. Wavell, quoted in ltr, Connell to Ismay, 6 September 1961, File (XII), Folder 2, [Wavell II], CP, MU.
15. Fergusson, ed., 134.
16. Maj. Gen. H Rowan-Robinson (ii), *Wavell in the Middle East* (London: Hutchinson, [1941]), 219.
17. Barnett, 76–77.
18. Ibid., 80. Italics in original.
19. Clausewitz, 87.
20. Harry L Coles, ed., *Total War and Cold War* (Columbus, Ohio: Ohio State University Press, 1962), 4.
21. Ltr, Fergusson to Ian G Wooster, 23 April 1965, ACC 9259/316, Ballantrae Papers, NLS.
22. Ltr, Wavell to Dill, 26 July 1941, Dill Papers. Original lent to author by Lady Dill.
23. Collins, 436.
24. Ltr, HJ Fischer to author, 17 October 1989.
25. Ltr, WJ Kennedy to author, 5 August 1989.
26. Ltr, Ernest A Mason to author, 14 May 1988.
27. Ltr, George A Rose to author, 8 August 1989.
28. Ltr, John Whyatt to author, undated [c. 3 June 1988].
29. Fuller, quoted in David Fisher, *The War Magician* (NY: Coward-McCann, 1983), 91–92.
30. Lee diary, 1 July 1941, quoted in James Leutze, ed., *The London Journal of General Raymond E Lee, 1940–1941* (Boston, Massachusetts: Little, Brown, 1971), 325.
31. [US] Military Intelligence Division, War Department General Staff, NY Office, MID Report Near East, Subject: 'Current Events 70', Report No. 1285, 9 July 1941, File No. 2017–744/34, RG 165, NA.
32. Woollcombe, 158.
33. Napoleon, quoted in Col. JFC Fuller, *The Foundations of the Science of War* (London: Hutchinson, 1926), 125.
34. A von Boguslawski, quoted in Maj. Gen JFC Fuller, *Generalship: Its Diseases and Their Cure* (London: Faber and Faber, 1933; rpt., Harrisburg, Pennsylvania: Military Service Publishing, 1936), 5.
35. Ltr, Wavell to Liddell Hart, 5 July 1935. Typescript copy in File (XII), Folder 7, [Wavell IX], CP, MU.
36. Frederick the Great, *Instructions for His Generals*, trans. Brig. Gen. Thomas R Phillips (1944; rpt., Harrisburg, Pennsylvania: Stackpole, 1960), 53.
37. Socrates, quoted in Wavell (viii), 2.
38. Wavell (viii), 2.
39. Ibid.
40. O'Connor, interview by Lewin, 9 November 1977.
41. Ltr, Ismay to Connell, 13 September 1961, File (XII), Folder 2, [Wavell II], CP, MU.
42. Wavell (viii), 4.
43. Playfair, 2:246.
44. O'Connor, interview by Lewin, 9 November 1977.
45. Wavell (viii), 6.
46. Ltr, Liddell Hart to Connell, 22 June 1962, File (XII), Folder 7, [Wavell IX],

CP, MU.
47. Ltr, Liddell Hart to Connell, 5 December 1960, File (XII), Folder 1, [Wavell I], CP, MU.
48. Wavell (viii), 6.
49. Lt. Col. KE Hamburger, *Leadership in Combat: An Historical Appraisal* (West Point, NY: Dept. of History, USMA, 1984), 9.
50. Wavell (viii), 7.
51. Ibid., 8.
52. Wavell (vii), 'Four Lessons of War', 79.
53. Wavell (viii), 11.
54. Wilson, quoted in 'Obituary: Lord Wavell, Leader in Peace and War', *The Times* (London), 1 June 1950, p. 9.
55. Ltr, Whyatt to author, undated [c. 3 June 1988].
56. Wavell (viii), 11.
57. Ltr, Connell to Ismay, 23 August 1961, Ismay IV/Con/4/3b, Ismay Papers, LHCMA.
58. FM Viscount Montgomery of Alamein, *The Path to Leadership* (London: Collins, 1961), 46.
59. Ltr, Wavell to O'Connor, 27 June 1945.
60. Wavell (viii), 14.
61. Ltr, Lt. Col. JAE Dene to author, 3 March 1987.
62. Wavell (viii), 15.
63. Lewin (i), 8.
64. Ltrs, SG Smith to author, 14 May 1988 (italics in original) and 12 June 1988 respectively.
65. Ltrs, Kennedy to author, 5 August 1989 and undated [c. 2 October 1989] respectively.
66. Ltr, Ashington to author, 28 October 1989.
67. Ltr, John H Barnard to author, 28 August 1988.
68. Ltr, Mathews to author, 17 November 1989.
69. Ltr, Harold E Van Santen to author, 3 May 1989.
70. Sykes, 236.
71. Clifford, 106.
72. Lt. Col. Vladimir Peniakoff, *Private Army* (London; Jonathan Cape, 1950), 239.
73. Wavell, (viii), 19.
74. Ibid., 20.
75. Norman Dixon, *On the Psychology of Military Incompetence* (1976; rpt., London: Jonathan Cape, 1984), 152–153.
76. Woollcombe, 42.
77. Harvey Arthur DeWeerd (ii), 'Wavell', chap. in *Great Soldiers of the Two World Wars* (1941; rpt., NY: WW Norton, 1969), 306.
78. Ltr, Wavell to O'Connor, 27 June 1945.
79. FM Earl Wavell (xi), 'A Note on Command', in *Soldiers and Soldiering* (London: Jonathan Cape, 1953), 127.
80. Ltr, Wavell to O'Connor, 27 June 1945.
81. Wavell (vii), 'A Note on Command', 77.
82. 'Britain's Soldier of the Hour', MR 21 (March 1941): 8.
83. Michael Howard, *British Intelligence in the Second World War: Strategic Deception,*

vol. V, History of the Second World War (London: HMSO, 1990), 32.
84. Cable No. 0/30117, 14 December 1940, PWT.
85. Colville diary, 3 June 1941, quoted in Colville, 394.
86. Pownall diary, 23 June 1941, Pownall Papers, LHCMA.
87. Ltr, Dorman-Smith to Connell, 11 September 1962, File (XII), Folder 11, CP, MU.
88. FM Lord Carver, interview by author, 11 April 1990.
89. Wavell, quoted in O'Connor, interview by Lewin, 9 November 1977.
90. Wavell, quoted in ltr, FM Lord Harding to author, 21 September 1987.
91. Moorehead, quoted in 'Funeral of Lord Wavell', *Red Hackle* 93 (July 1950): 8.
92. Wavell, quoted in Brian Bond, ed., *Chief of Staff: The Diaries of Lt. Gen. Sir Henry Pownall* (London: Leo Cooper, 1974), 2:95.
93. Wavell diary, 12 January 1947, quoted in Penderel Moon, ed., *Wavell: The Viceroy's Journal* (London: OUP, 1973), 409.
94. AP Wavell, comp., *Other Men's Flowers* (London: Jonathan Cape, 1944), 75.
95. Ibid., 193.
96. Philip Mason, *A Shaft of Sunlight* (NY: Charles Scribner's Sons, 1978), 184.
97. Ltr, Churchill to Eden, 13 August 1940, PREM 3/296/17, PRO.
98. Jacob, interview by author, 26 June 1989.
99. Wavell, quoted in ltr, Lt. Gen. Sir Arthur Smith to Connell, 1 January 1962, File (XII), Folder 2, [Wavell II], CP, MU.
100. Ltr, Benson to author, 2 March 1989.
101. David Walker, *Lean, Wind Lean* (London: Collins, 1984), 224. Italics in original.
102. Ibid.
103. Ltr, Burnaby-Atkins to author, 31 July 1989.
104. Wavell (xi), 'Military Genius: 2. From Hannibal to Foch', 51.
105. Donald Cowie, *The Campaigns of Wavell* (London: Chapman & Hall, 1942), v.
106. Walkling, 116.
107. Hamilton, quoted in ltr, CC Learmonth to Connell, 21 August 1961, File (XII), Folder 2, [Wavell II], CP, MU.
108. Ltr, Marshall-Cornwall to Connell, 14 July 1961, File (XII), Folder 2, [Wavell II], CP, MU.
109. Ltr, Ismay to Connell, 31 August 1961, Ismay IV/Con/4/4, Ismay Papers, LHCMA.
110. Ltr, Gen. Sir John Hackett to author, 24 February 1989.
111. FM Lord Harding, interview by author, 14 April 1988.
112. Rommel, quoted in Liddell Hart, ed., 520.
113. Playfair, 2:246.
114. Wavell (viii), 19.
115. A Correspondent, 'Obituary: Lord Wavell, Statesman and Leader', *The Times* (London), 27 May 1950, p. 6.
116. Ltr, Rose to author, 8 August 1989.

Select Bibliography

A. UNPUBLISHED MATERIAL

Official Documents

a. England

1. Public Record Office, Kew, Richmond, Surrey
   a) Admiralty and Naval Department Papers
      ADM 199 – War History Cases and Papers
   b) Air Ministry Papers
      AIR 40 – Directorate of Intelligence and Other Intelligence Papers
   c) Foreign Office Papers
      FO 371 – General Correspondence after 1906: Political
      FO 954 – Avon Papers
   d) Ministry of Defence Papers
      DEFE 3 – War of 1939–1945: Intelligence from Enemy Radio
               Communications
   e) War Cabinet Papers
      CAB 44 – Cabinet Office Historical Section: Official War Histories:
               Narratives (Military)
      CAB 65 – War Cabinet: Minutes
      CAB 66 – War Cabinet: Memoranda (WP) and (CP) Series
      CAB 67 – War Cabinet: Memoranda WP (G) Series
      CAB 69 – War Cabinet: Defence Committee (Operations)
      CAB 79 – War Cabinet: Chiefs of Staff Committee: Minutes of
               Meetings
      CAB 106 – Cabinet Office: Historical Section Files (Archivist and
                Librarian Series)
      CAB 120 – Minister of Defence: Secretariat Files
      PREM 1 – Prime Minister's Office: Correspondence and Papers
      PREM 3 – Prime Minister's Private Office: 'Operational' Papers
      PREM 4 – Prime Minister's Private Office: 'Confidential' Papers
   f) War Office Papers
      WO 106 – Directorate of Military Operations and Intelligence
      WO 165 – War of 1939–1945: War Diaries: War Office Directorates
      WO 169 – War of 1939–1945: War Diaries: Middle East Forces

WO 179 – War of 1939–1945: War Diaries: Dominion Forces
WO 201 – War of 1939–1945: Military Headquarters Papers:
Middle East Forces
WO 215 – War of 1939–1945: GHQ Liaison Regiment: War
Diaries and Papers
WO 216 – Chief of the (Imperial) General Staff: Papers
WO 217 – War of 1939–1945: Private War Diaries
WO 282 – Dill Papers

b. India

1. Historical Section, Ministry of Defence, New Delhi
   a) War Diaries
      4th Indian Division, 1940–1941
      5th Indian Division, 1941

c. United States

1. National Archives, Washington, DC
   a) Record Group 165 – Records of the War Department General and Special
      Staffs

II. Private Papers

a. Australia

1. Australian War Memorial, Canberra, ACT
   a) Allen, Major-General AS
   b) Blamey, Field Marshal Sir Thomas
   c) Lavarack, Lieutenant General Sir John
   d) Mackay, Lieutenant General Sir Iven
   e) Morshead, Lieutenant General Sir Leslie

b. Canada

1. William Ready Division of Archives and Research Collections, Mills Memorial
   Library, McMaster University, Hamilton, Ontario
   a) Connell, John [John Henry Robertson]

c. England

1. Astley, Mrs. Joan Bright, London
   a) Personal papers and correspondence
2. British Library, London
   a) Cunningham, Admiral of the Fleet The Rt. Hon. Viscount, of Hyndhope
3. Churchill Archives Centre, Churchill College, Cambridge

   a) Elmhirst, Air Marshal Sir Thomas
   b) Jacob, Lieutenant General Sir Ian
   c) Lewin, (George) Ronald
   d) Strang, The Rt. Hon. Lord, of Stonesfield
4. Dill, Lady NIC, Badminton, Glos.
   a) Dill, Field Marshal Sir John
5. Imperial War Museum, London
   a) Evans, Lieutenant General Sir Geoffrey
   b) Haining, General Sir Robert
   c) Platt, General Sir William
   d) Reid, Major General DW
   e) Wetherall, Lieutenant General Sir Harry
   f) Willis, Admiral of the Fleet Sir Algernon
6. Liddell Hart Centre for Military Archives, King's College, London
   a) Allenby, Field Marshal The Rt. Hon. Viscount
   b) Bartholomew, General Sir William
   c) Blakiston Houston, Lieutenant Colonel John
   d) Burnett-Stuart, General Sir John
   e) Caunter, Brigadier John
   f) Charrington, Brigadier HVS
   g) Chater, Major General AH
   h) Creagh, Major General Sir Michael O'Moore
   i) de Guingand, Major General Sir Francis
   j) Dill, Field Marshal Sir John
   k) Fergusson, Sir Bernard (Brigadier The Rt. Hon. Lord Ballantrae)
   l) Godwin Austen, General Sir Reade
   m) Gracey, General Sir Douglas
   n) Hobday, Brigadier R
   o) Ismay, General The Rt. Hon. Lord
   p) Liddell Hart, Captain Sir Basil
   q) Messervy, General Sir Frank
   r) O'Connor, General Sir Richard
   s) Platt, General Sir William
   t) Pownall, Lieutenant General Sir Henry
7. National Army Museum, London
   a) O'Connor, General Sir Richard
8. Public Record Office, Kew, Richmond, Surrey
   a) Kisch, Brigadier FH
   b) Lacroze, Major RA
   c) Oliphant, Captain KM
9. Ranfurly, The Countess of, Chesham, Bucks.
   a) Personal diaries
10. Rhodes House Library, University of Oxford, Oxford
   a) Cozens, AB
   b) Hallier, FC
   c) Mitchell, Major General Sir Philip
11. Royal Air Force Museum, Hendon, London
   a) Longmore, Air Chief Marshal Sir Arthur

12. Special Collections, University Library, University of Birmingham, Birmingham
    a) Anthony Eden, 1st Earl of Avon
13. Wilson, The Rt. Hon. Lord, of Libya, London
    a) Wilson, Field Marshal The Rt. Hon. Lord, of Libya

d. Scotland

1. Haig, The Rt. Hon. The Earl, of Bemersyde, Melrose, Roxboughshire
   a) Unpublished autobiography
2. National Library of Scotland, Edinburgh
   a) Ballantrae, Brigadier The Rt. Hon. Lord (Bernard Fergusson)

e. South Africa

1. South African Defence Force Archives, Pretoria
   a) Brink, Major General GE

f. United States

1. Author's Possession
   a) Whyatt, John
2. Franklin D Roosevelt Library, Hyde Park, New York
   a) Hopkins, Harry L
   b) Roosevelt, President Franklin D
3. Special Collections and Archives, Rutgers University Libraries, New Brunswick, New Jersey
   a) Fuller, Major General JFC
4. US Army Military History Institute, Carlisle Barracks, Pennsylvania
   a) Donovan, Major General William J
5. United States Military Academy Library, West Point, New York
   a) Stimson, Henry L (microfilm diaries)

III. Interviews

a. Conducted by author

1. Allendale, The Rt. Hon. Viscount (Aide-de-camp to Wavell, 1946–1947).
2. Arnaut, Duro (Yugoslavian Chetnik during World War II).
3. Astley, Mrs. Joan Bright, (operated War Cabinet Office's Special Information Centre during World War II).
4. Baker-Baker, Brigadier HC, (Aide-de-camp to Wavell, 1939–1940).
5. Barnett, Correlli, (Keeper, Churchill Archives Centre).
6. Benson, Lieutenant Colonel John (GSO3, GHQ, Middle East, August 1939-April 1940; GSO3, Western Desert Force/XIII Corps, October 1940-March 1941; GSO 3/2, HQ, British Troops in Egypt, March-June 1941).

7. Bond, Professor Brian (Department of War Studies, King's College, London).
8. Burnaby-Atkins, Lieutenant Colonel FJ (Aide-de-camp to Wavell, 1946–1947).
9. Caccia, The Rt. Hon. Lord (First Secretary, His Majesty's Legation, Athens, 1939–1941).
10. Carver, Field Marshal The Rt. Hon. Lord
11. Chandler, Professor David G., (Head, Department of War Studies and International Affairs, Royal Military Academy, Sandhurst).
12. Danchev, Dr. Alex (biographer of Field Marshal Dill).
13. Dill, Lady NIC (widow of Field Marshal Sir John Dill).
14. Emerson, Dr. William (Director, Franklin D Roosevelt Library).
15. Fergusson, The Hon. George D (son of Brigadier The Rt. Hon. Lord Ballantrae).
16. Harding, Field Marshal The Rt. Hon. Lord, of Petherton.
17. Hoger, Victor (Vladimir Vasiljevic) (member of Sokol, a Pan-Slavic organisation, during 1941 Yugoslavian *coup d'état*).
18. Humphrys, Lady Pamela (eldest daughter of Field Marshal The Rt. Hon. Earl Wavell).
19. Jacob, Lieutenant-General Sir Ian (Military Assistant to the War Cabinet, and Staff Officer to the Minister of Defence, 1939–1946).
20. Janic, Lazar (former Senior Captain, Yugoslavian Army, participant in the 1941 Yugoslavian *coup d'état*).
21. Le Moigne, Sergeant EJ, Royal Corps of Invalids (1st Queen's Regiment, 1939–1944).
22. Liddell Hart, Adrian (son of Captain Sir Basil Liddell Hart).
23. Mirkovic, Mihalo (son of Senior Captain Mirkovic, Yugoslavian Army Orderly Officer on day of *coup d'état*, 27 March 1941).
24. Murton, PG, (Keeper of Aviation Records, The Royal Air Force Museum).
25. O'Meara, Brigadier PHB (Ministry of Defence, London)
26. Ranfurly, The Countess of, (SOE, Cairo, 1941; wife of The Rt. Hon. Earl of Ranfurly, who served as Aide-de-camp to Lieutenant-General Philip Neame, VC, General Officer Commanding-in-Chief, Cyrenaica, 1941).
27. Stansbie, HC, Royal Corps of Invalids (7th Armoured Division, 1940–1943).
28. Ward, Miss AJ (Head of (British) Army Historical Branch).
29. Wilson, The Rt. Hon. Lord, of Libya (served in Middle East, 1940–1944; son of Field Marshal The Rt. Hon. Lord Wilson, of Libya).
30. Winkworth, John (Winchester College)

b. Conducted by others

1. Avon, The Rt. Hon. Earl of (Anthony Eden). Interview by David Elstein, 5 April 1972. Transcript on file in Department of Film, Imperial War Museum, London, England.
2. Bird, General Sir Clarence. Interview by Ronald Lewin, 6 April 1978. Notes on file in Lewin Papers, Churchill Archives Centre, Churchill College, Cambridge, England.
3. Blamey, Lieutenant-General Sir Thomas. Interview by Kenneth Slessor, 30 April 1941. Notes in Clement Semmler, ed., *The War Diaries of Kenneth Slessor:*

Official Australian Correspondent. 1940-1944 (St. Lucia: University of Queensland Press, 1985), 271-273.

4. Creagh, Major General Sir Michael O'Moore. Interviewer unknown, 13 July 1945. Transcript on file in Creagh Papers, Liddell Hart Centre for Military Archives, King's College, London, England.
5. Harding, Field Marshal The Rt. Hon. Lord, of Petherton. Interview by Peter Batty, 13 September 1972. Transcript on file in Department of Film, Imperial War Museum, London, England.
6. O'Connor, General Sir Richard. Interview by Peter Batty, 17 October 1972. Transcript on file in Department of Film, Imperial War Museum, London, England.
7. O'Connor, General Sir Richard. Interview by Ronald Lewin, 9 November 1977. Notes on file in Lewin Papers, Churchill Archives Centre, Churchill College, Cambridge, England.
8. Vesey, General Sir Ivo. Interview by John Connell, 26 August 1961, Gosfield Hall, Halstead, Essex, England. Notes on file in Connell Papers, Hamilton, Ontario, Canada.

IV. Correspondence

Abell, Sir George (Deputy Private Secretary to Viceroy (Wavell), 1943-1945; Private Secretary to Viceroy, 1945-1947) – 5 March 1986; undated [c. 13 May 1986].

Adams, Mrs. Cara – 6 January 1988.

Alberti, Mrs. PJ – 24 May 1989.

Alderton, Lieutenant Colonel E C, – 10 March 1988.

Allendale, The Rt. Hon. Viscount – 15 April 1986.

Amery, The Rt. Hon. Julian, MP – 25 October 1988; 31 January 1989.

Annan, The Rt. Hon. Lord – 11 September 1987.

Arbuthnott, Colonel (Retd.) The Hon. WD, (Colonel, The Black Watch) – 2 November 1987; 13 February 1989; 14 February 1989; 27 February 1989; 12 December 1990; 14 December 1990.

Arthur, Lieutenant General Sir Norman (grandson of General Sir John Burnett-Stuart) – 1 January 1989.

Ashington, Reuben (Natal Mounted Rifles, 1st South African Division, 1940-1942) – 22 August 1989; 28 October 1989; 24 January 1990.

Astley, Mrs. Joan Bright – 12 July 1986; 25 July 1987; 6 June 1989; 9 December 1989.

Barnard, JH (4th Indian Division, 1940-1942) – 2 August 1988; 28 August 1988.

Barringer, Miss TA (Librarian, Royal Commonwealth Society, London) – 24 October 1988.

Baynes, Lieutenant Colonel Sir John, Bt. – 17 March 1990.

Beale, Paul – 17 March 1987; 14/15 April 1987; 11 July 1987.

Benson, Lieutenant Colonel JE. – 3 June 1986; undated [c. 20 October 1988]; 15 December 1988; 24 January 1989; 2 March 1989; 7 June 1989; undated [c. 17 December 1990].

Bligh, Ms. KV (Assistant Archivist, Record Office, House of Lords, London) – 3

November 1987.

Bond, Professor Brian – 8 March 1990; 13 April 1990; 7 May 1990.

Boyden, Dr. PB (Archivist, National Army Museum, London) – 25 April 1988; 27 June 1988.

Bradley, Joyce (Curator, Information Services, Australian War Memorial, Canberra) – 14 December 1988.

Bridge, TD (Publisher, *Army Quarterly and Defence Journal*) – 11 November 1989.

Brookeborough, The Rt. Hon. Viscount (Aide-de-camp to Wavell, 1946–1947) – 21 January 1986.

Brooks, Mrs. Patricia – 16 August 1989.

Brown, PWH (Secretary, The British Academy, London) – 19 September 1988.

Bruntisfield, The Rt. Hon. Lord – 26 August 1987.

Burnaby-Atkins, Lieutenant Colonel FJ – 5 June 1989; 31 July 1989; 12 September 1989; 30 October 1989; 20 December 1989; 24 January 1990; 20 February 1990; 13 March 1990.

Burt, John (Assistant Librarian, Manuscripts Section, University of Sussex Library, Brighton) – 4 November 1987.

Caccia, The Rt. Hon. Lord – 31 January 1990; 26 February 1990.

Callahan, Professor Raymond – 20 October 1988.

Cane, MA (Hon. Editor, *Journal of the Society for Army Historical Research*) – 26 January 1987.

Carver, Field Marshal The Rt. Hon. Lord – 3 September 1987; 17 February 1990; 26 March 1990; 16 April 1990.

Chandler, Professor David G – 25 March 1990.

Cloughley, Colonel BW, – 24 May 1988.

Coats, Peter (Senior Aide-de-camp to Wavell, 1940–1945) – 11 April 1987; 23 March 1988; 19 December 1988.

Coats-Carr, Mrs. Camilla – 27 December 1990.

Collocott, Colonel ACJ (Senior Staff Officer Periodicals, South African Defence Force Archives, Pretoria) – 15 January 1988.

Combrinck, Colonel JA (Chief, South African Defence Force Archives, Pretoria) – 25 January 1988; 30 March 1988.

Commissariat, Colonel MD (Ret.) – 19 May 1989; 9 August 1989.

Cooper, Mrs. EM – 6 October 1989.

Crane, Wendy (Information Services, Australian War Memorial, Canberra) – 16 January 1989.

Custance, Roger (Archivist, Winchester College, Winchester) – 7 December 1988.

Danchev, Dr. Alex – 26 June 1987; 21 March 1988; 12 May 1988; 23 May 1988; 7 June 1988; 17 August 1988.

Davies, JM (Royal Navy, Port Mine Sweeping Officer, Tobruk, 1941) – 22 December 1989.

DeLease, LK (South African Medical Corps, 1940–1942) – Undated [c. 13 October 1990]; 16 January 1991.

Dene, Lieutenant Colonel JAE – 3 March 1987.

Dill, Lady NIC – 21 September 1987; 26 October 1987; 17 March 1988; 14 November 1988; 22 February 1989; 31 May 1989; 14 August 1989; 21 August 1989; 23 January 1990.

Dorge, Captain Marsha (Editor, *Sentinel*) – 17 December 1987.

310 WAVELL IN THE MIDDLE EAST 1939–1941

Douglas, WAB (Director, Directorate of History, Canadian National Defence Headquarters, Ottawa) – 10 February 1988; 13 April 1988; 30 June 1988.

Elder, Barry – 11 February 1987.

English, Roy (Senior Manager, Documentaries, Music and Arts, Thames Television, London) – 9 December 1988.

Feltham, Penelope (Archivist, New Zealand National Archives, Wellington) – 12 January 1988; 11 September 1989.

Fergusson, The Hon. George – 3 August 1987; 5 April 1988.

Fischer, H J (1st South African Brigade Group, 1939–1942) – 17 August 1989; 17 October 1989.

Fleming, Anne (Keeper, Department of Film, Imperial War Museum, London) – 15 December 1988; 20 March 1989.

Fleming, Carmela (Library Assistant, *Dallas Morning News*) – 29 December 1988.

Freyberg, Colonel The Rt. Hon. Lord (son of Lieutenant General The Rt. Hon. Lord Freyberg, VC) – 7 December 1987.

Frowe, Mrs. Margaret – 10 April 1987.

Garay, Dr. KE (Research Collections Librarian (since 1988), Mills Memorial Library, McMaster University) – 11 November 1988; 13 January 1989; 23 February 1989; 21 April 1989.

Garland, Lieutenant Colonel Albert N USA (Ret.) (Editor, *Infantry*) – 16 December 1987; 1 April 1988.

Garnett, Mrs. EA (granddaughter of General Sir John Burnett-Stuart) – 25 November 1988; 3 January 1989.

Gilchrist, Ron (Curator, Private Records, Australian War Memorial, Canberra) – 23 June 1988; 29 January 1991.

Gilliat, Martin (Private Secretary to Queen Elizabeth The Queen Mother) – 13 December 1989.

Grant, Gillian (Archivist, Middle East Centre, St. Anthony's College, Oxford) – 21 March 1988; 31 May 1988.

Griffiths, Sir Percival – 30 March 1987.

Hackett, General Sir John – 24 February 1989.

Haig, The Rt. Hon. The Earl, of Bemersyde (Aide-de-camp to O'Connor, 1940) – 8 December 1989; 9 January 1990; 9 February 1990.

Hand, William – Undated [c. 11 May 1988].

Harding, Field Marshal The Rt. Hon. Lord, of Petherton – 21 September 1987; 24 March 1988.

Harrison, Captain SHJ (1401/1402 (Aden) Companies AMPC Group, 1940–1941) – 9 April 1988.

Heathcote, TA, (Curator, RMAS Collection, Royal Military Academy Sandhurst, Camberley, Surrey) – 12 January 1989.

Higham, Professor Robin – 26 August 1986; 23 September 1986; 22 October 1986; 19 November 1986; 8 December 1986; 25 June 1990.

Holt, Robert (6th Australian Division, 1939–1945) – 19 September 1989; 15 October 1989; 9 December 1989.

Home, The Rt. Hon. Lord, of the Hirsel 8 September 1987.

Hudson, Major Roy – 2 April 1987; 18 June 1987.

Huggett, Major PS – 16 May 1988; 16 June 1988; 21 September 1988; 16 March 1989.

Humphrys, Lady Pamela – 26 April 1986; 28 June 1986; 18 November 1986; 29 May 1987; 9 November 1987; 18 March 1988; 4 February 1989; 19 February 1989; 20 March 1989.

Hyam, Dr. GFS (Royal Natal Carbineers, 1st South African Division, 1940–1943) – 7 May 1989, 23 July 1989; 7 August 1989.

Ironside, The Rt. Hon. Lord (son of Field Marshal The Rt. Hon. Lord Ironside) – 23 December 1987.

Irwin, Major Arthur (The Black Watch) – 7 June 1989; 30 July 1989; 16 September 1989.

Jacob, Lieutenant General Sir Ian S – 18 October 1988; 18 November 1988; 29 December 1988; 14 February 1989.

Jacobsen, Dr. Mark – 30 May 1988.

Jadhar, Lieutenant Colonel VP (Ret.) – 12 December 1987.

Jones, Professor RV, – 15 September 1987.

Kennedy, WJ (2nd New Zealand Division, 1940–1943) – 5 August 1989; undated [c. 2 October 1989].

Kruger, JP (1st Medium Brigade, South African Artillery, 1939–1941) – Undated [c. 26 August 1989]; 8 October 1989; 23 November 1989.

Kruh, Louis (Co-Editor, *Cryptologia*) – 23 February 1989.

Kucia, Alan (Archivist, Trinity College Library, Cambridge) – 4 November 1987.

Langley, Helen (Assistant Librarian, Bodleian Library, Oxford) – 29 March 1988; 19 April 1988; 9 June 1988.

Lavery, TJ (9th Australian Division, 1940–1941) – 10 November 1989.

Liddell Hart, Adrian – 3 May 1988; 21 May 1988; 17 June 1988.

Lloyd, Lieutenant Colonel Henry – 12 September 1987.

Lowe, J Austin – 1 January 1987.

Lyon, DJ (Head of Enquiry Services, National Maritime Museum, Greenwich) – 30 November 1987.

MacKenzie, Major Colin (Deputy Military Secretary to Wavell, 1945–1947) – 13 March 1986; 7 May 1986; 21 April 1987.

MacLeod, Chrissie (Manuscripts Section, National Maritime Museum, Greenwich) – 28 January 1988.

Marshall, CG (1st Battalion Royal Sussex Regiment, 4th Indian Division, 1939–1941) – Undated [c. 14 April 1988].

Mason, Ernest (13th Light Anti-Aircraft Regiment, 37th Battery Royal Artillery, 7th Armoured Division, 1940–1945) – Undated [c. 8 April 1988]; 14 May 1988; 6 June 1988; 19 September 1988; 2 November 1988; 26 February 1989; 18 April 1989; 22 May 1989.

Mason, Philip (Secretary to Chiefs of Staff Committee, India, 1941–1944) – 26 March 1986; 7 May 1986; 15 April 1987; 14 May 1987; 24 March 1988.

Mathews, RJ (7th Medium Regiment, Royal Artillery, 1939–1943) – Undated [c. 3 October 1989]; 17 November 1989.

Maunze, FW (National Archives of Zimbabwe, Harare) – 19 January 1988.

McGowan, Gordon (6th and 7th Australian Divisions, 1940–1941) – 4 October 1989; 13 November 1989.

McKenzie Johnston, HB – 30 December 1986.

McNiven, Dr. P (Archives, John Rylands University Library, Manchester) – 21 December 1987.

Mellenthin, Generalmajor Friedrich Wilhelm von – 14 April 1989.

Montgomery, Arthur – 5 May 1989; 26 May 1989; 26 July 1989; 3 August 1989; 19 August 1989; 30 August 1989.

Mourgels, Lieutenant General Grigorios – 10 March 1989.

Murray, James – 31 March 1987.

Murray, John – 3 May 1989.

Murtagh, Dr. Harman (Editor, *Irish Sword*) – 16 February 1987.

O'Farrell, GC (144th Field Regiment, Royal Artillery, 1940–1945) – 2 February 1990.

Osmond, WG, (State Secretary, Returned Services League of Australia, New South Wales Branch) – 26 November 1987.

Owen, AEB (Keeper of Manuscripts, Cambridge University Library, Cambridge) – 27 November 1987; 6 June 1989.

Palmer, Commander AB, RN – 19 December 1989; 12 July 1990.

Prior, DL (Curatorial Officer, Royal Commission on Historical Manuscripts, London) – 29 September 1988.

Ranfurly, The Countess of – 20 December 1989; 28 January 1990; 21 March 1990; 5 April 1990; 6 April 1990.

Reid, Stanley (16th Infantry Brigade, 1940–1941) – 20 June 1989.

Reynecker, GJ (Chief, Central Archives Depot, South African Government Archives Service, Pretoria) – 4 February 1988; 23 May 1988.

Robertson, Mrs. Ruth Connell – 13 July 1989.

Rose, George A (3rd Regiment, Royal Horse Artillery, 7th Armoured Division, 1939–1941) – 31 May 1989; 8 August 1989.

Rosenthal, Ken (3rd Transvaal Scottish, 1st South African Division, 1940–1941) – 30 May 1989.

Scott, Sir Ian (Deputy Private Secretary to Viceroy (Wavell), 1945–1947) – 9 April 1987; 21 May 1987.

Self, Bronwyn (Assistant Curator, Information Services, Australian War Memorial, Canberra) – 4 April 1989; 21 August 1989; 10 October 1989; 29 November 1989; 23 February 1990.

Shears, RJ – 10 March 1988; 19 April 1988.

Sheikh, Atique Zafar (Director General of Archives, Pakistan Department of Archives, Islamabad) – 8 December 1987.

Sims, MG (Librarian, Staff College, Camberley, Surrey) – 5 December 1988.

Sinclair, William (9th Australian Division, 1940–1945) – 15 September 1989; 28 November 1989.

Singh, GB (Historical Section, Indian Ministry of Defence, New Delhi) – 2 September 1988; 7 November 1988; 2 February 1989; 10 April 1989; 19 May 1989.

Singh, Air Commodore NB, IAF (Ret.) – 9 March 1988; 21 April 1988; 28 December 1988; 3 March 1989; 28 April 1989; 19 June 1989; 24 October 1989; 24 January 1990.

Sinha, Major General SC, (Ret.) – 27 January 1988.

Slim, The Rt. Hon. Viscount (son of Field Marshal The Rt. Hon. Viscount Slim) – 8 December 1987; 7 December 1988.

Smith, HJ – 31 March 1988.

Smith, SG (11th Hussars, 1938–1943) – Undated [c. 23 March 1988]; 14 May 1988;

12 June 1988.

Sommers, Dr. Richard (Archivist-Historian, US Army Military History Institute, Carlisle Barracks, Pennsylvania) – 25 August 1988; 21 December 1988; 15 February 1989.

Stafford, Professor David – 25 September 1989.

Sutton, G (Librarian, Royal Artillery Institution, Old Royal Military Academy, Woolwich) – 11 November 1987; 30 November 1987; 12 January 1988.

Thomson, Lieutenant Colonel Douglas – 27 March 1987; 28 April 1987; 3 June 1987.

Tubb, Richard (Librarian, Ministry of Defence Library, Whitehall, London) – 21 December 1983; 4 July 1984; 12 October 1984; 30 October 1986.

Van Der Waag, Lieutenant IJ (South African Defence Force Archives, Pretoria) – 14 December 1987.

Van Santen, Harold (Staff Officer, 2nd Infantry Brigade, 1st South African Division, 1939–1943) – 3 May 1989.

Vansit, G (National Archives of India, New Delhi) – 3 February 1988; 18 April 1988, 2 June 1988.

Verghese, GT (Editor, *Indo-British Review – A Journal of History*) – 16 February 1987; 3 April 1987.

Waddy, Colonel JL – 27 January 1987.

Wagland, Mark (Australian Archives, Belconnen) – 7 December 1987.

Walker, Lieutenant Colonel David – 24 April 1986; 23 May 1986; 13 March 1987.

Wark, Professor Wesley K – 17 February 1988.

Watkins, Brigadier HBC – 25 July 1984; 3 September 1984; 14 August 1989; 14 September 1989; 19 February 1990; 15 May 1990; 5 June 1990; 27 June 1990; 2 July 1990; 13 July 1990.

West, Jane (Curatorial Assistant, Private Records, Australian War Memorial, Canberra) – 6 January 1988; 17 February 1988; 22 February 1988; 2 February 1989; 7 June 1989; 4 July 1989.

Whiteman, Bruce (Research Collections Librarian (until 1988), Mills Memorial Library, McMaster University) – 28 October 1986; 13 October 1987; 7 December 1987; 15 February 1988.

Whyatt, John (2nd Battalion The York and Lancaster Regiment, Crete, 1940–1941) – 25 March 1988; undated [c. 3 June 1988].

Wilson, Brigadier ADRG, – 13 May 1987.

Wilson, The Rt. Hon. Lord, of Libya – 11 December 1988; 22 February 1989; 25 March 1989; 28 April 1989; 22 May 1989; 22 January 1990; 2 April 1990.

Wilson, The Rt. Hon. Lord, of Rievaulx – 16 September 1987.

Wolfe, Mrs. TA – Undated [c. 2 April 1987].

Woods, Vernon (South African Medical Corps, 1940–1943) – 4 May 1989; 26 May 1989; 24 July 1989; 28 August 1989.

Wright, Dr. MM (Senior Sub-Librarian, John Rylands University Library, Manchester) – 24 November 1987.

V. Newspapers and Magazines

a. England

1. *Daily Telegraph* – 20 July 1989.
2. *Illustrated London News* – 15 February 1941; 31 January 1948; 10 June 1950.
3. *The Times* (London) – 12, 14, 15 August 1936; 10 December 1940; 17, 18, 19, 20, 21, 24 February 1941; 3 March 1941; 5, 7, 9, 10, 11, 12 June 1941; 25, 27, 29 May 1950; 1, 7, 8 June 1950.
4. *The Times Literary Supplement* (London) – 4 July 1942; 29 September 1945; 26 September 1980.

b. United States

1. *Dallas Morning News* – 21 September 1941.
2. *Library Journal* – 1 November 1980.
3. *Life* – 3 March 1941.
4. *New York Times* – 9 February 1941.
5. *Newsweek* – 20 January 1941; 7 April 1941.
6. *Time* – 3 March 1941.

VI. Sound Records

a. England

1. Batty, Peter, writer and producer. *The World at War*. Program 4, *Alone*. Teddington, Middlesex: Thames Television Limited, 1974. Videorecording.
2. Batty, Peter, writer and producer. *The World at War*. Program 8, *Desert*. Teddington, Middlesex: Thames Television Limited, 1974. Videorecording.

VII. Photographic Records

a. Australia

1. Australian War Memorial, Canberra, ACT.

b. England

1. Imperial War Musuem, London.

c. Scotland

1. Regimental Headquarters, The Black Watch (Royal Highland Regiment).

Index